Success Studybooks

Biology
British History 1760–1914
Business Calculations
Chemistry
Commerce
Economic Geography
Economics
Economics: West African Edition
Elements of Banking
European History 1815–1941
Geography: Human and Regional
Geography: Physical and Mapwork
Investment
Law
Management: Personnel
Mathematics
Nutrition
Office Practice
Organic Chemistry
Principles of Accounting
Principles of Accounting: Answer Book
Statistics
Twentieth Century World Affairs

Success in

INVESTMENT

R. G. Winfield, B.Sc. (Econ.), F.I.B.

**Director of Banking Studies,
City of London Polytechnic**

and

S. J. Curry, M.A.

**Senior Lecturer in Economics and Finance,
Birmingham Polytechnic**

CONSULTANT EDITOR

Peter Roots, F.I.B.

Manager, Corporate Services Branch,
Midland Bank Trust Company Ltd

John Murray

First published 1981
by John Murray (Publishers) Ltd
50 Albemarle Street, London W1X 4BD

Typeset by Inforum Ltd, Portsmouth
Printed in Great Britain by
Richard Clay (The Chaucer Press) Ltd, Bungay, Suffolk

British Library Cataloguing in Publication Data
Winfield, R. G.
Success in investment. – 2nd ed.
1. Investment – Great Britain
I. Title II. Curry, S. J.
III. Roots, Peter. Success in investment
332.6′0941 HG5432
ISBN 0-7195-3839-4

Foreword

Books on investment usually fall into two categories. The first are the 'light-weights' – chattily readable but limited in scope; the second are the 'heavies' – theoretical, full of mathematical formulae and mainly for the specialist. In *Success in Investment* we have tried to strike a midpoint between the two, combining readability with instruction in a book designed to be of maximum practical help to its readers.

Investment is a wide subject touching many areas of business activity. We have therefore had to be selective and to concentrate on main topics that are relevant. We visualize three types of reader: first, the person who has money to invest and wants information on the investment scene today and the different kinds of investment that are available; second, the professional person, not an investment expert, who needs to be informed enough to give sound general advice to clients; third, the student working for professional qualifications.

In this book we aim to provide a comprehensive treatment of investment, integrating theory and practice, bearing in mind the changes of recent years. In the 1950s and 60s there was an important shift in the preference of investors from fixed-interest securities to equities, and new forms of investment, particularly those based on insurance, became popular. In the 1970s investors increasingly became aware of the problems of inflation and sought other forms of investment: index linking and floating interest rates were introduced and competition for investment funds was intensified. Alternative forms of investment in real assets, such as stamps, furniture and wine, also flourished. The 1980s began with a period of recession although a new stock market 'high' was reached in April 1981, and it is possible that further, higher peaks will be scaled before the end of the decade.

Although the day-to-day workings of the financial world fluctuate continually, basic structures and principles do not. In this book we keep these structures and principles in full focus, but it is frequently necessary to quote specific examples and readers must be on their guard about changes in interest rates, taxation, government policy and legislation. It is essential for students of investment to keep up to date by reading the financial columns of the press as well as specialist periodicals such as the *Investors Chronicle* and *Money Management*.

Success in investment depends on being aware of the opportunities available at a given time, and making decisions which prove to be good. There is no royal road to getting rich quickly but anyone who understands the main principles and knows the pitfalls and risks is well on the way to making the most of whatever resources are available.

This book replaces the original *Success in Investment* by Peter Roots; in that book the author gave wise and excellent advice, especially in his final summing up. We feel we cannot better this and have quoted from it liberally in our Unit 22 'The Successful Investor'.

Students on business or professional courses will find the text covers syllabus requirements of the following: the Institute of Bankers, London Chamber of Commerce, Business Education Council, Institute of Chartered Accountants, Association of Certified Accountants, Institute of Cost and Management Accountants. It also covers investment and finance aspects of examinations of the Stock Exchange, Chartered Insurance Institute, Institute of Chartered Secretaries, Society of Investment Analysts, and the relevant aspects of degree courses in Business Studies, Accounting and Banking.

R.G.W. and S.J.C.

Acknowledgments

In writing this book we have been helped by many people, especially those who appraised and criticized it at different stages. We are particularly grateful to Peter Roots, author of the original *Success in Investment* and Consultant Editor of this new text; W.J. Burnett, formerly Secretary of the Unit Trust Association; Martin Gibbs, Paul Nield and others of Phillips & Drew, stockbrokers; H.N. Morris of the National Westminster Bank Trustee and Income Tax Department; Norman Reynolds of Williams & Glyn's Trust Company Ltd; J. Sturges, Secretary of the Association of Investment Trust Companies; Peter Wells and others at the Stock Exchange; John Driver of Smith Keen Cutler, stockbrokers; Don Aston of Birmingham Polytechnic; Peter Bond of the City of London Polytechnic; David Cox of Worcester Technical College and Julia Tomkins.

We have also received help from various institutions and business companies and gratefully acknowledge: the Institute of Bankers, London, for permission to use questions from past examination papers, and in particular, John Mortimer, Assistant Secretary of the Institute, for his continued interest and support; the Bank of England for permission to reproduce material from the *Bank of England Quarterly Bulletin* (Figs. 4.1, 18.2); the *Financial Times* who provided information and source material for text and some of the diagrams, including Figs. 16.1, 16.2; Her Majesty's Stationery Office for material from the *Report of the* [*Wilson*] *Committee to Review the Functioning of Financial Institutions*, and for figures from *Financial Statistics*; Investment Research, Cambridge, for permission to reproduce charts (Figs. 15.2, 15.3); the *Sunday Times* for permission to reproduce graphs (Figs. 7.3, 11.1); the Stock Exchange for permission to reproduce material from their documents (Figs. 10.2, 10.3); the Midland Bank Ltd for permission to reproduce material from the *Midland Bank Review* (Fig. 8.1); the National Westminster Bank Ltd for permission to reproduce material from the *National Westminster Bank Review* (Fig. 15.1); *Money Management* for permission to reproduce tabular material (Tables 11.4, 12.3); *Money Which?* for permission to reproduce a graph (Fig. 13.1); de Zoete & Bevan, stockbrokers, for permission to reproduce material from *Equities and Fixed Interest Securities Since 1919* (Fig. 2.2, Tables 6.2, 6.3); Sotheby's for permission to reproduce material used in Table 13.2; the Treasurer of the City of Nottingham for permission to reproduce an advertisement for Fig. 5.1; Macmillan Publishers for permission to quote from

J.M. Keynes's *General Theory of Employment, Interest and Money*.

Thanks are also due to: W. Greenwell & Co, stockbrokers; Hinton & Wild (Insurance) Ltd, insurance brokers; the M & G Group; M.J.H. Nightingale & Co Ltd; the Save & Prosper Group Ltd; Towry Law & Co Ltd, insurance brokers.

Cartoons were kindly provided by: *Accountancy* (pages 120, 172, 188, 199, 204, 228, 238, 245, 275, 331); Basil Hone (Ben Shailo) (44, 79, 93); the Institute of Bankers (214); *Punch* Library (3, 17, 28, 37, 48, 162, 327).

Finally we must thank Jean Macqueen for her meticulous work in editing the typescript; Irene Slade, editor of the Success Studybook series, and Anne Webster, both of John Murray; and our wives, Margaret Winfield and Linda Curry (who also typed the manuscript and gave help with the index).

R.G.W. and S.J.C.

Contents

Unit 1 Investors and Investment 1
1.1 What is Investment? 1
1.2 Real and Financial Investment 1
1.3 Investment, Speculation and Gambling 3
1.4 Who are the Savers and Borrowers? 4
1.5 The Role of the Stock Exchange 7
1.6 The Personal and the Institutional Investor 10
1.7 Implications of the Growth of Institutional Investment 13
1.8 The Different Types of Investment 16
1.9 Success in Investment 16
1.10 Questions 17

Unit 2 Types of Investment 19
2.1 Fixed-income and Variable-income Investments 19
2.2 Quoted and Unquoted Investments 20
2.3 Direct and Indirect Investments 20
2.4 Risk in Investment 22
2.5 Cash Investments 24
2.6 National Savings Bank and National Girobank Accounts 25
2.7 Trustee Savings Bank Accounts 26
2.8 Bank Deposit Accounts 27
2.9 Finance House Accounts 28
2.10 Building Society Accounts 29
2.11 Cash Investments: Summary 30
2.12 Quoted Investments 31
2.13 Questions 32

Unit 3 The Government as Borrower 33
3.1 The National Debt 33
3.2 National Savings 33
3.3 Save As You Earn 34
3.4 National Savings Certificates 35
3.5 Second Index-linked National Savings Certificates 36
3.6 Premium Savings Bonds 36
3.7 National Savings and Deposits Compared 37

3.8	The Gilt-edged Market	38
3.9	Why are Gilts Issued?	38
3.10	Gilts and the Institutional Investor	38
3.11	Categories of British Government Securities	39
3.12	The Importance of Dates	40
3.13	Short-dated Securities	40
3.14	Sinking Funds	41
3.15	Dealing in Gilts	41
3.16	The National Savings Stock Register	42
3.17	Registered and Bearer Stocks	42
3.18	Payment of Interest	43
3.19	Pricing New Issues	43
3.20	Risk and Volatility	45
3.21	Tax Considerations with British Government Stocks	46
3.22	Questions	47
Unit 4	**Yield on Fixed-interest Stocks**	48
4.1	What is Yield?	48
4.2	Income Yield	49
4.3	Interest Yield	49
4.4	Gross Redemption Yield	50
4.5	Net Present Value and Yield	51
4.6	Net Redemption Yield	53
4.7	Grossed-up Net Redemption Yield	53
4.8	Yield Calculations in the Financial Press	54
4.9	Gross Funds and Net Funds	55
4.10	Interest Payments	55
4.11	Yield Curves	55
4.12	Questions	56
Unit 5	**Non-Government Fixed-interest Securities**	58
5.1	Introduction	58
5.2	Local Authority Quoted Stocks	58
5.3	Short-dated Local Authority Bonds	59
5.4	Loans to Local Authorities	60
5.5	Public Boards	61
5.6	Commonwealth Stocks	61
5.7	Foreign Governments' Bonds	61
5.8	Miscellaneous Fixed-interest Issues	62
5.9	Company Fixed-interest Finance	62
5.10	Debentures and Debenture Stocks	63
5.11	Unsecured Loan Stocks	64
5.12	Company Fixed-interest Stocks: Investment Criteria	64
5.13	Fixed-interest Stocks and the Investor	66
5.14	Questions	68

Unit 6	**Equities**	69
6.1	The Equity	69
6.2	The Dividend Yield	70
6.3	The Earnings Yield and the Price–Earnings Ratio	71
6.4	The Dividend Yield and the Growth Rate	71
6.5	Asset Values	73
6.6	Management	74
6.7	Nominal Values	74
6.8	Dividend Payments	75
6.9	Non-voting Shares	75
6.10	Risk	75
6.11	Yields and Risk	78
6.12	Comparison against Other Investments	78
6.13	Timing	80
6.14	Questions	81
Unit 7	**Other Direct Financial Assets**	82
7.1	Preference Shares	82
7.2	Convertible Stocks	84
7.3	Warrants	87
7.4	Foreign Currency Bank Accounts	89
7.5	Overseas Equities	89
7.6	Questions	91
Unit 8	**New Issues**	92
8.1	Going Public	92
8.2	Quotation and the Listing Agreement	93
8.3	Prospectus Issues	94
8.4	Offers for Sale	95
8.5	Offers for Sale by Tender	95
8.6	Placings	96
8.7	Introductions	96
8.8	Control over New Issues	97
8.9	The Prospectus	97
8.10	The Cost of Flotation	98
8.11	Stags and Stagging	98
8.12	Capitalization Issues	99
8.13	Rights Issues	101
8.14	Underwriting New Issues	103
8.15	Allotment Letters	106
8.16	Fractional Allotments	107
8.17	Offers of Different Classes of Capital	107
8.18	The Timing of New Issues	108
8.19	Questions	108

Unit 9 The Stock Exchange 110
9.1 The Exchange 110
9.2 Brokers and Jobbers 111
9.3 The Investor and his Broker 115
9.4 Quotation 116
9.5 *Stock Exchange Daily Official List* 116
9.6 Criticism of the Broking/Jobbing System 117
9.7 ARIEL 118
9.8 The Three-tier Market 119
9.9 Questions 121

Unit 10 The Transfer and Settlement Procedure 122
10.1 Cash and Account Transactions 122
10.2 The Account 122
10.3 The Contract Note 123
10.4 Brokers' Commission 125
10.5 Transfer Stamp Duty 130
10.6 Contract Stamp Duty 131
10.7 Transfer of Registered Securities 131
10.8 Talisman 134
10.9 Certificates 137
10.10 Depositories and Bearer Securities 138
10.11 Bulls and Bears 140
10.12 Options 142
10.13 Buying-in and Selling-out 144
10.14 Questions 145

Unit 11 Unit Trusts and Investment Trust Companies 147
11.1 What is a Unit Trust? 147
11.2 The Issue of Units 148
11.3 The Pricing of Units 150
11.4 Prices and the Unit-holder 151
11.5 The Role of the Department of Trade 152
11.6 The Duties of the Trustee 153
11.7 Investment in Authorized Unit Trusts 155
11.8 Timing of Unit Trust Purchases 156
11.9 Savings Schemes and Pound Cost Averaging 157
11.10 Withdrawal Plans 158
11.11 Share Exchange Schemes 159
11.12 The Choice Available 159
11.13 Distributions and Reports 161
11.14 The Taxation of Unit Trusts 161
11.15 Unauthorized Trusts 162
11.16 Investment in Unit Trusts 163
11.17 What are Investment Trusts? 164

11.18	Comparison with Unit Trusts	164
11.19	Split-level Trusts	166
11.20	'B' Shares	167
11.21	Taxation and Investment Trusts	167
11.22	The Decline in Status of Investment Trusts	168
11.23	Judging Performance	168
11.24	Questions	169
Unit 12	**Insurance and Investment**	171
12.1	Life Assurance	171
12.2	Endowment Assurance	171
12.3	Qualifying Life Assurance Policies	173
12.4	Conventional Endowment Contracts	174
12.5	Investment-linked Policies	175
12.6	Annuities	177
12.7	Single-premium Assurance Policies	179
12.8	Property Bonds	180
12.9	Managed Bonds	181
12.10	Income Bonds	182
12.11	Guaranteed Growth Bonds	182
12.12	Bond Switching	183
12.13	Friendly Societies' Bonds	183
12.14	Building-society-linked Contracts	183
12.15	Investment in Life Assurance	184
12.16	Questions	184
Unit 13	**Real Assets and Other Investments**	186
13.1	Investment in Property	186
13.2	Freehold Property	186
13.3	Leasehold Property	187
13.4	Mortgages	187
13.5	Investment in Freehold Rack Rents	188
13.6	Investment in Leasehold Property	191
13.7	Owner-occupation	191
13.8	Indirect Investment in Property	193
13.9	Unauthorized Unit Trusts	194
13.10	Investment in Chattels	198
13.11	Gold	201
13.12	Questions	202
Unit 14	**Portfolio Planning**	203
14.1	The Tax Environment	203
14.2	Income Tax	203
14.3	Capital Gains Tax	205
14.4	Capital Transfer Tax	209

14.5 Identifying the Investor 211
14.6 Income and Tax Position 211
14.7 Responsibilities and Commitments 213
14.8 Personal Feelings 214
14.9 Liquidity 215
14.10 Diversification 215
14.11 Net-of-tax Returns 216
14.12 Investing for Income 217
14.13 Protection Against Inflation 218
14.14 Case Studies 219
14.15 Investment Policies of the Institutional Investors: Principles 222
14.16 Investment Policies of the Institutional Investors: Practice 223
14.17 Questions 225

Unit 15 Selection and Review of Investments 227
15.1 Techniques of Investment Analysis 227
15.2 The Fundamental Approach 227
15.3 Technical Analysis 231
15.4 Interpretation of the Annual Report and Accounts 238
15.5 Income Statement 239
15.6 The Balance Sheet and Other Items 244
15.7 Ratio Analysis 250
15.8 Liquidity Ratios 252
15.9 Gearing Ratios 253
15.10 Activity Ratios 255
15.11 Profitability Ratios 256
15.12 Sources of Information 258
15.13 Conclusion 259
15.14 Questions 259

Unit 16 Portfolio Management and Review 262
16.1 The Stock Market Indices 262
16.2 Equity Switching 267
16.3 Gilt-edged Switching 269
16.4 The Efficient Market Hypothesis 274
16.5 Pound Cost Averaging 277
16.6 Performance Measurement 277
16.7 Questions 282

Unit 17 The Business of Shareholders' Meetings 283
17.1 Legal Personality and Limited Liability 283
17.2 Formation of a Company 284
17.3 The Memorandum of Association 284

17.4 The Articles of Association 284
17.5 Directors 285
17.6 The Quorum 286
17.7 Resolutions 286
17.8 Voting and Proxies 286
17.9 The Annual General Meeting 287
17.10 Extraordinary General Meetings 287
17.11 Class Meetings 287
17.12 Special Business and Special Notice 288
17.13 Auditors 288
17.14 The Audited Accounts 289
17.15 Stock Exchange Requirements 289
17.16 The Rights of Shareholders 289
17.17 Disclosure of Shareholders' Interests 290
17.18 Attendance at Meetings 290
17.19 Capital Reconstruction 291
17.20 Reduction of Capital 291
17.21 Sale of the Company under Section 287 of the Companies Act 1948 292
17.22 Scheme of Arrangement under Section 206 of the Companies Act 1948 292
17.23 Questions 292

Unit 18 Investor Protection 294
18.1 Introduction 294
18.2 Take-overs and Mergers 295
18.3 Take-overs: Strategy and Information 296
18.4 Take-overs: the Shareholders' Response 297
18.5 Obtaining Control 298
18.6 The City Code on Take-overs and Mergers 299
18.7 The Council for the Securities Industry 301
18.8 Other Voluntary Bodies 301
18.9 The Prevention of Fraud (Investments) Act 1958 302
18.10 The Banking Act 1979 304
18.11 Insurance Policyholders and the Law 305
18.12 Questions 305

Unit 19 Investment Advice and Professional Management 306
19.1 Advice 306
19.2 Professional Management 308
19.3 Questions 311

Unit 20 Investment by Trustees 313
20.1 The Investment Powers of Trustees 313
20.2 The Trustee Investments Act 1961 314

20.3	Investments Authorized by the 1961 Act	315
20.4	Division of the Fund	316
20.5	Transfers, Additions and Withdrawals	317
20.6	Retention and Postponer	319
20.7	Expert Advice	319
20.8	The Trustee Act 1925	320
20.9	Questions	321
Unit 21	**Investment Portfolios for Trustees**	322
21.1	Family Trusts	322
21.2	Valuation of Securities for Tax Purposes	324
21.3	Charitable Trusts	325
21.4	Pension Funds	326
21.5	Questions	328
Unit 22	**The Successful Investor**	329
22.1	A Sensible Approach	329
22.2	Conclusion	331
	Glossary	332
	Further Reading	351
	Index	353

Unit One

Investors and Investment

1.1 What is Investment?

The Multinational Motor company puts money into developing a new small car. Gushing Oil Incorporated spends millions of pounds in North Sea oil exploration. The Government decides it must step up its nuclear energy programme. At the same time Smith is buying Perfect Paints International ordinary shares, Jones is subscribing for Government gilt-edged securities while Sykes opts for additional life assurance as the means of saving some of his increased salary.

What all these actions have in common is that they are all forms of investment. Each involves the sacrifice of something now for the prospect of something later. This means that either individually, as a company or as a country, we forgo the consumption of goods today in order to achieve greater consumption in the future. The essence of investment is *time*, and also *risk*. The sacrifice takes place first and is unavoidable; the returns come later, if at all, and their magnitude is uncertain. (There is the apocryphal story of the two German brothers during the latter days of the Weimar Republic. One was honest and sober, the other wayward and drunken. The former put his savings into bonds which were wiped out by inflation; the latter made a million on the 'empties'.)

With some types of investment, such as Government securities, the time aspect predominates because future returns are absolutely certain in money terms (or as certain as anything can be). With others, such as options or warrants – which are sometimes not much more than a gamble on the price of the shares going up or down – the element of risk is dominant. Often both time and risk are important, as with ordinary shares, for instance.

1.2 Real and Financial Investment

It is useful to distinguish between investment in 'real' things, such as buildings, plant and machinery, houses or hospitals, and various types of 'paper' investment. This distinction is not made in any pejorative sense; it does not imply that 'paper' investment is any less valuable to the community.

In a highly industrialized economy, such as that of the United Kingdom, most industrial investment is undertaken by large-scale public and private business enterprises, but a significant proportion of the savings necessary to finance such investment comes from private persons. For example, if a company wished to undertake an expansion programme it could use its own savings (retained earnings and depreciation allowances) to finance the programme, but it might also raise funds from the general public by offering securities, like shares or debentures. Anyone buying this kind of offering would be acquiring a *financial asset*. In effect, the financial asset would be a claim on the future income from the underlying *real assets* financed by these savings. New financial investment is frequently a prerequisite for 'real' investment in the economy.

More often than not nowadays, a *financial intermediary* intervenes between the ultimate saver and ultimate borrower. For example, by buying a life assurance policy Sykes acquired a financial asset. He will pay the premiums to the life assurance company, which in turn might invest the proceeds in financial assets issued by companies and the Government. There may even be another link in the chain if the life assurance company invests in a unit trust or investment trust.

Risk cannot be eliminated from business ventures, but financial claims can be packaged to cater for the different time and risk preferences of investors. For this reason companies and governments rarely issue only one type of security. For example, those investors who desire low risk might choose a company's fixed-interest stock or preference shares, while those who are ready to accept a stronger element of risk might go for the ordinary shares. Thus different classes of financial asset appeal to different types of investor, even though they are all ultimately claims on the same real assets. Moreover, once 'real' investment is undertaken it is difficult or impossible to 'undo' by withdrawing resources. But financial assets, if negotiable, provide a means by which the original investor can recover the use of his capital, while the original funds remain 'locked' in the project.

Most, but not all, personal investment is of the 'financial' type, the most obvious exception being the owner-occupied house. This is the biggest investment for most people, and in recent years probably the most profitable. But even here 'financial' investment plays a part. The outlay involved in house purchase is greater than most people can supply from past or current savings, so a large part of the required funds is usually provided by a building society mortgage. The building society provides one of the best examples of a financial intermediary at work. It creates short-term financial liabilities, by borrowing usually at one month's notice of withdrawal, and acquires long-term financial assets by lending for periods of up to twenty-five years, or occasionally more. The short-term financial assets of one set of households (the lenders) is matched by the long-term financial liabilities of another set (the borrowers). Short-term lending finances long-term 'real' investment. The building society is willing to finance the borrower on terms that would not be acceptable to the original lender. It can only do this because of its ability to vary its borrowing and lending rates and because it holds sufficient *liquid assets* (assets which are in cash form, or which can be quickly turned into cash) to meet sudden withdrawals.

To sum up, saving inevitably implies investment, either direct 'real' investment or the *net acquisition of financial assets* (or the reduction in financial liabilities). Even if a saver, however unwisely, merely accumulates money in a current account at the bank or keeps it under the proverbial mattress, he is undertaking a form of financial investment. Incidentally, money should not be confused with *wealth*. Savings add to wealth, wealth being the net total of a person's assets and liabilities, real or financial. Sometimes money is used as a synonym for wealth, as in the famous aphorism that money, like muck, is no good unless well-spread. Money, or cash, correctly understood is merely the most liquid of financial assets, and only one component of overall wealth.

1.3 Investment, Speculation and Gambling

It is very difficult to distinguish precisely between these three kinds of activity. Certainly they have all been employed at various times in the stock market. Time and risk are two criteria that are sometimes used to differentiate them.

Investment was traditionally interpreted by trustees as long-term and low-risk, usually restricted to Government securities. Where equities were concerned, these were to be *blue-chip companies* (see Glossary), bought for their future dividends. *Speculation* is generally considered to be more short-

'Ready? Here it is – I wish for riches beyond my wildest dreams with no encumbering socialist guilt feelings.'

term, involving greater risk and based on anticipating market movements rather than judging the long-term fundamentals of a particular investment. Yet the distinction is not quite clear-cut, as many long-term investors consider timing to be an important part of investment strategy; and risk may be worth accepting, providing it is accompanied by the expectation of commensurate reward.

Gambling is considered to involve the shortest waiting period, and the greatest risk. But here, too, the dividing line is sometimes difficult to draw. Betting on the Football League Championship, or backing a horse ante-post, can involve a long wait before the outcome is known. Though risks are usually greater they are frequently more explicit or calculable, as in roulette or poker; and buying shares 'on the margin' or share options also involves the possibility of losing everything. Holding shares for the duration of a Stock Exchange fortnightly account might be termed speculation, but to bet on the course of the stock market over the same period with a bookmaker is considered by the Inland Revenue to be gambling.

1.4 Who are the Savers and Borrowers?

Savings in advanced industrialized societies come from the *personal sector* (households and unincorporated businesses), the retained profits and depreciation allowances of companies in the private sector, and the current surpluses of central government, local authorities and the public corporations. The net savers and investors are shown in Table 1.1.

In this table, the term *saving* excludes stock appreciation, but there is no deduction for depreciation and additions to reserves. It also includes net capital transfers to and from the Government. *Investment* here means 'real' investment, that is, gross domestic fixed capital formation plus the value of the physical increase in stocks and work-in-progress. For domestic sectors, the term *net acquisition of financial assets* equals savings less 'real' investment (or gross lending minus gross borrowing); for the overseas sector it equals the balance of payments current account with the sign reversed, plus net capital transfers to and from abroad.

Table 1.1. shows that during the 1970s personal savings overtook those of industrial and commercial companies. To some extent it depends on what definition of profit is used because if stock appreciation is included in company profits and savings, the gap with the personal sector is very much narrower. Nevertheless net personal savings are much larger than those of companies. Most corporate savings are invested directly in 'real' assets whereas, apart from housebuilding and 'real' investment by unincorporated businesses, most personal savings go into financial investment. The acquisition of financial liabilities (negative acquisition of financial assets) is not necessarily a cause for concern, however. In fact it can be a sign of success, rapid expansion of 'real' investment being financed by external funds.

Although overall savings in the United Kingdom are low by international

Table 1.1 Savings and investment by sector, 1968–79 (per cent of gross domestic product at market prices)

	Personal sector	Industrial and commercial companies	Financial companies and institutions	Public corporations	Central Government	Local authorities	Overseas sector
Saving:							
1968–72	4.8	7.2	0.8	1.7	4.3	1.3	
1973–77	8.3	6.3	1.2	2.0	−0.8	1.3	
1978	9.6	7.7	1.7	2.4	−2.6	1.1	
1979	10.8	5.5	1.8	2.0	−1.0	0.9	
Investment:							
1968–72	3.3	6.7	1.3	3.2	1.1	3.6	
1973–77	3.0	7.2	1.7	3.6	1.1	3.4	
1978	3.6	7.3	2.0	3.1	0.8	2.1	
1979	3.6	7.9	2.1	3.0	0.8	2.0	
Net acquisition of financial assets:							
1968–72	1.6	0.5	−0.5	−1.5	3.2	−2.3	−0.9
1973–77	5.4	−0.9	−0.5	−1.6	−1.9	−2.1	1.5
1978	6.0	0.4	−0.3	−0.7	−3.4	−0.9	−0.6
1979	7.2	−2.4	−0.2	−1.0	−1.8	−1.1	1.3

Source: *Committee to Review the Functioning of Financial Institutions (Chairman, Sir Harold Wilson) : Main Report (*hereinafter known as the *Wilson Report),* p.58

standards, the ratio of *non-discretionary savings* to disposable income is high. Non-discretionary savings schemes are those which involve a prior commitment to save a stipulated sum: they may be *contractual* (life assurance, for example) or *compulsory* (such as occupational pension schemes). These have been the main stimulus to savings growth in the United Kingdom since the end of the Second World War. Overall, personal savings rose from about 3 per cent of disposable income in the early 1950s to around 8 per cent in the 1960s. From 1972 there was a sudden upsurge in the personal savings ratio, mainly accounted for by discretionary savings (in building societies and banks, for instance), taking the ratio to 14 per cent in 1974 and as high as 19 per cent in early 1975. This behaviour, which was not confined to the United Kingdom, was unforeseen because it occurred at a time of severe squeeze on living standards and high nominal (but low or negative real) rates of return. Explanations put forward were the *precautionary motive*, especially strong during a period of economic uncertainty, *money illusion* (investors misled by higher prices and high rates of interest, ignoring higher incomes and the impact of inflation and tax on rates of return), and the desire to *restore financial assets* to their level in real terms before the investment market collapse of 1973–75. The personal savings ratio subsequently settled down to around 15 per cent.

Companies in the United Kingdom have traditionally had a high profit-retention rate, and this became accentuated during the 1970s due to the joint impact of inflation and divident control, the former almost certainly more than the latter. The corporate sector, particularly the industrial and commercial companies, has also traditionally never resorted extensively to external financing. Indeed for most of the 1950s and 1960s companies generated more cash than they required for 'real' investment. British economic and political circles have long discussed whether the relatively low level of manufacturing investment in the United Kingdom was the cause or the effect of such self-reliance. Only during the 1970s, with the problem of refinancing higher-priced stock, did the corporate sector seek substantial external funds (that is, run a large financial deficit), and even then it preferred to rely on credit creation by bank borrowing, rather than tapping savings through the capital market.

The public sector (central Government, local government and the public corporations) became a large-scale borrower during the 1970s. In the eight years to 1970, the *public sector borrowing requirement* (PSBR, which is the net acquisition of financial liabilities plus net lending to the private sector) averaged a little over £0.75bn (2 per cent of gross domestic product (GDP) at current market prices). From then until 1979 it averaged £6bn (6 per cent of GDP) with a peak of over £10.5bn (10¼ per cent of GDP) in 1975–76. It became a frequent cry of Government critics in the City that the public sector was 'crowding out' the corporate sector from the capital market. The argument was that the public sector as a borrower was not constrained by commercial considerations in the rate of interest it could afford to pay, and it could therefore always raise the rate to a level which would deter competing private-sector borrowing.

The alternative viewpoint was that Government deficit financing, in true Keynesian fashion, was necessary to counteract the recessionary effects of the OPEC export surplus and the poor investment intentions of the private sector. Moreover, the PSBR was to finance capital expenditure, so why should not the public sector run a financial deficit if the corporate sector refused to do so? The public sector traditionally ran a surplus on current account (though central Government no longer did so after 1975), although not sufficient to meet the investment demands of the local authorities and public corporations, particularly in the energy sector. If these industries were under private ownership would they not be large-scale borrowers?

The Conservative Government came to power in 1979 pledged to alter this picture radically. They proposed to cut the real PSBR drastically in order to reduce inflation and interest rates. Cheaper finance, together with the planned reduction in Government grants and subsidies, would bring companies into the marketplace for funds. Critics of this policy argued that investment is not sufficiently sensitive to interest-rate changes for this to be effective and that cuts in public spending, particularly capital items, would adversely affect sales and investment intentions of many firms in the private sector.

1.5 The Role of the Stock Exchange

The Stock Exchange, or capital market, is an institution where quoted investments (*stocks and shares*) may be exchanged between buyers and sellers. The term 'stocks and shares' is nowadays rather anachronistic, but still fixed in the popular imagination. *Stocks* are generally thought of as referring to fixed-interest capital in units of £100 and quoted at so much per cent, while the term *shares* is used for dividend-paying capital, either ordinary or preferred. But the distinction is not a precise one. 'Stock' can be quoted in units of any amount, and it can embrace dividend-paying capital; unlike share capital, stock transfers can take place in fractions of a unit.

Before the Companies Act 1948 many companies preferred ordinary stock units to ordinary shares because until that time all shares had to have distinctive numbers, a requirement which meant an enormous amount of work in the preparation of deeds of transfer and share certificates. So it was easier to issue, say, a 25p stock unit rather than a 25p share. Nevertheless the word 'shares' was frequently used for shares and ordinary stock alike, since for all practical purposes they were, and are, one and the same.

Because the word 'stock' encompasses both ordinary share capital and loan capital it is nowadays used as a generic term for all securities. The evidence of any property right is generally termed a *security*, although the word is often clearly inappropriate in its strictest sense. Broadly, it is a legal representation of the right to receive prospective future benefits under stated conditions, and it is in this sense that the words 'stocks' and 'securities' will be used interchangeably throughout this book. The Stock Exchange provides a market in a wide range of traded securities, generally of medium- to long-term maturities, issued by companies, governments and public organizations, both domestic and overseas.

Traditionally the Stock Exchange is thought of as both a primary and secondary market. (A *primary market* is where new funds are raised by the issue of new securities; a *secondary market* is where trade takes place in already-issued securities.) The two markets are closely related, in that the willingness of investors to subscribe to new issues in the primary market is crucially dependent on their ability to dispose of such securities, if necessary, in the secondary market, before the final maturity date. Some securities, such as ordinary shares or undated Government securities, have no guaranteed maturity date.

Strictly speaking, however, the Stock Exchange is only a secondary market, as no securities are initially sold on the Stock Exchange trading floor by the issuer. Instead they are sold first of all to institutions or individuals, who are then free to resell them on the floor of the Exchange provided that the Stock Exchange Council have signified their approval by quoting the security on their *Official List*. (There is one exception: whereas subscriptions for new issues of company securities are paid to the issuing house advising the company, application for Government issues has to be made to the Bank of England, either centrally or regionally.) The new-issue market is thus separate from, and off the floor of, the Stock Exchange.

The fund-raising operations of the public sector are largely dictated by fiscal policy – by the extent of the budget deficit, or occasionally surplus – and not by the cost of funds. But in company fund-raising the cost, or at least the likelihood of an issue being fully subscribed, should be more influential. This again illustrates the connection between the secondary market and the new-issue market, for the cost of raising new funds is determined by the current yields of existing securities being traded in the stock market. In theory, through the forces of demand and supply, the stock market is constantly reassessing the prospects of companies, so that at any time those securities offer a fair return for the risk involved. If the prospects of a company deteriorate, the value of its debt and equity (see Unit 6) will fall, so that at the lower price the securities offer the same return (or even an increased return if more risk is now involved) on the lower expected earnings. The converse applies if prospects improve.

So the efficiency with which the Stock Exchange discharges its role as an allocator of capital depends, among other things, on how well securities are valued in the secondary market. If they are fairly valued, and capital is in short supply, only the companies with the best investment prospects will be willing to raise funds on the high yields that have to be paid. But this view has to be qualified on several counts. First, most corporate investment is undertaken from retained earnings, and these may not be properly costed. Secondly, in times of boom allocation is more likely to be by queue than by price, because the Bank of England does not allow companies to come to the market all at the same time, but instead gives them dates in the future. Thirdly, the efficiency of the allocatory function depends on the degree of foresight of investors in the market. The stock market prides itself on being a barometer of the future, rather than a thermometer of the present but, in the absence of other information, investors perhaps tend to base the valuation of companies excessively on recent past performance.

Views on how successfully the Stock Exchange fulfils its allocatory function differ widely, partly because the Stock Exchange is seen as the symbol of capitalism. For example, Walter Bagehot in the nineteenth century opposed any changes, saying 'we must not let in daylight upon magic'. Even greater praise came more recently in F.E. Armstrong's book on the Stock Exchange; 'The Stock Exchange as an institution has been evolved by time and perfected by experience . . . It is the Citadel of Capital, the Temple of Values. It is the axle on which the whole financial structure of the Capitalistic System turns. It is the Bazaar of human effort and endeavour, the Mart where man's courage, ingenuity and labour are marketed.'

Lord Keynes was less impressed. 'Speculators may do no harm as bubbles on a steady stream of enterprise. But the position is serious when enterprise becomes the bubble on a whirlpool of speculation. When the capital development of a country becomes a by-product of the activities of a casino, the job is likely to be ill done.'

Keynes was writing in the mid-1930s but his views have been echoed in recent times. The establishment in 1977 of the 'Wilson Committee' to review the functioning of the financial institutions was partly in response to criticisms like his. Despite its protestations to the contrary, the Exchange's secondary role has appeared to predominate over the primary one in recent years, as far as industry and commerce are concerned.

The market capitalization of the ordinary shares of companies fluctuates a great deal, as instanced by the fall by over two-thirds between May 1972 and January 1975, but some generalizations can nevertheless be made about the size of the market. The market value of such shares on the London Stock Exchange is far below that of the New York and Tokyo Exchanges, but much bigger than that of any other country. Moreover, it is generally much easier to trade in United Kingdom ordinary shares and Government securities than in the equivalent stocks in these other countries. Yet at the same time industrial and commercial companies have been raising on average less than 5 per cent of their total funds from the new-issue market, as Table 1.2 shows.

Table 1.2 Sources of capital funds of industrial and commercial companies (£mn)

	Total from all sources	UK capital issues	
		Ordinary shares	Debentures and preference shares
1975	12 887	1 031	202
1976	18 163	785	42
1977	19 810	729	−67
1978	21 761	830	−71
1979	28 035	906	−21

Source: *Financial Statistics*, June 1980

There is some evidence that during the 1960s the United Kingdom new-issue market raised a smaller amount (relative to gross national product (GNP)) in new domestic industrial finance than did its main rivals. The Stock Exchange has disputed the consistency of the figures used for these comparisons, but the general picture nevertheless is clear.

The Stock Exchange can be defended on several points. First, it acts only in a regulatory capacity towards the new-issue market, laying down listing and minimum size requirements, which are not considered to be too onerous. Secondly, the administrative costs of fund-raising compare favourably with those in most other countries, although there are significant economies of scale. Thirdly, 'you can lead a horse to water, but you cannot make it drink'. If companies do not wish to borrow, if they are in the main satisfied with retained earnings to finance their investment programmes, then the Stock Exchange cannot force them to borrow. Fourthly, the Exchange has been successful in funding the increasing public sector borrowing requirement from 1974 onwards.

It may seem strange that during most of the 1970s, companies that needed to use external finance went primarily to the banks, while the public sector relied on capital issues. But the reasoning is quite straightforward. In the first place, there were reasons of financial prudence. Companies were unwilling to commit themselves to high nominal long-term rates of interest, in case inflation subsided, or to the expense of the initial servicing costs. They preferred to rely on bank overdrafts or medium-term loans with floating interest rates. Moreover, the Government was not commercially restricted in its issuing of debt (perhaps it was more pessimistic about inflationary prospects), and there was also the technical reason that borrowing short-term from the banks was liable to inflate the money supply because of the creation of reserve assets for the banking system; issuing gilt-edged securities (see Glossary) to the non-bank private sector would not do so.

Clearly, therefore, the new-issue market has in recent years been essentially one for public-sector rather than corporate fund-raising. But this is nothing more than a return to historical practice. Government financing has always been an important element in the life of the Stock Exchange. Even in the years shortly before the First World War, only about a tenth of real investment in Britain was financed by new issues on the Stock Exchange. Nevertheless, United Kingdom Government securities, which in 1853 amounted to 70 per cent of the nominal value of all securities quoted on the Exchange, shrank to only 9 per cent by 1914. Then followed the heavy Government borrowing necessary to finance the two world wars, and the depressed conditions of the 1920s and 1930s discouraged the creation of company securities. After 1945, however, the number of quoted industrial companies increased rapidly, and inflation (together with retentions) has boosted their market values, while diminishing those of long-term Government securities.

The mechanics of the Stock Exchange's operations are discussed in Units 9 and 10.

1.6 The Personal and the Institutional Investor

Personal sector savings that are not required for housebuilding (and real investment by unincorporated businesses) are largely lent to Government through the Stock Exchange. But this lending is indirect, via insurance companies and pension funds, rather than directly into Government securities. In recent years, private individuals have been increasing their overall savings ratios but simultaneously reducing their direct investments in the stock market at a dramatic rate, as Tables 1.3 and 1.4 demonstrate.

Table 1.4 shows that over the last two decades there has been a continuing

Table 1.3 Personal sector: acquisition and sale of financial assets (£mn)

	Company and overseas securities	Inflows to life assurance and pension funds
1975	1 039	4 549
1976	1 549	5 663
1977	1 885	6 366
1978	1 414	7 706
1979	1 845	9 499

Source: *Financial Statistics*, June 1980

Table 1.4 Percentage of total market value of United Kingdom listed equities held by different groups

31 December	1963	1973	1975	1978	1979
Insurance companies	(10.6)	(16.2)	(15.9)	(19.5)	(20.5)
Pension funds	(7.0)	(12.2)	(16.8)	(21.0)	(22.5)
Investment trusts	(6.7)	(6.5)	(6.1)	(5.5)	(4.5)
Unit trusts	(1.2)	(3.4)	(4.1)	(4.5)	(3.0)
Total institutions	25.5	38.3	42.9	50.5	51.0
Persons	58.7	42.0	37.5	30.0	29.5
Charities	2.6	4.4	2.3	2.5	2.5
Financial companies	2.3	3.3	4.0	4.0	4.0
Industrial and commercial companies	4.8	4.3	4.1	4.5	4.0
Government	1.6	2.5	3.6	4.0	4.0
Overseas	4.4	5.2	5.6	4.5	5.0
Total per cent*	100.0	100.0	100.0	100.0	100.0
Value (£bn)	27.5	40.5	44.6	63.3	70.0

*Subject to rounding differences.
Source: Phillips and Drew. Figures for 1963 and 1973 are from the Diamond Commission, those for 1975 from the Department of Industry, while those for 1978 and 1979 are Phillips and Drew's own estimates.

trend away from personal towards institutional ownership of ordinary shares. Between 1963 and 1979 the proportion of ordinary shares in United Kingdom listed companies held directly by individuals fell by almost exactly one-half – from 58.7 per cent to 29.5 per cent – while at the same time the proportion held by the major institutional investors exactly doubled – from 25.5 to 51 per cent.

An *institution*, in the broadest sense, is a body which takes funds from individuals and corporate organizations for the purpose of profitable investment. It invests as a principal (that is, in its own name), mainly in the stock market, using professional management and operating within the constraints provided by its own articles or trust deed and by tax and legal considerations. A full list would include merchant banks, charities, the Church Commissioners, trade unions, the Public Trustee and others, but for most purposes, as in this book, the term *institutional investor* is used to refer to the insurance companies, the pension funds (private, public and local authority), unit trusts and investment trusts.

The personal sector has been a net disposer of company and overseas securities every year since 1955, most recently at a rate of £1bn to £2bn each year. Most of these securities have been taken up by the institutions. If the proportion of equities held by private investors continues to fall at the past average rate of about 2 per cent per annum, all personal shareholdings will be eliminated within 15 years!

Combined institutional investors were net buyers of ordinary shares in each of the years between 1966 and 1979. Insurance companies, all three classes of pension fund, and unit trusts were net purchasers in all years, though investment trusts were net sellers in 1969, 1970, 1973, 1974 and 1978. Similar developments, although not so advanced, have been experienced in the USA. The demise of the 'small investor' has prompted one wag to comment that nowadays the term means a fund manager under five feet six!

But why should so many people prefer to hold a claim on a financial institution rather than one directly on the Government or a company? The main reasons are as follows:

(*a*) This is the most tax-efficient way to save. For example, for every 85p a person saves in life assurance he now receives a subsidy of 15p, which is effectively 17.65 per cent (for premiums up to one-sixth of income or £1 500, whichever is the greater). In the case of approved pension schemes the whole of the contributions are an allowable charge against taxable income (up to 17½ per cent of net relevant earnings for self-employed people). In addition, unit trust management companies offer life assurance schemes linked to their units. It is much more difficult for anyone to achieve equivalent returns by direct investment, especially when in the case of life assurance and pension schemes the investment income can be accumulated within the fund and be treated more generously than if received directly by an investor paying higher-rate tax.

(*b*) Institutional investors can provide a widely diversified portfolio for a relatively small outlay. This may be a broad spread of ordinary shares or, in the case of life assurance and pension funds, it may extend to gilt-edged stocks and property. Thus the small investor is far less exposed to risk than if his eggs were in one or two baskets – for even the most highly regarded companies have been known to go into liquidation. Modern financial theory suggests that diversification should be one of the prime objectives of the investor.

(*c*) The public is increasingly aware of the need for professional management. This in part reflects increased advertising and promotional activities, initially by unit trust groups, more recently by the life assurance companies. But professional management does not, or should not, imply an ability to make exceptionally high profits year after year. It means providing the highest return for the level of risk the investor is willing to undertake, having regard to his personal circumstances and tax position.

(*d*) Estate duty and capital transfer tax have forced private holdings on to the market to meet these liabilities, and frequently these holdings, if substantial, are sold directly to institutions.

(*e*) Finally, some small investors are made to feel unwanted by the generally poorer dealing and information service they receive compared with that accorded to institutional clients (although this is less marked in the case of smaller brokers in the provinces). Perhaps this simply reflects the broker's increased costs and the inevitable emphasis on the more lucrative institutional business. Of course, the small investor can buy shares through his local clearing bank, but anyone with less than £1 000 to invest would be well advised to choose a unit trust. Few brokers would be interested in managing a portfolio as small as this.

1.7 Implications of the Growth of Institutional Investment

The domination of savings flows and the increasing control of the equity market by institutional investors has become a topic of widespread political and economic debate. Concern centres around the following areas:

(*a*) Stock Market Efficiency

Institutional investors bring savings into the stock market which otherwise might have gone elsewhere, and the high commission they pay to brokers on large deals stimulates research to justify such rewards. These are good points which strengthen the size and efficiency of the market. But frequently institutions 'lock up' company securities in their portfolios, and so make it difficult to deal in the shares. When they do wish to deal it may be in larger amounts than the traditional jobbing system can cope with, thus leading to developments such as ARIEL (see Unit 9.7) whereby institutions deal between themselves outside the traditional market.

The minimum size of deal which interests the large institutional fund may preclude investment in small companies. There is a feeling that this raises the *de facto* minimum size requirements of the new issue market. Even worse is the position of unquoted companies, largely precluded from institutional backing.

Institutional activity makes a significant contribution to stock market turnover, and gives financial institutions considerable impact on security prices. There is a very high correlation between their net acquisitions of equities and movements in the market indices, suggesting that they are either following or making the market. They have frequently been criticized for their 'herd-like' attitude to investment, all trying to buy or sell at the same time, no one wishing to take an opposite view and be the odd man out. Such behaviour was perhaps responsible for the volatility of the market during the 1970s. This instability made rational capital allocation difficult, if not impossible; it was foreseen by Keynes, who wrote:

> It is the long-term investor, he who most promotes the public interest, who will in practice come in for most criticism, wherever investment funds are managed by committees or boards or banks. For it is in the essence of his behaviour that he should be eccentric, unconventional and rash in the eyes of average opinion. If he is successful, that will only confirm the general belief in his rashness; and if, in the short run, he is unsuccessful, which is very likely, he will not receive much mercy. Worldly wisdom teaches that it is better for reputation to fail conventionally than to succeed unconventionally.

(*b*) **Shareholder Democracy**

Traditionally shareholders have not interfered in company management – there has been a 'divorce of ownership from control'. This has been a consequence of the wide dispersion of shareholdings and the general ignorance and apathy of many investors. But institutional investors collectively now hold majority, or at least strategic, stakes in many companies. Their decisions are crucial in take-over bids. They are frequently invited, along with brokers, to meet top management. They have become the 'élite' investors. This is a situation the Stock Exchange has attempted to resist, because it challenges one of its fundamental tenets, that all investors are equal – the *Take-over Code*, for instance, was introduced in part to prevent differential offers being made to different classes of shareholder. Nevertheless a feeling remains that the small shareholder may be effectively disenfranchised by a body which has tremendous collective power but no real accountability to its own investors.

(*c*) **Company Management**

Some people believe that the institutions should be more forthright and interventionist towards companies, rather than worrying about treading on the toes of the small investor. The United Kingdom is frequently compared unfavourably in terms of economic performance with other industrialized countries, and one possible explanation lies in the differences in financial structure. In Germany, in particular, the banks have a strong say in company organization, and it may be that something similar is required in this country, to disturb sleepy and inefficient management. Until recently the institutional investors have always resisted such a role, preferring to sell shares that performed badly rather than trying to intervene directly in the company. They justified this policy on several grounds:

(i) lack of necessary management consultancy expertise;
(ii) fear that news of intervention would further depress the share price;
(iii) fear of nationalization if they were seen to be too powerful;
(iv) acquisition of 'inside' knowledge would preclude further share dealing;

(v) fear of adverse publicity if involved in redundancies, factory closures and so forth;

(vi) a belief that their first duty was to their own investors.

Slowly the attitude of the institutions has been changing. In 1970 the Prudential Assurance and other institutions initiated sweeping changes in the management of Vickers. In 1972, following the débâcle of Rolls-Royce, BSA and the Mersey Docks and Harbour Board, the Governor of the Bank of England persuaded the institutions to get together and the outcome was the formation of the *Institutional Shareholders Committee* in 1973. Its record to date is best summed up by a *Sunday Times* headline 'Will the Watchdog Awake?' Secrecy was one of the conditions laid down by the British Insurance Association before it agreed to join.

Despite the unpromising record to date, institutions are likely to become bolder in the future. They need to show their political critics that they are not neglectful of the national interest (which is also their own collective vested interest). More pertinently, such action may be unavoidable because of the large share stakes amassed. The Prudential Assurance, for example, in April 1977 held stakes of 5 per cent and above in either the ordinary or preference capital of more than 230 United Kingdom quoted companies. Its stake in GEC was valued at £60mn, and that in Marks and Spencer nearly £50mn. Increasingly institutions are becoming 'locked in' to their large shareholdings; they are too large to be disposed of through normal market channels. Intervention may be the only answer.

(*d*) **Take-overs and Mergers**

During the 1960s and early 1970s the United Kingdom had a higher incidence of merger activity than virtually any other major industrialized country. Some mergers turned out to be successful; most were disappointing. The economic rationale for many of them was mystifying, yet they had largely been supported by the institutions. This was because the institutions were willing to accept offers which were a significant improvement on the prevailing share price, thus at once improving the performance of, and rationalizing, their portfolios. In the long run, however, many of these businesses might have provided greater earnings and dividends if they had remained independent. So a great deal of economic reorganization may have been simply a consequence of administrative tidiness on the part of the institutions.

Companies have also been deterred from long-term investment plans for fear that any temporary depression of earnings or dividends might adversely affect the share price and thereby invite a take-over bid. Again contrast can be made with the continental habit of supplying long-term support, provided that the fundamentals of the company are satisfactory.

Institutional dominance certainly seems a mixed blessing. It has undoubtedly helped the Government fund its borrowing requirement. But it appears to conflict with the current interest in stimulating new entrepreneurial businesses, and there may well be moves in the future to remove the fiscal advantages accorded these institutions and those that invest through them.

1.8 The Different Types of Investment

One increasingly widespread area of investment is proving to be an extremely valuable method of employing available moneys, giving a real protection against the long-term effect of inflation. This is *owner-occupied house property*. It is without doubt the form of growth investment owned by the largest number of individuals. The provision of finance to enable people to buy houses to live in has become a highly organized business.

Almost everyone realizes that owning the house you live in is one of the best investments you can make. When the mortgage is at last paid off, most home-owners have an asset which has appreciated substantially over the purchase price. And the amount of interest paid, although considerable, has almost certainly been less than the rent payable for the occupation of similar property owned by someone else. The payment of mortgage instalments instead of rent will have given you a real opportunity to acquire something worthwhile to pass on to your children.

Another type of investment is the *personal chattel*, although it is the choice of relatively few investors. Everyone has personal possessions, of course, but the vast majority are acquired for use and consumption or as a hobby, rather than for investment. But precious stones, antiques, postage stamps and many other specialized fields of collecting can be profitable as investments. The *ownership of property for letting* is another area where few individuals are investors, although this is a regular and common area of investment for institutions.

Although we shall discuss the value of holding property and chattels in Unit 13, we shall in this book be concerned principally with the three other major types of investment: (*a*) loans, (*b*) shares, and (*c*) indirect investment through a financial institution. Later Units will show the use that investors, both individual and institutional, can make of these investments and also describe the workings of the market that serves (*a*) and (*b*).

1.9 Success in Investment

Success in most things is relative, and no less so in the field of investment. Success in investment means earning the highest possible return with the constraints imposed by the investor's personal circumstances – age, family needs, liquidity requirements, tax position and acceptability of risk. If possible, performance should be measured against alternative investments, or combinations of investments, available to the investor within those constraints. Genuine success also means winning the battle against inflation, against the fall in the real value of savings and capital.

'Money can't buy them happiness.'

The investor should be aware of, but not daunted by, the fact that investment markets, the stock market in particular, are largely dominated by professional investors. As a consequence, grossly undervalued investments are rarely easy to come by. Moreover, he should beware of books subtitled *How I Made a Million* and statements such as 'You can have a high return with no risk'. In reasonably efficient markets risk and return go together like bread and butter; in the words of Milton Friedman, 'there is no such thing as a free lunch'.

Success involves planning – clearly establishing one's objectives and constraints. Investments should be looked at in terms of what they contribute to the overall portfolio, rather than their merits in isolation. Institutional investment will probably play some part, and performance tables are available to give some guidance. But personal direct investment should not be overlooked, particularly in the obvious area of home-ownership, and one's own knowledge, skills, hobbies and acquaintances can also be put to advantage. Remember Francis Bacon's words:

> If a man look sharply and attentively, he shall see fortune; for though she be blind, yet she is not invisible.

1.10 Questions

1. Over the past 30 years there have been radical changes in the ownership of the share capital of United Kingdom companies. What have these changes

been and what, in your view, are the reasons for them? What is the effect of these changes on the stock market?

2. Who are the major borrowers and savers in the United Kingdom economy?

3. Discuss the relative importance of the Stock Exchange and the banking system in the financing of British industry.

Unit Two

Types of Investment

Today there is a very considerable variety of investment opportunity for the private individual, but it is difficult to discuss types of investment in broad terms because there are so many possible ways of classifying investments. While all are useful up to a point, because of the degree of overlapping none is entirely satisfactory.

2.1 Fixed-income and Variable-income Investments

Investments are often divided into *fixed-income* and *variable-income* investments. Most investments come into one of these two categories; for instance:

Fixed-income investments	*Variable-income investments*
Gilt-edged securities	Ordinary shares
Company loan stocks	Unit trusts
Preference shares	

There are such important differences between the securities within these groups, however, that such a division is sometimes a hindrance to understanding. Preference shares, for example, generally produce a fixed income but the security itself fundamentally has more in common with ordinary shares since preference shares are part of the share capital and are not a loan. Most unit trusts consist of holdings of ordinary shares but because there is a spread of investment – with the intention of eliminating severe fluctuations in prices – unit trust income tends to be more stable than the typical ordinary share.

Another objection to classifying investments in this way is that it ignores those investments which produce no income as such. Obviously in the long run all investments must offer some prospect of a return but the following investments all fall into a third group:

Premium savings bonds
Chattels (e.g. stamp collections, coins, Oriental carpets)
Owner-occupied property
Warrants

Premium savings bonds are well known to offer not interest but prizes. The prize fund is based on a notional sum which would otherwise be available for rest but the random distribution of the prizes, both large and small, makes the premium bond a very speculative investment, if indeed it really is an investment at all. Chattels purchased as investments – that is, to produce a gain – must be distinguished from those acquired for the enjoyment they give the collector. Owner-occupied property, as we saw in Unit 1.8, has proved to be an excellent investment in its own right. Warrants produce no income as such and their attractiveness as investments is wholly dependent on the related ordinary shares.

2.2 Quoted and Unquoted Investments

Another approach is to consider the division of investments into those which are *quoted* investments – that is, those in which dealings are permitted on the Stock Exchange – and those which are *unquoted*. This separation is not without problems because many types of investment can be in both categories: ordinary shares, loan stocks and warrants, for instance. These are all company securities, however, and investment in unquoted companies, in particular in the equity capital, must always be subject to special considerations. Most investors avoid them if only because, since there is no market in them, their disposal may present problems. Occasionally, however, they may be inherited, and they are therefore discussed later in this book. Examples of quoted and unquoted investments are:

Quoted	*Quoted or unquoted*	*Unquoted*
British Government securities	All company securities:	Bank and other deposits
	Ordinary shares	
	Preference shares	Unit trusts (with a few exceptions)
Public board stocks	Loan issues	
	Warrants	National Savings:
		Premium Savings Bonds
		National Savings Certificates

Many unquoted investments, excepting always the special cases of property and chattels, are 'cash' investments in that they can be redeemed for no less than the capital sum invested (sometimes with an interest penalty for early encashment). Unit trusts, however, stand out as examples of unquoted investments which, to cite the usual warning to prospective investors, 'can go down as well as up'!

2.3 Direct and Indirect Investments

In Unit 1.5 a distinction was made between primary and secondary investment. This book is mainly concerned with secondary investment, but to understand this thoroughly the need for the underlying real investment must always be borne in mind. Another distinction that can be drawn is that between *direct investment* and *indirect investment*. Most of the investments we have looked at in this Unit so far have been direct investments in that the securities concerned represent investment in a particular organization – government, bank, building society, company and so on.

One important group, however, can be designated indirect investments. These are essentially 'investments in investments'. They are particularly useful to the smaller investor, who is unwise if he puts money into the more speculative direct investments such as ordinary shares. It is usually uneconomic to invest less than about £500 in any one security and it is generally thought that an investor needs to spread his capital among at least fifteen securities. He must also be sure that he obtains a sensible spread between industries: it is not much use allocating his funds between fifteen different engineering firms, because many of the problems experienced by one company in that industry will adversely affect its competitors also. This spreading of investment, or *diversification*, is only possible for the small investor if he uses one of the available vehicles for indirect investment.

The number of these has increased considerably during the postwar years, corresponding with the decline of the direct private investor and the rise of the institutions. The oldest member of the group is the investment trust company. *Investment trusts*, as they are commonly called, are limited companies with capital structures not unlike those of other companies. They differ from the trading company, however, in that their assets consist of the shares of other companies. Thus a purchase of the ordinary shares in an investment trust is an indirect investment in perhaps as many as several hundred other companies.

Unit trusts, however, are not companies but trusts, with objects similar to those of the investment trust – they invest widely and their managers aim generally to produce a total return (both income and capital gain) which is at least better than average. The prices of units reflect the value of the underlying portfolio, whereas in the case of the investment trust prices are determined by market factors.

A most important type of indirect investment is in insurance or, more properly, *life assurance*. Life assurance is a contract whereby the insurance company agrees to pay a certain amount if the insured person dies during the course of the contract. The premiums for the cheapest form of life assurance, *term assurance*, are payable for a limited number of years only and payment of the sum assured is only made if death occurs during that period. In such a case there is no savings or investment element.

With an *endowment insurance policy*, however, premiums are payable for a limited period or until earlier death, whereupon the sum assured, which may be with or without profits, becomes payable. Such a policy combines both insurance and savings elements.

Another kind of policy may be linked to a specific fund such as a unit trust or an internal fund, as in the case of a *property bond* which is linked to a portfolio of direct property investment. Tax concessions actually make it possible for many investors to acquire a larger investment with the same cash in this way than they can by investing directly. Thus the investor prepared to spread his investment over a period can obtain the life assurance element at no real cost. For higher-rate taxpayers different tax considerations apply and several attractive forms of investment have been tailored to their needs.

Today the most widespread form of indirect investment is the *pension scheme*. The pension fund managers are now the second biggest of all the institutional investors (see Table 14.2) and exercise enormous market influence. Quite apart from the State schemes – the flat-rate pension and earnings-related scheme – many employers, both in the private and the public sector, now offer their employees attractive pension plans. A few of these are 'non-contributory' for employees but in most they make a contribution that is supplemented by the employer's contribution, which is usually the larger of the two. Large employers set up their own pension companies to run self-invested funds, while many smaller companies secure pensions for their employees by means of insurance contracts. Employees' contributions are wholly allowable for tax purposes but the pensions when received are chargeable to tax as earned income. Usually a substantial part of the pension can be taken as a lump sum.

Self-employed people, left out of the earnings-related state scheme for practical reasons, are now encouraged to make their own pension arrangements. This encouragement takes the form of tax relief at the highest marginal rate (inclusive of the investment income surcharge) on their contributions, the limit being 17½ per cent of net relevant earnings.

Fig. 2.1 shows the relative importance of the various kinds of investment.

2.4 Risk in Investment

Investments may be classified according to the degree of risk. Risk avoidance is an important topic in itself and may be regarded as one of the underlying themes not only of this book but of any serious approach to investment. There are two kinds of risk:

(*a*) that capital may be lost in part or altogether, and even if not lost, that short-term fluctuations in value may seriously affect the investor; and

(*b*) that income may not be paid when due, or may at least be unreliable. A threat to the income can be regarded as endangering the capital too, for if a business has difficulty in paying interest or dividends this is often the result of losses which are, in effect, forced reductions of capital.

Unfortunately, there are difficulties in categorizing investments in this way. The main reason is that within a category – loan stocks, for example – one could buy a range of securities extending from the fairly safe to the downright speculative. Even British Government securities have their attendant risks. The so-called 'undated' stocks such as 3½% War Loan are absolutely safe as regards interest, but must be regarded as risk investments so far as capital is concerned because there is no prospect whatsoever of repayment and the

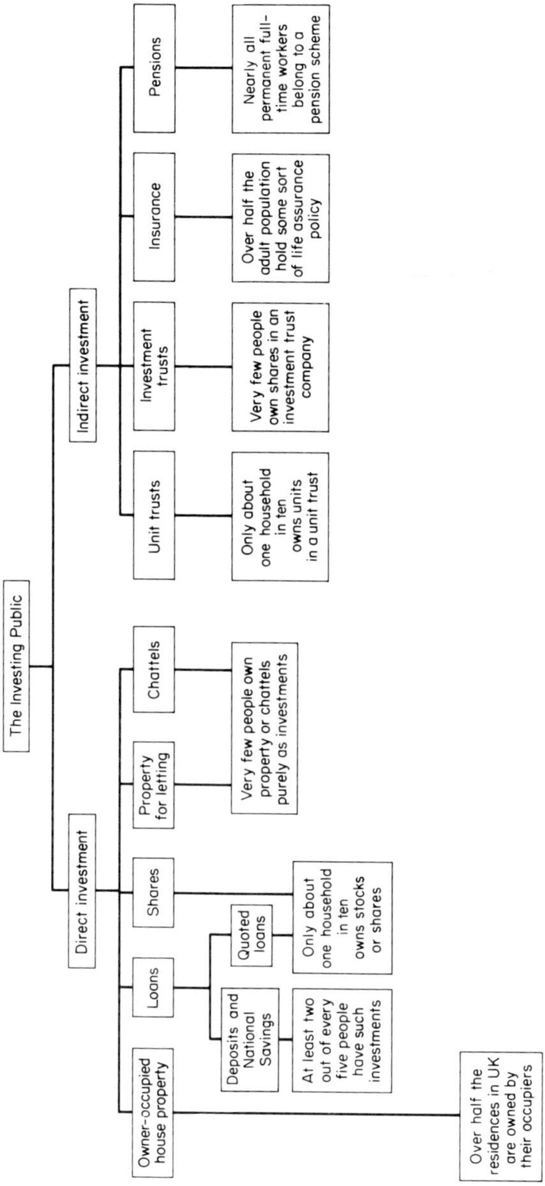

Fig. 2.1 The range of available investments

future price of the stock cannot be forecast. Even the dated securities carry risks because the stated repayment date may be much more remote than the investor's own investment time horizon. Time and risk are really always closely connected.

In the rest of this Unit we shall examine in some detail the various kinds of cash investment. The two main types of quoted investment, fixed-interest securities and ordinary shares or equities, will be discussed in Units 4 and 5 and in Unit 6 respectively.

2.5 Cash Investments

Cash investments are loans made by investors to the Government or to financial institutions and which are repayable without penalty on demand or after only a relatively short period of notice. Some cash investments give tax benefits to the investor, making it complicated to compare one with another for all categories of investor.

Every investor should keep part of his capital in a suitable cash investment so that he has money easily realizable in the event of an emergency. He would be unwise to rely for his unexpected cash needs on investments which have to be sold on the Stock Exchange, as he might have to realize them at a time when the market for those particular investments is depressed. Similar reservations apply to most National Savings investments, such as National Savings Certificates, for early withdrawal usually means some loss of 'interest'. Most loans to local authorities (see Unit 5.4) are not repayable on demand.

The disadvantage of cash investments is that they do not grow, that is to say, the amount of money available can never be greater than the amount originally invested, together with interest earned. Equally, it can never diminish but, as the value of the money is continually falling as a result of inflation, the holder of a cash investment is dependent on his net interest return to maintain the real value of his money. Unless the annual interest received, after allowing for any tax liabilities, is greater than the annual rate of inflation, the investment fails to maintain its value. For this reason the amount held permanently in this type of investment should normally not be greater than the sum required to maintain an adequate emergency reserve.

All temporary investments should be in the form of cash investments. If an investor provides his capital by savings out of income, he should make use of a suitable cash investment until he has accumulated sufficient funds to make a more permanent investment worthwhile. Any moneys which he knows he will need within a year or so should usually also be placed in this type of investment, so as to avoid loss in the event of market prices being lower at the time the cash is required.

There may also be times when the investor takes a particularly gloomy view about the alternative quoted investments. In such circumstances he will doubtless consider keeping a substantial percentage of his funds in this form; indeed he may decide to be 100 per cent liquid. For much of the early 1970s most of

Fig. 2.2 £1 000 invested in equities and building societies, with net income reinvested (1946–79)

the cash investments outperformed not only equities and the property market but Government securities too. Over the postwar years, however, equities have been a better investment on the whole (see Fig. 2.2).

2.6 National Savings Bank and National Girobank Accounts

The National Savings Bank, formerly called the Post Office Savings Bank, was set up in 1861 for the safe keeping of savings and the encouragement of thrift. The rate of interest paid was $2\frac{1}{2}$ per cent in 1861 and remained so until 1970. In recent years the rate of interest has been increased from time to time in order to encourage the use of the Bank and at the time of writing it stands at 5 per cent for ordinary accounts.

The attraction of an *ordinary account* with the National Savings Bank to the investor, apart from being able to deposit moneys and withdraw up to £100 at many Post Offices during their normal business hours, is the fact that the first £70 of interest paid is entirely free of income tax (although any interest, no matter how small, must be declared for income tax purposes – unlike gains made on National Savings Certificates or Save As You Earn contracts). This £70 represents the interest at 5 per cent on £1 400, and while this may be a useful concession to high-rate taxpayers, it is unattractive to most investors at times when interest rates are high. The maximum amount that may be held in an ordinary account is £10 000, but as interest in excess of £70 is fully taxable this restriction is of merely academic concern to serious investors.

The National Savings Bank also conducts *investment accounts*. There are no tax concessions on these accounts but the rate of interest varies with the level of interest rates generally, although it tends to be more rigid than bank or building society rates. The maximum investment is £200 000 at the time of writing, and one month's notice of withdrawal is required, compared to a few days in the case of ordinary accounts.

National Girobank is best known as the money transfer arm of the Government sector. Operations began in 1968 but in 1975 its structure was reorganized, and it now offers an increasing range of banking services including deposit accounts. Interest is taxable and an additional ½ per cent is paid on deposits held for six months or more.

2.7 Trustee Savings Bank Accounts

The trustee savings banks (TSBs), like so many other financial institutions, were founded in Scotland. In the early nineteenth century, as the Industrial Revolution gathered momentum, a need developed for institutions that catered for the savings of wage-earners. The TSBs have long been regarded as quasi-governmental organizations because in their early days it was Government which enabled them to place their funds at interest while still maintaining essential liquidity. The Fund for the Banks for Savings (FBS), as the Government fund was called, was guaranteed but in return the banks surrendered a substantial degree of control to the National Debt Commissioners. The TSBs were thus much restricted in the uses to which they could put the funds placed with them by savers and they were not permitted to open current accounts until 1964. In 1968 they extended their services by marketing a unit trust, and they now boast a range of services that rivals those of the clearing banks. The really radical changes in TSB business have been the opening of current accounts and the introduction of lending. This was one of the recommendations of the Page Committee on National Savings, which reported in 1973. A necessary precondition was that the TSBs concentrated their resources and today, whereas there were once over seventy separate TSBs, there are only seventeen. The Trustee Savings Bank Act 1976 provides for TSB funds held in the FBS to be withdrawn gradually over a transitional period and invested by the banks themselves, subject to Treasury and Bank of England control, instead of by the National Debt Office.

As quasi-governmental institutions the TSBs enjoyed certain privileges, but these are now gradually being withdrawn and will in time disappear altogether. Like the National Savings Bank the TSBs have two basic saving schemes: the *Ordinary Department* and the *Investment Department*. The first £70 of interest on Ordinary Department accounts used to be free of income tax but this privilege was withdrawn in November 1979. The Investment Department, first introduced in the 1880s, has long been regarded as the principal savings medium for a large number of TSB customers. Today some 60 per cent of balances are held in this Department.

2.8 Bank Deposit Accounts

One of the simplest forms of investment is a *deposit account* with a clearing bank. Most investors maintain a current account with a clearing bank and the transfer of part of the balance of that account to a separate deposit account requires only the completion of a form. The bank manager himself may suggest such a transfer. The very simplicity of such an investment might lead the suspicious to doubt whether, as an investment, the bank deposit account ranks among the most rewarding and these doubts may be justified. Of all borrowers, the banks are most flexible in their reactions to changes in Bank of England Minimum Lending Rate, the most influential of all interest rates. If this is raised sharply the interest rates of the clearing banks are the first to follow, and for a time at least offer a very satisfactory return. In the longer term, however, bank deposit rates are attractive only to non-taxpayers.

The clearing banks generally publish two rates of interest. *Base rate* is the rate by reference to which most of their advances are made; thus if base rate is, say, 12 per cent a first-class corporate borrower might be charged 13 per cent, while a private individual might pay 16 or 17 per cent. They also publish a *deposit rate*. This is not formally related to base rate and differs from one bank to another and from time to time; in recent years it has varied between $1\frac{3}{4}$ per cent and $2\frac{3}{4}$ per cent below base rate. Interest is calculated on a daily basis and deposit account moneys are held on seven days' notice. Deposits may be withdrawn at shorter notice on payment of a penalty, usually equivalent to seven days' interest.

Interest allowed on bank deposits is subject to income tax although paid without deduction of tax. Higher rates of interest may be allowed by banks on large deposits and for deposits subject to longer periods of notice. Whereas deposits of up to £10 000 are placed on seven-day call, the banks now offer more attractive rates for call and term deposits in the region of £10 000 to £25 000. For deposits above £25 000 the banks are naturally particularly keen to offer an attractive rate, for it is with larger amounts such as these that the investor has wider fields open to him.

In the latter part of 1980 the clearing banks all moved to compete more aggressively with the building societies, who for many years offered an imaginative choice of savings vehicles to their customers. Their main targets were deposits of £2 500 and above. The main emphasis was on deposits for fixed periods and deposits at longer periods of notice. One bank introduced a variable-rate scheme at three and six months' notice of withdrawal, while another offered high rates of interest for deposits of up to seven years duration with a withdrawal option.

Within the specialized interbank market the sums moved run into millions of pounds and access is naturally restricted. The investor with £25 000 or more could however find a discount house or a merchant bank a more attractive haven for his funds. Another alternative is a *sterling certificate of deposit* issued by a bank. The minimum sum necessary is £50 000 and these are issued at fixed rates of interest for periods ranging from three months to five years. Although issued for fixed periods such certificates can be readily negotiated in the secondary market. The longer-dated ones are, however, decidedly risky for, if interest rates rise after issue, the sum realized prior to maturity could involve the investor in a loss. Equally, of course, they could be profitable.

The other important money market investments – local authority deposits and bonds, Treasury bills and so on – are dealt with in Units 3 and 5.

2.9 Finance House Accounts

Finance houses is the correct name for those institutions, commonly called 'hire purchase companies', which provide credit to the general public to assist with the purchase of consumer goods. In contrast to bank lending, which is usually negotiated with established customers at the branch bank, most hire purchase finance is arranged at the 'point of sale' – the garage, television shop or furniture store. The growth in the personal loan business of the clearing banks has meant, and will continue to mean, a reduction in the provision of hire purchase finance to the more creditworthy customer. Hire purchase is a more expensive form of borrowing because it is provided for those less able to raise money and the risks are correspondingly higher.

Finance houses have, however, been able to expand other sections of their business which have a lower risk potential. Much of their activity now concerns

'Actually, I want to start a finance company.'

the provision of instalment finance to companies and firms to assist them in the purchase of capital equipment. There is also a growing demand for the leasing services of finance houses. To companies there may be tax advantages in leasing plant and machinery rather than in purchasing them. It certainly eases their cash flow problems.

When lending money to a finance house an investor should try to find out the exact nature of the major part of its activities, to ensure that he is not accepting an above-average risk. Generally he should be wary of houses offering unusually high rates of interest. If such high rates are paid to depositors, funds must be lent at correspondingly higher rates. Borrowers who are prepared to pay above-average rates must represent above-average risks, as their proposals clearly do not appeal to the more cautious and responsible lenders. The average investor probably looks no further for security than the finance houses that are wholly or partly owned by the big banks. He may have confidence that the banks would not permit the deposits to be lost and be comforted by the huge resources available for support. All finance houses advertising for deposits are required by the Banking Act 1979 to register with the Bank of England (see Unit 18.10), however, and this provides some extra measure of protection for investors.

The interest paid by finance houses is subject to income tax, although paid without deduction of tax if the period of deposit is less than one year. Because of the greater risk, rates are higher than those paid by banks on their deposits. Generally rates are quoted for deposits at one month's, three months' and six months' notice, although arrangements can be made for longer or shorter periods of notice, or for fixed periods at fixed rates. The rates obtainable on agreeing to give three or six months' notice are generally slightly better than the clearing banks' base rates.

2.10 Building Society Accounts

Building society deposit and share accounts are normally much more attractive to the average investor than the bank deposit account. Many building societies have accounts which may be operated by their members as though they were savings bank accounts – like ordinary bank accounts but with no cheque book or overdraft facilities. Strictly, societies may require notice of withdrawal but many may permit quite large sums to be withdrawn on demand. The two principal types of account are *deposit accounts* and *share accounts*, the former paying a slightly lower rate of interest as they have priority against assets should the society get into financial difficulties. As building societies borrow from their investors in order to lend to other members wishing to buy houses, they lend on a long-term basis moneys which, at the same time, they are offering to repay with little or no notice. Should a large number of investors all wish to withdraw at the same time a society could be in difficulties – the equivalent of a 'run on the banks'. To prevent such problems societies maintain reserves and liquid funds to meet contingencies, and where these exceed $7\frac{1}{2}$ per cent of assets and the society is of moderate size it may be granted *trustee status* by the Chief Registrar of Building Societies.

Many societies operate schemes under which investors can put aside a relatively small, regular sum over a period of years. These subscription shares usually receive rather more interest than other shares, reflecting the value to the society of funds not likely to be withdrawn at short notice. Most societies also offer higher, but usually variable, rates for *term shares* (investments for longer periods, usually for between one and six years).

Interest is paid net of basic-rate income tax. Special arrangements exist with the Inland Revenue under which societies pay a composite rate of tax based on an estimate of what investors would pay if they were assessed individually. This rate is fixed annually. The rates paid are adjusted by societies according to (*a*) the supply of moneys for investment and (*b*) the relative attractiveness of building society investment against other forms of cash investment. Smaller societies often pay higher rates than larger ones, reflecting their greater difficulty in attracting funds. The maximum amount that may be held with one society by any one individual is £20 000 (£40 000 by a married couple).

Although building society interest is received 'tax paid' this applies only to the basic rate of tax. To ascertain the further tax due, the building society interest must be 'grossed up'. Thus building society investments are not a very attractive proposition to a high-rate taxpayer, nor are they so to someone who pays no income tax, such as an elderly pensioner with just a small amount of capital invested.

Under one building society scheme – Save-As-You-Earn – no tax whatsoever is payable. Up to £20 a month (May 1981) is saved for five years. No interest is paid: instead the saver receives a bonus of fourteen monthly payments on completion of the term, the bonus being doubled if the funds are left for a further two-year period. The return is generally attractive only to higher-rate taxpayers.

Other building society schemes for investors are linked with life assurance (see Unit 12.14).

2.11 Cash Investments: Summary

The Post Office, an investor's bank and the local offices of the trustee savings banks and building societies can take care of most requirements for cash investment. Special problems arise, however, with the placing of large sums with financial institutions. Several firms in the City of London specialize in such business, and an investor should find little difficulty in getting in touch with one of them through his bank manager. These firms will quote the rates available from a range of institutions, for any period, for sums of £10 000 upwards. The investor himself may balance available rates against potential risk. The *Financial Times* quotes available rates from the local authority market daily.

Any individual adult can invest in any cash investment and, with the exception of finance houses and local authorities, the minimum amount required is

£5 or less. Investment can be made on behalf of a child and the National Savings Bank recognizes the signature of a child of seven years of age or over on withdrawal applications. Companies many not invest in the National Savings Bank or trustee savings banks unless acting as trustees. Building societies often refuse accounts to companies because of the tax complications. Clubs and other unincorporated societies may invest in any of the media described in this Unit.

2.12 Quoted Investments

None of the investments described above requires the services of a market. Most are open-ended investments from the borrower's point of view – that is to say, the amount borrowed by each institution from the investor is not limited and can be increased simply by accepting a further deposit. Equally, the amount the investor has lent to the institution can be reduced or withdrawn completely by giving the borrower the required period of notice. The services of an agent are not essential, and investing and withdrawing can be dealt with 'over the counter', or by letters between borrower and lender.

This is not the case with most investments. If you own 100 ordinary shares in British Petroleum Ltd, for example, you cannot walk into their offices and ask for a form to fill in to withdraw them in the same way that you can walk into the local office of a building society and complete a form to withdraw the balance of your share account. If you own £500 9% Treasury Stock 1994 (which is a Government security), you cannot complete a form to obtain £500 in one month's time, as you can if you own £500 of National Savings Certificates. The Government will not be prepared to encash Treasury Stock 1994 at its par (or face) value until 17 November 1994. The only way in which you can acquire or dispose of investments such as British Petroleum Ltd ordinary shares or 9% Treasury Stock 1994 is to find someone who wants to sell what you want to buy, or to buy what you have to sell.

With many kinds of trading it is difficult and expensive to get willing buyers and willing sellers together so that a deal may be done. If you want to buy a pound of frozen peas a willing seller will be found at a local supermarket. On the other hand, if you want to sell a few pounds of frozen peas it might be harder to find a willing buyer. With an original Rembrandt portrait to sell, you will need to seek a willing buyer at one of the world-famous London auction rooms and to pay a substantial commission for the service, which ensures a fair market price. If you want to sell a house, a fair market price can often only be obtained by employing an estate agent to advise and then test the market, and again the payment of commission will be necessary.

The Stock Exchange with its trading floors in London and elsewhere in Britain exists to provide a market for a very large number of investments. An investor does not need to look for someone with whom to deal. He must employ an agent, a stockbroker, to act for him, but generally there is no need to test the market so long as the amount involved is relatively small. A deal will be done with a jobber in the market at the prevailing market price. Under normal conditions a purchase or sale can be effected without delay so long as the current price is accepted. Without the services of a stock exchange the existing free market in investments would be impossible to maintain. The getting together of buyers and sellers would be a lengthy and expensive business, except in the case of those few stocks which are dealt in very frequently.

2.13 Questions

1. What are the merits and demerits of deposits with (*a*) a clearing bank, (*b*) a finance house, and (*c*) a building society? What consideration must be paid to the investor's tax position?

2. 'Every investor should keep part of his capital in a suitable cash investment.' Discuss.

3. Why, in general, would a small investor be advised to invest indirectly rather than in companies' securities – both equities and fixed-interest?

Unit Three

The Government as Borrower

3.1 The National Debt

Most governments are very large borrowers and the United Kingdom Government is no exception. The National Debt originated in the late seventeenth century and except for one brief period has progressively increased in volume, largely because of, first, the greater involvement of the State in the economy and, secondly, of wars, which have generally caused the most dramatic increases in the National Debt. Increases in this debt are technically referred to as the *Central Government Borrowing Requirement* (CGBR). In the post-war years there have been substantial increases, in part due to nationalization programmes, but in relation to the gross national product the National Debt has declined substantially since 1945.

Table 3.1 shows how the National Debt is made up. The figures shown are nominal amounts only. They correspond approximately to the actual amounts borrowed by the Government, and thus in general to the amount which the Government must in due course redeem. The market values of Government stocks at any time are generally lower than these nominal values, because since 1945 interest rates have risen inexorably and this in turn has tended to depress prices. The very substantial funds held by the National Savings Bank and National Girobank are not treated as part of the National Debt. This is because their funds are themselves invested in National Debt securities.

This Unit is concerned with British Government quoted securities and National Savings. The other large component of the National Debt – *Treasury bills* – represents the bulk of the Government's short-term borrowing. Treasury bills are issued in batches each week, and mature after three months. They are taken up in the first instance by the discount houses, foreign banks and other financial institutions, but are frequently negotiated before maturity by the clearing banks. They can be purchased on the secondary market by the individual investor in units of £5 000. They may be considered as a short-term alternative to sterling certificates of deposit (see Unit 2.8).

3.2 National Savings

The National Savings Movement is operated by the Department of National Savings in conjunction with the Treasury. Originally intended for small, unsophisticated savers, some of the investments offered today have considerable

Table 3.1 Components of the National Debt, 31 March 1978 (nominal values) (£mn)

British Government securities:	
under 5 years	18 625
5–15 years	9 013
over 15 years	20 322
undated	3 346
Total quoted securities	51 306
National Savings	5 832
Tax reserve certificates/deposits	452
Treasury bills	7 358
Ways and Means Advances	5 332
Overseas borrowings:	
International Monetary Fund	4 146
Other external debt	4 631
Other	123
Total	79 180

Source: *Financial Statistics*

appeal for the better-off, better-informed investor too. Even institutional investors can sometimes take advantage of the investment opportunities they offer, and National Savings Certificates are generally regarded as an excellent investment for the wealthy. The four principal types of investment offered and their relative importance in the National Debt are as follows:

	£mn
British Savings Bonds (no longer issued)	812
Save As You Earn	332
National Savings Certificates	3 394
Premium Savings Bonds	1 284
	5 822

In addition, some £10 million was represented by savings stamps and gift tokens.

3.3 Save As You Earn

This scheme encourages regular savings of between £4 and £50 a month over a five-year period. An earlier scheme offered a tax-free bonus equivalent to 12 per cent gross but the present scheme (the Third Issue) is index-linked in that the savings are revalued in line with the Retail Prices Index at the end of the contract period.

Each contribution must be separately revalued. Suppose, for instance, that the first instalment of £10 was made when the Index stood at 180 and that the Index at the end of the period was 300; the value of that contribution would be:

$$£10 \times \frac{300}{180} = £16.67$$

The final instalment made when the Index had reached 297 would be worth

$$£10 \times \frac{300}{297} = £10.10$$

Thus the sum payable in total would be the total of a series of contributions, each revalued in this way.

At the end of five years the saver has the option of leaving his funds for a further two years. At the end of this further period the funds are revalued again and in addition the saver receives a bonus equal to two monthly payments. There is some flexibility in SAYE contracts in that up to six monthly payments can be missed: thus if, say, three payments are missed the contract period is simply extended by three months. If seven payments are missed, however, the contract is cancelled and the saver is entitled only to interest at 6 per cent per annum. Withdrawal is subject to eight working days' notice but partial withdrawals are not allowed.

Savings fare so badly during inflation that it may seem strange that a scheme which merely guarantees the *real* value of contributions should be an excellent investment. SAYE is particularly useful for those people who are saving for a specific purpose such as a deposit on a house. Whether it proves to be a better investment than, say, National Savings Certificates depends very much on the rate of inflation over the contract period.

3.4 National Savings Certificates

Prior to the introduction of Save As You Earn in 1969, National Savings Certificates were the most attractive of the non-risk cash investments to the taxpayer. First issued in 1916 to help finance the First World War, there have been many issued with different terms, although only the latest issue could be purchased at any one time.

National Savings pamphlets refer to 'interest' on National Savings Certificates, but in fact they earn no interest. They increase in value by the addition of predetermined sums at regular intervals. These capital accretions are free of income and capital gains taxes. The current issue – the Twenty-first Issue – costs £10 per unit and the value at the end of five years from the date of purchase is £15.40, additions to the value being made as shown in Table 3.2.

Since nothing is added to the value of a unit until the end of the first year, National Savings Certificates should not be used as a very short-term investment. Moreover, the amount added increases as the years progress and the maximum return is obtained only if the certificates are held for the full period. The compound rate of return on certificates held for the whole five years is 9.02

Table 3.2 National Savings Certificate (Twenty-first Issue)

End of year	*Value (£)*	*Growth (£)*	*Return each year (%)*
1	10.75	0.75	7.50
2	11.59	0.84	7.81
3	12.58	0.99	8.54
4	13.78	1.20	9.54
5	15.40	1.62	11.76

per cent but the actual rate of return is higher than this in the last two years. Clearly, an investor who doubts whether he can leave his investment undisturbed for the whole five-year period should think carefully before buying National Savings Certificates. On the other hand, a high-rate taxpayer may find 9.02 per cent free of tax a thoroughly satisfactory return.

A maximum of £5 000 of the Twenty-first Issue can be purchased by an individual. For each issue, limits have been set on the number of units that can be purchased but the limits can be exceeded by units acquired by inheritance or gift. Units of earlier issues continue to increase in value. Encashment of all units is possible on a few days' notice.

3.5 Second Index-linked National Savings Certificates

The first index-linked National Savings Certificates were the Retirement Issue, nicknamed 'Granny Bonds', which were introduced in 1975. These were available to men aged sixty-five and over, and women aged sixty and over, whether or not they were retired. As investments they proved to be outstandingly successful, since because of the link with the Retail Price Index, they grew in line with inflation. Five years after launching £100 invested had grown to over £213, a compound return of 13½ per cent net.

In November 1980 this issue was withdrawn and the Second Index-linked Issue introduced, which in April 1981 was made available to all men and women over fifty years old; later that year the age limit was removed. The maximum holding is £3 000 (£6 000 for a married couple). A minimum terminal bonus of 4 per cent, not index-linked, is also payable. This issue does therefore offer a modest real return.

During the years 1975–80 inflation was always high, but when the Second Issue was launched at the end of 1980 the prospect of lower inflation seemed much better. Thus the investment merits of the present issue, certainly over a five-year period, appear less rosy, and certain other schemes, such as the guaranteed income bonds discussed in Units 12.10 and 12.11, must be considered to have their attractions.

3.6 Premium Savings Bonds

Introduced in 1956, Premium Savings Bonds have done valiant service for the National Savings Movement but they are not investments within the usual

'I very much doubt he'll accept as sufficient security the fact that you might be a delayed Ernie prizewinner."

meaning of the word. Now sold in £5 units, they produce no interest and there is no inherent capital growth element in them either. Instead what would otherwise be paid as interest is paid out in the form of prizes. The interest element has never been generous compared with other National Savings and at the time of writing stands at 7 per cent. In spite of this poor 'investment' return, this saving medium still appeals to many people. The 'computer' ERNIE (Electronic Random Number Indicator Equipment) selects the winning bond numbers each week, and the prizes now range from £50 to £250 000.

3.7 National Savings and Deposits Compared

An investor in any of these investments should periodically check the return he is receiving against that available from other similar investments, taking two principal factors into account:

(*a*) The effect of income tax should not be overlooked, in view of the tax relief on some investments.

(*b*) Some interest rates vary over quite short intervals of time, whereas others are fixed for periods of four or five years. National Savings investments, NSB deposits excepted, involve some sacrifice in the return if they are not held for the normal term. An investor should therefore avoid them if he anticipates that he might need the cash before maturity.

A potential investor should ascertain his own top rate of tax and calculate his *net* return on an investment at the rate of interest currently available. When comparing rates of return he should remember that rates can vary throughout the term of investment (see Unit 3.4).

3.8 The Gilt-edged Market

Gilt-edged securities comprise those British Government securities quoted on the Stock Exchange together with certain stocks guaranteed by the Government and the so-called *nationalization stocks*. The term 'gilt-edged' is often interpreted more widely, however, to include corporation and county stocks, public boards and Commonwealth Government stocks. Of the thousand or so stocks, more than three-quarters are corporation and county stocks. Seventy-nine British Government stocks with an average nominal value of around £600mn accounted for 93 per cent of the total market in 1980. The largest issue in existence is £1 909mn 3½% War Loan (although the market value of this stock is very much less). Several issues have a much larger market value – 15½% Treasury Loan 1996, for instance. The nominal value of this stock is £1 350mn but with the fall in interest rates its market value is now much higher.

3.9 Why are Gilts Issued?

There are several reasons why a Government issues debt securities.

(*a*) The principal reason is to finance budget deficits (when the borrowing requirement exceeds the amount of revenue raised by various means).

(*b*) The Government issues securities as a tool of monetary policy in order to control the money supply and so affect the structure of interest rates. This kind of intervention in turn affects such key indicators as the levels of prices, unemployment and the balance of payments.

(*c*) Government stocks have been issued to pay for the nationalization of industries such as coal, railways, steel and electricity.

(*d*) The Government must issue stocks from time to time simply to replace those stocks which it has to redeem.

(*e*) Issues by local authorities are frequently made to finance capital spending which cannot be properly financed out of rate receipts.

3.10 Gilts and the Institutional Investor

A very large volume of British Government securities is held by institutional investors and Table 3.2 shows that it is the institutions who are most active in this market. 'Official holders' include the Bank of England, Government Departments and the National Debt Commissioners, and 'others' include private investors, companies and a substantial overseas element. The overall institutional domination is evident; the United Kingdom banks and the building societies are most involved in the short-dated securities, while the insurance companies and pension funds alone account for nearly half of the remainder of the market.

Table 3.2 Holdings of gilt-edged securities, 31 March 1978

	Under 5 years		Over 5 years	
	£mn	%	£mn	%
Official holders	4 091	21.3	4 525	13.8
UK banks	2 914	15.2	195	0.6
Discount market	417	2.2	10	–
Insurance companies	953	4.9	10 263	31.2
Pension funds	375	1.9	5 775	17.5
Building societies	2 632	13.7	528	1.6
National Savings Bank	1 032	5.4	1 056	3.2
Investments and unit trusts	148	0.8	217	0.7
Others	6 647	34.6	10 334	31.4
Total	19 209	100.0	32 903	100.0

Source: *Bank of England Quarterly Bulletin*

3.11 Categories of British Government Securities

These stocks are usually divided into four categories:

short-dated (or 'shorts');
medium-dated (or 'mediums');
long-dated (or 'longs');
one-way option stocks (often called 'undated' or 'irredeemable' stocks).

These definitions refer to the remaining life of the security at the date of purchase. The *short-dated stocks* are redeemable within five years, *medium-dated* range from five to fifteen years while *long-dated* stocks are any which have more than fifteen years to run but are definitely repayable at some future date. For Stock Exchange commission purposes, however, the definitions of 'mediums' and 'longs' are five to ten years and over ten years respectively.

Most *one-way option stocks* are in fact dated stocks – 3½% War Loan (1952 or after) is an example – and are so called because they are redeemable only at the option of the Government. But since 3½ per cent is an extremely low interest rate by modern standards such stocks are regarded as virtually irredeemable today.

A problem of definition can arise because some stocks have two dates after the name: 9% Treasury Loan 1992–96, for instance. In 1980 this had a life of between twelve and sixteen years. Should it therefore be regarded as a 'medium' or a 'long'? The answer lies in the *coupon* – the nominal interest rate (see Unit 4.1). While 9 per cent is a good deal higher than 3½ per cent, it was still below the cost of long-term money in 1980. The Government can therefore be expected to redeem this stock as late as possible – in 1996 – and therefore during 1980 it was found among the long-dated securities.

3.12 The Importance of Dates

The investor can sell gilt-edged securities on the market at any time. Then why are the dates of any real significance?

Let us consider the case of three stocks at prices quoted in early 1981:

	Price
3% Exchequer Stock 1984	78⅝
3½% Funding Stock 1999–2004	39
3½% War Loan (1952 or after)	30½

All these stocks had similar coupons, but their prices were very different. The Exchequer Stock redeemable in 1984 was considerably more expensive than the others because of the close proximity of the latest possible redemption date. 3½% Funding Stock, however, is not redeemable until 2004. Its price was therefore markedly lower while War Loan, considered by investors as never likely to be redeemed, languished at 30½. The first two stocks have differing support from the latest possible redemption dates. This *pull to maturity* is a very important factor in determining the prices of gilt-edged securities.

Incidentally the exact redemption terms of securities can be found in the *Stock Exchange Official Year Book*. For example, 3½% Funding Stock 1999–2004 is redeemable at any time between 14 July 1999 and 14 July 2004 by drawings (see Glossary) or otherwise. It must be redeemed, of course, by 14 July 2004.

3.13 Short-dated Stocks

Unlike other gilt-edged stocks the 'shorts' are quoted *clean* which means that the gross accrued interest must be added or subtracted to arrive at the total price. If the price is quoted *cum (with) dividend*, interest for the period from the last interest date to the day after purchase (because 'gilt-edged' settlements are due on that day) is added to the purchase price. If the purchase is *ex (without) dividend* interest to the next payment date will be deducted.

Thus the price of £1 000 3% Exchequer Stock 1981 purchased on October 26 1979 at 90 is calculated as follows:

£1 000 at 90	£900.00
Accrued interest for 67 days (from August 21 to October 27, since interest on this stock is payable on 21 February and 21 August)	£ 5.50
	£905.50

3.14 Sinking Funds

The object of a 'sinking fund' is for the borrower to set aside a regular amount each year so that redemption can take place in accordance with the stated redemption terms. Two British Government stocks have sinking funds: 3% Redemption Stock 1986–96 and 3½% Conversion Stock 1961 or after. Redemption can be effected in total at maturity, by annual drawings (4% Victory Bonds were finally redeemed in 1976 on this basis) or by purchases by the Government Broker in the open market. Both these Government stocks are being gradually redeemed in this last manner.

3.15 Dealing in Gilts

Gilts can be purchased or sold in three different ways:

(*a*) through a stockbroker;
(*b*) through a registered agent, such as a bank, solicitor or accountant; or
(*c*) through the larger post offices.

When bought or sold through a stockbroker, gilts are dealt with for immediate or *cash* settlement – actually the day after the transaction – and therefore do not incur the 2 per cent transfer stamp duty. The usual dealing expenses are therefore brokers' commission on the *consideration* (the cost of the purchase), VAT and the nominal contract stamp duty. Commissions are much lower on gilts than on other securities, although there are different scales for the different categories of stocks – 'shorts', 'mediums' and so on. Although in share dealings it is not possible to deal in fractions of shares, in gilt-edged dealings one can deal to the nearest penny. This is especially useful to people who wish to invest a specific amount.

Thus the cost of buying £5 912.37 2½% Consols at 20½ is worked out as follows:

Consideration: £5 912.37 × 20½ ÷ 100 =	£1 212.04
Broker's commission at 0.625% on consideration	£7.58
VAT on commission (15%)	£1.14
Contract stamp	£0.30
	£1 221.06

The purchase through an agent (such as a bank) would cost rather more. In our example the commission rate would be 0.7812 per cent, involving commission of £9.47. The higher commission is shared with the agent. Banks generally receive a quarter of the commission, while other agents such as solicitors and accountants receive only one-fifth.

It is also possible to invest a fixed sum in gilts. Thus (ignoring expenses)

£5 000 invested in $2\frac{1}{2}$% Consols at $20\frac{1}{2}$ would purchase a nominal value calculated as follows:

$$£5\,000 \times 100/20\tfrac{1}{2} = £24\,390.24$$

3.16 The National Savings Stock Register

Most British Government stocks can be purchased and sold through larger post offices, which act as agents for the Stock and Bonds Office at Blackpool. Up to £5 000 cash value can be acquired in any one day but there is no limit to the amount that can be held or sold. Commission charges are lower than those of stockbrokers and are inclusive of VAT. On purchase the minimum charge is £1 and this increases by 50p for every £125 consideration (or part thereof) over £250. For sales, the scale is the same except that small sales are charged 10p for every £10 or part thereof. Thus the purchase of £5 912.37 $2\frac{1}{2}$% Consols at $20\frac{1}{2}$ would involve commission (including VAT) of £5.

The disadvantages of buying and selling through the Post Office can be briefly summarized:

(*a*) purchases are limited to £5 000 in any one day;
(*b*) transactions are normally effected on the day following receipt of the order but no guarantee can be given as to when dealing will take place;
(*c*) no advice is available;
(*d*) limit orders are not possible;
(*e*) dealings are not possible in the full range of British Funds, although many of them – about fifty – are available in this way;
(*f*) stock cannot be purchased 'specially ex-dividend' (see Unit 3.18).

Using the National Savings Stock Register is cheap for very small transactions (compare the minimum Stock Exchange commission on gilts of £4). For larger transactions it may well be worth paying a higher commission in the knowledge that the transaction can be affected immediately and settled on the following day.

The most professional service can be given by a broker but an agent, in particular the investor's bank, may have a better overall idea of its client's financial situation and has less pecuniary interest (only one-quarter of the commission) in seeing the transaction made.

3.17 Registered and Bearer Stocks

Most holdings of gilt-edged stocks are in *registered* form, that is:

(*a*) The issuing body or its registrars (the Bank of England in the case of gilts) keeps a register in which the names and addresses of holders together with the amount of stock held is recorded.

(*b*) The holder receives a certificate proving his title to his holding.

(*c*) Transfer is generally in accordance with the Stock Transfer Act 1963; the seller alone is required to execute a stock transfer form.

On the other hand, a considerable number of British Government stocks – for example, 3½% War Loan – have a small part of the issue in *bearer* form, that is, payable to the individual who has possession of the stock, without formal transfer. Interest on most of these is payable on application free of tax to residents abroad.

3.18 Payment of Interest

All paying agents, including the Bank of England, close their transfer books for interest and dividend purposes a few weeks before payment is due. An *ex dividend* (*ex div* or *xd*) date is announced shortly before the books close. On or after this date, the seller will be entitled to the next payment and the buyer will not receive his first interest for a further six months.

Certain gilts can also be bought *specially ex dividend*. This means that for a further period of up to twenty-one days before the normal xd date the shares can be bought at the buyer's or seller's request on this basis. There are three exceptions to this rule:

(*a*) short-dated stocks;
(*b*) 3½% War Loan;
(*c*) any stocks bought on the National Savings Stock Register.

This facility is attractive to those investors who are more interested in capital appreciation than in highly taxed income and makes it somewhat easier to obtain tax-free capital gains after holding gilts for more than one year.

3.19 Pricing New Issues

Gilt-edged securities are issued in a number of different ways. The most substantial issues are advertised by prospectus. The price of a new stock is determined by reference to a similar stock already in issue but the terms are generally marginally better to induce investors to subscribe for the issue.

Establishing the right price is usually relatively easy because of the substantial volume and range of securities already available with redemption dates stretching from a few months until well into the next century. The main problem lies in the volatility of the market. A relatively small change in the economic environment can suddenly make the issue extremely attractive, or conversely ruin its prospects.

Issues are rarely taken up in full (the dramatic oversubscriptions of early 1979 were quite exceptional) so that the bulk of the issue is frequently taken up by the Bank of England Issue Department and other Government departments. The stock is then sold to the public *on tap* over a period through the Government Broker at prices that reflect market conditions and official policy.

Such stocks are known as *tap stocks*. One or more 'taps' may be available at any one time. Gilt-edged issues are sometimes made direct to banks. Because such 'directed loans' are an instrument of monetary policy, banks do not lightly refuse to subscribe for them, though they are not legally bound to do so.

In May 1977 the Government issued its first variable- or floating-interest loan in the form of £400 million variable-rate Treasury Stock 1981. This stock was issued by tender, the lowest acceptable bid being £98. £75mn was sold on the first day alone and the complete issue in 16 days. The interest rate payable is $\frac{1}{2}$ per cent above an *indicator rate* which is arrived at by reference to the average Treasury bill rate.

This important innovation has been followed by two further issues which mature in 1982 and 1983 respectively. But this method of Government finance is unlikely to displace fixed-coupon issues. Variable-rate issues have much to commend them to investors for whom safety of capital is paramount, because their market price tends to remain reasonably close to par. They are less

appealing to the life assurance companies for whom a fixed return, essential to their actuarial calculations, is of vital importance.

Another recent trend in new issues has been to issue stock payable by instalments, the final instalment being the largest. For instance, on 2 June 1977 £700mn $11\frac{3}{4}$% Treasury Stock 1991 was issued at 94, with £15 payable on application, £15 a month later and the balance in August. Since 1979 many fixed-interest issues have been made *by tender*, a minimum tender price being stipulated (see Unit 8.5). This method is particularly appropriate when markets are volatile.

The most radical approach so far has been the issue in March 1981 of an index-linked gilt-edged stock – 2% Index-linked Treasury Stock 1996. Both interest and capital are tied to the Retail Price Index. Thus the new stock offers a real return of 2 per cent over a fifteen-year period. This important innovation also combines features of the other recent trends, it being issued by tender with payments by instalments. Unlike other gilts, however, the index-linked issue is not generally available. Only certain domestic financial institutions – friendly societies, pension funds and the pensions business part of life assurance companies – are allowed to own them.

3.20 Risk and Volatility

Clearly, the purchase and holding of gilts can involve risks that are not associated with investments such as National Savings Certificates. Subject to due notice, National Savings can easily be withdrawn (although the interest penalties are often severe) and the investor can transfer them to a better-yielding investment if the opportunity arises. Marketable securities are less flexible, and a better immediate return can often be found in the gilt-edged market; in addition there may be prospects of capital gains, free of tax if the stock is held for more than one year. While the interest return is absolutely certain if the price of the security subsequently falls, the price of other similar securities will fall too and the investor will find it difficult to obtain a better return elsewhere. Selling will involve a loss on his present investment.

The risks to capital are most obvious in the case of the one-way option stocks. Because there is no pull to maturity such stocks have no fundamental price support at all and over the post-war years there has been a steady downward trend. But there are also risks to capital in the dated stocks, even though they are all repayable at par at some future date. Few investors intend to hold stocks indefinitely so they are interested to know what the prospects are in the short and medium term. It would be better to remain liquid for a time than to buy prematurely. The longer the date the more volatile the price performance, but even the 'shorts' can fall sharply in price if interest rates in general move upwards.

Stock prices tend to be more volatile the longer their life. Consider as an example the price range of two stocks in 1980:

	Prices (1980)		*Difference as*
	Low	*High*	*percentage of 'Low'*
12% Treasury Stock 1985	$88\frac{3}{8}$	$99\frac{3}{8}$	12.4%
12% Treasury Stock 1995	82	$97\frac{1}{8}$	18.4%

Of the two, the fluctuations in the longer-dated stock were appreciably the wider.

Another general feature of price behaviour concerns the coupon. Given the same (or similar) dates, the lower-coupon stocks are usually the more volatile:

	Prices (1980)		*Difference as*
	Low	*High*	*percentage of 'Low'*
$13\frac{3}{4}$% Treasury Stock 1993	$93\frac{1}{2}$	$107\frac{7}{8}$	15.4%
$6\frac{1}{2}$% Funding Loan 1993	$54\frac{5}{8}$	$66\frac{1}{4}$	21.3%

Volatility is thus an important factor in decision-making.

3.21 Tax Considerations with British Government Stocks

Income tax is deducted from most payments of interest on British Government stocks. The principal exceptions are as follows:

(*a*) Income tax is not normally deducted from payments of interest on $3\frac{1}{2}$% War Loan. Where the stock is held on the Register maintained by the Bank of England income tax will be deducted if a form requesting deduction is completed.

(*b*) Interest on stocks registered on the National Savings Stock Register is paid without deduction of income tax.

(*c*) Where the gross interest payable on a holding of a British Government stock or certain other 'gilt-edged' securities is not more than £2.50 per half-year it is paid without deduction of income tax.

In these three instances the income received is liable for tax in the hands of the investor and should be included in his income tax return as untaxed income. Payment of income without deduction of tax does not imply exemption from tax in respect of that income.

The interest on British Government stocks may be paid without deduction of income tax where the beneficial owner is resident abroad for income tax purposes. Application must be made by the investor to the Inspector of Foreign Dividends and, if approved, the Bank of England is authorized to pay the interest gross. This applies whether the stock is registered in the name of the stockholder resident abroad or whether it is in the name of a nominee, or even if it is held in a trust so long as the person resident abroad is entitled to the income received. Naturally no request to the Inspector of Foreign Dividends is required with $3\frac{1}{2}$% War Loan, as the interest is paid without deduction of tax in any case.

All British Government stocks are exempt from capital gains tax after they have been held for one year. This means that profits on sales of stocks *more* than one year after they were purchased do not attract a liability but equally any losses are not available to be set against other profits. When sales are carried out *within* one year from the date of purchase, capital gains tax applies in just the same way as for any other investment liable to tax.

3.22 Questions

1. Briefly describe the investment opportunities available in the gilt-edged market. What special advantages do they have over other types of investment?

2. Your customer says he has heard about index-linked investment. He asks you (*a*) to explain what this means, (*b*) to describe briefly the available index-linked investments, (*c*) to advise him on whether any of them is suitable for his circumstances, and (*d*) to let him know whether any of them would be suitable for the investment of £300, which his mother has left to her unmarried sister aged 62. What questions would you first ask? How would you answer his queries?

3. A customer asks you to purchase a gilt-edged security 'specially ex-dividend'. What do you understand by 'specially ex-dividend' and for what reason would the customer want to deal in this way? Does this facility extend to all gilt-edged securities?

Unit Four

Yield on Fixed-interest Stocks

4.1 What is Yield?

All fixed-interest quoted securities bear a nominal rate of interest, the *coupon*, which relates to the rate of interest on £100 nominal of the stock, even though the stock may have been issued at 98 per cent or 101 per cent and irrespective of whether the current market price is lower or higher. The two vital considerations when buying fixed-interest securities are (*a*) the amount of income which the investment will produce or *yield* in relation to the market price, and (*b*) the period of time before the issue will be redeemed (if indeed it is likely to be redeemed at all).

In the case of irredeemable stocks the yield consists only of interest, but where the stocks are dated the capital appreciation (or depreciation) to the maturity date must also be taken into account. The investor's tax position is also of the utmost importance. The basis of yield calculations is the price at the date of purchase, together with the total costs of purchase (the consideration

plus all dealing costs), but for simplicity's sake we shall ignore dealing costs in this Unit. In considering the various kinds of yield – there is no simple definition – we will take as our first example a hypothetical stock:

£100 9% Government Stock 1990–92
Interest payable 1 January, 1 July
Purchased 1 May 1980 at 85

4.2 Income Yield

This is the simplest concept of yield and gives the return on our stock over the following 12 months:

$$\frac{\text{Nominal rate} \times 100}{\text{Price}} = \frac{9 \times 100}{85} = 10.59\%$$

This is not wholly satisfactory, however, because the stock was purchased between the two interest payment dates. On May 1 1980 it will have been purchased 'cum div' (that is, with the interest accrued due from 1 January) so the actual return is rather better than this implies. Income yield is thus of little practical use.

4.3 Interest Yield

To obtain the interest yield we must *clean the price*, that is to say, strip it of the accrued interest element. This is normally calculated on a daily basis but months will be quite accurate enough for our purpose.

Interest for 4 months (1 January 1980 to 1 May 1980 – from last payment date to date of purchase) = £100 × 9% × 4/12 = £3.00

Now we can calculate the interest yield, otherwise known as the *flat* or *running yield*, given by the expression

$$\frac{\text{Nominal rate} \times 100}{\text{Clean price}} = \frac{9 \times 100}{85 - 3} = \frac{900}{82} = 10.98\%$$

This calculation provides the *gross interest yield*, which is the yield applicable to the non-taxpayer. The *net interest yield* is found by (*a*) reducing the actual price only by the net interest and (*b*) reducing the resulting yield by the relevant tax rate. Thus for the basic-rate taxpayer:

(*a*)	Gross accued interest =	£ 3.00
	Less income tax at 30% =	£ 0.90
		£ 2.10
	£85 − £2.10 =	£82.90

(*b*) $$\frac{9 \times 100}{82.90} \times \frac{70(\text{i.e. } 100 - 30)}{100} = 7.60\%$$

For individuals with a higher marginal rate of tax the net yield is correspondingly lower. For a 60 per cent taxpayer it amounts to 4.3 per cent.

4.4 Gross Redemption Yield

This yield takes into account the capital gain (or loss) if the security is assumed to be held to the date of redemption. Calculating the redemption yield is more complex because it consists of two elements: the interest yield and the capital gain or loss if the stock is held to maturity. Interest is usually paid half-yearly but the capital gain (or loss) only occurs at the end of the period. Therefore in calculating the yield compound interest must be taken into account. This involves a rather complex formula. Resort to the formula is rarely necessary, however, because bond yield tables and specialist lists are readily available. The following approximate expression is generally regarded as quite satisfactory but because it ignores the compound interest factor it is not really accurate enough for an informed investment decision:

$$\text{Redemption yield} = \text{Interest yield} + (\text{or} -) \frac{\text{Gain (or loss) to maturity}}{\text{Period to maturity}}$$

As an example, consider a 14% company fixed-interest stock redeemable in exactly ten years, the price of which is 95. Thus the interest yield (assuming no cleaning of the price is required) is 14.7 per cent. What is the redemption yield?

Interest yield	14.7
Average gain to maturity $\frac{(100-95)}{10}$	0.5
Redemption yield	15.2%

Now in this example the gain to maturity is very small and this method produces virtually the same answer as the strictly mathematical one. As the maturity period lengthens or the gain or loss to maturity is increased, however, this method becomes less reliable. Take for example the case of a 3% stock standing at 75 and redeemable in five years' time:

Interest yield	4.0
Average gain to maturity	5.0
Redemption yield	9.0%

4.5 Net Present Value and Yield

In fact the true redemption yield is 9.84 per cent, a significant difference. To calculate a true redemption yield can be quite laborious (even with a calculator) but an appreciation of the principles involved is necessary.

Clearly, what the investor can expect from an investment of £75 in £100 of 3% stock is:

10 half-yearly interest payments of £1.50	=	£ 15
1 final payment on redemption	=	£100
		£115

Now each of the successive payments of interest is really less valuable than the previous one. Just as £1 invested at 10 per cent will grow in value to £1.33 after three years:

Initial investment	£1.00
Interest 1st year	10
	£1.10
Interest 2nd year	11
	£1.21
Interest 3rd year	12
	£1.33

so £1 receivable in three years' time will have a lower present value than £1 receivable now.

The future value of £1 is shown by the formula

$$\text{Value after } n \text{ years} = (1 + i)^n$$

where i is the rate of interest. Thus

$$\text{£1 invested for 3 years at 10\%} = (1 + 0.10)^3 = \text{£1.33}$$

The present value of £1 receivable in three years is found by inverting the formula. Thus:

$$\text{Present value of £1 receivable in 3 years when interest is 10\%} = \frac{1}{(1 + 0.10)^3} = \text{£0.75}$$

Table 4.1 Present value tables

Present value of 1

$(1 + i)^{-n}$

Period	1%	2%	3%	4%	5%	6%	7%	8%	9%	10%	12%	14%	15%
1	0.990	0.980	0.971	0.961	0.952	0.943	0.935	0.926	0.917	0.909	0.893	0.877	0.870
2	0.980	0.961	0.943	0.925	0.907	0.890	0.873	0.857	0.842	0.826	0.797	0.769	0.756
3	0.971	0.942	0.915	0.889	0.864	0.840	0.816	0.794	0.772	0.751	0.712	0.675	0.658
4	0.961	0.924	0.889	0.855	0.823	0.792	0.763	0.735	0.708	0.683	0.636	0.592	0.572
5	0.951	0.906	0.863	0.822	0.784	0.747	0.713	0.681	0.650	**0.621**	0.567	0.519	0.497
6	0.942	0.888	0.838	0.790	0.746	0.705	0.666	0.630	0.596	0.564	0.507	0.456	0.432
7	0.933	0.871	0.813	0.760	0.711	0.665	0.623	0.583	0.547	0.513	0.452	0.400	0.376
8	0.923	0.853	0.789	0.731	0.677	0.627	0.582	0.540	0.502	0.467	0.404	0.351	0.327
9	0.914	0.837	0.766	0.703	0.645	0.592	0.544	0.500	0.460	0.424	0.361	0.308	0.284
10	0.905	0.820	0.744	0.676	0.614	0.558	0.508	0.463	0.422	0.386	0.322	0.270	0.247
11	0.896	0.804	0.722	0.650	0.585	0.527	0.475	0.429	0.388	0.350	0.287	0.237	0.215

Present value of annuity of 1 per period

$$\frac{1 - (1 + i)^{-n}}{i}$$

Period	1%	2%	3%	4%	5%	6%	7%	8%	9%	10%
1	0.990	0.980	0.971	0.962	0.952	0.943	0.935	0.926	0.917	0.909
2	1.970	1.942	1.913	1.886	1.859	1.833	1.808	1.783	1.759	1.736
3	2.941	2.884	2.829	2.775	2.723	2.673	2.624	2.577	2.531	2.487
4	3.902	3.808	3.717	3.630	3.546	3.465	3.387	3.312	3.240	3.170
5	4.853	4.713	4.580	4.452	4.329	4.212	4.100	3.993	3.890	3.791
6	5.795	5.601	5.417	5.242	5.076	4.917	4.766	4.623	4.486	4.355
7	6.728	6.472	6.230	6.002	5.786	5.582	5.389	5.206	5.033	4.868
8	7.652	7.325	7.020	6.733	6.463	6.210	5.971	5.747	5.535	5.335
9	8.566	8.162	7.786	7.435	7.108	6.802	6.515	6.247	5.985	5.759
10	9.471	8.983	8.530	8.111	**7.722**	7.360	7.024	6.710	6.418	6.145
11	10.368	9.787	9.253	8.760	8.306	7.887	7.499	7.139	6.805	6.495

To calculate the true redemption yield, we would have to make no less than eleven different calculations. Fortunately tables are available, such as Table 4.1. Applying those figures to our example, the calculations are as follows:

Present value of £100
receivable in 5 years = £100 × 0.621 = £62.10

Present value of £1.50
per ½ year for 5 years = £1.50 × 7.722 = £11.58

The toal present value, £73.68, is actually rather less than £75, the original cost. This implies that the yield is rather less than 10 per cent. Further calculations show it to be 9.84 per cent – appreciably more than indicated by the approximate method and a very material difference to an investor in a sensitive market where modest price changes can signal a change of policy.

The gross redemption yield is thus made up of two elements:

Interest yield	4.00 %
Gain to redemption	5.84 %
	9.84 %

Thus the investment will yield an interest return of 4 per cent and grow in theory at 5.84 per cent per annum or rather 2.92 per cent per half-year.

Initial cost	£75.00
Gain (1)	£ 2.19
Gain (2)	£ 2.25
etc.	...
	£100.00

4.6 Net Redemption Yield

The interest bears tax at the investor's marginal rate while the gain is entirely free of capital gains tax provided the stock is held for more than one year. Clearly, therefore, the gross redemption yield has little meaning for anyone but the non-taxpayer. To ascertain the actual yield, tax must be deducted at the appropriate rate from the interest yeild for the basic- and higher-rate taxpayers.

	30% tax	*60% tax*
Interest yield (gross)	£4.00	£4.00
Less income tax	£1.20	£2.40
	£2.80	£1.60
Gain to redemption	£5.84	£5.84
Net redemption yield	£8.64	£7.44

Thus the higher-rate taxpayer is not much worse off than the basic-rate taxpayer. Contrast this with what their positions would be in the case of the company 14% stock selling at 95 (see Unit 4.4).

4.7 Grossed-up Net Redemption Yield

This yield calculation also provides a most useful means of comparison. Not all investments have a redemption element. How, for example, does the 3% Government stock compare with a bank deposit at 11 per cent where the return is all taxable? Although these instances are hardly comparable, such comparisons may have to be made from time to time.

The grossed-up net redemption yield is also useful in deciding whether or not a particular investment is suitable for a certain type of taxpayer. The calculation is simple; the net redemption yield is simply 'grossed-up' at the individual's marginal rate of income tax, thus:

$$30\%\text{ taxpayer receives } 8.64 \times \frac{100}{70} = 11.97\%\text{ gross}$$

$$60\%\text{ taxpayer receives } 7.44 \times \frac{100}{40} = 17.95\%\text{ gross}$$

Such a stock therefore represents a good investment for the higher-rate taxpayer but is less satisfactory for the investor paying only basic-rate income tax.

Until quite recently, the highest marginal rate of tax was 98 per cent (83 per cent plus investment income surcharge), and this gave rise to some quite phenomenal grossed-up net redemption yields – for instance, on this stock it was 283 per cent! At the current top rate (75 per cent) it is a mere 26.3 per cent.

The grossed-up net redemption yield is also known as the *gross equivalent yield*.

4.8 Yield Calculations in the Financial Press

Yield calculations in the financial press are 'cleaned' yields and so can be relied upon by the intending investor. For example, on 12 November 1979 the *Financial Times* stated the gross interest yield of 4% Consols quoted at 30½ as 13.62 per cent. This was derived as follows:

Quoted price	£30.50
Accrued interest, 1 August to 12 November (103 days)	£ 1.13
	£29.37

$$\text{Gross yield} = \frac{4}{29.37} \times 100 = 13.62\%$$

Every Monday the *Financial Times* gives details of interest payment dates and when stocks were last 'ex-dividend'. If a stock is quoted 'xd' then the cleaned price is found by adding accrued interest to the next payment date.

Since the 'shorts' are quoted exclusive of interest, however, their yields do not require any adjustment. Thus on the same day Treasury 3% 1982 was quoted at 84¼, eighty-nine days after the last interest payment. The stated yield, 3.56 per cent, is simply $\frac{3}{84.25} \times 100$. But a purchaser would be charged:

Quoted price	£84.25
Accrued interest	£ 0.73
	£84.98

4.9 Gross Funds and Net Funds

Those institutions that are generally not taxable at all (such as pension funds) look to the gross redemption yield for ascertaining the return on their investment, and are therefore known as *gross funds*. Life assurance funds, building societies and, of course, individuals face tax at different rates on income and capital gains, however, and are accordingly known as *net funds*. The net redemption yield, or grossed-up net redemption yield, provides the better guide to these investors.

4.10 Interest Payments

Government securities, company loan stocks and other forms of debt are subject to regular interest payments. The normal procedure is for the paying agents (the Bank of England in the case of the British Government securities) to pay interest half-yearly after deduction of basic-rate tax. The investor receives a *negotiable warrant* for the net interest together with a *certificate of tax deducted*.

Interest payments are made at various dates throughout the year; a holder of 13% Treasury Loan 1993, for example, would receive interest on 23 May and 23 November. Companies usually pay interest every six months, normally on dates relating to their accounting period.

Non-taxpayers can make a claim for repayment of the tax but higher-rate taxpayers will have to make a further payment. Interest is also subject to the investment income surcharge, where this is applicable.

Interest is payable not half-yearly but quarterly in the case of 2½% Consolidated Stock (Consols) and the Annuity Stocks. Interest is payable gross on Government stocks in four separate cases, though it is taxable in the hands of United Kingdom residents. These are:

(*a*) interest on 3½% War Loan;
(*b*) interest on Government stocks not exceeding £2.50 per half-year;
(*c*) interest on certain Government stocks held by overseas residents;
(*d*) interest on Government stocks held on the National Savings Bank Register.

4.11 Yield Curves

The normal pattern of return is for yields to increase relative to the length of the period to redemption. This can be clearly shown by a *yield curve*, which plots the yields of a number of dated stocks against years to maturity, at a specific point in time. Fig. 4.1, for instance, shows that yields in general increased considerably between October 1977 and October 1978. The yield curve drawn for 31 October 1977 is very steep in the one- to four-year period and then gradually flattens out. This phenomenon is generally considered 'bearish' (see

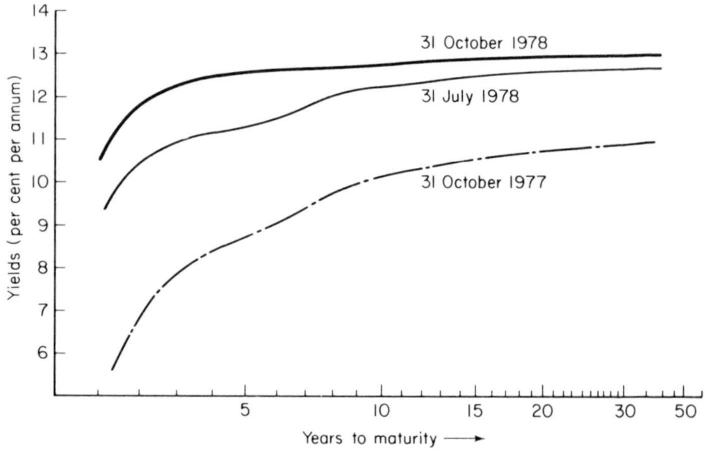

Fig. 4.1 Yield curves of British Government stocks

Glossary) for fixed-interest securities and indeed so it proved to be in this case. A year later there was an enormous narrowing of the interest differential between the 'shorts' and the 'longs'. Occasionally 'short' yields are higher than 'long' yields, a factor that points positively to a likely increase in gilt prices and thus a fall in interest rates.

4.12 Questions

1. (*a*) What do you understand by the term *redemption yield*? Illustrate your answer by calculating the approximate redemption yield of two 10 per cent stocks both dated 1985–90, one quoted at 95 and the othr at 110.

   (*b*) On one day in August 1979 the *Financial Times* showed the prices and yields of two stocks as follows:

	Price	*Yield*	
		Interest	*Redemption*
British Transport 3% 1978–88	66	4.57	8.62
Treasury 7¾% 1985–88	85½	9.11	10.45

   Which of these two stocks on that day would have been the more suitable for (i) Mr A with a total taxable income of £16 000 per annum, and (ii) Mr B with a total taxable income of £7 000 per annum, assuming that each had £1 000 available for investment and that neither was liable to the investment income surcharge? Show the calculations in support of your answer.

2. Describe the purpose of constructing a yield curve. On graph paper construct a yield curve for all Government stocks carrying a coupon in the region of 8 per cent (i.e. 7¾–8¼ per cent). How do you interpret your results?

3. What do the terms *ex div* and *cum div* mean? On what basis would a taxpayer whose marginal rate of tax is 75 per cent prefer to make a purchase? If the purchase was of a British Government security would your answer differ?

Unit Five

Non-Government Fixed-interest Securities

5.1 Introduction

Unit 3.1 showed that the National Debt consisted principally of marketable securities – the quoted British Government funds – and those National Savings securities which can be purchased over the counter at post offices and which though not quoted can readily be encashed if necessary. The former are generally referred to as *gilt-edged securities*, but historically the description 'gilt-edged' has also been applied to certain other kinds of quoted securities, such as British corporation and county stocks, issues by public boards and stocks issued by Commonwealth governments (see Unit 3.8). In recent years there has been a tendency to narrow the definition to exclude those stocks which are clearly not in the same category as securities issued by the central Government. Although no corporation or county stocks have ever failed, changes in the political spectrum have clearly led investors to reappraise the attractions of Commonwealth government stocks.

In this Unit we deal with these other gilt-edged stocks as well as some other major issues, including the fixed-interest stocks issued by companies. Such issues are now a less important source of company funds, however.

5.2 Local Authority Quoted Stocks

After British Government stocks and a few others that are guaranteed by the British Government, British corporation and county stocks are the most secure investments available. Many stocks are issued by British local authorities, and are a charge on the rates income of those authorities. There are dated and undated stocks, including a few genuinely irredeemable stocks (stocks which by their terms of issue can never be redeemed). Some pay their interest quarterly and others half-yearly, and interest rates and redemption dates vary widely. And a great many authorities issue such stocks, from Aberdeen and Barking to Warwickshire and York.

(*a*) Availability

The main problem connected with investing in local authority stocks is that of availability, which contrasts sharply with the very free market in all British

Government stocks. Many issues are comparatively small and by their nature tend to be held by the institutions and so rarely come on the market. The larger issues are made by the bigger corporations; generally speaking, the larger the issue the freer the market. The freest market in this sector is in the stocks of the Greater London Council, some of which carry the earlier names of Corporation of London and London County Council.

(*b*) Factors Influencing Prices

Profits made on local authority stocks (unlike those on British Government stocks) are subject to capital gains tax irrespective of how long the stock has been held. Equally, losses on these stocks are available for set-off against other gains. This of course affects prices, since net redemption yields must always be calculated net of capital gains tax as well as net of income tax. The yields obtainable on local authority stocks are slightly higher than those obtainable on equivalent British Government stocks because of the slightly greater risk and the tax position.

The tax element in the gain to redemption results in investors looking for a higher gross redemption yield than they would do otherwise. This benefits the small investor who can avoid capital gains tax. It is of little advantage to the big institutional investor, even though the fund may not be liable to capital gains tax, because the comparative difficulty in marketing these stocks offsets the advantages of investment at slightly more attractive rates.

5.3 Short-dated Local Authority Bonds

Many of the larger local authorities issue negotiable 'yearling' bonds, so called because most of them are repaid after one year. These are usually issued in weekly batches; the names of the issuing authorities, together with the amounts issued, the interest rate and the issue prices are announced every Tuesday morning.

An investor interested in a particular week's issue will ask his bank manager or stockbroker in the preceding week to see that his name is entered on the placing list. While the applicant cannot predict the rate of interest, he can make a fairly close estimate based on the previous week's rate and the trend in interest rates. He can, if he wishes, instruct his agent as to the minimum interest rate he is willing to accept. Dealings start in the newly issued bonds on Wednesdays in minimum denominations of £1 000, with accrued interest being added daily (as with short-dated Government securities). Over the years interest rates have fluctuated sharply, from as low as 5 per cent in early 1972 to over 17 per cent in the autumn of 1980. The *Stock Exchange Daily Official List* contains details of such short-dated bonds, which are transferred free of stamp duty. The names of the borrowing authorities are not published in the *List*, but can be found in its sister publication, the *Stock Exchange Weekly Official Intelligence*.

Fig. 5.1 Local authority advertised loan

5.4 Loans to Local Authorities

In addition to the quoted securities described above, some local authorities accept deposits and loans from investors for periods ranging from seven days to several years at fixed rates of interest. The minimum amount that can be invested varies from £250 upwards depending upon the authority and its supply of money in relation to its immediate needs, although few authorities are interested in small sums for short periods. The Treasury became concerned about the tendency among the authorities to bid up short-term rates of interest in the hope of avoiding higher rates in the long term, with the result that authorities now tend to take longer-dated deposits. This trend has been strengthened since the introduction of a voluntary code of conduct, the aim of which is to lengthen the average period of local authority debt to seven years.

The rates of interest paid on the longer loans are generally slightly above the rates obtainable on similarly dated local authority stocks quoted on the Stock Exchange. The rates paid on three months' and six months' notice deposits are somewhat lower than those obtainable from finance houses (reflecting the virtual absence of risk). Interest is subject to income tax but is paid without deduction of tax on loans of less than one year. Small deposits receive a lower rate of interest than large ones.

Loans exceeding one year are usually mortgages (so called because they are charged on the authority's assets and revenues) and are normally repayable before maturity only on the death of the lender. If the rate of interest payable exceeds the current rate, the authority may be happy to repay should some emergency arise, because it could then re-borrow elsewhere more cheaply. There is a limited market in these mortgages but prices are relatively unfavourable to the vendor. Such mortgages should only be entered into if the investor is sure that the capital will not be required during the stated period of the loan. These 'town hall' or 'over-the-counter' bonds are regularly advertised in the press (see Fig. 5.1).

5.5 Public Boards

Another sector of the public authority loan market is that comprising public boards such as water boards, port authorities and the Agricultural Mortgage Corporation. Some of these resemble local authority stocks insofar as security is concerned, but there are others in which the investor should not place as much confidence. They are all free of transfer stamp duty but are subject to capital gains tax. A prospective investor in this market should always ascertain the exact terms of a stock and the nature of the security so that it may be properly compared with other loans.

5.6 Commonwealth Stocks

Many stocks quoted on the Stock Exchange are issued in London by governments and local authorities of Commonwealth countries. Of all the gilt-edged stocks these least deserve the 'gilt-edged' label, which ought really to be reserved for stocks where the security is virtually undoubted. Although the political risks attaching to stocks issued by foreign authorities are well known, the realities of the situation were not brought home to holders of Commonwealth stocks until Rhodesia's Unilateral Declaration of Independence in 1965. It was not until 1980 that settlement terms for investors were agreed.

The confidence placed in certain Commonwealth governments causes their stocks to be quoted at prices comparable with those of United Kingdom local authority stocks. The doubtful stability of a few governments results in their stocks being quoted to give yields very much above those available on any other gilts, however. In comparing Commonwealth and United Kingdom stocks the investor should weigh up the political risks to the best of his ability and assess the yields obtainable accordingly.

Commonwealth stocks are free of all United Kingdom taxes to residents abroad.

5.7 Foreign Governments' Bonds

Very many foreign government stock and bond issues are quoted on the London Stock Exchange. Generalization over these is impossible. Apart from the variety of terms and borrowers involved, political factors play an important part in price movements and many issues are purely speculative.

In the past, some foreign governments have defaulted on their liabilities to bondholders and often, after such a default, proposals have been put forward for schemes under which some form of payment might be made. Thus it is now frequently possible to find two types of the same issue, namely *assented* and *unassented bonds*, where holders of the former have accepted amended terms and those of the latter have not. Assented bonds are sometimes described as being *enfaced* because the revised terms are set out on the face of the certificate. The Hungarian 7½% Sterling Bond issue of 1924 is one such issue: new terms were assented to in 1968, the interest rate being reduced to 4½ per cent as part of the agreement.

The foreign bond market is one for the specialist and the private investor is usually advised to stay in markets that are less complicated and speculative.

5.8 Miscellaneous Fixed-interest Stocks

Some fixed-interest investments do not fall into any well-defined category.

A few stocks are issued in the United Kingdom by the International Bank for Reconstruction and Development (better known as the World Bank). They qualify as 'gilt-edged' stocks and their prices compare with corporation stocks and the better-quality Commonwealth loans. They are free of transfer stamp duty and free of United Kingdom taxes to non-residents.

A number of foreign and Commonwealth governments, consortium banks and foreign companies have issued fixed-interest stocks in US dollar and other currency denominations. These are commonly known as *Eurobonds* and can be traded on the secondary market.

We should also count among fixed-interest stocks the preference and ordinary stocks of water boards in the United Kingdom. For historical reasons only, these stocks are named as though they had the characteristics of preference and ordinary shares issued by companies but they are in fact to be regarded as public board fixed-interest stocks. Many of these authorities also have debenture stocks quoted and the rights of repayment of the various issues follow the normal company rules in the event of a winding-up.

Other important issues include those of the Inter-American Development Bank and the British institutions Finance for Industry (FFI) and its subsidiary companies.

5.9 Company Fixed-interest Finance

The capital of companies in the United Kingdom may be divided into two principal classes: *share capital* and *loan capital*. Each of these may be subdivided into various classes of capital for any particular company. It is unusual for a company of any size to have only one class of capital. Companies must have a share capital but they may have various classes of share capital and no loan capital, or a combination of different classes of both share and loan capital.

In simple terms, the owners of the share capital of a company own the company itself, and the holders of loan capital are creditors of the company. Thus the holders of share capital are not creditors and have no security, and the holders of loan capital have no rights in the company beyond the payment of interest on their loans and repayment of the loans in accordance with the terms on which they were issued. The amount which a company may borrow by way of loan capital is laid down in its articles of association.

Loan capital may be secured or unsecured and companies frequently issue both kinds of stock. Where the loan is secured the capital is charged on certain assets of the company to which the holders of that capital may look for repayment in the event of the company being wound up. Unsecured loan stock holders on the other hand are entitled to repayment equally with the ordinary creditors of the company. Some creditors may be secured and therefore rank before unsecured loan capital, for example, when a company, wishing to borrow from its bankers, is required to give the bank security for its overdraft. For the protection of its holders, the terms of issue of loan capital usually limit the company's borrowing powers, not only in respect of debts which would take priority over the loan capital, but also in respect of further loan capital which would rank equally.

A few companies (notably the clearing banks) issue *subordinated* loan stocks, repayment of such stocks being subordinated to all other creditors. Such stocks clearly involve a greater risk than the more usual kinds of loan capital and the investor can accordingly obtain a better return.

Another class are the *convertible* loan stocks, which are often, though not necessarily, unsecured. These usually carry a lower coupon than a straightforward loan stock, because they carry the right of conversion into ordinary shares at some future date; they are discussed in Unit 7.2.

Not all classes of a company's capital need be quoted on a stock exchange, even though some classes may be. Thus a company might have only one or two classes of loan capital quoted and the share capital retained within a family, or it might have one or more classes of loan stock issued privately to institutions and not quoted on an exchange while its share capital is quoted.

5.10 Debentures and Debenture Stocks

The statutory definition of a *debenture* (Companies Act 1948, section 455) is very wide and does not necessarily imply that the security gives any charge over the assets of the borrower. This should stand as a warning to the incautious investor, but as the term is generally used in investment it is taken to imply that some form of security is given. Thus debenture and debenture stocks are usually similar to mortgages and indeed the word 'mortgage' is commonly used to describe them – 6% First Mortgage Debenture Stock, for instance.

Debentures 'pure and simple' are rarely issued nowadays and not many are still outstanding. Recent issues of this nature have been in the form of *debenture stocks*. The amount of the debenture is expressed in the form of stock and transactions on the market are carried out in the same way as for any other type of stock. Whereas Government stocks are transferable in multiples of 1p, debenture stocks may be transferable only in multiples of £1, £5 or even £100, the minimum amount being written into the terms of issue of the stock.

Usually, trustees are appointed for the assets charged as security for debentures and debenture stocks; generally they are banks or insurance companies. A trust deed is drawn up and completed by the company and by the trustee, setting out the terms of the issue, the security charged, the powers of the trustee and the duties of the company in respect of the stock and the security. The trustee's duty is to act on behalf of the holders of the issue, even though the company pays his fee. He usually has the power to approve any changes in the security and minor amendments to the requirements of the trust deed in the light of changing circumstances. If he believes that a proposed change may be prejudicial to the interests of the holders of the issue he may require the company to obtain approval of its proposals from a meeting of debenture-holders.

Debenture stocks are quite commonly secured on certain specific assets of the company, with a floating charge over the rest of the company's assets. It is not strictly necessary for there to be a specific or *fixed charge*, however; and a *floating charge*, a form of security which only a limited company can give, embodies the right to take possession of the company's assets as they stand at any particular time.

All secured debt ranks for repayment before unsecured debt in the event of the company being wound up. If the trustees consider that the security of the holders is in danger through the company's actions they may apply for a receiver to be appointed to liquidate sufficient of the charged assets to repay the capital of the issued stock and any arrears of interest.

5.11 Unsecured Loan Stocks

Unsecured loan stocks, as their name indicates, are stocks representing loans to the company which are not secured or charged on the company's assets. In the event of liquidation they rank after secured loans, equally with general creditors and before share capital.

Trustees are appointed for unsecured loan stocks in the same way as for debenture stocks, but they of course hold no assets. They watch the interests of stockholders, particularly with regard to restrictions on borrowing, which are usually included in the terms of issue of these stocks. This protects the position of stockholders by limiting the amount of capital and other borrowing ranking both prior to the stock and also equally with it. A limit on total borrowing of, say, twice the share capital is a common provision, but this will exclude short-term borrowing in the normal course of business and inter-group loans.

5.12 Company Fixed-interest Stocks: Investment Criteria

The prospective investor in the company fixed-interest market is faced with a bewildering choice if he looks at the whole range of available stocks. There are redeemable and irredeemable stocks; debentures, debenture stocks and unsecured loan stocks; unsecured loan stocks in companies which have no debenture stocks in issue; first, second and even third mortgage debenture stocks charging the same assets; unsecured loan stocks where charges ranking in priority are not quoted in the market; subordinated loan stocks; and stocks that are only one issue among as many as twenty by the same company with different terms for interest and repayment.

(*a*) **Common Factors**

All fixed-interest stocks have certain things in common. They carry a fixed rate of interest, usually payable half-yearly, and the rights attaching to them are ascertainable. The yields obtainable from company stocks are always somewhat higher than those obtainable on local authority stocks with similar coupons and redemption dates, because of the higher risks to the investor. All interest is subject to tax and paid with income tax deducted at source by the company and passed over to the Inland Revenue. All stocks are liable to capital gains tax. Stamp duty is payable only on transfers of convertible loan stocks.

(*b*) **Yield**

Yields on apparently similar stocks may differ. Differences in price, and therefore yield, reflect the market's assessment of the issuing company's standing and of the risk elements in the particular stocks. A high yield in relation to the market in general shows an above-average risk element. Investors wanting a high yield from a redeemable fixed-interest investment will find suitable stocks, but should not be tempted by exceptionally high yields. Stocks issued by sound companies are generally found to give flat yields at least 1 per cent higher than equivalent local authority stocks, with redemption yields correspondingly higher. In calculating yields, however, it must be remembered that the rate of broker's commission chargeable on company fixed-interest stocks is higher than that on 'gilt-edged' stocks.

Marketability can be a problem with stocks in this sector and it may not be possible to buy exactly the stock selected. New issues usually command a free market and most of the stocks of the largest companies can also be bought and sold freely.

The yield structure of a hypothetical company is illustrated in Fig. 5.2.

(*c*) **Security**

An investor assessing the quality of a company fixed-interest stock must take into account the amount of other issues ranking in priority to the stock, the security (if any), the rights of the company to issue further stock ranking in priority or *pari passu* (on an equal footing) and the earnings of the company available to meet the interest.

(*d*) **Sinking Funds and Redemption**

The vast majority of stocks issued are redeemable with reference to some future date or dates. Many companies anticipate redemption by setting aside a

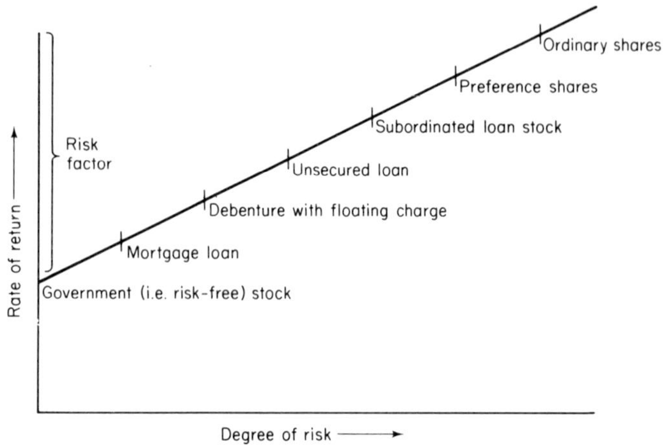

Fig. 5.2 Yield structure: loan capital in relation to Government stocks and share capital (in the case of ordinary shares, 'yield' really means 'total return', for ordinary shares are the one investment in this diagram where there are prospects of an increasing return)

part of each year's profit in a *sinking fund*.

An equivalent cash amount may be used in various ways:

(*a*) To purchase the stock itself in the open market. Because the company is buying at current market price there is then no question of preferring some creditors at the expense of others.

(*b*) To redeem part of the issued stock at par (or as otherwise agreed) on the basis of drawings (the stock to be redeemed is determined by ballot).

(*c*) To purchase other investments which are then held until the company considers it prudent to redeem the stock, perhaps not until the final redemption date.

The existence of a sinking fund improves the marketability and market rating of a stock.

5.13 Fixed-interest Stocks and the Investor

We can summarize the usefulness of fixed-interest investments to the main types of investor as follows:

(*a*) Yield

For the private individual, yield is usually the most influential factor in his investment decisions. Because yields from fixed-interest investments are generally higher than those from most others, an investor may choose to include such a stock in a larger portfolio to 'sweeten' the immediate return from his total investment. This can be so even when, owing to tax considerations, the immediate net return on a building society account is higher than that obtainable from a gilt-edged stock. This is because the immediate flat yield on the fixed-interest investment remains constant until redemption, whereas building society rates fluctuate.

(*b*) **Redemption**

Sometimes a private investor purchases a redeemable fixed-interest stock in order to be sure of receiving a known sum at a particular time with a good income return in the meantime – for instance, a man in his early sixties may want to provide for a cash sum to be available to him when he retires. Such a stock might prove a better prospect for him than a cash investment or a marketable investment which may stand at a lower price when he eventually wants his cash.

(*c*) **Non-residents**

A private investor living outside the United Kingdom may find that the attraction of freedom from taxes on certain gilt-edged stocks outweighs their disadvantages, particularly if he is able to avoid capital transfer tax. If an investor is receiving a tax-free yield approximately double that obtainable from growth investments (where the income is taxable) coupled with a substantial tax saving for his dependants, the growth required from another investment to equal the eventual net return is very large indeed.

(*d*) **Companies' Investments**

Gilt-edged, debenture and loan stock interest is liable for corporation tax in the hands of companies and generally such investments are unpopular with them. They find *franked income* (income which has already borne corporation tax – see Unit 7.1(*a*)) more attractive. Thus preference share dividends have a particular appeal to companies seeking a high fixed-income return. Special considerations apply to investment companies where a small amount of non-franked income is desirable for offsetting management expenses.

(*e*) **Trustees**

Trustees of private trusts usually hold a proportion of the trust funds in fixed-interest stocks (see Units 20 and 21).

(*f*) **Institutions**

The institutions are large holders of fixed-interest stocks, particularly British Government stocks. Where pension funds and charities are concerned, there is no tax liability to take into account and the higher gross yields are attractive (see Unit 21). Other institutions usually keep a proportion of their funds in gilt-edged stocks for the security of income and capital which they offer, generally managing their gilt-edged portfolio separately from the rest of their investments. The very free market in Government stocks and the comparative cheapness of dealing in large amounts of these stocks together give rise to a constant movement between stocks in this sector.

5.14 Questions

1. In comparing the merits of the 12% loan stocks of different companies, what factors would you take into account?
2. What investment opportunities are available in the local authority sector?
3. What are the chief factors in determining yield? Suggest possible yields at which the following securities might be quoted. Place them in order from the lowest yielding security to the highest-yielding.

   Burnley 13% 1987
   Treasury 10½% 1999
   Midland Bank Ordinary shares
   Midland Bank 10¾% 1993–98
   Exchequer 13¼% 1987
   General Electric Company Ordinary shares

   Compare your answer with figures quoted in the *Financial Times*.

Unit Six

Equities

In discussing other forms of investment, apart from those where tax concessions apply, we have seen that higher risk means higher expected income returns. A yield from an investment higher than that obtainable from similar investments should signal caution on the part of the investor. As far as investment in companies is concerned, the highest risk is carried by the holders of the ordinary share capital. Other things being equal, then, yields obtainable on ordinary shares should be higher than those obtainable on prior-charge capital and preference shares. They represent the type of investment that transfers to the investor a part or share of a business enterprise. Ordinary shares are not loans and their holders have no specific rights against the company. The ordinary shareholders, on the other hand, *are* the company insofar as together they can control the company's activities and future.

6.1 The Equity

Ordinary shares as a whole are usually referred to as *equities*. This accurately describes their significance, as the holders of the ordinary capital of a company usually own between them the equity of that company. Equity in this sense means *that which remains after the rights of creditors and mortgagees are cleared*. The equity in a private house, for instance, is the market value less the amount of an outstanding mortgage. The equity in a company is the value of the assets remaining after creditors, debenture and loan stockholders and preference shareholders have been paid what they are entitled to.

The equity is usually owned by the ordinary shareholders but this is not invariably so. The equity must be owned by the holders of share capital but there can be several classes of share capital, and the names given to these classes can be misleading. Thus the equity may be owned by deferred shareholders and, if there are also ordinary shares in issue, these may be preferred ordinary, and therefore a type of preference share. Alternatively, the equity may be owned in various degrees by participating preference, preferred ordinary, ordinary, 'A' ordinary, deferred ordinary and deferred shareholders, or in any combination of any two or more of them. Fortunately a large number of public companies do not have very complicated share capital structures.

The rights of the holders of the equity of a company do not extend to the assets alone but also to the earnings. Thus the profits made by a company after providing for all debts, interest and taxation are applied to the holders of the share capital according to their rights. With a straightforward capital structure, therefore, the preference shareholders receive their fixed dividend and the balance belongs to the ordinary shareholders. Not all of this balance is normally paid out by way of dividend. What is not distributed is retained by the company and increases the assets attributable to the ordinary capital.

6.2 The Dividend Yield

The calculation of yield on fixed-interest investments is relatively simple, as one is dealing with a fixed-income return. By their very nature equities do not have a fixed return, however, and no investor can know for certain what rate of dividend will be declared in the future. The *dividend yield* is an historic measure; it looks backward, not forward, since calculations are based on the latest annual dividend rate (unless the company has already indicated what rate of annual dividend will be paid in the current year). The formula is:

$$\text{Gross dividend yield} = \frac{\text{Gross dividend per share}}{\text{Market price of share}} \times 100$$

Dividends used to be declared in gross terms as a percentage of the nominal share capital. This figure then had to be expressed as a percentage of the current market price. Nowadays the common practice is simply to declare dividends in absolute money terms per share. However, these figures are usually 'net' – the dividend is declared net of the tax credit which the shareholder receives – so in order to work out the equivalent gross yield the net dividend needs to be 'grossed-up' at the basic rate of tax. For example, if the net dividend per share is 5p, the quoted price of the share is 75p, and the basic rate of income tax is 30 per cent, then:

$$\text{Gross dividend yield} = \frac{5\text{p}}{75\text{p}} \times \frac{100}{100 - 30}\% = 9.52\%$$

The dividend yield is frequently quoted as a measure of the return on an equity because of its ready availability (in the *Financial Times* for most large companies) and because it is analogous to the interest yield on debt capital. But it takes no account of future trends or variability in dividends; it is a totally static measure. The dividend yield is also very dependent on the company's payout policy. Dividends declared may be only a small proportion of the profits of the company available for the equity shareholders, but the earnings retained are not 'lost' to the shareholders but rather represent deferred income, that is, they provide for the financing of assets to produce greater future profits and dividends. On the other hand, dividends are sometimes in excess of earnings, and the historic yield is misleading if the dividend cannot be maintained.

6.3 The Earnings Yield and the Price-Earnings Ratio

The *earnings yield* is frequently regarded as a better measure of the shareholder's return than the dividend yield, because it is unaffected by payout policy. The formula is:

$$\text{Earnings yield} = \frac{\text{Earnings per share}}{\text{Market price of share}} \times 100$$

The yields can be derived from companies quoted in the *Financial Times* by multiplying the dividend yield by the 'cover'. No calculations are necessary to obtain the *price-earnings (PE) ratio*, however, since these are published. PE ratios were an import from the USA when corporation tax was introduced into the United Kingdom in 1965, and are given by the formula:

$$\text{Price–earnings ratio} = \frac{\text{Market price of share}}{\text{Earnings per share}}$$

Although since the mid-1960s it has been fashionable to talk in terms of PE ratios, these of course convey the same information as do the earnings yields. The PE ratio is the reciprocal of the earnings yield, expressed as a number – a ratio – rather than a percentage. If the market price of the share is 50p and the earnings per share $2\frac{1}{2}$p, the earnings yield is 5 per cent and the PE ratio 20. If the earnings yield is 25 per cent, the PE ratio is 4. The product of the two is always 100 per cent.

The only complication arises because different definitions of earnings are used for earnings yield and PE ratio purposes (see Unit 15.5). Earnings yields are expressed 'gross', the earnings per share being calculated on a 'full distribution' basis. This represents the maximum gross dividend the company could pay if it adopted a 100 per cent payout policy. It is therefore also the figure used to calculate *dividend cover*, the number of times dividends could be paid out of earnings. On the other hand, for PE ratio purposes earnings are normally calculated on the 'net' basis (retentions plus net dividends). In theory, we could derive the PE ratio as follows:

$$\text{PE ratio} = \frac{100}{\text{Dividend yield} \times \text{Cover}}$$

but the differences in earnings definitions prevent us from doing this with the data provided in the *Financial Times*.

6.4 The Dividend Yield and the Growth Rate

PE ratios can be used for comparing one share with another. At first sight it would appear that the lower the PE ratio is the better, since it takes fewer years

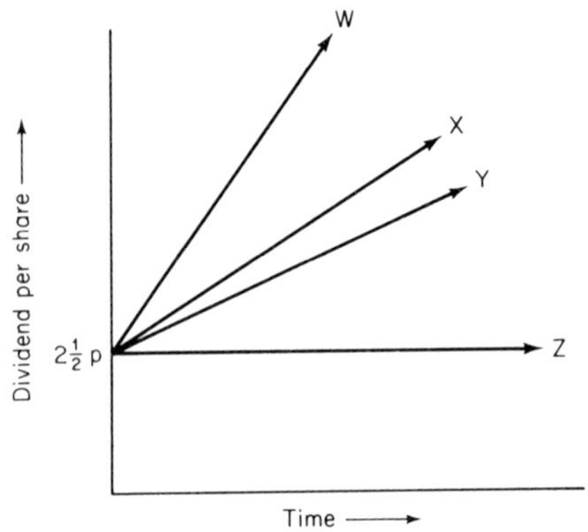

Fig. 6.1 Four companies with different growth rates (all taxes are ignored)

to return one's capital in the form of earnings. But to the shareholder earnings are not cash unless paid as dividends, and the earnings figures are historic. They are the last reported earnings (updated in the *Financial Times* where possible on half-yearly figures). A cursory glance at the financial press reveals an enormous range in PE ratios, as with dividend yields, and frequently the most sought-after shares have been those with the highest PE ratios! Fig. 6.1 will help to explain this seeming paradox. This diagram illustrates the future earnings and dividend profiles of four companies, W, X, Y and Z. The earnings and dividends per share of the four companies are expected to grow perpetually at rates of 18, 12, 10 and 0 per cent respectively. Purchase of a share entitles the investor to a future stream of dividends from that share.

The shareholder's total return is composed of two parts: an initial dividend yield, based on the next expected dividend, and a growth factor, representing the expectation of higher future dividends to the long-term investor, and of capital gain (if share prices rise with dividends and earnings) to the investor who decides to sell. On this basis, investors will be prepared to bid up the price of 'growth stocks', causing the dividend yields to fall to relatively low levels.

Referring back to Fig. 6.1, if all investors were aware of the expected growth rates and all investors required a total return of 20 per cent, we could predict the dividend yields of the four shares.

	Annual growth rate (%) +	Dividend yield (%) =	Total return (%)
W	18	2	20
X	12	8	20
Y	10	10	20
Z	0	20	20

By assuming no taxes of any form, we remove the problem of defining dividends and earnings. If each company pays out half of earnings as dividends (all dividends are 2½p), earnings will be twice dividends, and the earnings yield twice the dividend yield. We can then derive the PE ratio and the share price (share price = PE ratio × earnings per share of 5p).

	Earnings yield (%)	PE ratio	Share price
W	4	25	£1.25
X	16	6¼	31p
Y	20	5	25p
Z	40	2½	12½p

Thus the PE ratios range from 2½ to 25, dividend yields from 2 to 20, and earnings yields from 4 to 40, even though each share offers a return of 20 per cent! Both dividend and earnings yields dramatically understate the shareholder's return with 'super-growth' shares. The dividend yield of Z accurately measures the shareholders' return only because dividends are static. The earnings yield of Y likewise is a good indicator only because the retained earnings are reinvested in the company at the shareholder's rate of return, 20 per cent (that is, one-half of earnings are reinvested at 20 per cent so that total earnings grow at 10 per cent).

This model is highly simplified, but the principles are sound. A glance in the *Financial Times* will show that the sectors with the best growth prospects, such as property, stores, electricals, and electronics, have relatively high PE ratios and low dividend yields; the reverse is true of textiles, tobacco and metals.

6.5 Asset Values

The holders of the equity of a company own between them the earnings and assets of that company after prior claims have been discharged. Apart from earnings, therefore, the other tangible factor in assessment of ordinary shares is the value of the assets attributable to the equity. This information is given in the balance sheet of the company but assets should not be assumed to be worth the figures stated there. Briefly, the balance sheet value of assets attributable to the equity is the nominal value of the equity plus the total reserves. The real value of the assets may be more or less than the balance sheet figure and be different in different circumstances. For instance, the value of a factory might be very much higher as a going concern than as an empty building on the liquidation of the company. The balance sheet value of the factory – cost less accumulated depreciation – reflects neither circumstance. Trade investments in the balance sheet may be worth more or less than the figure shown. This sort of situation can arise with many balance sheet items; we shall look at the calculation of asset value in more detail in Unit 15.

In general asset values are less important than earnings in determining share prices. A company's earnings are available for distribution or for investment in expansion. The value of the assets employed can be realized only on liquidation, although their value may be significant in the event of a take-over bid being made for the company. But if earnings on assets employed fall to low levels, the asset value may underpin the market price in the anticipation of another company becoming interested in those assets for use in an amalgamated concern. In other words, assets producing inadequate earnings are meat and drink to the take-over specialist.

6.6 Management

The third important factor in the assessment of the equity of a company is an intangible one: the quality of the management. This will not be found in the company's balance sheet, and analysis of the published results will show it only after a number of years. With the benefit of hindsight it is possible to distinguish those companies where management has been exceptional. These are companies where profits have increased regularly over a long period at a rate greater than that achieved by their competitors.

The quality of a company's management is the most difficult factor to assess and evaluate. It has a marked influence nevertheless on the level of market priceof the equity capital. Whereas asset value and past earnings are a guide to the true value of an equity share, it is the ability of management to recognize changing circumstances, and to amend policy to take account of those changes, which is the principal growth factor in the success of the best companies. Market price reflects the views of investors as to the future potential of a company. Good management is normally taken fully into account in the market price of a share.

6.7 Nominal Values

You might find it confusing that some companies have ordinary shares of £1 each, some have ordinary shares of 25p each (all shares quoted in the *Financial Times* are 25p shares unless otherwise stated) and others have 50p, 5p or some other value expressed in the title of the shares. To the investor such distinctions are irrelevant. It makes no difference whatsoever what denomination the shares are quoted in. If a company has net assets of, say, £5 000 000, it cannot have any significance to the investor whether there are 4 000 000 £1 shares issued and £1 000 000 of reserves or 16 000 000 25p shares and £1 000 000 of reserves, except that the quoted price of the nominal £1 shares would be four times that of the 25p shares.

The law of the United Kingdom requires shares of companies to have a nominal value. This is in contrast to some countries, such as the United States of America and Canada, where shares may have no nominal value and are then described as *of no par value*. In the example here, the equity capital could be expressed as £5 000 000 divided into a number of shares of no par value. The reserves of a company belong to the holders of equity equally with the nominal amount of equity capital and the distinction in this country is really an artificial one. It may be that in due time shares of no par value will be issued here.

6.8 Dividend Payments

Dividends on ordinary shares are declared in respect of the company's trading period, usually a year. There are two types of dividend, *interim* and *final*. Interim dividends may be declared by the directors but final dividends may only be paid on approval by the annual general meeting of the company.

The directors usually declare and pay an interim dividend during the second half of the company's year, and propose a final dividend to be paid the day after the annual meeting. Thus dividends are usually paid at about six-monthly intervals. More often than not the final dividend is at a higher rate than the interim one.

Sometimes companies pay more than two dividends for one year, sometimes only one. Sometimes two interims are paid and no final. The annual meeting has the power to reduce a final dividend but not to increase it, although the exercise of such power is very rare in quoted companies.

All dividends are paid net of tax which has to be accounted for by the company as *advance corporation tax* (see Unit 15.5).

6.9 Non-voting Shares

Although frowned on by the Stock Exchange, which prevents further issues of them, some issues of equity shares that have no voting rights are still outstanding. These are usually called 'A' ordinary shares. They were devised to keep the voting control in a company in the hands of a minority while bringing in capital from general investors. Where they still exist they are usually quoted at slightly lower prices than the voting ordinary shares.

It is difficult to justify the existence of non-voting ordinary shares. Those who carry the risk in a company should be able to control its future together. In recent years several companies have enfranchised these shares, and at the same time given a bonus issue to the previous voting shares to compensate them for the dilution in control.

6.10 Risk

An investor in ordinary shares should never forget that he is in a risk situation. The degree of risk attached to an individual share depends on the amounts of business and financial risk. *Business risk* is largely determined by the type of economic activity in which the company is involved: it is the risk of profit fluctuation due to changes in demand (arising from changes in tastes, new products, competitors' strengths, overall economic activity and so on) or in supply (due to factors such as new methods of production or varying costs of labour or raw materials). To a certain extent, companies can reduce business risk by means of diversification.

Financial risk is measured by the fluctuations in shareholders' returns and the probability of liquidation, brought about by the use of borrowed funds and especially short-term borrowings. The ratio of borrowed funds to overall capital is called the *gearing ratio*, and the ratio of short-term ('current') assets to liabilities the *current ratio*. The more highly geared and the more illiquid the company, the greater the financial risk. It is a 'voluntary' risk, however, in the sense that it could be avoided by having a 'clean' balance sheet – no borrowed funds – but many companies believe that the risk is justified by the enhanced return to the shareholders. As long as the company can earn a higher return on its total assets than the cost of borrowed funds, the shareholders will benefit from the 'surplus' on the debt-financed assets.

To take a simple example, imagine three companies – A, B and C – identical in every respect except their financial structures, which are as follows:

Company A:		*Company B:*		*Company C:*	
Total debt	–	12 per cent debt	£ 50mn	12 per cent debt	£ 75mn
Net worth	£100mn	Net worth	£ 50mn	Net worth	£ 25mn
Total capital	£100mn	Total capital	£100mn	Total capital	£100mn

Company A is financed entirely by shareholders' funds (net worth), while Company C has a book value capital gearing ratio of 75 per cent. Accordingly A's shareholders are relatively better off in bad times, C's in good times. This is illustrated in Table 6.1, where it is assumed that under very difficult economic conditions a rate of return of only 4 per cent on assets can be expected, that a normal rate of return is 16 per cent and that under exceptionally favourable circumstances the rate of return can reach 28 per cent. Table 6.1 shows that the volatility of returns for the highly geared Company C is much greater than that for B, which in turn is greater than that for A. The *indifference level* is the overall rate of return, equal to the cost of debt capital, where the returns to the shareholder are the same in each company.

The *volatility* of a share is nowadays frequently expressed in terms of its *beta coefficient*. The rate of return on a share (dividend income and capital change expressed as a percentage of the opening market value) for successive periods is plotted on one axis of a graph, and the return on a share index – representing the average performance of a large number of shares – on the other axis (see Fig. 6.2). The slope of the line, defined as the beta coefficient, measures the volatility, or riskiness, of the share relative to market as a whole. Fig. 6.2 makes it clear that Company A's share price is much less volatile than that of Company C. A is said to be a *defensive* share and C an *aggressive* one. The volatility depends on both business and financial risk, but also on the extent to which the fortunes of the company are correlated with those of other firms. It is not only important how much the share price moves up and down, but also to

Table 6.1 Returns to shareholders in different types of company

	Economic conditions			
	Very poor	Indifference level	Normal	Very good
Rate of return on assets before interest and taxes	4%	12%	16%	28%
Company A:				
Earnings before interest and taxes	£4mn	£12mn	£16mn	£28mn
Less interest	0	0	0	0
Taxable income	£4mn	£12mn	£16mn	£28mn
Corporation tax (say, 50 per cent)	£2mn	£6mn	£8mn	£14mn
Attributable to shareholders	£2mn	£6mn	£8mn	£14mn
Net return to shareholders	2%	6%	8%	14%
Company B:				
Earnings before interest and taxes	£4mn	£12mn	£16mn	£28mn
Less interest	£6mn	£6mn	£6mn	£6mn
Taxable income	−£2mn	£6mn	£10mn	£22mn
Corporation tax (say, 50 per cent)	0	£3mn	£5mn	£11mn
Attributable to shareholders	−£2mn	£3mn	£5mn	£11mn
Net return to shareholders	−4%	6%	10%	22%
Company C:				
Earnings before interest and taxes	£4mn	£12mn	£16mn	£28mn
Less interest	£9mn	£9mn	£9mn	£9mn
Taxable income	−£5mn	£3mn	£7mn	£19mn
Corporation tax (say, 50 per cent)	0	£1½mn	£3½mn	£9½mn
Attributable to shareholders	−£5mn	£1½mn	£3½mn	£9½mn
Net return to shareholders	−20%	6%	14%	38%

what extent it does so together with, or independently of, the stock market as a whole. The greater the degree of independence the better so far as risk minimization is concerned, because risk can then be reduced by holding a combination of shares. Diversification enables the investor to eliminate 'independent' risk so that only 'systematic' risk remains, and it is this risk that is measured by the beta coefficient. In our example, the greater financial gearing of Company C means that its earnings are more volatile than those of companies A and B, and so also its dividends and share price are likely to be.

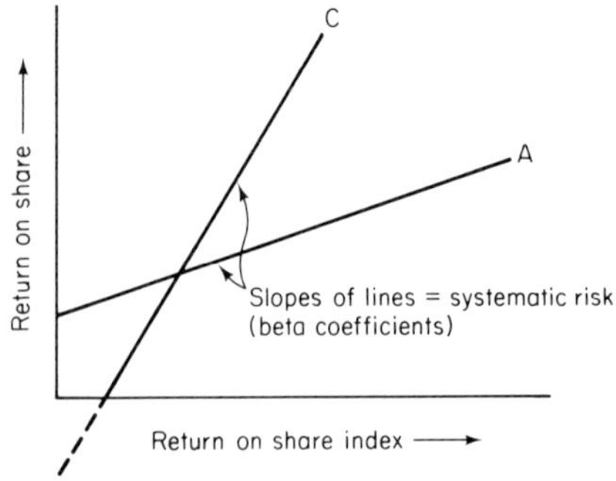

Fig. 6.2 Measuring the beta coefficients of shares

6.11 Yields and Risk

In a competitive market risk must be compensated for by extra return. High-risk fixed-interest stocks should yield more than low-risk ones, equities more than stocks and high-risk equities more than low-risk ones. Considerable evidence exists to confirm that the greater the volatility of a share, on average the higher the return (see Fig. 6.3).

It should be remembered that the total return is the sum of the dividend yield and the expected growth rate in income and capital. There is nothing surprising in the existence of a 'reverse yield gap', which is the difference between the dividend yield on a share index and the yield on a long-dated or undated gilt-edged security such as 2½% Consols. In September 1979 the *Financial Times* All Share Index had a gross dividend yield of approximately 6 per cent, while 2½% Consols yielded just over 10½ per cent, giving a reverse yield gap of 4½ percentage points. But we should not assume that investors were irrational in purchasing low-return and high-risk equities, but rather that they expected capital gain and income growth to more than compensate for the initial shortfall, and so provide a higher overall return on equities than gilts.

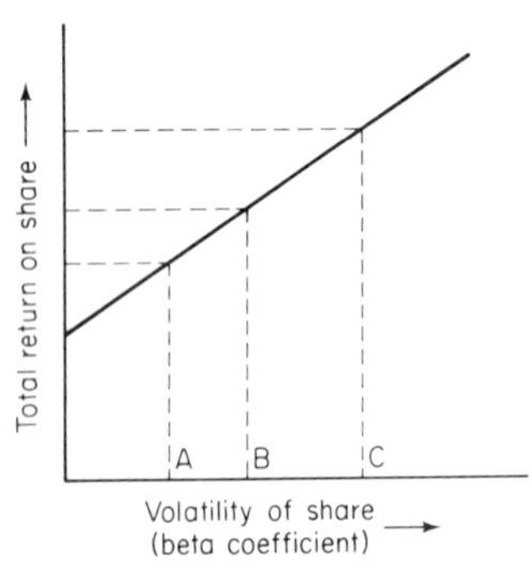

Fig. 6.3 The relationship between risk and return

6.12 Comparison against Other Investments

At the end of 1980, the Equity Income Index published by the stockbrokers De Zoete and Bevan stood at almost nine and a half times its value for the year 1946, equivalent to a compound growth rate of 6.6 per cent per year. Income was erratic between 1919 and 1945, but since 1945 income growth has been much more consistent, although, adjusted for inflation, the Equity Income Index at the end of 1980 was about 7 per cent below its 1946 level, and less than half the high point reached at the end of 1965.

The corresponding Equity Price Index at the end of 1980 was 5.5 times the figure for 1 January 1946. In real terms, however, the adjusted Index was only 54 per cent of the 1946 figure, only 30 per cent of the highest figure ever recorded (that of 1 January 1969) and lower than that for any year-end (except for three years) since 1922.

Even worse has been the performance of Government securities, as illustrated by the Consols Index. In the thirty-five years from 1947 to 1980 it rose in only eleven, which included the three consecutive years ending 31 December 1977. On 1 January 1981 it was still 79 per cent below the 1947 level – adjusted for inflation, only 2 per cent of its value in that year.

'A little medium-term finance for the small businessman?'

Treasury bills have performed better than either equities or Consols in fourteen of the years between 1946 and 1980. Consols came out on top overall in only four years, equities in the remaining seventeen. The superior relative performance of equities is emphasized by the comparisons made in Tables 6.2 and 6.3.

Table 6.2 Performance of investments of £1 000 made on 1 January 1946, assuming gross income reinvested (1 January 1981)

Equities	£33 082
Consols	£2 694
Treasury bills	£6 750

Source: De Zoete and Bevan

Table 6.3 Average overall returns per annum, with gross income reinvested, for different types of investment (per cent)

	Equities	Consols	Treasury bills
1946–51	3.0	−2.0	0.5
1951–56	17.3	−0.5	2.0
1956–61	15.9	0	4.7
1961–66	6.9	3.4	4.8
1966–71	6.6	−0.5	7.0
1971–76	9.0	3.6	8.8
1976–81	15.8	17.2	11.8
1946–81	10.5	2.9	5.6

Source: De Zoete and Bevan

6.13 Timing

The secret of short-term success in equity investment is *when* you buy and sell rather than *what* you buy and sell, as nearly all shares tend to move upwards in price during a 'bull' market and downwards in a 'bear' market (see Glossary). All investors would like to buy at the bottom of a bear market and sell, or 'go liquid', at the top of a bull market. In this respect the personal investor and the small unit trust have much greater flexibility than most other investors, particularly large insurance companies and pension funds, who would find it both very difficult, and imprudent, to reduce their share holdings suddenly and drastically.

For the personal investor the difficulty lies in knowing when the top or bottom has been reached. Is he watching a primary change in the trend, or merely a temporary aberration? One can only say with hindsight. Although bull and bear markets regularly follow each other their duration and amplitude are not consistent enough for us to discern a regular pattern. Changes in the market still tend to precede changes in economic activity, but the 'trade cycle' itself is much less regular and much more 'politically' determined than it was a century ago. Stock market folklore used to talk of a cycle of something like four years from peak to peak, with the market retracing itself by about a third in the 'bear' phase. Such believers had a rude awakening, however, when the FT 30 Share Index fell 73 per cent in a bear phase of 31 months from May 1972 to January 1975. (There was a 52 per cent fall in 49 months between 1929 and 1932, and a 61 per cent fall in 43 months from 1936 to 1940.)

6.14 Questions

1. Extract from the *Financial Times* the names of the companies and sectors which have (*a*) the highest price–earnings ratios and lowest dividend yields, and (*b*) the lowest price–earnings ratios and the highest dividend yields. How would you account for these differences?

2. Most types of Stock Exchange investment involve some kind of risk to the investor. What are these risks and what can be done to minimize them?

3. Given below is financial and operating information for Companies A, B and C:

Capital structure:	A	B	C
Ordinary shares and reserves	£ 200 000	£ 500 000	£1 000 000
10% debentures	£ 800 000	£ 500 000	Nil
	£1 000 000	£1 000 000	£1 000 000

In the followings years each company made a profit (return on total capital) as detailed below:

1974 : 8 per cent
1975 : 15 per cent
1976 : 20 per cent

Taxation can be ignored

(*a*) What fundamental factor, apparent in the figures, could have considerable importance for the potential investor in ordinary shares in these companies? Illustrate the impact of this factor by using the information supplied.

(*b*) What conclusion can be drawn from the experience of these companies in 1974 and 1976 about the factor referred to in (*a*) above?

(*c*) What further conclusions would you draw?

Unit Seven

Other Direct Financial Assets

7.1 Preference Shares

Preference shares are not loans, they do not form part of loan capital, and on a winding-up they do not rank for repayment until all creditors have been repaid in full.

(*a*) The Effect of Corporation Tax

Preference shares are a *fixed-income* investment but not a *fixed-interest* investment. As they form part of the share capital of a company the income paid to the investor is dividend and not interest. This may seem an artificial distinction to the average investor but it is in fact an important one. All loan interest is a charge on company profits and the cost of loan capital to a company is consequently the interest paid, less the corporation tax that would have been payable on that interest. Preference share dividends are payable out of taxed profits and therefore cost the company more than loan stock interest on the same amount of capital. For a corporate investor, however, preference share dividends are *franked income* for corporation tax, whereas loan stock interest is not. (Franked income is that part of a company's income which is paid to it out of profits that have suffered corporation tax and is thereby exempt from further corporation tax, whereas other investment income is unfranked and therefore liable for corporation tax in the hands of a company investor.) Thus, from the tax point of view alone, preference shares are a better investment for companies than loan stocks.

Following the introduction of the imputation system of corporation tax in 1973, the coupons of preference shares were changed from a gross to a net basis at the prevailing basic rate of income tax (30 per cent). Thus a 10 per cent gross preference share became 7 per cent net. This meant that if the basic rate of income tax changed then so did the gross return. For example, at basic-rate income tax of 35 per cent, the gross yield of our example would become $7 \div 0.65 = 10.77$ per cent.

(*b*) Lack of Attraction

The vast majority of preference shares are irredeemable. To the private investor it is difficult to find anything to commend them as investments. They have all the disadvantages of British Government fixed-interest undated stocks with none of the advantages. The interest on the Government stock is guaranteed, whereas the dividends on preference shares depend on the availability of company profits. There are many preference shares of large companies on which it is hardly conceivable that the dividend would not be paid. But the gross yield on these shares is lower than that on British Government undated securities, and any capital profits that might be made on them are liable to capital gains tax (while those on Government stocks are exempt if held for more than one year). This situation makes preference shares – attractive to corporate investors – unattractive to the private investor.

It is of course possible to buy preference shares whose yield far exceeds that obtainable on any gilt-edged stock. This is again a reflection of risk. Except where tax benefits can accrue, yield is a measure of the market's view of the risk attaching to the particular stock or share. Investors should always be suspicious of a yield which is significantly higher than that obtainable from similar investments.

Loan capital of a company is generally referred to as the *prior charges* of that company. This term indicates that, along with creditors, the holders of that capital have a prior claim on the assets of the company in the event of liquidation. Some prior charges have priority over others. In the share capital of a company, preference shares have priority (or preference) over other types of share, but here again some preference shares may have a prior claim over others. As with debentures and unsecured loan stocks, an investor should be aware of the nature of the investment he is purchasing.

(*c*) Types of Preference Share

It is quite common for a company to have several issues of preference shares. These may rank either in priority to each other or *pari passu* (on an equal basis). They may be classified as first and second preference shares but the absence of such classification does not guarantee that they rank equally. Often preference shares with different rates of dividend rank *pari passu*. The order of priority usually relates equally to the availability of profits out of which to pay a dividend and to capital priority on winding-up.

Preference shares may be either *cumulative* or *non-cumulative*. If there are insufficient profits in one year to pay a cumulative preference dividend, the right continues for that dividend to be received before any payment is made to the holders of a lower class of capital. Even though a cumulative preference share dividend may be years in arrear, all arrears must be paid off before a dividend is declared on preference shares ranking lower in priority, and on ordinary shares. With non-cumulative preference shares, once a dividend is passed for one year the right to receive it is lost and on resumption of payment no arrears are due. Preference shares are understood to be cumulative unless specifically stated otherwise.

Some companies have preference shares with rights to participate in profits beyond the fixed dividend. These *participating preference shares* vary enormously in their terms, but the investor is fortunate if he can find one where there is still scope for increases in dividends. Very few, if any, are now available, as there is always an upper limit to the amount of participation, and in the course of time this effectively converts the share to a preference share with a higher fixed dividend than that available when it was first issued. Some participating preference shares are called *preferred ordinary shares*, but there is generally no difference in the rights of holders. Reference to the terms of issue will always clarify any doubts.

Some preference shares are described as redeemable, but care is needed when assessing these. Redemption may either be set for a particular time or be at the option of the company. Redemption must take place out of accumulated profits or from the proceeds of a new issue so as not to affect the security of creditors and the holders of prior charges.

(*d*) **Voting**

Holders of preference shares, although 'proprietors' of the company by the holding of share capital, usually cannot vote at general meetings of the company. This is not always so; some preference shares do carry voting rights, often in a limited form. Even those shares which do not normally have voting rights usually carry votes when the dividend is in arrears, however. The articles of association of the company or the terms of issue of the shares will give full details of any such rights.

7.2 Convertible Stocks

Convertible debentures or loan stocks are fixed-interest securities with rights for conversion into ordinary shares at the holder's option and under specified terms and conditions. There are many different convertible loan stocks with various conversion rights, and it is impossible to generalize about them. Some have a short conversion period, such as a month, in each of a number of consecutive years. Some have a precise date on which conversion can be carried out. Some may be converted a few years after the stock is first issued, others not for many years ahead. All convertible loan stocks have redemption dates but these are often of only academic interest as the company usually retains a right to redeem any stock outstanding once a certain percentage of the stock has been converted.

The *conversion ratio* is the number of shares the holder of a convertible receives when he surrenders his security on conversion. This number can be fixed, or may vary depending on when conversion takes place. The *conversion price* is the effective price paid for a way into the ordinary shares; that is:

$$\text{Conversion price} = \frac{\text{Market value of convertible}}{\text{Number of shares on conversion}}$$

This can then be compared with the actual market price of the ordinary shares to determine the *conversion premium*:

$$\text{Conversion premium} = \text{Conversion price} - \text{Market price of ordinary share}$$

The larger the conversion premium the more expensive the convertible is as a way of buying ordinary shares. The *option cost* or *rights premium* is how much more expensive a convertible is as compared with a 'straight' debenture or loan stock (one without conversion rights):

$$\text{Option cost per share} = \frac{\text{Market value of convertible} - \text{Value as straight loan stock}}{\text{Number of shares at conversion date}}$$

Conversion rights are worth having, but the likelihood of exercising them will depend on the remaining life of the convertible and the size of the conversion premium. If the convertible has a long conversion period remaining and the conversion premium is small, the conversion rights are valuable, and the convertible will sell at a substantial premium over a comparable straight issue.

As an illustration, on 5 October 1979 Wilkinson Match had £11.1mn of 10 per cent convertible outstanding, redeemable 1984–98. The stock, selling at a market price of £80, could be converted into 40 ordinary shares between 1976 and 1983. The ordinary shares were selling for £1.70. The conversion price was thus £2.00 per share and the conversion premium therefore 30p a share, or 18 per cent. The convertible had a redemption yield of nearly 13½ per cent, suggesting that investors did not consider the conversion rights particularly attractive and were not willing to buy the stock on a much lower yield than comparable straight debentures.

Because convertibles can be valued either as a straight loan stock or as a means into the equity, the minimum price tends to be set by the higher of these two figures. In an efficient market the convertible should never sell for less than an otherwise identical straight loan stock, but as the share price rises it tends to pull the convertible's price up with it. In our example, if Wilkinson Match's share price rose to £3.00, the convertible would be worth a minimum of £120 (40 × £3.00).

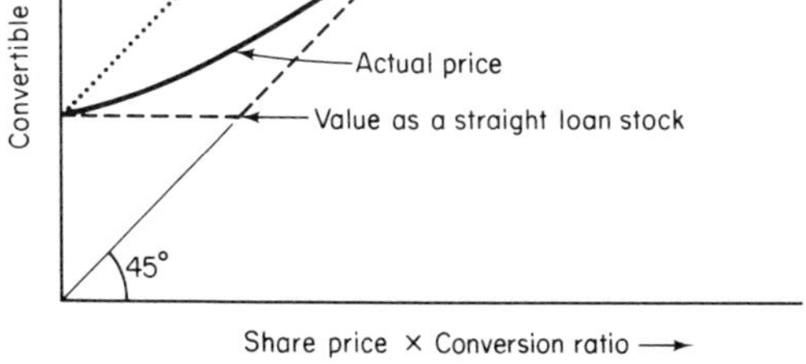

Fig. 7.1 The price range of a convertible stock

The valuation of a convertible is illustrated in Fig. 7.1. The conversion premium exists because of the *downside protection*, the 'floor', provided by the convertible as compared with direct ownership of the equity; because of the income differential, the interest yield on the convertible usually exceeds the dividend yield from the equivalent shares. As the share price increases, and the remaining conversion period shortens, so the conversion premium narrows.

When a possible conversion day is imminent, the convertible should never sell for less than the value of the shares into which it is convertible, or the straight loan stock, and never for more than the shares plus the loan stock.

The attractions of convertibles are as follows:

(*a*) **To the Company**

(i) Initially convertibles were issued as unsecured loan stock by companies without sufficient assets for a full mortgage debenture. The extra risk was compensated for by the opportunity to participate in the success of the business, through conversion, without the full risks of equity-holders.

(ii) The cash flow implications are attractive in that convertibles can be sold on lower yields than straight loan stocks if the conversion rights are attractive. Allied to tax relief this means that the debt servicing can be relatively light in the early years, and so may be useful in the finance of projects with long gestation periods.

(iii) It is sometimes suggested that convertibles are a way of selling deferred equity at a premium when the stock market is depressed. This can be misleading, however, since although the conversion price is at a premium over the share price at the time of issue, it may well be at a significant discount when compared with the price of the equity at the time of conversion. Moreover, the company cannot set the conversion price totally independently of the prevailing share price, since the initial conversion premium will determine how much investors are willing to pay for the option element and the convertible as a whole.

(iv) Convertibles have in the past been part of the currency of take-over bids. In this respect they have provided an indirect method of selling highly priced equity to 'outside' investors.' The convertible gives the vendor shareholders a continuing, but secure, stake in the business taken over.

(*b*) **To the Investor**

(i) There is no limit to the 'upside' potential of a convertible, but the downside is generally limited to the value of a straight loan stock. This can be a more effective protection against risk than a 'stop-loss' order (see Glossary) placed with a broker. Convertibles are most suitable for investment in enterprises where the outcome is uncertain.

(ii) They are attractive to trustees of funds where there are restrictions on the equity content of the portfolio. They are regarded as 'narrower-range' investments in the Trustee Investments Act 1961 (see Unit 20.2). When converted they must be transferred into the wider-range section of the portfolio, but in the meantime provide a 'backdoor' way of boosting the equity content of the fund.

7.3 Warrants

A variant on the convertible loan stock is the loan stock with warrants (subscription rights) attached. A *warrant* is a quoted option certificate issued by a company, entitling the holder to subscribe for a given number (or fraction) of ordinary shares in the company at a predetermined price (the *exercise price*) on any one of a selection of specified future dates. Most companies that have issued warrants have done so as part of a 'package deal', with the warrants having been originally attached to loan stock. Subsequently the warrants have been detached, quoted and dealt in separately from the loan stock, but usually such warrants can be exercised either by subscribing for shares in cash or by exchanging the loan stock.

Warrants produce no income; they are not part of a company's share capital, although they threaten to dilute the equity. In the balance sheet they are normally shown as part of capital reserve. They usually have a limited life, although a very few are perpetual. The company is required by the Stock Exchange to protect warrant-holders from suffering loss due to rights issues or bonus issues reducing the price of the ordinary shares.

At or near any of the stipulated exercise dates the floor to the market price of the warrant will be the difference between the share price and the exercise price (multiplied by the number of shares to which the warrant entitles the holder). But frequently warrants sell for considerably more than their minimum conversion value. For example, at the time of writing Ladbroke Group have warrants outstanding that give the holders the right to buy one ordinary share at a cash price of 171.2p for every warrant held. The warrants expire at the end of 1987. At one point during 1974, the warrant was selling for 30p when the ordinary shares were quoted at 95p, giving a *conversion premium* (warrant price plus exercise price minus share price) of 106.2p. It may seem incredible that the warrant could be worth anything when the exercise price was nearly double the share price itself! The answer lies in the fact that at that time the warrant had a remaining life of over thirteen years, while the company's growth prospects were above average. As long as there is any probability of the share price exceeding the exercise price during this period the warrant will have a value. But a warrant can never sell for more than the value of the shares into which it can be converted.

The size of the conversion premium depends on the remaining life of the warrant, the volatility of the share and the exercise price relative to the share price. The greater these three factors the larger the conversion premium, as all three features are attractive to warrant-holders. Obviously, as the end of the warrant's life approaches the premium will disappear as the warrant must either be exercised or become worthless. As the share price and the dividend income increase the *gearing attraction* (the extent to which the price of the warrant changes more proportionately than that of the underlying share) is reduced and it becomes increasingly expensive to forgo income by not exercising the option. Sometimes the exercise price increases periodically and this may encourage early exercising of the warrant. In Fig. 7.2 we plot on the vertical axis the price

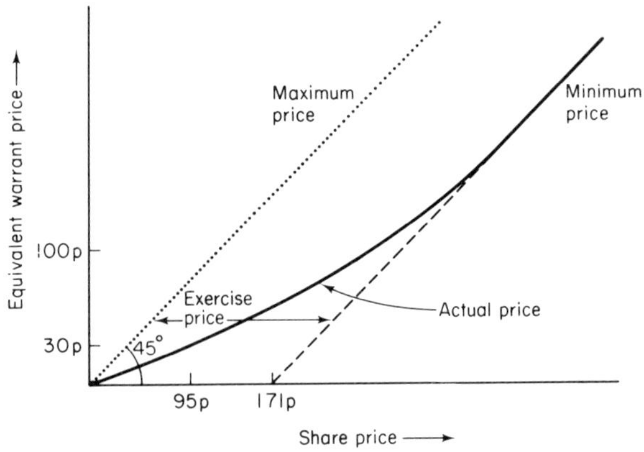

Fig. 7.2 The price range of a warrant (the figures for Ladbroke Group are applied to the model)

of an equivalent warrant, by which is meant the price of that fraction of, or multiple of, a basic warrant which will enable one share to be purchased.

If it can be exercised in the very near future, the warrant should never sell for less than the difference between the share price and the exercise price, and never for more than the share price.

The attractions of warrants are as follows:

(*a*) **To the Company**

(i) No initial servicing costs are involved, as no interest or dividends are paid on the warrant itself. As warrants are not normally converted early in life (as long as the premium exists) this situation may extend many years into the future.

(ii) They are an attractive supplement for unsecured loan stock where adequate security is lacking.

(iii) They provide a means of selling deferred equity to 'outsiders', particularly when the company believes its share price to be overvalued. If the market is grossly over-optimistic the proceeds of the issue may be obtained without conversion taking place, that is, the warrants become worthless. The Stock Exchange regulations, however, provide that quoted companies must obtain the consent of their ordinary shareholders in general meeting to an issue of warrants other than to existing shareholders.

(*b*) **To the Investor**

(i) As warrants provide no income, all return is in the form of capital gain, and they are therefore attractive to high-rate taxpayers.

(ii) Warrants offer high risk/return opportunities to the investor, particularly where the exercise price is close to the share price. For example, if the share price is £1 and the exercise price 90p, then the minimum value for the warrant is 10p. A 10 per cent rise in the share price would lead to a 100 per cent increase in the value of the warrant (that is, minimum value of warrant = £1.10 − 90p = 20p). The ratio of the market price of the ordinary share to the adjusted market price (per share) of the warrant is one which some technical analysts calculate and refer to as a measure of gearing.

7.4 Foreign Currency Bank Accounts

With the complete removal of exchange controls on 24 October 1979, there is no longer any restriction on a United Kingdom resident having a foreign currency bank account. Current and deposit accounts can be opened with a clearing bank, a United Kingdom branch of a foreign bank or directly in the countries concerned. These accounts are convenient for holidays, are a handy way of investing in foreign securities and provide a hedge against a fall in the sterling exchange rate.

By no means all countries have dismantled their own exchange controls. France, Italy and Spain, for example, have restrictions at the time of writing. The non-resident cannot credit his 'external account' from inside these countries, although he can draw on it freely. On the other hand, in the USA and West Germany the facilities offered to resident and non-resident customers are identical. At the end of 1979, Switzerland abandoned the negative interest-rate provision on large foreign-held accounts, because of the weakness of the Swiss franc.

7.5 Overseas Equities

Overseas security issues, particularly equities, can be attractive to the investor, as they offer scope for further diversification of the portfolio and an opportunity to partake in the success of faster-growing economies than that of the United Kingdom (although this may be reflected in their valuations). The principal markets are North America, South Africa, Australia, the Far East and the rest of the European Community.

The investor should be aware of the problems of investing from a distance, and of the dangers of being exploited by unscrupulous local dealers. In many countries, accounting policies and disclosure requirements are highly unsatisfactory (the USA is an obvious exception). In the remainder of the European Community equities have been distrusted as a savings medium in the past, and there are restrictions on institutional investment; moreover, the financial systems of many countries are controlled by the government and/or the banks. Consequently the equity markets are poorly capitalized, and dealing more restricted than in the United Kingdom.

Some overseas equities have a United Kingdom quotation; others, quoted on their domestic markets, can be bought through the Stock Exchange under

Rule 163(1) (see Unit 9.8), although using a United Kingdom-based broker to invest abroad entails higher commission costs than dealing directly through a local broker. (Equally, British investors may buy British securities on foreign bourses, and thus avoid stamp duty.) Nevertheless, despite the removal of exchange controls, the personal investor is still well advised to use a means of indirect investment, such as a unit or investment trust (see Units 11 and 13.9), because of the specialized knowledge required of these markets and also because of tax complications.

In general, all the income of a United Kingdom resident is liable to United Kingdom tax, irrespective of whether it is derived at home or overseas. This applies to all types of financial asset, including equities. Moreover, income from overseas investments is usually already taxed in the country in which it originates. The United Kingdom Government has made agreements with a large number of countries to limit the extent to which income may be taxed twice over, however. Under one of these *double taxation agreements*, the British investor is credited with tax paid overseas. Most double taxation agreements provide for a 15 per cent withholding tax on dividends by foreign governments, with the balance, depending on the investor's marginal tax rate, being paid to the Inland Revenue; but investors paying tax at a rate less than has been deducted under a double taxation agreement are unable to claim back the extra foreign tax paid. If income is paid direct to the investor from abroad, rather than to an agent such as a bank, it is the responsibility of the investor to apply to the Inland Revenue in order to have the foreign tax deducted at the reduced rate, and receive a credit against the United Kingdom tax liability.

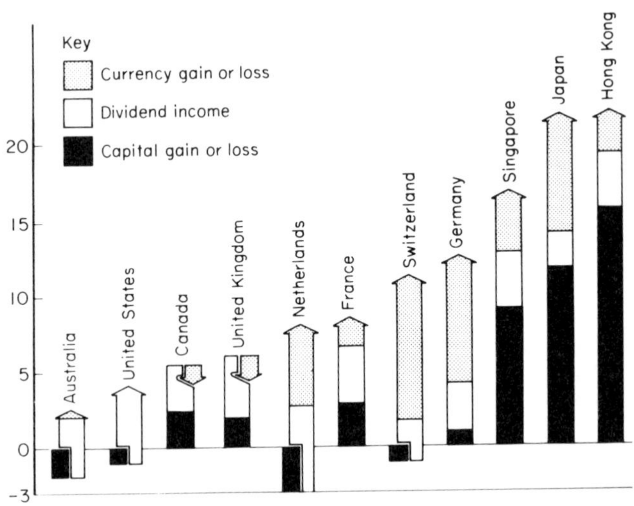

Fig. 7.3 Total return of major stock markets, 1969–78: percentage compound rate of growth in US dollar terms

With regard to the choice of markets, those of the Far East have been the clear winners over the last decade (see Fig. 7.3). The Tokyo Dow-Jones Index and its better known Wall Street version both stood at 1 000 in December 1965. By the end of 1979 Tokyo had surged to 6 400, while the US market languished around the 800 level. Moreover, the yen stood at 360 to the dollar in 1965, whereas by the end of the 1979 one dollar bought only 240 yen. So a theoretical purchase of the Tokyo index in December 1965 would, after fourteen years, have been worth twelve times more than if it had been made in Wall Street.

7.6 Questions

1. Which type of investor finds preference shares attractive? Why is this? Would you recommend them to a personal investor?

2. (*a*) What do you understand by a convertible debenture/loan stock? How would you assess such a stock as an investment?
   (*b*) Discuss briefly the advantages and disadvantages of convertible stocks, (i) from the issuing company's point of view, (ii) as a personal investment.

3. Outline the attractions and risks of warrants from the viewpoint of the personal investor.

Unit Eight

New Issues

In this Unit we shall discuss two types of new issue:

(*a*) the bringing to the market of companies that have not been previously quoted;

(*b*) the raising of additional capital by companies that already have a quotation.

A recently introduced means of quotation for smaller companies, the Unlisted Securities Market, is discussed in Unit 9.8.

8.1 Going Public

Most large public companies have had modest beginnings. Except for companies which have been floated off larger concerns and certain investment companies, most of today's household names started as small businesses, sometimes a very long time ago. Many companies whose names will be equally familiar to the next generation are now small businesses and obscure private companies.

The small business is often turned into a company because of tax considerations. All profits made by a sole trader or a partnership are taxed as the income of the proprietor or partners. With certain restrictions to avoid abuse, the profits of a company are taxed as company profits at the rate of corporation tax and profits may be carried forward. In addition, the company structure enables friends and relatives of the founder to put their money into the business to facilitate expansion by means other than private loans. They can take up ordinary capital which gives them in return for their investment at least the nominal right to have a say in the way the company is run.

There comes a time with a successful and expanding company when both the resources of the founder's friends and relatives and the willingness of the company's bankers to extend credit facilities come to an end, and it is necessary to look elsewhere for funds for further expansion. At this point a merchant bank may be persuaded to take a financial interest in the company, or perhaps stock or shares will be taken up by a company in the Finance for Industry group (FFI itself being owned by the large clearing banks), or Estate Duties Investment Trust Ltd, itself a quoted public company.

Once outside finance from sources like these has been brought in, the next step must be the eventual flotation of the company. At some time in the future the general public will be offered shares to enable the merchant bank or other institution to realize part, at least, of its investment, and for further outside finance to be raised. This is often achieved by the issue of a large number of bonus shares (see Unit 8.12) which are renounced by the existing shareholders for sale to the public.

Another reason for a company to go public is the effect of capital transfer tax. If a majority of the shares of a large company are held by one person and he does not have substantial assets outside that company, his death may precipitate a flotation at an inconvenient time. Alternatively, some form of capital reorganization may have to be carried out, so that company assets can be released to the shareholder's personal representatives to provide funds for the payment of taxes. In any case, the death is likely to cause difficulties of one sort or another and frequently principal shareholders dispose of part of their holdings to the general public during their lifetimes merely to provide other assets from which capital transfer tax can be paid at the appropriate time.

8.2 Quotation and the Listing Agreement

The advantages of quotation may be summarized as follows:

(*a*) shares become more readily realizable;
(*b*) share valuation depends on market forces, rather than negotiation or the

'However, if you want a bit of a flutter . . .'

subjective views of people like accountants, surveyors or stockbrokers;

(*c*) the existence of a ready market facilitates the disposal of shares on death for capital transfer tax purposes;

(*d*) the company itself will find it easier and less expensive to raise capital;

(*e*) it will facilitate take-over activity.

The Stock Exchange will not consider granting a quotation for a company with a total market capitalization below £500 000, the minimum for any one quoted security being £200 000. Since the cost of obtaining a quotation is itself very substantial, however (see Unit 8.10), it is usually very much larger companies who seek them. The Stock Exchange also lays down that at least 25 per cent of the shares must be made available to the public.

The issuing body approaches the Stock Exchange at an early stage to ascertain its requirements for the granting of a quotation. Permission to quote is not given until after the quotation is made, but if all the requirements are met it is very unlikely to be withheld. Should a quotation not be granted, all moneys would have to be returned since issues are made subject to the granting of a quotation on the Exchange.

Companies receiving a quotation execute a *Listing Agreement* with the Stock Exchange. The Stock Exchange requires listed companies to provide fuller disclosure in their annual accounts than is required by the Companies Acts; in addition, immediately after shareholders' meetings are held, companies must notify the Stock Exchange of all dividends, profit figures, proposed capital issues and any other 'price-sensitive' information. Take-over bids are an area about which the Stock Exchange is particularly concerned.

If the information provided is inadequate, the only penalty the Stock Exchange can effectively impose is the withdrawal of quotation. This sanction is never applied without considerable thought as it obviously tends to affect the shareholders' interests adversely. It is expected, therefore, that shareholders will make use of the powers granted by company law to protect themselves against inadequate management.

8.3 Prospectus Issues

This method of issue was predominant in the early twentieth century but has now largely been superseded by the offer for sale (see Unit 8.4). In the prospectus issue the company (or other body issuing the stock or shares) itself invites applications from the public. One disadvantage of this method is that unless underwriting is arranged, the issuing body cannot be cesrtain that the total number of shares will be applied for. If underwriting is to be arranged it is far simpler to have a specialized issuing house arrange the whole issue. Another drawback is that a prospectus issue does not provide for the offer of *vendor* shares – shares already owned by exisiting shareholders – but is restricted to the offer of new capital. Prospectus issues are now almost entirely restricted to the issue of Government and public authority stocks, except occasionally for the launch of a new investment trust company.

8.4 Offers for Sale

The most common method of bringing new companies to the market is the offer for sale. A City institution, such as a merchant bank that is a member of the Issuing Houses Association, buys a block of shares from the existing shareholders and offers them to the general public at a fixed price. The offer is advertised in the press, usually in the 'serious' newspapers. The prospectus of the issue is published together with an application form which the investor can fill in and send off with his cheque to the bank or other institution handling the issue. Copies of the form can also be obtained from other leading banks and financial institutions.

Usually about three to five days elapse between the date of the advertisements and the closing date for application. All applications submitted by 10 a.m. on that day are accepted if they are in order, but if the offer is oversubscribed at that time the subscription lists close officially after about one minute. If the offer is not fully subscribed, the lists remain open in the hope of further applications arriving, although only applications delayed in the post are likely to be received. Oversubscription means that the offer is a success and the extent of the oversubscription is some guide to the price at which dealings will open on the Stock Exchange.

If the offer is oversubscribed the issuing house scales down the applications and quite often the smaller applications are subject to a ballot. Many small investors thus receive no shares and their money will be returned to them. Applications for very large numbers of shares, usually those from institutions, will receive only a small percentage of the shares applied for.

If the offer is undersubscribed, all applications are allotted in full and the issuing house could find itself left with a large block of shares. To avoid this the issue may be underwritten by certain institutions (see also Unit 8.14).

8.5 Offers for Sale by Tender

A tender is exactly like an offer for sale except that the price of the shares is not fixed in advance. Tender issues are not common but they have been used from time to time, and are sometimes used by the Government to launch a new issue (see Unit 3.19). Their principal advantage to the issuing body is that they avoid difficulties over fixing the issue price. Such difficulties can occur in volatile markets on an offer for sale, as the issue price has to be decided far enough in advance for all the printing and advertising to be arranged. With a tender issue the applicant has to state the price at which he is prepared to purchase the number of shares applied for. To take a very simple example, assume that 1 000 000 shares are offered at a minimum tender price of £1 and applications are received as follows:

200 000 shares tendered for at £1.25
300 000 shares tendered for at £1.20

500 000 shares tendered for at £1.15
800 000 shares tendered for at £1.05
700 000 shares tendered for at £1.00

The issue is oversubscribed and the one million shares offered will be allotted at £1.15 per share to those who tendered at or above this price. Those who tendered more than this will receive a refund with their allotment. Usually the number of shares applied for at the striking price exceeds the number available and a ballot of those tendering at that price may have to be held, although those tendering more will receive allotments in full. Occasionally, when allotment by this method would produce a narrow range of allottees, the Stock Exchange may require the larger allotments to be scaled down and the striking price reduced accordingly to increase the number of successful applicants.

8.6 Placings

A placing is sometimes used to bring new companies to the market and is most often used for the issue of fixed-interest stocks. A City institution may buy the stock or shares and arrange for the placing of the issue with various funds or companies known to be interested in taking up such issues. Alternatively the company itself may ask its stockbrokers to place the issue with their own clients.

Placings are only allowed where there is not likely to be a significant demand for the securities and where the market value of the securities does not exceed a prescribed maximum amount. Although a prospectus is required, advertising and other costs are much lower than for an offer for sale (see Unit 8.10). Shares that are placed frequently go to an even more substantial premium than shares offered for sale, however, suggesting that one of the 'costs' – too low an initial price – is not always fully taken into account.

Under a Stock Exchange rule, one-quarter of an ordinary share placing and one-fifth of a fixed-interest stock placing must be made available to jobbers to enable them to make a market in the issue.

8.7 Introductions

An introduction to the market is used when a company already has a fairly large number of individual shareholdings. It involves only the granting of a quotation by the Stock Exchange for the company's shares. This provides a market for the shares which previously could only be dealt in privately or on a restricted basis. Overseas securities which are well-established public companies in their own countries frequently come to the market by way of an introduction.

Because no capital is being offered for sale no published prospectus is required under the Companies Acts, although the Stock Exchange does insist on a similar document being made available so that the intending shareholder has a measure of protection. It may be that a number of shares will be made available to the market at the time dealings begin, but in any event this method does permit the sale of large numbers of shares by a few shareholders to the general investing public over a period of time.

8.8 Control over New Issues

The Bank of England, in order to maintain an orderly capital market, exercises control over the timing of new issues where the amount of money being raised exceeds £3 million. In such cases the sponsoring broker applies to the Government Broker for a date known as *Impact Day*. This day is the first day on which any publicity may be given to the issue and it is essential that this rule should be observed by all parties to the proposed issue.

No control is exercised over placings, because of their small size, nor over introductions because no new money is being raised. For offers for sale, however, there is sometimes a long 'queue' of prospective issues.

8.9 The Prospectus

Apart from the requirements of the Stock Exchange, prospectus issues and offers for sale are governed by the provisions of the Companies Acts. When the public are being invited to subscribe for shares in enterprises, the law requires certain information to be disclosed in a prospectus which, in the case of an offer for sale, takes the form of a letter by the company's chairman to the issuing house. This is to enable the prospective investor to assess the merits of the company and the price asked for participation. The penalties for including a false statement in a prospectus are severe.

The information required by law to be included in a prospectus is laid down in the Fourth Schedule to the Companies Act 1948. The requirements of the Stock Exchange that are to be met before shares may be quoted are set out in the Listing Agreement, which requires additional information to be disclosed. The prospectus will include information relating to the history of the company, details of the directors, information about other classes of capital and their rights, details of the issue, a balance sheet, an auditors' report including profit statements for five years, details of dividends paid, options and unusual contracts, and details of who is disposing of the shares on offer and the amount payable to them.

This mass of information may not materially assist the average investor to assess the merits of the issue. But the fact that a prospectus has been published does protect him substantially, since it will have been carefully prepared and checked and will have passed through the hands of many expert professional people. The prospects for the shares at the price of issue will be discussed by financial journalists in the daily papers and their comments may be more readable and more interesting than the prospectus to the average investor.

8.10 The Cost of Flotation

The cost of an offer for sale or a prospectus issue greatly exceeds the cost of either a placing or an introduction, and the cost for an equity issue is greater than that for a fixed-interest issue. The chief reasons concern the greater risk involved – equity more than fixed-interest stock, offer for sale greater than placing – and the costs of publicity and distribution. Usually an equity offer for sale is wanted by a large number of individual investors whereas, in contrast, the fixed-interest placing is generally readily taken up by the institutions in the absence of individual investor interest. Estimated costs for three different kinds of issue are shown in Table 8.1.

Table 8.1 Typical costs (£) of issues to raise £2mn

	Offer for sale (fixed-interest)	Offer for sale (equity)	Placing (equity)
Capital duty	–	20 000	20 000
Advertising	12 500	25 000	–
Legal and accounting fees	20 000	35 000	8 000
Bankers and registrars	15 000	15 000	2 000
Stock Exchange listing	1 200	2 400	1 200
Allotment commission	2 500	–	–
Underwriting commission	25 000	25 000	–
Broker's fee	5 000	5 000	5 000
Issuing house	15 000	10 000	10 000
Printing	18 000	15 500	6 500
Total	114 200	152 900	52 700

Source: *Evidence on the Financing of Industry and Trade (1978)*, HMSO

8.11 Stags and Stagging

A *stag* is generally defined as a speculator on the Stock Exchange who subscribes to a new issue with no intention of holding the shares allotted to him permanently, but hoping to sell his allotment at a profit as soon as dealings begin. The public 'offer for sale' is said to be the most democratic method of issue because the general public is given the opportunity of subscribing. It is, however, always difficult to fix the 'right' price, and while orthodox opinion holds that the perfect issue is one that goes to a small premium, others maintain that a heavy oversubscription is good publicity; the share gains popularity and the issuing house is regarded as successful.

The abuse of stagging is brought about by multiple applications – perhaps dozens of applications by a single applicant – and, worst of all, applications accompanied by cheques either only partly covered or not covered at all by cash at the banks. In order to curb these abuses the following remedies have been suggested or attempted:

(*a*) a requirement that all cheques sent with applications should be cleared before allotment is made;
(*b*) the exclusion of multiple applications;
(*c*) a requirement that applicants should send banker's drafts or certified cheques with their applications;
(*d*) tender issues.

Certainly stagging is not without its merits. It ensures that the issue is fully subscribed and, because many stags sell in early dealings, the new shares quickly make an impact on the Stock Exchange. Nothing could be worse than a debut at which the shares open at a discount. Nor would it be very satisfactory if all the applicants were intent on holding on to their shares (though market prices would doubtless induce some of them to do otherwise).

8.12 Capitalization Issues

Capitalization issues may be referred to as *scrip* issues or *bonus* issues. They represent only an adjustment to the share capital of a company.

In the course of its normal activities the reserves of a company may increase, perhaps as a result of retaining part of its earnings or of an upward revaluation of fixed assets such as land and buildings. As a consequence, the value of the assets permanently employed in the business may come to exceed substantially the nominal value of the issued capital, the balance forming part of the various reserves. At this stage the company may decide to *capitalize* part of the reserves, that is, to convert reserves into issued share capital. As the reserves belong to the owners of the equity this normally means that new ordinary shares are issued to existing ordinary shareholders in proportion to their holdings. No payment is due from the shareholder.

The effect on the market price of ordinary shares of a capitalization issue is, other things being equal, to reduce the price in exact proportion to the issue. Thus, if a company with 2 000 000 ordinary shares of £1 in issue decided to reduce its reserve accounts by £1 000 000 and to create £1 000 000 of new ordinary capital, it would issue to shareholders one new ordinary share of £1 for every two such shares already held, and the price of the ordinary shares on the market would fall by one-third. In fact other things are rarely equal, and usually the price after a bonus issue is slightly more than the equivalent price beforehand. This is mainly because a bonus issue is usually accompanied by either a profit statement, an increased dividend rate, an encouraging forecast of future profits or an upward revaluation of fixed assets – any of which would have the effect of increasing the price of the shares – or by more than one of these. Another reason is that the reduction in the price of a share has the effect of increasing its marketability. There is a freer market for lower-priced shares, for no good reason except that many private investors seem to be put off by 'heavy' (high-priced) shares.

No investment decisions need to be made with capitalization issues. The shares are received in the form of a renounceable share certificate and no specific action has to be taken unless the holder wishes to sell or otherwise dispose of the bonus shares. In this case all he should do is to sign the certificate in the place indicated on the reverse side and hand it to his broker or to the transferee. A bonus issue has only marginal benefits for a holder. If a dividend rate is being maintained on capital increased by a capitalization issue, this is oply equivalent to a corresponding increase in rate without an issue. The making of a capitalization issue should not of itself be understood as good news for shareholders, although good news frequently accompanies such an issue.

A capitalization issue, in which new fully paid shares in the same denomination are issued, must be distinguished from a *share split* or subdivision. The share split involves the creation of a larger number of shares with a lower nominal value – for instance, 100 000 £1 shares might become 400 000 25p shares.

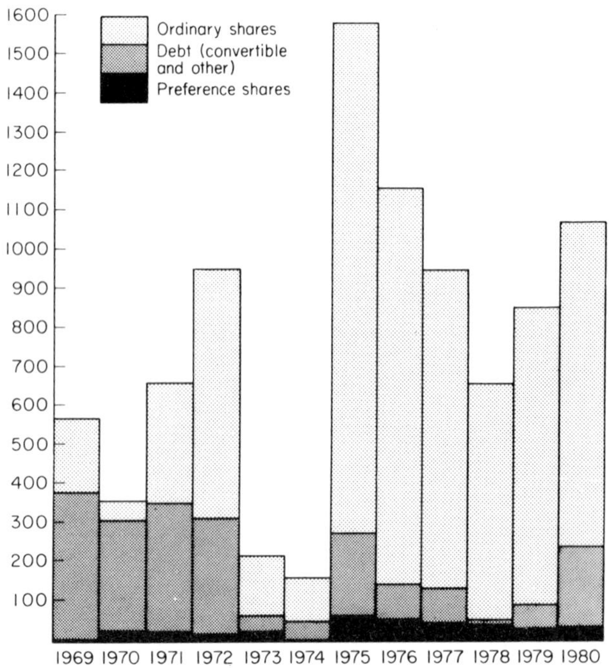

Fig. 8.1 New issues by companies by type of security (£ million)

8.13 Rights Issues

Rights issues are the issue of new shares to existing shareholders for cash. Companies often find it necessary to raise additional funds for general expansion, for particular projects or for the repayment of short-term borrowing which has been incurred for these purposes. Banks and insurance companies in particular have to maintain adequate capital bases and thus quite frequently raise new capital in this manner. This can be done in several ways, and one of them is the issue of additional equity capital. As Fig 8.1 shows, this was the predominant type of issue even in the depressed conditions of 1973–74. In 1975, when the stock market dramatically improved, there was a huge increase in equity issues.

Additional equity capital must be issued at less than the market price, or else no one would buy the new shares. An issue below the market price to the public at large would adversely affect existing equity-holders, so the issue is made to existing holders in proportion to their holdings. They may either take up the new shares offered to them or dispose of the rights to them to another person. A person acquiring rights pays the market price of the right (the *premium*) to the allottee and the issue price (the *call*) to the company.

(*a*) The Theoretical Value of Rights

When rights issues are announced, the value of the rights to existing holders and the anticipated premium on the market can be calculated. Assume that a company whose shares are quoted at 180p each is about to make a rights issue of one new ordinary share for every five held, at 120p per share. A holder of ordinary shares would then have this position:

5 old shares at £1.80 each would cost	£ 9.00
1 new share will cost	£ 1.20
6 shares therefore would cost	£10.20
Each share is therefore worth	£ 1.70

The rights are said to be worth 10p per share, as this is the amount by which the value of each old share would fall when the issue is made. The rights would be expected to command a premium of 50p on the market as this is the amount by which the value of a share (£1.70) exceeds the sum payable to the company (£1.20). In fact, of course, prices fluctuate as a result of supply and demand and these calculations are only theoretical.

(*b*) Market Factors

A rights issue generally has the effect of depressing the market price of the underlying shares, for several reasons. One is that, initially, many shareholders will sell their rights, thus depressing the theoretical price of those rights. The mere fact that the supply of shares has been increased relative to demand is a depressing factor. More fundamental, however, is the investor's reaction to the purpose of the issue. Quite frequently the issue is made to replace short-term borrowings and represents a reduction in the company's gearing. This is good for the company but it may reflect adversely on its future distributions by way of ordinary dividends. (Of course, if the announcement of the rights issue is accompanied by news of future highly profitable projects, the price of the underlying shares could well increase.)

Any fall, however, is likely to be only a short-term phenomenon and the rights issue can therefore provide a good buying opportunity for the investor. Purchase of the rights – technically the shares in nil-paid form – or of the fully paid new shares for a limited period is free of stamp duty but this benefit is usually more or less absorbed by the slightly higher price which the new issue will carry reflecting this benefit.

(*c*) Dealing with Rights

A rights issue is made by means of a *provisional letter of allotment* which acts as a receipt for moneys paid to the company as well as a negotiable document on the stock market. Provided that a premium is quoted for the rights, an investor should take up his entitlement, or sell it, or sell part of it and take up the balance. If he fails to act on the allotment letter he may lose the value of the rights. Sometimes an issue is made in adverse market conditions and the rights prove to have no value. In this case the shares should not be taken up and the rights will prove unsaleable.

The net 'cost' to a shareholder of taking up the rights or of selling them is exactly the same if the costs of sale are ignored. Sometimes lack of finance prevents a shareholder from taking up all the shares, but shareholders should nevertheless generally base their decision not on the cost of the issue but on the investment merits of the shares themselves. Consider the case of a shareholder holding 1 700 shares (quoted at £1.80) and £940 cash.

	Shares		*Cash*		*Total value*
	Pre-rights value	Post-rights value	Pre-rights holding	Post-rights holding	
	£	£	£	£	£
(i) All rights sold	3 060	2 890	940	1 110	4 000
(ii) All rights taken up	3 060	3 468	940	532	4 000
(iii) 100 rights taken up, 240 rights sold	3 060	3 060	940	940	4 000

In case (i) the 340 rights are sold at the premium of 50p, realizing £170, and the price of the shares falls to £1.70. In case (ii) 340 new shares are purchased at

£1.20. The 2 040 shares now held are worth £1.70 each. In case (iii), the shareholder chooses to take up just as many rights as he can afford using the proceeds of the sale of some of the rights. Whereas he formerly had 1 700 shares worth £1.80 each he now has 1 800 shares valued at £1.70. The cost of taking up the shares (100 × £1.20) is found by selling 240 of the rights (240 × 50p). Where the shareholder wishes to take up some of the rights without depleting his cash, or to put it another way, to maintain the same proportionate interest in his portfolio, the number of rights he should take up is found by the formula:

$$\text{Number of rights taken up} = \frac{\text{Nil-paid price}}{\text{`Ex rights' price}} \times \text{Number of rights allotted}$$

Only when the shareholder takes up his full entitlement does he maintain his proportionate stake in the company.

Occasionally a rights issue fails because for some reason the share price falls dramatically just before or after it is announced. If the price drops below that of the new shares the rights will command no premium and the shareholder will allow them to lapse. As rights issues are usually underwritten, however, the company will receive the money from the underwriters.

8.14 Underwriting New Issues

Underwriting commission is payable to those who undertake to subscribe for a certain number of shares or debentures if shareholders and members of the public do not take up the whole of the issue for which subscriptions are invited. It is usual for both offers for sale and rights issues to be underwritten: in the first case to ensure that the issuing house is not left with a large number of shares it cannot easily sell and, in the second, so that the company concerned is sure of obtaining the cash it requires. Even when an issue appears certain to succeed an unforeseen event, such as the death of one of the promoters or a sudden slump in share prices generally, may endanger the issue's success. Hence the practice of underwriting an issue.

The issuing house arranges the underwriting contracts, and the underwriting commission of perhaps 2 per cent on the total amount to be subscribed is paid direct to them. The issuing house does not usually take on all the responsibility of the issue, but shares it out among other issuing houses, insurance companies investment trusts and stockbrokers: it pays these sub-underwriters a commission on the amount each of them is willing to underwrite, say 1½ per cent. The sub-underwriters are primarily responsible for accepting, *pro rata* (in proportion), shares not taken up by the public and if they fail to do this, the issuing house accepts responsibility. The issuing house receives an *overriding commission* for this contingent liability, in our example ½ per cent.

When the underwriter or a sub-underwriter considers an issue to be a good investment, he may underwrite so much of the issue *firm*; this means that, if the

THIS DOCUMENT IS OF VALUE AND IS NEGOTIABLE. IF YOU DO NOT UNDERSTAND IT YOU SHOULD CONSULT YOUR STOCKBROKER, BANK MANAGER, SOLICITOR, ACCOUNTANT OR OTHER PROFESSIONAL ADVISER IMMEDIATELY WHETHER OR NOT YOU WISH TO TAKE UP ANY NEW SHARES. THE OFFER EXPIRES AT 3 p.m. ON 15 SEPTEMBER, 19...

To:

No. ....

X Y Z COMPANY LIMITED

Issue of 1 000 000 ordinary shares of 25p each at 80p per share

Payable in full on acceptance not later than 3 p.m. on 15th September 19..

PROVISIONAL LETTER OF ALLOTMENT

Number of Shares held Aug. 19 . .	Number of new Shares provisionally allotted	Amount payable at 80p per share	At ABC Bank Ltd, New Issue Dept. London EC99	
			Last date for:	at 3 p.m. on:
			SPLITTING (nil paid)	13 September
			ACCEPTANCE	15 September
			SPLITTING (fully paid)	10 October
			REGISTRATION OF RENUNCIATION	12 October

To the Holders of Ordinary Shares.

20 August 19.

DEAR SIR (*or* MADAM).

As explained in the Company's Circular Letter dated 20 August, and enclosed herewith, your Directors have decided to issue 1 000 000 Shares of 25p each at 80p per Share. You have been provisionally allotted the number of Shares shown above being in the proportion of one new Share for every twenty held by you on the 1st August 19 . . fractions of a new Share being disregarded.

The new Shares, when fully paid, will rank *pari passu* with the existing ordinary shares of the Company.

If you wish to accept this provisional allotment this Allotment Letter, together with a remittance for the sum shown above, must be lodged with ABC Bank Ltd, New Issue Dept., London EC99 not later than 3 p.m. on 15 September 19 . . This Allotment Letter will be appropriately marked and returned to the person lodging it. Cheques must be payable to 'ABC Bank Ltd'.

Share Certificates will be available in exchange for this allotment letter on and after 15 November 19 . .. After 31 December 19 . . any remaining certificates will be despatched to the registered holders and Allotment Letters will cease to have any value.

By Order of the Board,
T.O. MANN,
Secretary.

Payment received for ABC BANK LTD	XYZ COMPANY LTD
....	Payment due £................................

Fig. 8.2 Specimen allotment letter for a rights issue

FORM OF RENUNCIATION

FORM X

To the Directors of

XYZ COMPANY LIMITED

I/We hereby renounce my/our right to the Shares comprised in this Allotment Letter in favour of the person(s) named in the Registration Application Form relating to or including such Shares.

Dated..................day of..................19......

SIGNATURE(S) OF ALLOTTEE(S)
....
....
....

(In the case of joint holdings ALL must sign. A corporation must affix its seal.)

FORM Y

REGISTRATION APPLICATION FORM

If Form X is completed this Allotment Letter must be lodged for Registration with Form Y completed.

To the Directors of

XYZ COMPANY LIMITED

I/We request registration in the following name(s) of the shares specified in this Allotment Letter.

This form must be lodged by an Authorized Depositary unless the following Declaration can be made.

I/We declare that the person(s) in whose name(s) the Shares are to be registered is/are not resident outside the Scheduled Territories and is/are not acquiring the Shares as the nominee(s) of any person(s) so resident.

***Signature of Declarant* ....**

Dated this..............day of..............19......

Full name(s) and address(es) of the persons in whose name(s) the shares are to be registered.	
Lodged by:	

Fig. 8.3 Specimen forms of renunciation and registration, to be found on reverse of allotment letter in Fig. 8.2

whole issue is subscribed for by the public so that the underwriters are not called upon to take up any of it, the underwriter may be allotted the shares which he has applied for 'firm'.

8.15 Allotment Letters

In offers for sale, successful applicants receive *letters of acceptance*, but for prospectus offers and rights issues the document received is an *allotment letter*. There is no practical difference between the two documents and we shall term them both 'allotment letters.'

Allotment letters all follow a fairly standard form (see Figs. 8.2 and 8.3). Apart from the name of the company, the name of the allottee and details of the issue, there are several important sections. First, there is the calculation of allotment, based on either the underlying holding or the amount applied for. Secondly, there is the timetable: the date and time by which payments (if any) must be made, the place where payment must be made, the last dates for splitting, renunciation and registration, and the date when the certificates will be issued. There is, thirdly, a form of renunciation and, fourthly, a registration application form.

(*a*) Renunciation and Splitting

If the original allottee signs the form of renunciation he converts the allotment letter into a valuable, negotiable document. During the period up to the last date for registration the document may pass *by delivery* (that is, no transfer form is required) and free of stamp duty in the same way as a bearer security. After that date the shares represented by the allotment letter can be transferred only by a transfer form in the usual way.

Splitting is a means of facilitating negotiation of the allotment. A renounced allotment letter can be lodged with the company or its registrar with a request for a number of separate letters in smaller denominations. This is necessary to complete market deliveries or when the allottee wishes to take up part of the allotment and dispose of the rest.

(*b*) Calls

Payment is normally made in full on application. Sometimes, however, further payments known as *calls* also have to be made. Where calls have to be paid in respect of an allotment the most important part of the allotment letter is that dealing with the date and place of payment. Strictly speaking, any earlier payments can be forfeited if a later payment is overdue, but even issuing houses have hearts and by concession often accept later payment. Failure to make a first payment on time, however, will result in a lost allotment.

Incidentally the freedom of allotment letters from stamp duty gives a welcome opportunity to many shareholders to effect gifts to relatives and trusts at a lower-than-usual cost.

(*c*) **Registration**
If the shares are being taken up and retained by the original allottee, it is not usually necessary for application for registration to be made. But if the allotment letter is disposed of on the market or by gift, the eventual owner must complete the registration application form and lodge the document where indicated to ensure that a certificate in his name is issued in due course. This is usually seen to by the investor's stockbroker on his behalf. Once the registration application form is completed the document cannot pass by delivery.

8.16 Fractional Allotments

Bonus and rights issues often involve fractions of shares. The terms of issue do not usually produce whole numbers of shares to be allotted, except of course with bonus issues on a one- or two-for-one or similar basis. Where a bonus issue gives rise to fractions these are not allotted to holders but the shares representing fractional allotments are sold by the company and the proceeds distributed to the holders entitled.

Fractions arising on rights issues are not usually allotted or sold. Sometimes a form is sent to shareholders with their allotment letter enabling them to apply for *excess* shares – shares in excess of their *pro rata* entitlement – at the same price as the rights issue. Allotments are made to those applying out of unallotted fractions and from shares not dealt with by original allottees. Allotments of excess shares are always small but they do represent a genuinely cheap purchase where a reasonable premium applies on the market.

More often, a company sells rights that are not taken up and distributes their value to the shareholders entitled. In these cases no excess share application forms are issued and fractions are ignored altogether. The allotment letters will indicate what is being done but an allottee should always take action himself if he is able to do so.

8.17 Offers of Different Classes of Capital

Sometimes holders of equity capital are sent forms or allotment letters in respect of issues of other classes of capital. Where the recipient is the holder of ordinary shares and the document represents a bonus issue of preference shares, there is no problem as only a capitalization of reserves into non-voting capital is taking place. From time to time, however, application forms are received giving the right, sometimes a preferential right over the general public, to apply for an unsecured loan stock or similar issue. Sometimes allotment letters or application forms are received in respect of issues of shares in other companies.

All these documents require careful consideration. A document that has value must say so at the top of the first page. Other application forms may or may not present opportunities for investment on favourable terms and may or may not be negotiable. Any document of this nature requires careful evaluation before any action is taken or before a decision to do nothing is made.

8.18 The Timing of New Issues

With companies coming newly to the market the question of timing is fairly simple. Unless it is essential for the issue to be dealt with as soon as possible most companies try to avoid the troughs of the market fluctuations and wait until a firm bull trend is established before considering a flotation. Not only does this give a better chance of success, but a higher price can be obtained as investors inevitably compare companies new to the market with others already quoted for a guide to a valuation of their shares.

When a company wishes to raise additional capital there is not only the question of general timing but also of the class of capital to be selected. When equity prices are depressed a rights issue is to be avoided because of the high cost of paying a dividend on increased capital at the same rate as previously. If a period of moderate interest rates accompanies a depressed equity market, it is probably cheaper to issue a prior charge, as the interest payable costs the company only the equivalent of the initial yield, net of corporation tax.

When equity prices are high, a leading company can make a rights issue which gives only a low initial yield and this can be cheaper, in the short term, than a prior charge issue. In the long run, however, the company has to take into account the overall cost. Ordinary dividends are normally expected to increase as time goes by, and for tax reasons are much more expensive to the company than interest payments.

In assessing the investment merit of new issues it is desirable to look at the reasons for the issue being made. All companies making issues take advice from leading City brokers and institutions. If a company chooses to make a rights issue at a time when it appears that fixed-interest issues are more appropriate, extra care is called for in deciding whether to invest. This situation may mean that the company is already overgeared. On the other hand, a fixed-interest issue could indicate that it is unable to support an equity issue with an attractive profit forecast. In any event a warning signal is sounded for the prospective investor.

8.19 Questions

1. Differentiate between the methods of bringing securities, not previously quoted, to the market, and discuss the merits and demerits of each method.

2. A British registered quoted company is proposing to make a rights issue of ordinary shares to raise enough money to enable it to discharge its bank loans.

(*a*) What factors are likely to have persuaded the directors to take this course, rather than to have issued an unsecured loan stock?

(*b*) What other methods of raising cash might the directors of the company have considered?

(*c*) The issue is made on the basis of 1 for 10 at 155p. If the ordinary shares of the company are quoted at 210p on the day before the allotment letters are posted:

(i) What is the value of the rights to existing shareholders?

(ii) What is the likely premium?

(iii) What is likely to be the quotation of the ordinary shares after the allotment letters are issued?

3. Mr D has made an application for £5 000 nominal of a new public offer for sale of a 15 per cent unsecured loan stock. The issue price is 95 payable as to 10 per cent on application, 15 per cent on allotment and the balance in three months' time. The issue is oversubscribed and he receives an allotment of £2 000 nominal of stock. He wishes to transfer the allotment equally to his wife and adult daughter. Tabulate the procedure in relation to these transactions from the completion of the application form to the issue of the certificates.

Unit Nine

The Stock Exchange

Although the role and historical development of the Stock Exchange were briefly discussed in Unit 1.5, a detailed study of its functions and operations is beyond the scope of this book. But any investor buying or selling investments through the market needs to have a general idea of what it is all about, and should understand the pieces of paper that pass through his hands. He should also be aware of what he is paying for the market's services, and why.

9.1 The Exchange

Before 1965 the various stock exchanges throughout Great Britain and Ireland were independent of each other. Naturally, a great deal of business was conducted between them, but each was a self-governing institution. Then in that year the Federation of Stock Exchanges was formed and, although each exchange maintained a large degree of autonomy, there has since been more co-operation between them and a slow movement towards a single national exchange. Full integration into a national exchange took place in March 1973. Apart from London, the headquarters of the new exchange, there are 'trading floors' at Birmingham, Bristol, Cardiff, Liverpool, Manchester, Edinburgh, Glasgow, Belfast and Dublin, but only Birmingham, Glasgow, Belfast and Dublin are really active centres.

The London Stock Exchange building is an office block with a tower on a piece of land in the City of London surrounded by Threadneedle Street, Old Broad Street, Throgmorton Street and Bartholomew Lane. It is the administrative centre of the national organization; it also contains the largest and most active trading floor.

Membership of the Exchange consists of brokers and jobbers, with brokers outnumbering jobbers by about eight to one. Only members of the Exchange and their authorized clerks may deal on the floor of the Exchange, and only members may deal on their own account. Apart from those authorized to deal, only 'unauthorized' clerks of members are permitted on the floor, to convey messages, obtain prices and so on. The general public is only permitted to view the proceedings from special galleries provided for that purpose.

9.2 Brokers and Jobbers

Brokers act on behalf of investors and buy and sell securities on their behalf as their agents. *Jobbers* are not permitted to deal with the public and may only transact business with other jobbers and with brokers. Jobbers specialize in certain sections of the market such as the shares of oil companies, breweries or banks, or in British Government securities. Jobbers *make a market* in particular investments by buying lines which are for sale and selling lines which are to be bought. A jobber makes his living by buying and selling stocks and shares. Brokers make their living from commissions earned by acting on behalf of clients.

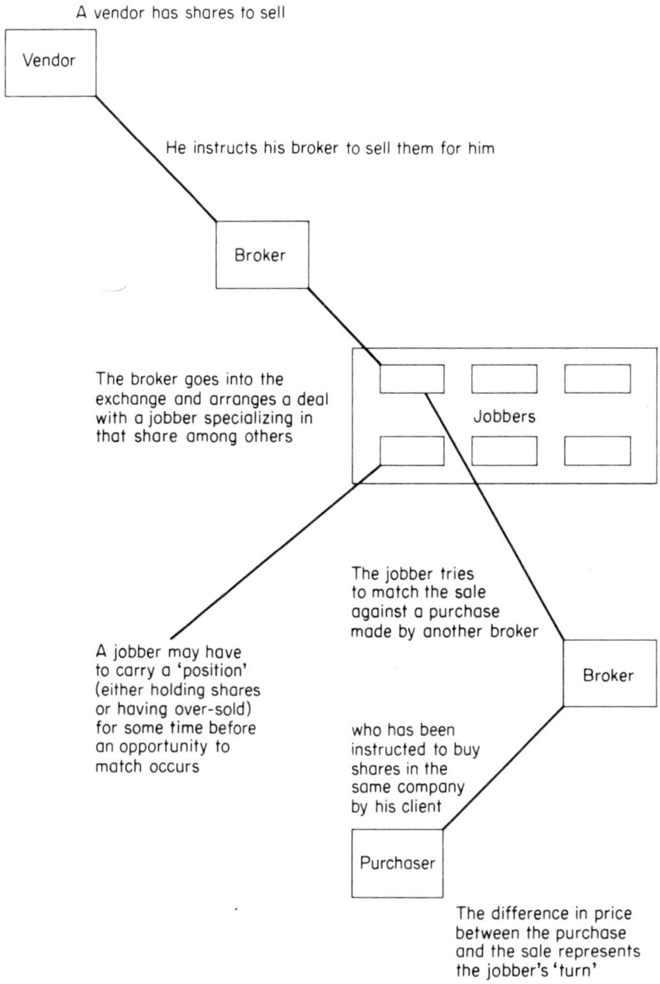

Fig. 9.1 The Stock Exchange at work

(*a*) **The Market at Work** (see Fig. 9.1)
The market for stocks and shares is the best example of a pure market existing today. The price of shares, like that of everything else, depends upon supply and demand. If the demand for manufactured goods or farm produce falls far enough, supply will be cut off completely. Competition between manufacturers ensures that artificial shortages cannot be created. With the market in stocks and shares, prices rise and fall entirely as a result of supply and demand (actual or anticipated) and no other factors apply. This arises from the use of the jobber system, which is unique to the United Kingdom.

When a broker enters the Exchange with instructions from clients to buy or sell on their behalf he approaches jobbers who specialize in the particular markets in which he is seeking to deal. If he has an order to buy, say, 1 000 ordinary £1 shares in a particular company where there is a free market, he will probably approach more than one jobber dealing in the shares of that company. From each he ascertains the price at present quoted by that jobber for that particular share. He may receive three different sets of prices from three different jobbers. For example, he may be quoted as follows:

Jobber A	298–301
Jobber B	299–303
Jobber C	296–300

Each of these pairs of figures means that the jobber is prepared to buy that particular share at the lower of the two prices and to sell it at the higher. At this stage the jobbers do not know whether the broker has an order to buy or an order to sell. As, in this example, he wishes to buy 1 000 shares, he will deal with Jobber C who is required to sell him that number at the price quoted (300p). As the price is quoted in pence the cost to the broker's client is £3 000. Had the broker had an order to sell instead of to buy he would have dealt with Jobber B who is bidding the highest price of 299p.

Once a jobber has 'made' a price for a share he must deal at those prices although only in a small number of shares. He may amend his quote for a large number of shares or he may place a limit on the number of shares to which the quote relates. For example, he may quote a share as '75–7p for 500 only'. This means that he will buy up to 500 shares at 75p each or sell up to 500 shares at 77p each. If the broker wishes to deal in a larger number he must say so and the quote will be altered – probably widened, perhaps to 72–80, which will discourage business in a large number of shares. If he wishes, the broker may still accept the quote and deal in the smaller number of shares. Sometimes a jobber may not wish to buy a particular share, in which case he may quote one price only, for example, '87p offered'. This means that he is offering shares in that company at 87p each but will not buy. If he is a buyer only he may quote a price such as '80p bid', which indicates that he has no shares to sell.

As a jobber does not know whether a broker who approaches him is a buyer or a seller his prices must reflect the balance of buyers and sellers. If his bid price is higher than that of other jobbers in the same share, all the shares being sold will come to him. If his offer price is lower than that of his competitors he will be selling shares continually but not buying any. As the aim of a jobber must be to *balance his book* – that is, to match buying orders with selling orders as far as possible – he cannot afford to have all his dealing in one share going in the same direction. If he buys shares continually without selling any, he must lower his bid price and his offer price to discourage sellers and encourage buyers. Equally, if brokers are buying shares from him continually and no shares are being sold to him he must raise both bid and offer price to correct the balance. Thus prices move according to supply and demand.

A jobber naturally moves his prices in anticipation of a change in the balance of buyers and sellers. Thus a press recommendation that a share is cheap causes jobbers to raise prices in anticipation of buyers appearing. An announcement of lower profits than expected may cause jobbers to drop prices in anticipation of sellers. The expected does not always happen, however, and often prices have to be returned to previous levels very quickly to offset a rush of trading in the opposite direction.

(*b*) The Jobber's Turn

The difference between the lower and upper prices in a jobber's quote – that is, between the bid and offer price – is called the *jobber's turn*, and if prices remained stable and the jobber's book remained even, this is the profit he would make on each share dealt in. With an active share his price may be moved quite often and the actual profit on shares purchased and then sold may be very different from the 'turn' quoted at any time. For instance, a jobber may quote 95–100p for a particular share and sell 100 000 of them in two or three deals when he has only 5 000 shares in that company on his book. As the deals are all in one direction and he has oversold his book he may have to raise the price to discourage buyers and bring out sellers. If his quote is raised to, say, 98–105p he may be able to buy 20 000 shares but it may be necessary to raise the price again to, say, 99½–107p, before he can buy enough shares to balance his book. He will then have had to pay an average of over 99p per share for them. His 'turn' therefore on those shares is less that 1p per share, although the quoted 'turn' has been 5p to 7½p during the operation.

Making a living at jobbing is clearly only for skilled market operators, able to assess the probable trends in the demand for particular shares and to react quickly and accurately to market influences. Changes in the prices of shares are made by jobbers but are caused principally by the operations of the large financial institutions in the market. Their decisions to buy or sell large numbers of shares on the market determine the level of prices in the long run.

(*c*) How Stocks and Shares are Quoted

(i) **Stocks**. Stocks are generally priced per £100 unit and are quoted in percentages. Thus a Government stock might be quoted at 42¾, indicating that £42.75 would buy £100 stock. (British Government stocks are transferable in multiples of one penny.) Most corporation and county stocks, Commonwealth stocks and public board stocks, as well as many stocks of other governments, are quoted similarly. A few public boards have fixed-interest stocks quoted as annuities. They are not redeemable and quotation is by reference to the income rather than the amount of stock represented. The Stock Exchange quotation for these annuities is a multiple of £1 of income.

(ii) **Company capital**. Company fixed-interest stocks are also generally quoted in percentages even though they may be transferable in units of 25p, 50p or £1. Thus an unsecured loan stock certificate may show a holding of 400 25p units of stock, but if the quotation is 90, the holding is worth £90, as it represents £100 stock. Ordinary stocks are quoted in pence per unit. Thus if an ordinary stock certificate shows a holding of 400 25p units of stock and the quotation is 90 the holding is worth £360, being 400 times 90p. Ordinary stocks are always referred to in the units in which they are transferable. The ordinary capital of many companies is expressed in shares and they are quoted individually (the price per share in pence); preference stock and preference shares are quoted in the same way. Where the quotation of ordinary or preference shares or stock units exceeds £10 the quotation will be in pounds and fractions of a pound; £11¼, for example, means £11.25 per share whereas 11¼ means 11.25 pence per share.

(iii) **Fractions**. Divisions of pounds or pence, depending on the unit of quotation, are always quoted in fractions. These fractions are always divisions by two so that a stock may be quoted as half, or in quarters, eighths, sixteenths, thirty-seconds or even sixty-fourths; no other type of fraction is used.

(iv) **Ex and cum**. Before a dividend or interest payment is made the register of a company or undertaking must be closed to enable the warrants to be prepared. It is clearly impossible for all transfer forms lodged with the registrar up to the day on which a dividend payment is due to be registered, and for the transferees to receive the dividend warrant. If transactions took no account of this, dividends would be paid to many one-time holders who had recently sold their shares and who owed these dividends to the purchasers. To restrict these 'wrong' payments to a minimum, bargains during a few weeks prior to the payment date are executed without regard to the dividend to be paid, which will belong to the vendor. Shares are thus quoted *ex dividend* during that period (abbreviated to *xd*). A vendor of shares xd keeps the next dividend payment; similarly, a purchaser xd has no right to the next dividend payment. Bargains not specifically marked xd are assumed to be *cum* (with) the next dividend or interest payment, but transactions on either basis are allowed in certain Government stocks for a period of three weeks before the stock is first quoted 'xd'. If there is any doubt about the matter a contract note may be marked *cd* (cum dividend).

When a new issue of shares to existing holders is made, the original shares are marked *xr* to mean ex the rights issue, or *xc* meaning ex the capitalization issue, or even *xa* meaning *ex all* to cover more than one 'ex' quotation, such as both a dividend and a rights issue.

9.3 The Investor and His Broker

Stockbrokers are now permitted to advertise, but the majority of investors may not know whom to approach when they want to carry out their first transactions. A broker is unlikely to accept as his client someone who just walks into his office, or calls him on the telephone, with an order to buy. Many investors deal through their banks and if the sums involved are relatively small this is a reasonably satisfactory way of going about matters. Brokers generally prefer to deal with the small investor through banks. This reduces the amount of paperwork and eases the routine since they will be dealing with a larger number of small transactions through one agent.

An investor wishing direct contact with a broker should preferably be introduced to one either by a friend or relative, or through his bank. Alternatively he can write to the Secretary of the Council, The Stock Exchange, London, EC2, who will, on request, send out lists of broking firms willing to accept business introduced in this way. A prospective investor should write to one of these firms, mentioning that its name has been supplied by the Stock Exchange and giving a reference, preferably a bank.

Brokers will advise clients on their investment problems but the question of investment advice will be dealt with in later Units. Here we shall assume that the investor has received all the advice he needs and has made up his mind to make an investment.

When placing an order with a broker, an investor must ensure that the order is clear and that there can be no misunderstanding as to his requirements. If the order is for ordinary shares it is usually necessary only to give the name of the company to identify the shares and this can often be abbreviated to an acceptable Exchange nickname. For example, if he wished to buy 500 ordinary 50p shares in B A T Industries Ltd there would be no misunderstanding if the order to the broker was 'Buy 500 BATS'. If the order related to Imperial Chemical Industries 5 per cent cumulative preference shares, it would be necessary to say 'Buy 500 ICI 5 per cent pref' to avoid confusion with other stocks and shares issued by that company. The investor would also have to make clear to his broker whether the shares were to be bought at the best available market price at the time of dealing ('at best'), or if he wished to place a limit on the price to be paid ('300 or better'). These same details would be required in the case of sales.

The broker will go into the Exchange with his order and, after finding out the prices quoted by the various jobbers dealing in the particular share, will strike a bargain with the one making the best price for his particular transaction within the client's limit. Details of the bargain will be entered in the bargain book of both jobber and broker and having agreed the transaction both will stand by it. The motto of the Stock Exchange is *Dictum meum pactum* (my word is my bond) which implies that a verbal agreement has the force of a written contract. The broker will send to his client a contract note (see Unit 10.3) which is evidence that he has dealt in the Exchange on the client's behalf.

9.4 Quotation

Dealings are permitted in securities for which a full Stock Exchange listing has been granted, and, additionally, in:

(*a*) certain short-term securities of central and local government authorities and public boards of the United Kingdom;
(*b*) securities quoted on certain stock exchanges overseas;
(*c*) certain securities traded 'over-the-counter' in the United States and Canada;
(*d*) securities registered on the Unlisted Securities Market (USM).

Additionally, permission may be sought for specific bargains in securities not covered by this general authorization (see the discussion of Rule 163(2) in Unit 9.8).

9.5 *Stock Exchange Daily Official List*

The *Stock Exchange Daily Official List* (SEDOL) is published by the Council of the Stock Exchange on each working day. It lists all stocks and shares quoted on the Exchange and gives particulars of the last dividend paid, the date last quoted 'ex dividend', the dates of dividend payments, the quotation at 2.15 p.m. and prices at which business was transacted. It also shows the SEDOL code number and the Classification Group Number allocated to each issue. For USM securities, no quotation is given.

The quotations are supplied by the jobbers and are usually far wider than a normal business quote. That is to say, the difference between buying and selling prices (the jobber's turn) is greater than any jobber would normally quote to a broker seeking to do business. The quotations listed are the 'official' quotations at the close of business, however, and are the basis of valuations for capital transfer tax and capital gains tax.

The prices shown for deals done are derived from two sources. Most are now supplied by the Talisman computer (see Unit 10.8) which has a complete record of all bargains in securities covered by the Talisman system. For those 'residual' securities not included in Talisman, principally gilt-edged, the previous system of recording bargains through *markings* still applies. Under this method, when a deal is done on the Stock Exchange the name and type of security may be entered on a slip, together with the price, and the slip put into a box. These are collected and published in the daily list. The information is, however, of limited use since it is incomplete, because members are not obliged to 'mark' such bargains. Prices are arranged in ascending order and only one bargain in any one security at any one price is recorded. No indication is available as to whether a bargain represents a sale or purchase.

9.6 Criticisms of the Broking/Jobbing System

Only the British Stock Exchange maintains a distinction between brokers and jobbers. The complete separation of the broking and jobbing functions, known as the *single-capacity* system, took place in 1910, and since then members have carried on business as either brokers or jobbers, but not both. The essence of the system is that jobbers should provide a competitive market for the more popular shares, with competition between them for brokers' business forcing down the jobbers' turn (which can be one of the most expensive costs of dealing), while also providing a continuous market for securities in which deals occur less frequently. In addition, because jobbers deal on their own account, it is often claimed that they perform an essential service by counterbalancing speculative price movements and thus stabilizing the market.

In recent years the competitive nature of the market has been undermined by the contraction in the number of jobbing and broking firms (see Table 9.1).

Table 9.1 Numbers of brokers and jobbers on the Stock Exchange

Year	Jobbing firms	Broking firms
1920	411	475
1950	187	364
1960	100	305
1970	31	192
1975*	21	284
1979*	20	245

Source: *Stock Exchange Fact Book*, March 1979 *after amalgamation

By July 1980 the number of jobbers had fallen to seventeen; on the London trading floor alone there were eleven jobbers and fewer than a hundred broking firms. To the surprise of many people, the Stock Exchange argues that this trend has not harmed competition because mergers have largely come about between firms who previously dealt in different sectors of the market. In its evidence to the Wilson Committee it stated that 'in fact, because jobbing firms are larger and more powerful, the market is more competitive than when there was a greater number of smaller firms'.

Not only have their numbers fallen, but to protect themselves many jobbers have entered into agreements with rival firms to maintain joint books in particular shares and to quote similar prices to any brokers attempting to deal with them, thus reducing competition even further and allowing them to make a wider 'turn'. Jobbers would argue that such measures were necessary to counteract the pressures they faced. More funds were required to maintain their capital base, but high income and capital taxes were simultaneously taking capital out of the system. So were deaths and retirements. Jobbers also faced a decline in income through the growth in 'put-through' business, where buyers and sellers are matched by brokers privately. This is largely institutional business, and although it has to be offered to jobbers in the normal way it is at a much lower 'turn' than that for conventional deals. The dominance of institutional investors has created further problems because of their desire to deal in large 'lines' of shares, and because of their general tendency to think alike, so that collectively they all wish to buy, or to stay on the sidelines. Thus it is very difficult for jobbers to stabilize market movements, especially in the gilt-edged market. When there is a preponderance of sellers over buyers, rather than taking ever-increasing amounts of shares on their books, jobbers react by restricting the size of deals and 'going short' (that is, selling shares that they do not themselves possess). The volatility of the British stock market, the dealing margins and frequent inability to deal in size have combined to focus attention on alternative systems, perhaps dispensing with the jobber as a 'middle-man', or combining his role with that of a broker in a system of *dual capacity*, as in the USA.

At the time of writing, there are no plans to adopt an American-style system in the British Isles, despite its attractions. In fact, the last of the dual-capacity firms (which were allowed in the old provincial exchanges before full integration) disappeared in 1975. But in recent years there have been two significant developments; one is ARIEL, and the other the over-the-counter markets.

9.7 ARIEL

ARIEL (Automated Real-Time Investments Exchange) is neither a jobber nor a broker, but simply a system for matching institutions' buying and selling orders in equities, for amounts of £5 000 or more. (It does not extend to gilt-edged securities.) Subscribers make known their wish to deal in a particular stock through a network of television screens and negotiate directly when they get a response. The system was established by the Accepting Houses Committee in February 1974, and aimed at the institutional market. It was expected to provide greater flexibility of dealing for large institutions, especially in 'second line' shares which were difficult to trade in large amounts through the jobbing system without provoking sharp price movements. In addition, it was hoped that its use would reduce the cost of large deals. It was felt that the large investor was subsidizing the small one in terms of commission rates, and that many brokers could not justify the commissions paid on large deals and could reduce their commission rates, charging institutions directly for research work.

Predictably the Stock Exchange opposed the introduction of ARIEL on the grounds that it would fragment the securities market, make share prices more volatile in 'thinner' markets, expose brokers and jobbers to further financial pressure and make listing regulations more difficult to operate. Their fears were largely unfounded.

ARIEL hoped for about 5 per cent of institutional turnover, but by 1980 it was achieving less than ½ per cent, as the number of subscribers had fallen from a peak of sixty to about forty, of which a minority were active users. ARIEL failed to win converts among the insurance companies and pension funds because of the difficulties in negotiating deals and the disclosure of investment intentions. It does not serve unit trusts, because a broker's certificate of value is required where deals are not done through a recognized stock exchange. In April 1979, ARIEL introduced the 'matchmaker' and 'call over' systems to induce more response and provide greater confidentiality. At the same time transaction fees were changed from a flat 0.3 per cent to a two-tier system. For those shares most favoured by the institutions, such as ICI and Marks and Spencer, the fee is 0.25 per cent; for the rest it is 0.5 per cent. In addition, big users qualify for a progressive rebate of up to 90 per cent of all fees in excess of £1 500. Even with these changes, however, the future of ARIEL remains uncertain at the time of writing, unless there is a significant improvement in dealing activity.

9.8 The Three-tier Market

On 10 November 1980 the Stock Exchange offered for the first time a three-tier market in company securities.

(*a*) **First Tier**

This market is for companies with a full Stock Exchange listing (see Unit 8.2).

(*b*) **Second Tier**

This is known as the *Unlisted Securities Market* (USM) and was established to meet the needs of the smaller but fast-growing entrepreneurial type of company. Its requirements differ in three respects from those of the first tier:

(i) Companies are required to offer only 10 per cent of their equity to the general public (as compared with a minimum of 25 per cent for those in the first tier).

(ii) Companies must provide considerable financial detail to potential shareholders but only for the past three years (instead of five), and there is no requirement for it to be backed by an independent accountant unless new capital is being raised.

(iii) Shareholders must be informed of details of acquisitions or disposals involving more than 15 per cent of assets or earnings (instead of 25 per cent).

Apart from these three points, second-tier companies are treated almost exactly as first-tier, fully listed companies. They must sign a 'General Undertaking', which is a commitment to follow a set of rules of future behaviour, disclosure, dealings and financial probity, very similar to those in the full Listing Agreement (see Unit 8.2). In fact the very name 'Unlisted Securities Market' is a misnomer, as the *Stock Exchange Daily Official List* carries records of bargains marked, although various fiscal and legal provisions distinguish between 'listed' and 'unlisted' securities, and could limit institutional investment in this market. The Stock Exchange has therefore deliberately maintained the distinction between the USM and listed securities, both to provide an incentive for companies to 'move up' and to maintain the status of listed companies. For the personal investor, from the dealing point of view, there is no difference between dealing in the first- and the second-tier markets; commission and other expenses are the same, although if a deal is done on the USM the contract note must state the fact.

'He passed away unlisted and unquoted.'

(*c*) **Third Tier**

The USM developed out of the third tier, commonly known as the *over-the-counter* market. Prior to the introduction of the USM it was possible to deal in unlisted securities through Rules 163(1), 163(2) and 163(3). Rule 163(1) provides for dealing in securities that are quoted on a recognized overseas stock exchange. Rule 163(3) specifically applied to North Sea exploration companies. Rule 163(2) provides a means of investing in other small unquoted companies.

Rule 163(2) was originally intended to enable relatively infrequent transactions to take place in the shares of small public companies, often with sporting connections, such as Aston Villa Football Club or Wimbledon Lawn Tennis Club. Each company is briefly scrutinized by the Stock Exchange and, unlike deals under Rules 163(1) and (3), each subsequent deal requires specific approval. This is not a Stock Exchange guarantee; it is simply an attempt to ensure a fair 'arm's length' price for each transaction. On the contrary, companies whose shares are traded under this rule are themselves totally unregulated by the Stock Exchange.

Following publicity in 1978 the number of deals done under Rule 163(2) grew very rapidly. The USM was established in order to exercise some control over the companies most actively traded. Such companies, together with those dealt under Rule 163(3), will be induced to join the USM. From 1982 onwards the third tier of the market will consist of 163(2) transactions, confined to less actively traded securities as originally intended, and 163(1) deals. For the investor the expenses of 163(2) and USM deals are the same. Prices are published regularly in the *Financial Times*.

Competition to the Stock Exchange's Rule 163(2) is provided by another 'over-the-counter' market operated by the investment bankers M.J.H. Nightingale and Co Ltd. They provide a market in a small number of securities, via the telephone rather than on a trading floor, and their prices are quoted daily in the *Financial Times*.

9.9 Questions

1. (*a*) Describe briefly the role of the Stock Exchange in the economic and financial life of the United Kingdom.
   (*b*) The jobbing system is unique to the Stock Exchange of Great Britain and Ireland, but critical comment often appears in the press and elsewhere about the future of this traditional pattern of stock exchange dealing. What are these criticisms? State briefly the reasons for them.
2. In what way has the Stock Exchange eased its rules to help smaller companies?
3. Explain the significance to an investor of the terms *xd, xr* and *xc*.

Unit Ten

The Transfer and Settlement Procedure

10.1 Cash and Account Transactions

The date on which a bargain should be settled is shown on the contract note. There are two types of settlement, *for cash* and *for the account*. The following securities are almost always dealt with for cash, that is to say, settlement is theoretically due on the following business day:

British Government stocks;
Commonwealth government and provincial securities;
United Kingdom corporation and county stocks;
bearer securities;
US and Canadian securities in 'good' names;
new issues in allotment letter or renounceable certificate form.

All securities other than these are dealt with for the account, unless special arrangements for settlement are made. Company loan stocks are for account settlement, even though they are dealt in free of stamp duty like the above.

10.2 The Account

The *account* system is used for securities that are not dealt in for cash. The account is normally a fortnight, from Monday to Friday week, although there are three-week accounts at holiday times such as Christmas and Easter. All transactions taking place within an account are due for settlement on *Settlement Day* (also known as *Account Day*) which is now the second Monday after the end of the account. (It was the second Tuesday until 6 August 1979, when it was brought forward one day following the introduction of the Talisman clearance system discussed in Unit 10.8.)

Account Day is the earliest day on which a broker can receive stock for delivery to his client, and the client should ensure that the broker receives payment on or before Account Day. If shares are bought and sold within the account, no transfer stamp duty is payable and only one broker's commission is paid; and if during the account the shares appreciate sufficiently to cover the jobber's 'turn' and the brokerage, the client receives the net difference between purchase and sale price minus charges, on or shortly after Account Day. If the difference is negative, this sum must be forwarded to the broker by

Account Day. In the autumn of 1979, for example, the account system worked as follows:

	September						October				
Sunday		2	9	16	23	30		7	14	21	28
Monday		**3**	10	**17**	24		**1**	8	**15**	22	**29**
Tuesday		4	11	18	25		2	9	16	23	30
Wednesday		5	12	19	26		3	10	17	24	31
Thursday		6	13	20	27		4	11	18	25	
Friday		7	14	21	28		5	12	19	26	
Saturday	1	8	15	22	29		6	13	20	27	

The Account Days were 3 and 17 September and 1, 15 and 29 October. Taking the 1 October Account Day as an example, the first dealing day was Monday 10 September and the last was Friday 21 September. All transactions for the account between 10 and 21 September inclusive were due for settlement on 1 October. By that date, of course, the market was into the second week of dealings for settlement on 15 October. Dealing for future accounts is not allowed except during the last two dealing days of the account, when special bargains may be done for the following account. Thus bargains for the 1 October settlement could have been made from 9 a.m. on Thursday 6 September as *new time* dealings. New time dealings may cost fractionally more than the normal offer price, for the privilege of the extended account.

The six working days from the last day of dealings and leading up to the Account Day form the *settlement period*. Each day is given a name. The last Friday of the old account is called *Contango Day*. The first Monday of the new account is called *Preliminary Day*. The Tuesday is *Making-up Day*. Wednesday is called *Ticket Day* or *Name Day*. The Thursday and Friday are the first and second *Intermediate Days* to the Account Day on the second Monday. With the introduction of the Talisman computerized settlement procedure, however, these names now appear anachronistic.

10.3 The Contract Note

The contract note (see Fig. 10.1) gives the investor the details of the transaction carried out on his behalf. The following information is shown:

(*a*) the name and address of the broking firm;
(*b*) the names of the partners in the firm;
(*c*) whether the transaction was a purchase or a sale;
(*d*) the number of shares or amount of stock;
(*e*) the name of the company or authority and the type of share or stock dealt in;
(*f*) the price at which the bargain was done;

(*g*) the consideration, that is, the number of shares or amount of stock multiplied by the price;
(*h*) the commission charged by the broker;
(*i*) value added tax thereon;
(*j*) contract stamp duty;
(*k*) the transfer stamp duty, if any;
(*l*) CSI levy, if applicable (see Unit 18.7) – payable on bargains with a consideration of £5 000 or more;
(*m*) the total cost of the purchase or the net proceeds of sale, whichever is applicable;
(*n*) the settlement date (no date is given where settlement is for cash);
(*o*) the settlement date;
(*p*) the client's name.

The investor should retain the contract note as evidence of the existence of the contract for the sale or purchase between him and his broker. It will also usually be required in connection with capital gains tax liability.

A. BROKER & CO.

In accordance with your instructions we have today

Partners
A. PARTNER
B. PARTNER
A. N. OTHER
C. PARTNER

789 COPTHALL COURT
LONDON E.C.2.
and Stock Exchange.

Telephone 01-001-0010
Telegrams ABROKELONDON EC

BOUGHT

This contract note should be carefully preserved for tax purposes.

I. INVESTOR ESQ.
10 HIGH STREET
ANY TOWN

Reference	Date	Settlement
AS2914	13 MAR 19..	12 APRIL 19..

2 000 A COMPANY and SONS LIMITED Ordinary Shares of 25p each @ 150p		3 000.00
Commission @ 1.5	45.00	
Contract Stamp	0.60	
Transfer Stamp	60.00	
Value Added Tax	6.75	112.35
Total Cost £		3 112.35

Yours faithfully

A. Broker & Co.

Contract Stamp

Subject to the Rules and Regulations of the Stock Exchange including any temporary regulations made by, or under the authority of the Council of the Stock Exchange.

MEMBERS OF THE STOCK EXCHANGE LONDON

Fig. 10.1 Specimen contract note

10.4 Brokers' Commission

The scales of minimum commissions chargeable by stockbrokers for acting on behalf of clients are laid down by the Rules of the Stock Exchange. In practice few brokers charge more than the minimum scale (Table 10.1) for handling normal transactions except for small transactions where a higher minimum commission than that recommended may be charged. There are two scales of commission, one for use where the commission charged is not divisible with an agent, and the other where the Rules provide that the broker may share his commission with an agent placing the business with him. Where the business is given to the broker by a bank, one-quarter of the commission charged by the broker may be allowed to that bank. Where other agents such as solicitors, accountants, licensed dealers in securities and others introduce the business to the broker, one-fifth of the commission may be allowed to the agent. Small investors would be well advised to check the minimum commission charge of a broker before placing an order as, although many brokers do not charge more than the £7 shown in the scale, others now charge as much as £15 as a minimum on small transactions in ordinary shares. Value added tax is payable on brokers' commissions.

(*a*) Concessions

There are three types of concession the broker may make in the charging of commission.

(i) If a client makes a series of transactions in the same security within a certain time limit, the subsequent contract notes may be marked *continuation* and the commission rate charged is the marginal rate for the cumulative sum. As each bargain is done the considerations of that bargain and the previous bargains are added together and the commission on a single transaction of that size is calculated. From this calculation the commission already paid is deducted and the balance represents the commission payable on the latest transaction. The time limit is normally a period of three calendar months from the date of the first bargain. This concession does not apply to transactions in most British and Irish Government funds, however, for which commission rates are based on total deals in any one security in any one day.

(ii) If the same stock is bought and sold during the same Stock Exchange account, the second or *closing* bargain may be executed free of commission. If the commission on the second bargain is higher than that on the first the balance may be charged on the closing bargain, so that in effect the higher of the two commissions is charged. The same applies where dealings are for cash if the reverse bargain takes place on or before the twenty-eighth day after the day of the original bargain. Whenever this concession is applied to any part of a continuation transaction, the period of continuation is terminated and any further bargain in the security for the same principal is regarded as a new transaction.

(iii) Finally, in the case of a *put-through*, commission to one principal only may be charged on an order to buy made together with a simultaneous order to

Table 10.1 Minimum scales of brokers' commission (abridged) (%)

A. (i) British Funds, etc.
Irish Government Funds.

	Not divisible	*Divisible*
1. Securities having no final redemption date within ten years:		
up to £2 000 consideration	0.625	0.7812
next £12 000	0.25	0.3125
next £986 000	0.125	0.1563
2. New issues and securities having ten years or less to final redemption:		
up to £2 000 consideration	0.625	0.7812
next £2 000	0.125	0.1562
next £996 000	0.0625	0.0782

Sums in excess are subject to further reduced rates; this applies also to all other scales.

(ii) Securities issued by the International Bank for Reconstruction and Development
Securities issued by the Inter-American Development Bank
Corporation and county stocks (Great Britain and Northern Ireland)
Public boards, etc. (Great Britain and Northern Ireland)
Commonwealth Government and provincial securities
Commonwealth corporation stocks
Irish Land Bonds
Irish corporation stocks and public boards

	Not divisible	*Divisible*
1. Securities having no final redemption date within ten years:		
up to £2 000 consideration	0.625	0.7812
next £12 000	0.25	0.3125
on the excess	0.125	0.1563
2. Securities having ten years or less to final redemption:		
up to £2 000 consideration	0.625	0.7812
next £2 000	0.125	0.1562
on the excess	0.0625	0.0782

B. Debentures and bonds and any other securities representing loans (debenture stocks, loan stocks, notes, annuities, etc.) other than those included in Section A above.

	Not divisible		*Divisible*
Registered:			
up to £5 000 consideration	0.75	up to £10 000	0.75
next £45 000	0.375	next £40 000	0.5
next £50 000	0.325		0.45

Separate rates apply to bearer bonds, Eurocurrency bonds, and fixed-interest securities issued by or guaranteed by any foreign government, government institution or public authority, payable in the currency of the country of the borrower.

C. Stocks and shares, registered or bearer (other than those in Sections A, B or D) whether partly or fully paid

Not divisible		*Divisible*	
up to £7 000 consideration	1.5	up to £7 000 consideration	1.5
next £93 000	0.5	next £3 000	1.25
		next £15 000	1.00
		next £25 000	0.75
		next £70 000	0.625

D. American and Canadian shares have different commission rates from the above (0.9% on the first £5 000, 0.4% on the next £5 000 and 0.3% on the balance). Separate rates also apply to listed units of unit trusts, options, probate valuations of £5 000 or over, and small bargains. In the case of small bargains, the minimum commission is £4 for securities in Section A and £7 for securities in all other sections except where commission is at the broker's discretion.

In the following transactions commission is at the broker's discretion:
(i) securities having five years or less to final redemption and not in default;
(ii) certain Eurocurrency bonds;
(iii) all unlisted and certain listed units in unit trusts;
(iv) options for one account and traded options under £20;
(v) bargains for consideration under £200;
(vi) valuations, with the exception of probate valuations over £5 000 (although for valuations over £5 000 the broker may, to the extent that he subsequently earns commission from business received from the estate, remit all or part of the fee charged);
(vii) sponsorship of a new issue in respect of the underwriting and placing of such an issue.

---

sell the same security, provided these orders originate either from one client (including an agent acting for more than one client) or from clients who are associated with each other, perhaps as members of the same family or as associated companies.

(*b*) Anomalies

The rates of commission laid down produce a strange effect where the divisible scale is applied. If an investor places orders for transactions in ordinary shares through his bank, it makes no difference to him financially whether the bank shares in the commission or not, so long as the consideration does not exceed £7 000. Up to that point, the divisible and non-divisible scales are the same. Between £7 000 and £15 250, however, the investor pays more commission and value added tax when the divisible scale applies, but the broker receives less than he would under the non-divisible scale. But when the consideration is larger than £15 250, not only does the investor pay more in commission and tax on the divisible scale but the broker then retains a larger sum than he would have done if the non-divisible scale were applied. The following examples show how this comes about:

Transaction 1. Consideration £7 000:

Non-divisible commission 1.5%		£105.00
Divisible commission 1.5%		
Charged to investor		£105.00
Allowed to bank agent (one-quarter)		£ 26.25
Retained by broker		£ 78.75

Transaction 2. Consideration £10 000:

Non-divisible commission		
1.5% on £7 000	£105.00	
0.5% on £3 000	£ 15.00	
Charged to investor		£120.00
Divisible commission		
1.5% on £7 000	£105.00	
1.25% on £3 000	£ 37.50	
Charged to investor		£142.50
Allowed to bank agent (one-quarter)		£ 35.63
Retained by broker		£106.87

Transaction 3. Consideration £16 000:

Non-divisible commission		
1.5% on £7 000	£105.00	
0.5% on £9 000	£ 45.00	
Charged to investor		£150.00

Divisible commission		
1.5% on £7 000	£105.00	
1.25% on £3 000	£ 37.50	
1.00% on £6 000	£ 60.00	
Charged to investor		£202.50
Allowed to bank agent (one-quarter)		£ 50.63
Retained by broker		£151.87

As the consideration rises so the difference gets greater.

There are practical advantages for a broker in dealing with clients through their banks. First, when making purchases he can be assured that default in payment is extremely unlikely, and when selling he can be confident that the client does in fact own the particular shares being sold. Secondly, he can usually settle the transaction through the bank's stock office in London and the bank will obtain the client's signature and/or cash when necessary. It is reasonable that banks should receive part of the commission charged by the broker for their part in the transaction. It seems strange, however, for the broker to be remunerated at a higher rate when a bank acts as intermediary between its customer and his broker and shares commission as a result.

The commission-sharing arrangements work perfectly satisfactorily for the investor in transactions where the consideration does not exceed £7 000, except in Government and similar stocks where the greater cost to the investor begins where minimum commission ceases to apply. An investor dealing regularly in sums greater than £7 000 should obviously either deal directly with a broker or else ensure that deals are done at 'best terms', that is, with the commission charged on the non-divisible scale.

An agent receiving a share of commission from a broker may not pass any part of it on to his principal, the investor. This is to ensure that only agents authorized by the Stock Exchange share in commission. When institutions assess their fees to investing clients they may take into account what additional income they may receive from shared commissions. Where the sums involved are substantial, it should generally benefit the investor to pay larger fees and insist on all deals being done at 'best terms'. Otherwise not only is the institution getting a share of the commission, but the broker is also receiving more, at the investor's expense.

(*c*) **Licensed and Exempted Dealers**

Even if all deals are done at 'best terms', an institution can still make part of its income from commission. This can occur where the institution is a licensed or exempted dealer in securities (see Unit 18.9) or buys and sells through a licensed dealing company associated with it. If a licensed dealer deals through a broker on behalf of several clients at the same time he can retain part of the commission payable by the clients even though the deal is done at 'best terms'.

This is possible because licensed dealers can issue their own contract notes to clients in place of those issued by brokers. An example will illustrate how the system works.

> Licensed dealer buys shares with consideration of £50 000 and allocates them to five clients in blocks of £10 000 each. He pays commission on the broker's contract note on non-divisible terms on the following scale:

1.5% on £7 000	£105.00
0.5% on £43 000	£215.00
	£320.00

> He receives commission from each client on his own contract notes on non-divisible terms on the following scale:

1.5% on £7 000	£105.00
0.5% on £3 000	£ 15.00
	£120.00
Total received from five clients	£600.00
Paid to broker	£320.00
Retained by licensed dealer	£280.00

Any investor using a professional agent, adviser or other intermediary between himself and a stockbroker should be aware of the effects of the various methods of dealing and commission charging. Whatever else may occur in the course of a transaction, however, he will never pay less commission than the non-divisible scale.

10.5 Transfer Stamp Duty

Stamp duty must be paid on any registered stock, shares or marketable securities passing by transfer, with the exception of British and Commonwealth Government securities and United Kingdom non-convertible loan capital. The rate of stamp duty is 2 per cent, payable by the transferee (the purchaser). It is charged on the consideration (money value of securities excluding expenses) in accordance with the following scale:

Up to £10	10p for every £5 or part thereof
Exceeds £10 but does not exceed £100	20p for every £10 or part thereof
Exceeds £100 but does not exceed £300	40p for every £20 or part thereof
Exceeds £300	£1 for every £50 or part thereof

Charities and non-residents pay a rate of 1 per cent based on the above scale.

Certain stocks and shares pass from one person to another by delivery only

Since no transfer exists to be stamped for these *bearer securities*, no duty is payable except on first issue. Similarly, if shares are bought and sold within an account, no stamp duty is payable.

Transfer stamp duty on the normal scale is also paid by the transferee of securities passing for no consideration, again with certain exceptions. Thus the donee of a gift of shares is liable for stamp duty *ad valorem* (according to the value) on the value of the gift at the date of the transfer. The principal exceptions, apart from those securities where no stamp duty is payable on transfer, are as follows:

(*a*) transfers where no beneficial interest passes, for example, from old trustees to new trustees of an existing trust, or from a beneficial holder to his nominee (or vice versa), or from one nominee to another nominee of the same beneficial holder;

(*b*) transfers to beneficiaries of estates or trusts, for example, to a residuary beneficiary of an estate, or to a specific legatee of the subject matter of the transfer, or to a beneficiary of a settlement of assets to which he has become absolutely entitled;

(*c*) transfers as part of a transaction where another document in the same transaction has suffered *ad valorem* duty, for example, to trustees of a settlement made in consideration of marriage where the settlement deed is stamped *ad valorem*.

In these three cases, and a few others, stamp duty is payable on each transfer document at a nominal rate of 50p. The transfers to beneficiaries of estates do not, however, include transfers of stocks or shares in satisfaction or part satisfaction of pecuniary legacies or debts, nor the widow's statutory legacy in the case of intestacy. These have to be stamped *ad valorem*.

10.6 Contract Stamp Duty

Stamp duty is payable on all contract notes on the following scale:

Up to £100	nil
Exceeds £100 but does not exceed £500	10p
Exceeds £500 but does not exceed £1 500	30p
Exceeds £1 500	60p

The stamp duty is paid by the broker and charged to the client on the contract note. Separate duties are thus charged for each security bought or sold.

10.7 Transfer of Registered Securities

Almost all the securities issued in the United Kingdom are *registered* securities, meaning that a register of holders is maintained by or on behalf of the issuing body. The register shows the name and address of the holder, the amount of stock or number of shares held and any instructions which the holder may have given in connection with the payment of interest or dividends. When stocks or shares pass from one holder to another the register must be amended, and this is usually effected by the completion either of a stock transfer form (see Fig. 10.2) or a Talisman sold transfer form (see Fig. 10.3). When the change of ownership arises as a result of a transaction on the Stock Exchange, the procedure differs from that used in respect of a gift, a private sale or the distribution of an estate.

STOCK TRANSFER FORM

(Above this line for Registrars only)

Consideration Money £...........		Certificate lodged with the Registrar **(For completion by the Registrar/Stock Exchange)**
Full name of Undertaking.		
Full description of Security.		
Number or amount of Shares, Stock or other security and, in figures column only, number and denomination of units, if any.	Words	Figures (units of)
Name(s) of registered holder(s) should be given in full; the address should be given where there is only one holder. If the transfer is not made by the registered holder(s) insert also the name(s) and capacity (e.g., Executor(s)) of the person(s) making the transfer.	In the name(s) of	

Fig. 10.2 Stock transfer form

If a holder of shares in a company agrees to sell them to another person without the deal going through a broker, all the vendor needs to do is to fill in and sign a stock transfer form and hand it, with his stock certificate, to the purchaser against payment of the agreed proceeds. The purchaser then completes his own name and address on the form and pays the transfer stamp duty, if any, at an Inland Revenue Stamp Office. The duty paid is shown by means of impressed stamps on the form. He then lodges the certificate and stock transfer form with the registrar of the company concerned and in due course receives a new certificate in his own name.

Stock Transfer Form *continued*

I/we hereby transfer the above security out of the name(s) aforesaid to the person(s) named below *or to the several persons named in Parts 2 of Brokers Transfer Forms relating to the above security.* **Delete words in italics except for stock exchange transactions.** Signature(s) of transferor(s) 1 .... 2 .... 3 .... 4 .... **Bodies corporate should execute under their common seal.**	**Stamp of Selling Broker(s) or, for transactions which are not stock exchange transactions, of Agent(s), if any, acting for the Transferor(s).** *Date*..........
Full name(s) and full postal address(es) (including County or, if applicable, Postal District number) of the person(s) to whom the security is transferred. **Please state title, if any, or whether Mr., Mrs. or Miss.** **Please complete in type-writing or in Block Capitals.**	

I/We request that such entries be made in the register as are necessary to give effect to this transfer.

Stamp of Buying Broker(s) (if any)	**Stamp or name and address of person lodging this form (if other than the Buying Broker(s))**

This type of transaction usually takes place in shares that are not quoted on the Stock Exchange. Where the transfer arises from a gift, the Stamp Office usually requires a valuation in support of the amount of duty tendered. Where the transaction is one which is exempt from *ad valorem* stamp duty a certificate on the back of the form must be completed by both parties to the transaction or by some acceptable agent, such as a bank or solicitor, having knowledge of the circumstances of the transaction, before the Stamp Office will stamp the transfer form with the nominal duty of 50p.

As a stock transfer form does not have to be signed by a purchaser, any fully paid stocks and shares can be transferred into anyone's name without their knowledge, as the transferor can pay any stamp duty himself and lodge the form with the registrar. This was not possible prior to the passing of the Stock Transfer Act 1963 as it was then necessary to complete a transfer deed where the signatures of both transferor and transferee were required and had to be witnessed. A transfer deed is still required with the stocks and shares of overseas companies and bodies to whom the 1963 Act does not apply, and in the case of partly paid securities.

The procedure necessary for transactions dealt with on the Exchange is described in Unit 10.8.

10.8 Talisman

The Stock Exchange system for dealing in account securities, based on 'tickets' passing between brokers and jobbers, operated almost unchanged for a century, until the introduction of the *Talisman* computerized settlement procedure in 1979. Under the old system, *Ticket Day* (or *Name Day*) was the day on which the buying broker would pass his 'name' to the jobber from whom he had bought shares. He would do this by preparing a *ticket* which showed the details of the shares purchased, the price, the consideration, stamp duty and his own firm's name, and delivering it to the jobber. The jobber matched tickets as far as possible with brokers from whom he had bought shares, and then passed them on. Selling brokers then knew to whom they had to deliver by Account Day. Where necessary a jobber would 'split' tickets, making out new ones for lesser amounts for passing to different brokers.

This system was replaced in 1979 by Talisman (Transfer Accounting Lodgement for Investors, Stock MANagement for jobbers), which covers the settlement of all securities with a United Kingdom or Irish register that are listed on the Stock Exchange and normally dealt in for account settlement. It excludes bearer securities, new issues and gilts, all of which are normally dealt in for cash, but it is being extended to include certain foreign registered securities – initially those of South Africa, and later those of Australia.

The basis for Talisman was the establishment of a Stock Exchange nominee company – SEPON Ltd (Stock Exchange POol Nominees) – into which all sold stock is registered during the course of settlement. SEPON has a single undesignated shareholding account in the register of every company participating in the scheme. All sold stock is transferred from the seller into the 'pool' account, and purchasers receive their stock by transfer out of SEPON. The Talisman Centre maintains separate accounts for each jobber dealing in the stock, and these record the movement of stock during the settlement process.

TALISMAN SOLD TRANSFER

This transfer is exempt from transfer stamp duty by virtue of section 127 (1) of the Finance Act 1976

Above this line for Registrar's use only

Bargain Reference No:

Name of undertaking

Description of Security

Certificate lodged with Registrar

(for completion by the Registrars/ Stock Exchange)

Amount of Stock or number of Stock units or shares or other security in words

Figures

In the name(s) of

Account Designation (if any)

Name(s) of registered holder(s) should be given in full; the address should be given where there is only one holder.

If the transfer is not made by the registered holder(s) insert also the name(s) and capacity (e.g., Executor(s) of the person(s) making the transfer.

I/We hereby transfer the above security out of the name(s) aforesaid into the name of SEPON LTD and request the necessary entries to be made in the register.

Balance Certificate Required for (amount or number in figures)

Bodies corporate should affix their common seal and each signatory should state his/her representative capacity (e.g. 'Company Secretary' 'Director') against his/her signature.

Stamp and Firm Code of Selling Broker

PLEASE SIGN HERE

1 ______

2 ______

3 ______

4 ______

Date

SEPON LTD is lodging this Transfer at the direction and on behalf of the Member Firm whose stamp appears herein ('the Original Lodging Agent') and does not in any manner or to any extent warrant or represent the validity or genuineness of the transfer instructions contained herein or the genuineness of the Transferor's signature. The original Lodging Agent by delivering this Transfer to SEPON Ltd authorises SEPON Ltd to lodge this Transfer for registration and agrees to be deemed for all purposes to be the person(s) actually lodging this Transfer for registration.

Stock Exchange Operating Account Number (if applicable)

TAL 112/1

Fig. 10.3 Talisman sold transfer form

When the selling broker receives the share certificate and the signed Talisman 'sold transfer' (see Fig. 10.3) from his client, he applies his office stamp, as before, to warrant the genuineness of execution and the general validity of the documents. He then passes them to the Centre where they are checked for 'good delivery' (that they are in proper order) and then forwarded to the registrar for registration into SEPON. Although the legal title passes to SEPON only on registration, the Stock Exchange is a trustee of the stock from the moment it comes into its hands and holds the stock to the order of the seller (that is, effective voting control remains with the seller) until Account Day and to the order of the buyer afterwards. On Account Day the stock is transferred to the jobber's trading account and the selling broker receives payment from the Centre on the jobber's behalf. The stock in the jobber's trading account is then allocated to his sold bargains in the correct sizes by a process known as *apportionment*. The registration details of the buying clients must be submitted to the Centre by the broker by the last business day before Account Day.

Once apportionment has taken place the stock is held to the order of the various buyers, and 'bought transfers' authorizing the removal of the stock from the SEPON account into the name of the buyers are prepared by the Centre and lodged for registration. When the Talisman bought transfer is registered, legal title passes from SEPON to the buyer and a new share certificate is issued by the registrar through the Centre.

Talisman in no way affects the dealing arrangements between broker and client; the investor is expected to benefit from the greater efficiency of the system, however. It should result in fewer delays in receiving share certificates and dividends, and considerably fewer occasions where dividends and other entitlements are paid to a shareholder who has already sold the stock, so that they must later be reclaimed. Delays resulting from dilatory sellers should also be reduced because the apportionment process first allocates stock to bargains with the earliest settlement date. Investors generally receive a single share certificate for their purchases, in contrast to the old system where, quite frequently, a number of certificates were received at different times eventually adding up to the amount of the initial purchase.

The Stock Exchange (Completion of Bargains) Act 1976 allowed for the introduction of new transfer forms for Talisman settlement. A further provision of the Act was introduced for the benefit of trustees and ensures protection from action for breach of trust by reason only of their having deposited stock at the Centre in advance of receiving payment or having paid for purchased stock in advance of obtaining transfer of the securities.

One of the main objectives of Talisman is to smooth the peaks of work for member firms, institutions and registrars, and a key factor in achieving this is the facility for sold stock to be deposited at the Centre before Account Day. Under the old system institutional investors were reluctant to release stock early because they had to sign an 'open' transfer with the buyer's details left blank, with the consequent risk of fraud or misappropriation. These risks have disappeared as the Talisman 'sold transfer' includes the name of SEPON Ltd pre-printed as the transferee, and registrars reject any Talisman 'sold transfer' which is not received directly from the Centre or on which any alteration has been made to these words.

Stock transfer forms are still used for non-Talisman transactions on the Stock Exchange, principally those in gilt-edged securities. The selling broker has a stock transfer form signed by his client for the total amount of stock sold. (This will have been sent to the client with the contract note.) If the stock sold has to be delivered to more than one buying broker the selling broker cancels the transferee part of the stock transfer form. He then completes separate brokers' transfer forms and takes the certificate, the stock transfer form and the brokers' transfer forms to the Certification Office of the Stock Exchange, where the brokers' transfer forms are certified to the effect that a certificate has been deposited to cover them. The brokers' transfer forms once certified are good delivery and they are presented to the buying brokers for payment. The stock transfer form and certificate are sent by the Stock Exchange to the Bank of England to await the presentation by the buying brokers of the brokers' transfer forms completed with the details of the purchasers. In due course the Bank sends each buying broker a new certificate showing the purchaser as the registered holder.

Sometimes a certificate provided by a seller is for more stock than has been sold. When this happens, the stock transfer form or Talisman transfer is certified and the certificate sent to the registrar by the Stock Exchange. In due course, a balance certificate is sent to the selling broker (for Talisman deals, via the Talisman Centre) for returning to his client.

10.9 Certificates

An investor in registered stocks or shares on the Stock Exchange, unless he sells his holding very soon after acquiring it, receives a certificate showing the details entered in the register of holders. The certificate shows the name of the company or undertaking, the type of stock or share, the holder's name and the amount of stock or number of shares which the certificate represents. It may or may not show the holder's address, and it is unlikely to show the address of the company or its registrar.

A certificate is merely a record of an entry in the register of holders. Transfers are not normally registered without production of the certificate as a protection against fraud. As the signature of a transferee is not required on a stock transfer form nor on a Talisman sold transfer form, however, the registrar has no record of the signature of a holder. Thus anyone coming into possession of a stock certificate could fraudulently complete a transfer form out of the holder's name in order to negotiate the holding. The risk is small, as it would be comparatively easy to trace anyone acting fraudulently. No broker would act for someone unknown to him without a reference. A cheque which might be issued by a broker for proceeds would have to be negotiated. Nevertheless, a prudent investor keeps his certificates in a safe place.

If a certificate is lost, or destroyed by accident, a registrar issues a duplicate or registers a transfer of the holding on receipt of an indemnity signed by the holder and guaranteed by a bank, an insurance company or, sometimes, a stockbroker. Many holders, when asked to get their bank to join in an indemnity, feel that this is unnecessary but, as the registrar has no means of knowing whether the person completing the indemnity is the real holder or an impostor, the request is intended as much for the protection of the holder as of the registrar. A guarantee of an indemnity is a continuing liability and, as a claim based on the original certificate could theoretically be made at any time, banks or insurance companies often make a charge for joining in. Where a certificate is lost in the post to the holder and has never come into his possession and his bank wishes to charge him for joining in an indemnity which only he, as the registered holder, can complete, an understandable difference of opinion can arise between the bank and its customer. It is difficult, however, to arrive at a compromise solution to a problem of this kind which protects all parties from the consequences of a possible misappropriation of a certificate.

10.10 Depositories and Bearer Securities

Certain stocks and shares do not have a register showing ownership, and certificates issued do not include the holder's name. These stocks and shares, known as *bearer securities*, belong to the person holding the certificate at any particular time and ownership passes by delivery alone. Most bearer securities are issued by overseas companies or bodies, but some British companies, such as Shell Transport and Trading, have part of their share issues in bearer form. Certificates of deposit, both sterling and foreign currency denominated, are bearer securities, and many British Government stocks also have a small part of their issue in bearer form.

Many investors use a *depository*, such as a broker or solicitor, as a custodian of their bearer securities. Since actual possession of these securities denotes ownership, all that is necessary in order to transfer title in a sale is for the seller to deliver the stock to the buyer. Depositories provide some protection against loss, which would mean complete forfeiture of both capital and income rights. Holders receive no direct notice of meetings, circulars or reports issued by the company. Because of the possibility of forgery of documents, bearer securities must be delivered in a reasonable condition, not badly torn or the wording materially obliterated.

The principal complication arising from the ownership of bearer securities is connected with the payment of interest or dividends. As the registrar does not know who holds the security he cannot send off a warrant for the amount due as he can with registered securities. The holder of the bearer security must claim the amount payable from the registrar or paying agent. This is done by detaching a numbered coupon from the bond or certificate and claiming against delivery of that coupon. Normally when a dividend is about to be paid an advertisement appears in the financial press informing holders of which coupon to submit, when to submit it and to whom, and dates of meetings, new issues of shares and related matters are similarly advertised. The last coupon is usually larger than the rest and is called a *talon*, and can be exchanged for a new sheet of coupons.

This procedure makes the holding of bearer securities a troublesome matter, compared with registered securities. On the other hand, they are not subject to transfer stamp duty, which is only payable on the certificate on issue.

(*a*) **American and Canadian Securities**

Shares in United States and Canadian companies are registered securities. The name of a registered holder appears on the face of the certificate, and a register of holders is maintained in the United States or Canada in the usual way. The reverse of the certificate contains a form of transfer which can be completed and the whole certificate sent to the registrar who will issue a new certificate in the name of the new owner. Dividends are naturally remitted in dollars to the registered holder. Stamp duty is payable on each certificate when it is first negotiated.

Because of the time and cost factors of transfer and the problems of currency conversion, however, United States and Canadian securities in this country are usually registered in the name of an institution. If the registered holder signs the form of transfer but the remainder of the form is left blank it becomes in effect a bearer security, and ownership passes by delivery. Institutions prepared to fulfil this function and which are acceptable to the market are known as *recognized* or *good marking names*. They can be stockbrokers, jobbers, banks or any other financial institution involved in some way in share dealing. Such status is awarded by the Stock Exchange in return for an undertaking to pay interest and dividends at the approved rate of exchange. Dividends and interest may have to be claimed from the marking name by the beneficial owner.

Anyone purchasing a security registered in a marking name can, if he wishes, have the holding re-registered in his own name and receive the interest or dividends direct. Securities in 'other names' command lower prices than those registered in 'good marking names', however, so this course of action is not to be recommended.

(*b*) **Other Overseas Securities**

Overseas securities come in various different forms and generalization is difficult. Some are purely bearer; some, like Unilever NV, resemble 'American-type' certificates, being endorsed in blank by the registered holder. Others are registered in their country of issue and the investor here is subject to the regulations and customs of the country concerned. As investment becomes more international the practice of securities being held only within the country of issue is growing and has often facilitated dealing, particularly for the professional dealer in securities.

In such cases, the British institutions appoint agents, often banks, in the various countries where they wish to deal. When they purchase securities they instruct their brokers to arrange delivery to the appointed agent. The agent is advised of the number of shares to be accepted and whether the shares are to be delivered to them against payment or free of payment. Payment can be arranged either in the United Kingdom or the country concerned. On a sale, the agent is instructed to deliver the shares to the buyer's agent, whose name is obtained from the buying broker, and again delivery is either free of payment or against payment. The shares are at all times registered in the names of the agents, who deal with all transfer formalities. The agents charge fees for their services, but the cost should be set against the delay and difficulty often experienced by investors trying to operate from a distance. Many British institutions, such as the overseas branches of the banks, act similarly in the United Kingdom for foreign investors.

In some countries the dealing system has gone one step further. For example, the extreme postal delays experienced between Britain and Australia, caused by the use of sea mail by registrars and often resulting in lost rights, brought about the Bearer Deposit Receipt Scheme in 1970. Shares in many Australian companies may be deposited at certain Australian banks (*depository banks*) and registered in the name of the bank's nominee company. *Bearer deposit receipts* are issued in London against these securities and pass as bearer securities. Thus on sales and purchases the share certificates do not change hands and the holder of a receipt has the ownership of the shares represented thereby and held by the nominee. Similar arrangements to these have grown up in many other countries.

10.11 Bulls and Bears

The two most famous words of Stock Exchange jargon and the best-known animals in the market are the *bull* and the *bear*. Both are speculators looking for quick profits from short-term market fluctuations. A bull buys shares during an account in the hope of being able to sell them at a profit before the end of the account. The credit given by the account system enables him, if successful, to profit with no cash outlay at all. A bear sells shares which he hopes to be able to buy back at a lower price before the end of the account. Thus the account system allows him to sell what he does not own as he is not required to deliver at the time of sale. (If he owns the shares in question he is referred to as a *covered bear*.) Thus a bull is looking for a quick increase in price and a bear for a quick fall in price. From this has derived the application of the words to market movements in general: a *bull market* is a rising market and a *bear market* is a falling one.

A bull may take up the shares purchased if the hoped-for quick profit does not materialize and he has the money available to do so. If he is very wrong and no price rise comes he may be termed a *stale bull*. If he does not have the cash available at the end of the account and wishes to 'carry over' (or 'continue') the bargain to the next account, he may be able to do so by arranging a *contango*.

This is an arrangement between a buyer of a security, who does not wish or is unable to take delivery and pay for his purchase on the due settlement date, and a seller who does not wish or is unable to deliver the security he has sold.

A contango is, for practical purposes, two transactions conducted at the same time, one of which closes the open position for the current settlement period while the other opens the position again for the next settlement period. Thus when the bull 'carries over' shares, he has to sell the shares he has bought in the old account, and buy them back again for the new account. Conversely, the bear has to buy back his shares in the old account and then sell them again for the new account. With this arrangement the bull does not have to pay for the shares, and the bear does not have to deliver them. In effect, the bull lends shares to the bear, and, in return, the bear lends money to the bull.

The bull (or *giver*, because he 'gives on' the shares he has purchased) is entitled to any dividends or rights declared on the shares after he has bought them and before he has sold them again. Normally he pays a rate of interest – the *contango rate* (which is expressed as a rate per cent per annum) – for the facility of not having to pay for the shares until the next but one Account Day. The bear (or *taker* of shares) receives this contango interest, minus broker's share, in compensation for his delayed receipt of payment (and the bear must hand over to the buyer any dividends or rights declared on the shares after he has sold them).

Generally there are more people wishing to effect bull contangos than bear contangos. If the bears predominate, however, the contango may be done at *evens* (that is, no contango rate at all), or the bears may have to pay a rate to the bulls. This is called a *backwardation* (which is a flat rate of so much per share); a *back* is the payment made by a bear on the shares which he borrows to deliver against his sale – it is the opposite of a contango. Thus the contango rate depends not only on prevailing interest rates but also on the volume of demand for contango facilities in either direction.

Since for each 'giver' there must be a corresponding 'taker' it is not always possible to effect a contango. Instructions are given to the broker on the penultimate day of the account (the second Thursday). Contangos are then arranged if possible by the broker the following day, usually through a jobber, and confirmed on the first day of the new account. Transactions take place at the *making-up price*, which is the middle-market price at the close of the market on the final day of the account. Any difference between this price and the price of the matching deal earlier in the account is settled with the broker on Account Day. So profits or losses are taken at the end of each account during the period in which the particular contango is in operation.

The risks faced by a bull and a bear are not symmetrical. A bull's maximum loss is limited to the amount he paid for the shares (assuming fully paid), while his possible profit is theoretically unlimited. It is easier to arrange a bull contango, as money can usually be borrowed if the rate of interest is high enough. If the worst comes to the worst, the broker could 'take up' the shares and charge stamp duty and interest on the money. On the other hand, an *uncovered* (or 'naked') bear is exposed to the possibility of unlimited loss, with the maximum gain possible being the sale price. Many bears, however, are 'covered' but prefer to arrange a bear contango because they wish to repurchase at a lower price but without stamp duty, or because the rate of interest for 'taking in' the shares is higher than they could obtain elsewhere with the funds.

Although contango business was once extremely popular, with large speculative positions being carried over from one account to the next, nowadays many brokers are unwilling to accept instructions to arrange them. An alternative to contango is *cash-and-new*. The expression is something of a misnomer, because no cash settlement is involved. The term is used when shares bought during the account are sold again at the end of the account, and are immediately repurchased 'new time' for the new account. Normally a premium is payable when shares are bought for 'new time' but, at the jobber's discretion, this is reduced for dealing 'cash-and-new'. The operation is much the same as contango as it postpones payment for the shares from the next Account Day to the following one.

10.12 Options

An *option* is a right to buy or sell a security at a fixed price at some time in the future (unlike a warrant, however, it is not a company security). Options can be taken on most securities, with the exception of gilt-edged. Some can be traded but most, known as *conventional* options, cannot.

Conventional options are contracts by which a 'giver' pays a sum of money, called *option money*, to a 'taker' for the right to buy (*call option*) or right to sell (*put option*) a stated amount of a particular security at a stated price, known as the *striking price* or *exercise price*. As well as 'call' and 'put' options, there are *double options* which confer the right to buy or sell. This right lasts at the most for two and a half to three months (to be more precise, for a period encompassing no more than seven ensuing Account Days). Furthermore, during this period the exercising of the right under the option is restricted to certain specified days, known as *Declaration Days* (normally the second Thursday or each fortnightly account period).

With a call option, the striking price is the offer price of the security in the market at the time of dealing, plus about $2\frac{1}{2}$ per cent for *contango*, which is the cost of financing the option over the period until its expiry date. The striking price of a 'put' option is usually simply the bid price of the security, although it is sometimes increased by part of the contango interest being passed on to the potential seller. The striking price of an option is *cum all*, but any rights which accrue to the security only become effective if the option is exercised, in which case they follow the security from the seller to the buyer. The striking price of a double option is fixed somewhere between the ruling bid and offer prices of the security.

In general the amount of option money (or *rate*) that is paid for an option depends on demand and supply; in bull markets 'call' options are more expensive than 'put' options, whereas in bear markets the reverse is true. Three-month call rates and details of option deals are published daily in the *Financial Times*. The rate for a three months' option on a blue-chip company is probably around 5 to 10 per cent of the share price; for instance, on 13 October 1979 a three-month call option in ICI cost 20p, while the middle market price of the share was £3.64.

The attractions of options to the investor are:

(*a*) They are high-risk, high-return investments. As with certain warrants, the gearing effect is enormous. In our ICI example, assuming that the striking price was £3.72, a 20 per cent increase in the share price to £4.37 would mean the option was worth 65p (£4.37 – £3.72) if exercised immediately – a capital profit of 225 per cent, ignoring expenses. Equally, if the share price fell, or if it failed to reach £3.72 during the three months, the option would be worthless. These features are nevertheless attractive to short-term speculators and investors seeking capital gain rather than income.

(*b*) They provide a means of 'hedging one's bets'. For example, suppose that an investor had made a reasonable gain on his shares in ICI and believed that the time was ripe to take his profits, but felt that the shares might go still higher. In order to protect his gain while still retaining an interest in any further capital appreciation, he could take out an option as an 'insurance policy'. He could either retain his shares and take out a put option, or sell them and buy a call option. Put options are sometimes used in this way to provide protection against a fall in the market when securities in a deceased's estate cannot be sold immediately because of a delay in the granting of probate. Selling shares and similtaneously taking out a call option also provides a means of raising short-term funds, as an alternative to using the shares as collateral for borrowing.

Options are more the province of the professional market operator, close to market information and able to keep a close eye on trends, than of the amateur. The share price must move by about 12 to 15 per cent before any profit can be made. This is partly because of the cost of the option itself, but also because the broker's commission (for options of more than one account) is assessed on the striking price rather than the option price. Commission on sixteen-day options is negotiable with the broker, but is usually much lower than on a three-month option. Similarly, because of the shorter period, the option itself is cheaper, usually around 3 per cent for a put or call in a leading share. Sixteen-day options run from the second Tuesday of one account to the second Thursday of the next.

Many options are bought which are never taken up. Furthermore, unlike traded options, conventional options do not come within the net of capital gains tax unless they are exercised, so that the loss from an unexercised option cannot be set off against an investor's capital gain elsewhere. Again, they differ from traded options in that a conventional option is regarded by the Inland Revenue as a wasting asset whose value, for capital gains tax purposes, declines steadily until its expiry date.

Dealings in traded options – options that can be bought and sold before their expiry dates – began in London in April 1978, five years after the successful introduction of such a system in Chicago. The market initially dealt only in call options for three, six or nine months, until puts were introduced in June 1981.

For each of the three expiry dates there is at least one striking price below the price of the underlying security (referred to as *in the money*) and at least one above (*out of the money*). These six permutations of expiry date and striking price are officially designated as six *series* of the same *class* of option. As the price of the underlying security moves, a new series is introduced whenever the share closes outside the range of striking prices for at least two days. Series are also replaced as they expire with the passage of time.

The initial seller of a call option is said to be the *writer* of the option. 'Writers' are investors who accept premiums for taking the risk that they will have to deliver stock in the event of an option being exercised. The difference between the conventional and traded option markets lies not only in the extension of the option period to a maximum of nine months, but also that both buyers and sellers of options can close their bargains whenever they like during the life of the options, simply by completing a counterpart transaction. The 'writer' buys an equivalent option; the buyer sells one. This is not possible with conventional options, where both parties are 'locked in' until the option is exercised or expires. This secondary market can only exist because of the common striking prices and expiry dates of series within a particular class.

Dealing in traded options takes place only between 10 a.m. and 3.30 p.m. on the Stock Exchange trading floor. Normally one option contract relates to 1 000 shares; deals for amounts larger than this figure require multiple contracts. Unlike conventional options, traded ones can be exercised at any time except the last two days of an account. The market is conducted by means of an auction system of bids and offers made in open competition; there is a facility for members of the public whereby any frustrated orders can be placed on the public limit book of a *board dealer* and they then take precedence over all other business at their price. They must, however, be designated either *good for the*

Table 10.2 Some traded call options, 13 October 1979

	Exercise price	October		January		April		Equity close
		Closing offer	Vol.	Closing offer	Vol.	Closing offer	Vol.	
ICI	360p	4p	27	25p	1	30p	8	364p
ICI	390p	$\frac{1}{3}$p	15	10p	5	19p	21	364p
ICI	420p	$\frac{1}{4}$p	–	$3\frac{1}{2}$p	6	–	–	364p

Source: *Financial Times*

day (GD) or *good till cancelled* (GTC). The commission rates are $2\frac{1}{2}$ per cent of the first £5 000, $1\frac{1}{2}$ per cent on the next £5 000, and 1 per cent on the excess (minimum £10) plus £1.50 per option contract clearing agents' fees.

By June 1981 there were traded options in seventeen major companies, and their prices are published daily in the *Financial Times*. One of the original ten was ICI; Table 10.2 shows the prices for some ICI options. Clearly, the later the expiry date and the lower the exercise price, the more valuable the option.

10.13 Buying-in and Selling-out

Buying-in and *selling-out* are procedures to which investors may resort should the settlement procedures not be complied with. Buying-in is the last resort of a purchaser who cannot obtain delivery of securities bought. Application is made to the Buying-in and Selling-out Department of the Stock Exchange to buy-in the security purchased. An official of the Department attempts to buy an equivalent amount of the undelivered security. If he succeeds, the original sale is cancelled, and the delivery on this purchase fulfils the delivery due on the original purchase. The original seller is responsible for the difference between the cost of the security bought-in and the price at which he sold. In fact, buying-in is very uncommon and the Buying-in and Selling-out Department officials find it difficult to transact business. A threat to buy-in is usually sufficient to produce delivery from a vendor.

Selling-out is resorted to by a vendor not receiving a name for delivery and settlement. Here the securities are sold again to cancel the original purchase and to obtain a name. This may be done if a name is not received by 2.30 p.m. on the first Intermediate Day. Any expenses and any loss are due from the party responsible for the non-delivery. Selling-out now applies only to 'residual' securities (those not covered by the Talisman settlement procedure).

A jobber may protect himself from buying-in when dealing in shares in which there is only a narrow market by completing a bargain *ntp* standing for *not to press* for delivery. In effect it means that the purchaser will not buy-in despite non-delivery. In fact a purchaser does not suffer from non-delivery, because a jobber who has oversold his book (sold shares he does not own) is liable to the purchaser for any dividends declared and any other rights which may be due.

10.14 Questions

1. (*a*) Outline the Stock Exchange procedure from the time an investor gives his stockbroker instructions to purchase a UK-registered security to the time the certificate in the investor's name is received.
   (*b*) Explain what is meant by the 'account' system of the Stock Exchange.
   (*c*) Under what circumstances does settlement not occur on settlement day?

2. (*a*) What information would be shown on a contract note for the purchase of 5 000 XYZ Company Limited ordinary 25p shares at 205p per share? Calculate the total cost of these shares to a private individual when the deal is done (i) at best terms, and (ii) with commission shared with a bank.
   (*b*) What is a *put-through*? In what circumstances would it arise?

3. (*a*) What is the difference between a standard stock transfer form and a Talisman sold transfer form, and for what types of transaction are they respectively used?
   (*b*) What is the purpose of brokers' transfer forms?

Unit Eleven

Unit Trusts and Investment Trust Companies

Indirect investment in stocks and shares or in property means the purchase of an interest in a managed fund. Instead of making direct purchases of stocks and shares on the market or through new issues, or buying land and buildings, the indirect investor entrusts his money to professional investment managers, who themselves place the total amount entrusted to them in direct investments. The indirect investor has no rights of ownership over the individual investments made by the investment managers, whereas a managed private portfolio belongs to its owner at all times. There are two traditional modes of indirect investment, *investment trusts*, which first came to the fore in the 1860s, and *unit trusts*, which had their fullest flowering a century or so later.

11.1 What is a Unit Trust?

The unit trust is one of the best known forms of managed fund investment. The law controlling its operation is not company law, but the law of trusts. The purchaser of units in a unit trust – the *unit-holder* – becomes a beneficiary of a trust fund and his interests are safeguarded by the *trustee* of the fund. The unit-holder can at any time require that his share of the fund be paid to him in cash.

A unit trust is constituted by a trust deed made between the managers and the trustee, who must be independent of each other. The *managers* of a unit trust are its promoters. They try to persuade the investing public to entrust its money to them for investment, they are responsible for the day-to-day management of the fund, they make a market in the units and they are entitled to charge the fund for their services. And, of course, they aim to make a profit out of promoting the trust. The *trustee*, invariably a bank or insurance company, has custody of the trust assets, controls the issue of units, maintains a register of holders and generally watches over the management of the trust. The trustee does not interfere with the day-to-day management of the trust unless the actions of the managers conflict with the interests of the unit-holders.

The money entrusted by the public to the managers of the trust is invested in stocks and shares. The investments are chosen so as to achieve the expressed objects of the trust. Some unit trusts aim at maximum capital appreciation and others at maintaining a reasonably high level of income return with some prospects of appreciation of capital value; still others concentrate on achieving the highest possible income return. Some specialize in certain sectors of the market. Most of the money invested in unit trusts is placed in the equity share market, although many trusts at times hold cash and Government and other fixed-interest stocks, and a few specialize in fixed-interest issues.

At any time the price of units reflects the value of the investments and cash held. A demand for units in a particular trust does not result in a rise in price as with direct investments. It merely means that more cash is available for investment in the shares selected by the investment managers and it is the fluctuations in prices of those underlying investments which cause the price of the units to move.

A unit trust has no capital and therefore it cannot have a capital structure such as investors are accustomed to with investment in companies. The whole of the fund and the income received from it belong to the holders of units in proportion to their holdings. At any time the value of a unit is the value of the investments and cash held, together with the income in hand and receivable, divided by the number of units issued.

Any attempt at gearing by means of borrowing or overinvestment is not permitted by the Department of Trade or the trust deed. If foreign currency is borrowed for investment overseas, a deposit in sterling of equivalent amount has to be made in the United Kingdom.

11.2 The Issue of Units

A unit trust is an *open-ended* fund. The number of units in issue changes as units are created by the managers to meet purchases by the public, or are liquidated as a result of sales of units by the public back to the managers. Most unit trusts are not quoted on the Stock Exchange and the market in the units is made by the managers.

(*a*) Purchases

When an investor decides to invest in a unit trust, he contacts the managers either directly or through his bank, broker or other agent. The managers issue a contract note showing the number of units he has purchased, the price and the total amount payable. No additional commission or transfer stamp duty is payable. A name ticket is included and this must be completed and returned; a certificate will be issued in due course showing the details on the name ticket.

(*b*) Sales

Similarly, when an investor is selling units it is the managers who buy them. A sale is arranged at the price ruling on the day the order is received and a contract note is issued showing the price and total proceeds. The investor must sign an endorsement on the back of the certificate giving up his rights of ownership of the units and send this to the managers, who then send a cheque for the proceeds to the investor.

(*c*) Creations and Liquidations

The managers are thus making a market in their units and at the end of each day they have a position in their units in the same way that Stock Exchange jobbers have a position in the stocks in which they deal. The managers will have sold more units than they have bought, or vice versa – it would be an unusual day in which sales and purchases were equal. If they have sold more units than have been sold back to them, they must create more units to meet their sales (unless they have a stock of units). If they have bought back more units than they have sold, they must decide either to take the excess on their books to meet sales in the future, or to liquidate units.

Creations and liquidations of units represent transactions between the managers and the trustee. To *create* units the managers prepare a calculation showing the cost of the units to be created and lodge this with the trustee. They must then pay the trustee the total cost, usually by the next Stock Exchange settlement day. This transaction increases the number of units in issue. To *liquidate* units a similar calculation is prepared and lodged with the trustee. The trustee reduces the number of units in issue accordingly when he has received endorsed certificates to the total number of units to be liquidated, and pays the managers the proceeds out of the fund to enable them to settle with the unit-holders.

The progress of the unit trust movement over the ten years to 1980 is shown in Table 11.1

Table 11.1 Unit trusts: a ten-year picture

Year	Value of funds (year-end) (£mn)	Sales (£mn)	Repurchases (£mn)	Net investment (£mn)
1971	1 991.2	204.10	127.45	76.65
1972	2 647.5	436.86	195.59	241.27
1973	2 060.4	357.90	171.75	186.15
1974	1 310.8	194.87	110.17	84.70
1975	2 512.4	321.21	130.90	190.31
1976	2 543.0	333.40	165.88	167.52
1977	3 461.3	372.32	257.90	114.42
1978	3 873.4	529.68	294.08	235.60
1979	3 936.7	411.95	353.87	58.08
1980	4 968.0	531.50	423.90	107.60

Source: Unit Trust Association

(*d*) Certificates

It is an important part of the trustee's duty to ensure that at no time are there certificates in issue for more units than those for which he holds assets in the fund. So when units are created he issues no certificates until he has received the moneys for the creation from the managers. When units are liquidated he does not pay the managers until endorsed certificates are lodged with him. When units are bought and resold by the managers he does not issue certificates to the new holders until he has endorsed certificates from other holders to an equivalent number of units. This protects the investor against the possibility of fraud by the managers when dealing in their units with the public. At any time the number of units issued may be less than the number for which the trustee holds assets. These surplus units belong to the managers beneficially and are available for resale, liquidation or holding as an investment as the managers wish. Managers can create units in advance of demand if they wish, and often do so in expectation of a rise in prices generally.

11.3 The Pricing of Units

All creations of units by the managers with the trustee must be on an *offered* price basis. All liquidations must be on a *bid* price basis. The Department of Trade requires these two methods of calculating the price of units to be in accordance with prescribed formulas laid down in the trust deed. The offered price is the maximum price at which units are sold by the managers to the public and the bid price is the minimum price at which the managers will repurchase units from the public. They are effectively the notional figures for establishing or realizing the entire fund. The offered price is based upon each investment in the fund at the lowest offered price in the market. To this is added a percentage for stamp duty payable on the purchase of the underlying investments, a percentage for brokers' commission on the purchase of the investments, the unit trust settlement duty (¼ per cent) payable on the creation of units, the amount of the managers' initial charge and the income in hand and receivable, the resulting figure being rounded off to the next convenient price. The bid price is based on each investment in the fund at the highest bid price in the market, less a percentage for brokers' commission on the sale of the investments, the resulting figure being rounded down to the next convenient price.

Until December 1979 charges were governed by Department of Trade regulations. Management charges, out of which the managers must meet the trustee's, registrar's and audit fees and the costs of all promotional material, were limited to 13¼ per cent of the value of the fund spread over a twenty-year period. Of this 13¼ per cent, a maximum of 5 per cent could be charged initially, restricting the annual charge to ³/₈ per cent. A few trusts charged less at the beginning and more annually. For many years the industry regarded the price structure as inadequate and campaigned for reform, with the result that it has now achieved complete freedom. Most trusts now charge ¾ per cent annually, leaving the initial charge unaffected. Competitive pressures tend to ensure that the public is not exploited. Indeed, the increase in management charges may be no bad thing for investors. When charges were regulated, the emphasis was clearly on the marketing of new units. Now managers have a greater incentive to manage the investment portfolio and retain the goodwill of existing investors.

Few unit trusts are quoted in line with the official bid and offer price calculations, which can give values as much as 12 to 13 per cent apart. Quoted prices usually give a spread of 6 to 8 per cent where the initial charge is 5 per cent. If the trust is a net seller of units the offer price often tends to be fixed at or near the maximum permitted level, the bid price being somewhat higher than the minimum. If on the other hand the managers face heavy demands for repurchases, the price structure will reflect their need to sell units, the minimum price being paid on repurchases with units being offered below the maximum formula price.

11.4 Prices and the Unit-holder

Two factors govern the price of units in a unit trust: the value of the underlying investments and the managers' pricing policy. Bid and offer prices are quoted daily in most newspapers and it is often a cause of dissatisfaction to holders and prospective purchasers when managers refuse to deal at those prices. There are two reasons why they may do so.

In the first place, the value of the underlying investments may have moved materially. Most unit trusts quote a daily price, and purchases and sales may be carried out on any business day. The portfolio of such a trust is valued daily by the stockbrokers to the trust and this valuation has to be prepared in time for the resulting offered and bid price calculations to be notified to the newspapers. If prices move substantially between the time of the valuation and the time of an intended deal, the published price may be quite different from that which may have to be paid. If the managers have a stock of units, or are prepared to take units on to their books, they may be content to deal at the published price. If they must create or liquidate to complete the proposed transaction, dealing at published prices may cause them substantial losses and they may then require a new valuation to be produced before they will deal. This is fair not only to the managers but also to other holders.

The second reason why managers may refuse to deal at published prices concerns their pricing policy. For instance, if the managers have been net buyers of units, the price may be quoted on a bid basis. If a proposed purchaser of a large number of units appears, units will have to be created at the full offered price to meet that transaction. The managers will then wish to recalculate their price on an offered price basis before dealing (although in these circumstances they would probably offer a discount off the full offered price basis out of their initial charge, to encourage the transaction).

Some unit trusts do not deal daily, but only weekly, fortnightly or monthly. In these cases the published price is out of date more often than not, and the current price can be ascertained on the dealing day only by reference to the managers.

Dealing in units is one method by which managers can profit from promoting a trust (in addition to their published charges). The trustee should watch to ensure that the managers do not sell more units than have been created.

11.5 The Role of the Department of Trade

The Department of Trade has an overriding authority over the operations of any unit trust which seeks to attract money from the general public. Any trust which the managers wish to make available to investors at large must be an *authorized* unit trust, under the provisions of the Prevention of Fraud (Investments) Act 1958. Authorization is the responsibility of the Department of Trade and, apart from certain requirements laid down in the Act, the Department requires the trust deed to contain certain provisions in connection with the management of the trust before authorization is granted. In fact, the terms of the deed must be agreed by the managers' solicitors with the Department of Trade, line by line, if authorization is to be obtained.

(*a*) Investment Powers of Managers

The Department of Trade does not authorize any trust that can invest in forms of investment other than stocks and shares and certain types of cash investment: no trust that invests in property, for instance, can be an authorized unit trust.

There must also be restrictions on the amount which can be invested in individual holdings. Generally, no more than 5 per cent of the fund can be invested in any one investment, although there are certain exceptions to this. If, by reason of changes in the value of the investments in a fund, one holding becomes larger than the limits laid down in the deed, the holding need not be reduced until the fund is reduced by reason of liquidation of units, resulting in the realization of investments to enable the managers to settle with outgoing unit-holders. Then a sale of part of the overlarge investment should be made.

A deed must also limit the amount of capital of one company that can be purchased in the unit trust. Usually this limit is 10 per cent of the issued equity capital.

(*b*) Requirements of the Act

All these requirements for authorization of a trust are Department of Trade regulations, not provisions of the Prevention of Fraud (Investments) Act. The Act lays down certain requirements for the deeds of authorized unit trusts, including provisions for price and yield calculations, control of advertising, audit and circulation of accounts and the powers of trustees, but the Department of Trade exercises a far larger measure of control on the content of the trust deed of every authorized unit trust.

(*c*) Approval of Managers

Perhaps the most important part played by the Department of Trade in the authorization of unit trusts is their examination of the two companies who propose to act as manager and trustee. Both must be limited companies and they must be controlled independently of each other. In practice trustees are invariably banks and insurance companies. Anyone with sufficient capital to set up a unit trust can do so and can, in fact, employ specialist companies to carry out all functions of the managers. The Department will wish to be satisfied as to the probity of the persons controlling the operation before granting the authorization which enables the managers to solicit funds from the general public. The powers of the Department extend to the withdrawal of authorization if it considers that there has been a material change in circumstances since authorization was granted.

The Department of Trade exercises a general supervision over the operations of authorized unit trusts, including examination of accounts and a watch on advertising standards. Its protection of the interests of the public investing in authorized unit trusts is invaluable.

11.6 The Duties of the Trustee

The primary duty of the trustee of an authorized unit trust scheme is to ensure that the terms of the trust deed are complied with. This includes the duties relating to the issue of certificates, the creation and liquidation of units and the general supervision of the administration on behalf of the unit-holders already discussed. The trustee may agree with the managers to enter into supplemental trust deeds to amend the provisions of the trust deed if he is satisfied that the interests of unit-holders are not prejudiced by the amendment. If he is not so satisfied, he must require the managers to call a meeting of unit-holders to which the proposed amendments will be put.

(*a*) Advertising

In the early days of unit trusts advertising – sometimes less than 'full and fair' – was responsible for substantial sales of units, but today the volume of advertising is much reduced. It is a statutory requirement that managers must state the commencing gross yield in advertisements, and the Unit Trust Association rules now provide that its member companies must also state the aims and objectives of funds, initial and annual management charges and distribution dates. Furthermore, statements to the effect that the investment must be considered long-term, and that the price of units may go down as well as up, must also appear. Where past performance records are quoted they must be for a reasonable period, at least five years in the case of established trusts, and a representative market index must be used. Graphs, if employed, should not be misleading.

The trust deed will require all advertising matter to be submitted to the trustee before publication if it contains an invitation to buy units or any reference to the price at which units may be purchased or the yield from the units. In practice trustees see advertisements, circulars and reports before issue and they naturally require amendments to be made from time to time. A trustee's concern must be that all statements are true and that there is nothing misleading in the content of such material.

(*b*) **Pricing**

By the terms of most trust deeds, the trustee is not required to check the price calculations produced by the managers unless specifically requested by a unit-holder to do so. From time to time, however, a wise trustee will check carefully the calculation of the unit price as errors can arise in the portfolio of investments, or in the brokers' valuation of the securities, or in the balance of cash held. Similarly, the trustee is not required to check yield calculations but he will check that distributions bear a close relation to published yields.

(*c*) **Custody**

The most time-consuming and labour-intensive part of the trustee's duties is the custody of the assets of the trust. The investment managers of a unit trust deal through their brokers in the name of the trustee. The trustee is nominally the principal in all purchases and sales on behalf of the trust. Many trusts are actively managed funds, with as many as a hundred stock or share transactions in a year for every £1 000 000 of value.

An order to buy a large line of stock may be completed in a number of relatively small deals over a period of some days. Some holdings will be held for only a short period and in an active fund many holdings may be purchased and sold within a six-monthly accounting period. All these transactions have to be recorded and settled with the brokers by the trustee. Active dealing also gives rise to problems in the collection and payment of dividends. Purchases normally outnumber sales, especially where a trust is expanding. The cost of dealing may discourage investment activity, although in practice the managers of unit trusts are substantially more active than are the pension fund managers.

(*d*) **Control of Investments**

One of the functions in the operation of a unit trust that is definitely not the trustee's province is the investment management. The trustee has no jurisdiction over the selection of shares for investment, and in consequence the investment performance of the fund is entirely the responsibility of the managers. This having been said, however, the trustee should watch the investments made by the managers to satisfy himself on five points.

(i) The investment policy to be followed by the managers is not laid down in the trust deed but will be stated in advertising matter. The trustee should therefore ensure that all investments made are in accordance with advertised policy. He should not, for example, permit a purchase of a stores share in a trust which advertises that it invests exclusively in shares in the financial sector.

(ii) He should ensure that purchases do not bring holdings above the permitted limits on investments and, if they do, that the trust does not lose on their sale.

(iii) He should check that purchases are of freely marketable investments and not, for instance, in other types of managed fund where sales back to the managers can be suspended.

(iv) He should ensure that no bear transactions are entered into (except covered bear transactions – see Unit 10.11) and if shares which the trust does not hold are inadvertently sold, that the trust does not suffer on their subsequent purchase.

(v) No transactions should be carried out by the managers with themselves or any associated company, not even through the Stock Exchange.

(*e*) Registration

The maintenance of a register of unit-holders is the responsibility of the trustee, although in these days of computerized registers this function is often delegated to the managers themselves or to a specialized registrar. The trustee remains responsible for the correctness of the register and usually arranges for checks to be carried out to ensure its accuracy.

(*f*) Liaison

The managers of a unit trust normally maintain close contacts with the trustee, consulting with him on any unusual matter and discussing problems as they arise. The agreement of a reputable trustee to a course of action is a valuable support to a management company. The co-operation of the Department of Trade, the trustees and the managers in the interests of unit-holders has proved a real protection to the investor.

11.7 Investment in Authorized Unit Trusts

Several arguments are put forward in favour of investment in unit trusts as opposed to direct investment in stocks and shares on the market. First, there is the argument that, for the small investor, investment in a managed fund gives a spread of interest over industries and companies that cannot be achieved with direct investment of a modest amount of cash. Secondly, it is argued that investment in a unit trust gives the small investor professional investment management that is not otherwise available. Neither of these two arguments is entirely valid.

(*a*) Spread of Interest

The first is a sound argument in many cases but an investor buying units for this reason should choose his trust with special care. Many unit trusts specialize in certain sectors of the market and an investor seeking spread of interest should ensure that he chooses a general trust with a relatively large number of holdings. The valuation of portfolios of unit trusts is based on the theory that all the shares held could be sold at the prevailing prices. This would not be so in practice. Where many different holdings are included in the portfolio quite a high proportion of repurchases can be accumulated without upsetting the prices of the underlying holdings, by the sale of smaller holdings and small parts of large holdings. But where there is undue concentration in relatively few holdings there is a danger of severe price falls unless the holdings are in large companies with a free market in their shares.

(*b*) **Management**

There is no real evidence that an investor obtains better value for money by investing in unit trusts than by using some other form of professional management, such as investment trusts or property bonds. Many unit trusts are used as 'shop-windows' by institutions providing investment management services to show the public at large what they can achieve. Merchant banks generally do not accept private portfolios of less than £100 000, but run unit trusts for their smaller clients. Many unit trust management companies offer fund management in other types of investment such as investment trusts and insurance schemes. There is no evidence from the performance records of unit trusts to suggest that the quality of the investment management offered by merchant banks is in general any better or worse than that offered by investment companies or other institutions offering private portfolio management. The performance of unit trusts managed by the clearing banks and by insurance companies is steady and unspectacular, these trusts appearing only infrequently in the top and bottom of performance tables.

(*c*) **Charges**

The initial charge imposed on unit trust investments can prove expensive where quite large sums are involved. If an investor is proposing to place a sum exceeding, say, £10 000 in one authorized unit trust, he would be well advised to try to negotiate a reduced initial charge with the managers. Some trusts, in fact, reduce the initial charge automatically on large investments and others, by the imposition of a high minimum investment, have low initial charges. (It is, of course, the management company which stands any reduction and not the trust itself.) In return the investor may have to agree to accept limits on the numbers of units he can resell to the managers on any one day.

(*d*) **Timing**

The most important point about investment in unit trusts, as for all equity investment, is that of timing. Unit trusts make regular investment easy, in a way which is not available to the direct investor, through the operation of savings schemes.

11.8 Timing of Unit Trust Purchases

Unfortunately, the public at large has not invested in unit trusts at times when prices are depressed, and has usually waited until a rising trend has been clearly established before entrusting funds to the unit trust industry. As a result, very many people have become disenchanted with unit trusts. They have seen the value of their investments fall to below their cost during the first bear market after purchase, and have had to wait a long while to see a profit in their units.

Management companies have frequently been criticized for advertising for funds when markets are high and refraining when they are low. They cannot entirely be blamed for this. Too many of them have lost money by advertising extensively in depressed markets to encourage a reversal of the trend. Unless the initial charges paid on units sold through an advertisement are sufficient to cover the cost of its insertion, there is no encouragement to advertise frequently. Unfortunately, many people do not realize that units are almost always available for purchase at the daily quoted price. The Department of Trade requires that managers must buy back on any dealing day.

11.9 Savings Schemes and Pound Cost Averaging

One argument in favour of the unit trust as a form of investment is wholly valid, and that is the facility it offers for the regular investment of small sums. Some trusts have a relatively high minimum investment requirement and few permit the investment of less than £250 initially, but most provide savings schemes which accept monthly sums from about £10 upwards. This is an ideal way for the investor who can provide only a few pounds each month from his income to invest in the share market. Direct investment out of savings is only possible by the purchase of one holding every now and again. At present Stock Exchange commission levels, a minimum of £40 a month would have to be set aside to make one new equity purchase a year at an economic cost. This is unsatisfactory in many ways. The regular purchase of units in an authorized unit trust scheme not only gives a spread of interest with the smallest sum, but also levels out the fluctuations in the market, disposing of the problem of timing. In addition, the monthly investment of a fixed sum, as opposed to the purchase of the same number of units, brings in the benefits of what is known as *pound cost averaging*. This merely means that more units are bought when prices are low. Its advantages are illustrated in Table 11.2 (on page 158).

The figures in Table 11.2 are hypothetical, but whatever figures are taken, the average cost per unit is always less than the average of the prices over the period, and in the long term substantially less. Obviously the average cost per unit is higher than if the total investment were made at the time that prices were at their lowest, but no investor can be certain of recognizing that moment. In practice, units bought through savings schemes are either calculated to three places of decimals, to absorb fully the monthly subscription, or else they are allocated as whole units with any cash balance remaining carried forward to the next month. Pound cost averaging is discussed again in Unit 16.5.

Savings schemes can also be linked to life assurance, which can give not only the benefit of pound cost averaging, but also that of income tax relief on the sum saved (see Unit 12.5).

Table 11.2 Pound cost averaging: investment of £10 in a unit trust per month for ten months

Month	Unit price (pence)	Number purchased
1	50.0	20.000
2	49.2	20.325
3	47.8	20.920
4	45.0	22.222
5	48.3	20.703
6	50.2	19.920
7	51.2	19.531
8	53.0	18.868
9	54.2	18.450
10	55.0	18.181
	Total units purchased	199.120
	Total cost of units	£100
	Average cost per unit	50.22p
	Average unit price	50.39p

11.10 Withdrawal Plans

Many unit trusts offer withdrawal plans, under which the investor receives not only his share of the income of the trust, but also a regular realization of his capital. With such a scheme in operation the investor is paid a regular sum which is made up of the income to which he is entitled together with the proceeds of sale of part of the fund.

Most commonly, either a half-yearly payment is fixed by the management company in offering the plan, or else the payment is selected by the unit-holder from a range offered by the managers. The payments are usually between 3 per cent and 8 per cent per annum of the amount invested, paid in half-yearly instalments of one-half the agreed rate. The sums received consist of income after tax plus the proceeds of sufficient of the holding of units to make up the agreed half-yearly percentage. A tax certificate is issued to the unit-holder in respect of the income proportion of the payment and can be used to support a repayment claim where this is relevant. The big disadvantage of this type of withdrawal plan is that the unit-holder loses the facility of timing his sales of units. During bull markets the plan works satisfactorily but during bear markets the sales of units take place at depressed prices and therefore eat severely into the value of the investment.

The problem is partly overcome by using the withdrawal unit method, in which the payment consists of a fixed percentage of the value of the units held, rather than of the amount invested. Each half-year the predetermined percentage of the fund is paid to unit-holders, and this consists of both income and capital, as in the other method. Because the payment is related to the value of the fund, the distribution is less when prices are depressed than it is when prices are high, and so the holder cannot be certain of a particular return. On the other hand approximately the same proportion of the fund is realized each time, varying only by the amount of income available, so overcoming in part the disadvantage of using the other method of operation in bear markets. Although withdrawal plans seem to appeal to some people, the disadvantages of forced sales at times of low prices make them unattractive in general.

11.11 Share Exchange Schemes

The drift of the private investor from the stock market has been encouraged by share exchange schemes. Many unit trust companies are prepared to accept quite small quantities of shares, perhaps as little as £500 worth, in exchange for units. Usually these schemes are attractive because the terms offered are better than a straight sale of the shares and a purchase of the unit trust. For the unit trust managers, some of the shares acquired in this way are of little interest and for these the terms offered may not be so good. If, on the other hand, the shares can be taken into their existing portfolio they could pay as much as the market 'offer' price. For capital gains tax purposes a share exchange represents a disposal and the tax implications must therefore be taken into account.

11.12 The Choice Available

Once a decision has been made to invest in a unit trust the choice available is bewilderingly wide. With hundreds of trusts to choose from, there is likely to be a trust to suit any requirement. The way to select a trust is to tackle the list methodically.

Funds fall into four broad categories: income funds, growth funds, balanced (or 'middle-of-the-road') funds and specialized funds. A prospective investor must decide which type of trust he requires.

(*a*) Income Funds

Income funds offer a higher-than-average immediate return and, to maintain this, they have to be invested in stocks with less capital growth potential than those that a growth fund would choose. An investor seeking an above-average income return will look for a general income trust that gives an immediate return at about the level he requires. The immediate return on different income funds varies considerably.

(*b*) Growth Funds

If the investor requires a general fund concentrating on capital growth he may be influenced in his choice by the past performance of various trusts which appear to be suitable for his requirements. He should examine the three-year and five-year records which are published from time to time in financial journals. A unit-holder in a growth fund often requires his income to be reinvested. This can usually be arranged by one of two methods: either through a *reinvestment scheme*, under which distributions are retained by the management company and used to buy additional units, or else through *accumulation units*. The latter do not qualify for distributions but the income is reinvested in the trust, increasing the value of each unit. Some trusts have only accumulation units. Reinvested income is, of course, subject to tax and the higher-rate taxpayer using such a scheme must find the additional tax due out of other income.

(*c*) Balanced Funds

A purchaser wishing to hold a 'middle-of-the-road', or balanced, fund will also study performance tables. These trusts aim to give reasonable income return with some capital growth. Naturally these trusts do not often figure in the 'top twenty' performance tables but both income records and capital performances can be compared against a suitable index and, of course, against each other.

(*d*) Specialized Funds

Specialized funds present a problem of their own. Generally speaking, an investor should not look to a specialized trust if it is to be his sole equity investment. Only if he already has a spread of investment elsewhere should he invest in unit trusts specializing in speculative areas such as gold mines, raw materials and recovery situations. These trusts provide an excellent way of including such investments in a more widely based portfolio. Similarly trusts specializing in overseas securities should be used only to increase the spread of larger portfolios.

Trusts which, although specialized, give a wide base in their specialization can be purchased by the small investor with more confidence, but they require more careful watching than the general funds as prospects for different sectors of the market fluctuate. In this category fall trusts specializing in the financial sector, in investment trusts and in consumer goods. In a general trust the investment managers can be expected to concentrate on different sectors from time to time, but in specialized trusts they are committed to a particular sector.

(*e*) Information

Lastly, and most important, the investor should always be aware of what he is buying. If he seeks an income fund based on equity investment, he must avoid those trusts which maintain an above-average income return by holding a high proportion of the fund in fixed-income investments. Some trusts in fact hold nothing but preference shares, and many holders fail to understand why capital performance is not in line with other trusts. The managers always supply information about their trusts on request. Their addresses appear in the leading newspapers daily, and details of most trusts are published annually in the *Unit Trust Year Book*. Copies of trust deeds may be obtained from the managers on payment of a fee but few investors will find that the provisions of the deed assist them in any way with their assessment of the trust. The investor who knows what he wants can make his choice on the basis of present policy and past performance.

11.13 Distributions and Reports

Most unit trusts distribute income received at half-yearly intervals, and for a few weeks before the date of distribution the units are dealt in *ex distribution* in the same way as stocks and shares are quoted ex dividend. Some trusts distribute quarterly, some only annually and, of course, accumulation units have no distributions. In all cases unit-holders are supplied with a tax credit certificate at the end of the accounting period. Distributions are rounded off to a convenient figure and any balance of income carried forward.

One unusual feature of unit trust distributions is *equalization*. The distribution is in respect of dividends and other income received and is not like a dividend declared by a company. The price of a unit at any time is calculated by including income received and receivable at that time. A purchaser of units is entitled to his share of income received after the date of purchase. Part of the price he pays for his units is in respect of income received before his money was introduced to the trust. On the first distribution date he receives the same amount per unit as all other holders. Part of this is taxed income and represents his share of income received after the date of purchase. Part is not taxed and is in effect a return of part of the purchase price, that part which represented income receivable up to the date of purchase. This sum is termed 'equalization'. Most modern trust deeds provide for equalization to be *averaged*. This means that all units purchased during an accounting period receive the same amount of equalization and the same amount of taxed income, irrespective of the day on which they were purchased. Outgoing unit-holders are not entitled to certificates in respect of any income included in the bid price of their units.

At least once a year, and in most cases every half-year, a report is sent out to unit-holders. This shows the calculation of the distribution, the composition of the trust portfolio, the managers' report for the period covered, the auditors' report and the names of the managers, trustees, auditors and solicitors to the trust. Copies of the last report of any trust may be obtained from the managers, who are also required to publish annually accounts for the trust showing the amount of their charges and expenditure on the trust.

11.14 The Taxation of Unit Trusts

Income received by trustees on behalf of unit-holders of an authorized unit trust consists mostly of dividends paid by companies. It is therefore net of

'What do you mean, Them? We are *Them.'*

tax when received. Some income may be received without tax having been deducted (for example, interest on moneys on deposit). Other income may be interest received on holdings of Government or other gilt-edged stock, or company debentures and loan stocks. This interest is normally taxed before receipt, but will not have borne corporation tax in the hands of the payer.

The income of unit trusts is liable for corporation tax as the trust is treated as a corporation for tax purposes. Dividends, however, are not taxed again as they represent franked income to the trust. Nor, following the Finance Act 1980, is unfranked income arising from fixed-interest securities, provided the unit trust in question is one which invests exclusively in fixed-interest securities. The Finance Act also freed unit trusts from tax on capital gains, thus transferring the onus for this tax entirely to the unit-holder.

11.15 Unauthorized Trusts

Not every unit trust is an authorized trust: very many unauthorized trusts are in existence. They may not be advertised in any way, and details of them may only be supplied to professional advisers. They are discussed in Unit 13.9.

11.16 Investment in Unit Trusts

In the past few years unit trusts have generally been out of favour with the investing public and have been criticized in the press and elsewhere; their failure to attract new funds is illustrated in Fig. 11.1. Between 1970 and 1980, out of the 134 funds listed in *Planned Savings* only 66 managed a return better than the All Share Index. Good results were achieved by most of the income trusts, however, twenty-five out of thirty beating the Index. This segment of the industry also substantially outperformed its less-exciting rivals, the building societies and bank deposits (see Table 11.3).

Table 11.3 Income unit trusts, building societies and bank deposits compared (investment of £1 000 over period 1.1.70 to 1.1.80) (£)

	Total income (net)	Capital growth	Value of investment, 1.1.80 (net income reinvested)
Income unit trusts	650	670	2 686
Building societies	660	nil	1 890
Bank deposits	440	nil	1 543

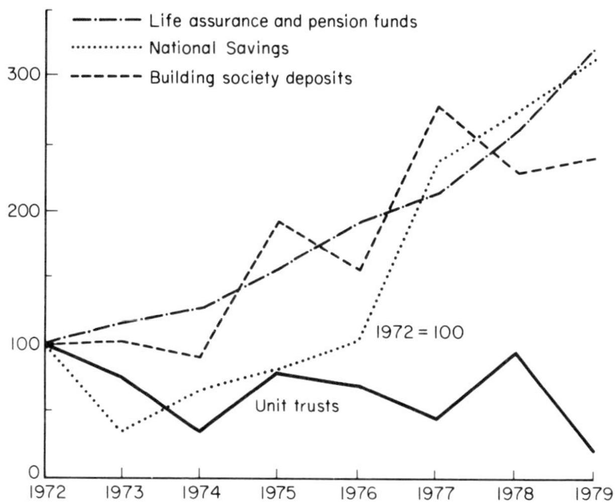

Fig. 11.1 Unit trusts: comparative growth in annual cash inflows (1972 = 100)

11.17 What are Investment Trusts?

Unlike unit trusts, investment trusts are not trusts but companies, subject to the provisions of the Companies Acts like all other companies. The Companies Act 1980 created an entirely new class of public company, the *investment company*, and such companies are subject to special rules relating to the distribution of profits. Investment companies provide another way in which the small investor can obtain a spread of interest and professional investment management. They use their capital and reserves for direct investment and a holder of ordinary shares in such companies has an indirect interest in the underlying portfolio.

Investment trust companies are a long-established form of indirect investment; some were formed over a century ago. They control more assets than do the unit trusts but they have suffered many problems in recent years and have not grown anything like as quickly as their more popular rivals. Their merits are less well known to the average private investor, and most of their shares are owned by other institutions, whereas most units in unit trusts are owned by the general public.

There are investment trust companies to suit most investment requirements, from above-average income return to nil income return, from specialized investment to a wide-ranging general investment policy, and from those concerned principally with United Kingdom investment to those that concentrate their attention overseas.

11.18 Comparison with Unit Trusts

There are several differences for the investor between an investment in an investment trust company and an investment in a unit trust.

(*a*) Closed Funds

An investment trust company is a *closed-end* fund as opposed to a unit trust which is *open-ended*. Issues of new capital can be made as in any other company but, unless these are prior charges to increase the gearing (see (*b*) below), only to existing ordinary shareholders by way of rights issues. Unit trusts, however, being open-ended, may grow in size as new unit-holders buy themselves into the trust at asset value.

(*b*) Gearing

Investment trust companies usually have an element of *gearing* – that is, part of their capital consists of fixed-interest issues such as debenture stocks. This gives the shareholder an advantage during periods of rising market prices. Conversely in bear markets the shareholder suffers from a fall in the value of his shares greater than the fall of prices generally. Unit trusts may not borrow and the price of units moves in line with the value of the underlying portfolio.

Gearing by investment trust companies is sometimes produced by the issue of convertible debenture stocks or loan stocks, giving a right to convert into the ordinary capital at some future date. Gearing can also be introduced by means of foreign currency loans. Investment trust companies can use their equity portfolios as security for the borrowing of foreign currency, thus increasing the total amount available for equity investment. Investment trust gearing is at present very low; at the end of 1980 it represented only about 8 per cent of total assets on average. (For a fuller discussion of gearing see Unit 15.9.)

(*c*) **Prices and Cost of Dealing**

The price of shares in investment trust companies is governed by the market forces of supply and demand. Unit trust prices are governed by the value of the underlying portfolio. Many investment trust company shares are dealt in on the Stock Exchange and therefore may be priced at above or below their asset value.

Investment trust company charges vary considerably from company to company. Fees and expenses frequently amount to ¼ per cent per annum of the value of the assets. As shares are purchased on the market there is no initial charge as such, but the normal expenses of the purchase of shares apply, equivalent to about 3½ per cent except for the smallest transactions. Similarly about 1½ per cent will be paid on sale. Generally, therefore, investment trust company investment is cheaper than other forms of indirect investment.

(*d*) **The Discount on Net Asset Value**

When share prices are rising, investment company shares are a particularly strong market and it is at such times that new issues abound. This was so during 1971 and 1972 and it was then quite common to find companies whose shares were sold at a premium over the net asset value of the underlying shares less borrowings. For many years, however, it has been more usual for investment company shares to sell at a substantial discount. The average discount amounted to around 30 per cent in late 1979, compared with only 3 per cent in 1972.

The prevalence of discounts ought to warn any investor against investing in a new investment trust company. It may be argued, however, that buying existing shares is quite another matter, given that substantial discounts are available. Generally speaking, the lower the discount the better the management record, so a large discount does not necessarily imply the shares are cheap. Many small investors find the existence of discounts disconcerting. They feel more at home with unit trusts where price is directly related to the value of the underlying securities.

(*e*) **Income**

Unit trusts generally distribute all their income except in the case of accumulation trusts. Investment trust companies, like other companies, declare dividends which may or may not exhaust the available income. Most of them have a 'plough-back' which increases the invested capital for the benefit of the ordinary shareholders.

(*f*) Investment Powers

The investment powers of unit trusts are limited by the terms of the trust deed; only a certain proportion of the fund may be invested in a single stock, and only a percentage of the share capital of a company may be acquired. The investment powers of investment companies may instead be limited by their articles of association and the Stock Exchange Listing Agreement. It is possible, however, for an investment trust company to acquire assets other than stocks and shares.

(*g*) Marketability

Marketability is no problem with a unit trust; only rarely are sales to the public suspended and the managers are required to repurchase any units offered to them. The shares of many investment trust companies are tightly held by institutions and just not available for purchase. This creates a very narrow market in some smaller companies and it is often difficult to deal. This problem does not arise in the larger companies.

(*h*) Information

Unit trust management companies supply information on all their trusts to inquirers. Because only a few trusts are quoted on the Stock Exchange, stockbrokers' advice on unit trusts is usually restricted to a small number of trusts where they have special connections. Advice and information on investment trust companies is not normally available from the directors. Stockbrokers expect to be asked to advise on the choice of investment trust companies and information is available from the usual sources concerned with public companies.

11.19 Split-level Trusts

The split-capital company, often called a *split-level trust* or a *dual trust*, was first introduced in 1965. In this type of investment trust company there are two classes of equity capital: *income shares* and *capital shares*. During the life of the company, which is usually a fixed period (often twenty years), the income shares are entitled to all the income received from the underlying portfolio and the capital shares are entitled to the assets but have no rights to income. At the end of the company's life the income shares are paid out at a pre-arranged figure, usually their par value, and the value remaining is paid out to the capital shareholders.

Split-level trust shares are an interesting investment. During the life of the company the income shareholders should receive a growing return to help offset the reduction in purchasing power caused by inflation. Some capital growth can be achieved by the sale of income shares fairly early in their life as the increasing yield on the value ultimately to be repaid makes the price of the shares on the market rise above the nominal value, although the price must fall again towards the end of the company's life. The income shares give a gearing element to the capital shares which, at the end of the period, are entitled to the value of the investments, less the nominal value of the fixed-capital income shares.

Capital shares may be useful to the high-rate taxpayer who finds income an unwelcome embarrassment. Their volatility, because of the gearing, makes them an investment to be in and out of rather than one to stick to through the usual succession of bull and bear markets. Sometimes additional gearing is introduced by the issue of fixed-interest capital, which makes a *triple trust*. Triple trusts can be very highly geared indeed and their capital shares the most volatile of all.

11.20 'B' Shares

'B' shares, introduced in 1967, have equal rights with ordinary shares of the investment trust company except that they have no rights to dividends. Instead of a dividend the holder receives additional shares equivalent in value to the amount of the dividend paid on the same number of ordinary shares. This makes 'B' shares very similar to a unit trust income reinvestment scheme. Originally there was a difference; the shares issued were not liable to the tax surcharge on investment income, unlike income reinvested in unit trust schemes. Under the Finance (No. 2) Act 1975, however, such scrip issues became assessable as income, and so no further issues have been made.

11.21 Taxation and Investment Trusts

The taxation of an investment company is very similar to that of a unit trust (see Unit 11.14), except that fixed-interest income is always subject to corporation tax. In order to qualify for exemption from tax on capital gains the company must be approved by the Inland Revenue as conforming with the definition of an investment trust company contained in the Income and Corporation Taxes Act 1970. The vast majority of investment trust companies do so conform.

The chief requirements of thc Act are that:

(*a*) the company's income is derived wholly or mainly from securities;

(*b*) no holding must represent more than 15 per cent of the investment trust company's investments;

(*c*) its own shares are quoted on the Stock Exchange;

(*d*) the company is debarred by its own memorandum or articles of association from distributing as dividends profits arising from the sale of investments;

(*e*) the company must not retain more than 15 per cent of the income derived from securities.

11.22 The Decline in Status of Investment Trusts

Investment trust shares were a strong market in the early 1970s, and this gave rise to a number of new issues. Several of the better managed companies' shares were selling at a premium and the average discount narrowed to around 3 per cent. Yields were low, in line with their growth-oriented portfolios. In late 1979, however, discounts averaged 30 per cent and the yield on the *Financial Times* Actuaries Investment Trust Index had risen to the level of the All Share Index, an unprecedented occurrence.

After the spate of new issues and the general market euphoria of the earlier period, a reaction set in. The oversupply of investment trust company shares coincided with investors' disillusionment both with the 'cult of the equity' and with the mistakes of many investment trusts in overseas markets. The drift of the private investor from the stock market and the counter-attractions of unit trusts also occasioned heavy selling of investment trust shares. With the growth of other institutional investment, particularly the pension funds, managers have tended to make direct investments rather than rely on the expertise of the investment trust managers.

Recently, however, there have been signs that the situation is improving. Several pension funds have invested in the purchase of the whole of the issued capital of some investment trusts and the excess supply problem has been assisted by a number of liquidations. At the same time several investment trust companies have been 'unitized' (that is, converted into unit trusts).

11.23 Judging Performance

Performance naturally varies, and the investor will examine the market price of different companies over a period when selecting established trusts. The *Financial Times* Actuaries Investment Trust Index forms a useful yardstick. With newer trusts it is now often possible to examine the record of other trusts under the same management, as investment trust companies have largely become concentrated in the hands of several specialist investment management concerns. The 1970s were a particularly difficult period for investment trust companies but on balance the investor with moderate funds could find such companies a better long-term investment than unit trusts. Because of gearing, which serves him well in bull markets, he should be more ready to sell after a reasonable price rise, as in a bear market the corresponding fall in market prices is generally accentuated. The smaller investor with less than, say, £20 000 might well prefer unit trusts because their prices are so much less volatile. For the person wishing to invest in equities out of income, a unit trust is usually preferred to an investment trust company, since units can be acquired through a qualifying life assurance policy with a consequent substantial tax saving.

Table 11.4 compares the best-performing investment trust companies with the worst-performing ones. The 'total' return comprises the value of £1 000 invested for five years together with the reinvestment of all dividends. It is interesting that, despite the poor record of the British economy over the period, the best-performing investment trusts were those largely invested in small United Kingdom companies.

Table 11.4 Best- and worst-performing investment trust companies: 5 years to 30 April 1979

Investment trust	Management group	% UK	Type of fund	Market capitalization (£mm)	Total return* (£)	Dividend contribution (£mn)
North British Canadian	ICFC	100	UK small companies	6.9	4 525	331
Moorgate	Philip Hill (Management)	92	UK small companies	5.5	4 090	293
London Atlantic	ICFC	90	UK small/medium companies	9.8	3 754	309
Young Companies	Singer & Friedlander	100	UK small/newly quoted companies	7.0	3 634	359
Family	Kleinwort Benson	99	UK small companies	5.3	3 611	354
Montagu Boston	Drayton Montagu	55	North American specialist	5.0	831	81
Scottish European	Stewart Fund Managers	40	European specialist	6.0	890	179
F & C Eurotrust	F & C Management Ltd	33	European specialist	3.6	1 091	91
Viking Resources	Ivory & Sime	52	Oil and gas exploration and development	10.9	1 116	55
Drayton Far Eastern	Drayton Montagu	20	Japan and Australia	4.0	1 146	146

* Based on initial investment of £1 000; return and dividends net

Source: *Money Management*

11.24 Questions

1. Mr A asks your views as to whether he should invest in stocks and shares directly, or in unit trusts. He also asks how he should decide in what unit trusts to invest. What factors would you consider of importance in answering these questions?

2. ‘Investment trusts are for the larger investor only.’ Is this statement true? Give full reasons for your answer.

3. What do you understand by *pound cost averaging*? To which types of investment does it apply?

Unit Twelve

Insurance and Investment

12.1 Life Assurance

Every *life assurance* policy – the term 'assurance' is reserved for this kind of insurance only – consists of a contract between an insurance company and its customer covering an agreed sum of money, the *sum assured*, and a period of time, *the term*. The customer agrees to pay certain sums, the *premiums*, usually at regular intervals over the term. The company agrees to pay the sum assured in the event of the customer's death before expiry of the term or, in certain cases, on survival at the end of the term. There are three basic types of life assurance:

(i) *Whole life*: premiums are paid throughout life or to a specified age and the sum assured is payable only on death or survival to an advanced age.
(ii) *Term*: premiums are paid throughout a limited period and the sum assured is payable only on death before the term ends.
(iii) *Endowment*: premiums are paid for a specified number of years only. The sum assured is payable on completion of the term or on earlier death.

Whole life and term policies are similar in that the sum assured is normally payable only on death, whereas endowment assurance premiums have to take into account the probability of survival to the end of the specified term. Term assurance is generally inexpensive, whereas endowment assurance is by far the most costly of the three kinds.

12.2 Endowment Assurance

Assurance policies that only provide for payment of the sum assured at death can hardly be regarded as investments, although they should be an important feature of any investor's overall financial strategy. Endowment policies, however, contain a very substantial savings or investment element. On taking out a policy the customer knows for certain the minimum sum payable should he die before the end of the term, and he will also be notified of the anticipated maturity value of the policy on his survival. The endowment policy may be *with profits* or *without profits*, the former type giving the customer the right to share in the life assurance profits of the insurance company. The life companies commonly estimate profits conservatively, and a 'with profits' policy is usually much the better investment of the two. The premium is of course higher, though not in proportion to the anticipated return.

The profits on endowment policies are of two kinds.

(i) *Reversionary bonuses* are based on the sum assured and are declared during the life of the policy. Over the years they have steadily increased and have never yet been reduced. It is therefore possible to ascertain the extent of the minimum reversionary bonuses likely to accrue over the life of the policy.

(ii) *Terminal bonuses* reflect the investment performance of the company up to the maturity date. They are thus more volatile and in 1974, a very bad year for investors, terminal bonuses were cut back sharply.

The life companies generally invest premium income in a balanced portfolio which usually includes substantial elements of gilt-edged securities and equities. The holder of a straightforward endowment policy does not know how his premiums are being used, but a wide variety of life assurance schemes are now linked to some specific type of fund such as equities, property or gilts or some combination of these investments. Whole life policies can also be taken out on the same basis.

'If you care to back your message with money . . .'

The life assurance element is important because of the substantial tax advantages available to the investor. The whole premium is generally reduced by tax relief of 15 per cent. Since the assurance element is frequently only about 5 per cent of the premium, not only is the life assurance 'thrown in' for nothing but there is a useful bonus available where units are purchased in this way.

Policies do not have to be maintained throughout the whole term. The holder of a whole life or an endowment policy nearly always has the options of *surrender* or *conversion to a paid-up policy*. Many companies now publish their terms for surrender or conversion; these vary considerably, although this is often reflected in the level of premiums. Nevertheless, these options are usually on terms that bear harshly on the policyholder. Conventional life assurance contracts, therefore, should only be entered into for the long term after careful consideration. They should be surrendered or paid up only in circumstances of extreme necessity, or where surrender after a specific period is a planned feature of the policy (as, for example, with building-society-linked assurance – see Unit 12.14).

12.3 Qualifying Life Assurance Policies

At the time of writing, an investor can obtain tax relief of 15 per cent on gross life assurance premiums on 'qualifying' policies. The relief is limited to life assurance premiums which are *the greater of* £1 500 per annum or one-sixth of taxable income. Qualifying policies at maturity are exempt from capital gains tax in the hands of the policyholder.

A gross premium of, say, £100 actually costs the taxpayer £85. The insurance company claims back £15 from the tax authorities. If the insurance company's expenses and the life cover cost, say, £6 per annum this actually leaves £94 (£9 more than is paid in premiums) invested in the fund. Thus if the fund is successful, life assurance can be a very good investment. Straightforward life assurance policies, however, are not always particularly good: but the best 'with profits' policies, after deduction of the element covering the risk of death, can produce an annualized return of around 12 per cent. Investing in a suitable investment bond (see Unit 12.7) could achieve a substantially better result.

To obtain the maximum benefits of life assurance the policy must be a so-called *qualifying policy*. The rules are inevitably complex but the following criteria are the most important:

(*a*) premiums must be payable for at least ten years, except in the case of term assurance;

(*b*) premiums must be paid annually or more frequently;

(*c*) the sum assured must be not less than a certain percentage of the premiums payable – 75 per cent for endowment policies. For policyholders over 55 years of age the rule is relaxed somewhat.

All these rules exist to prevent abuse of the tax system. If, for example, a policy is surrendered within ten years or three-quarters of the term (whichever is less) the taxpayer could find himself assessed for income tax at a higher rate. Furthermore, any surrender or conversion to a paid-up policy in the first four years means that the policyholder must forgo some or all of the premium relief. The *clawback*, as it is called, works as follows:

Surrender	*Basic clawback*	*Maximum clawback*
2 years or less	$15\% \times$ gross premiums paid	
Between 2 and 3 years	$15\% \times {}^{2}/_{3} \times$ gross premiums paid	Surrender value less (gross premiums paid minus basic clawback)
Between 3 and 4 years	$15\% \times {}^{1}/_{3} \times$ gross premiums paid	

Thus suppose a policyholder decides to surrender his policy after two and a half years having paid £306 net premiums (£360 gross), the policy then having a surrender value of £330:

Basic clawback $15\% \times {}^{2}/_{3} \times$ £360 =	£ 36
Maximum clawback £330 − (360 − 36) =	£ 6
The policyholder therefore receives	£324

12.4 Conventional Endowment Contracts

These are the traditional kinds of life assurance contract on which most companies still rely, even though many of them now offer life assurance linked with specific funds. The main features of the conventional contracts are:

(*a*) The insurance company itself is responsible for the investment of premium income.

(*b*) Premiums are thus invested in an internal fund about which the policyholder has no knowledge.

(*c*) The policyholder knows at the time of entering the contract the minimum value payable on death, and he usually has a good idea of the anticipated maturity value based upon estimated profits.

(*d*) While the maturity value is not subject to capital gains tax, the profits of the insurance company are subject to corporation tax at the reduced rate of $37\frac{1}{2}$ per cent.

12.5 Investment-linked Policies

This development owes much more to the unit trust movement than to the life assurance companies. Left to themselves, the latter would doubtless have preferred the greater flexibility which is permitted them in providing conventional policies. Unit trust managers, however, saw the regular collection of premiums and the purchase of units as going hand in hand.

Life assurance as such is one of those essential services which normally requires to be actively sold. In general, people do not seek out life assurance and so traditionally it has been sold by the doorstep salesman calling on homes and offices. The marketing of unit trusts at first depended largely on newspaper advertising, and more recently on sales through agents such as stockbrokers and insurance brokers, but they could not be sold door-to-door because of the provisions of the Prevention of Fraud (Investments) Act. So unit trust managers found that, either by arrangement with life assurance companies or by forming their own companies, they could very effectively promote the sales of their products.

Today linked life assurance also covers those investments, such as property bonds (see Unit 12.8) and managed bonds (see Unit 12.9) that can also be purchased on the basis of regular premiums. Table 12.1 illustrates the percentage of premiums invested in the unit trusts or bonds of a well-known management company.

Table 12.1 Regular investment plan

Age at entry	Percentage of payment invested during first two years	Percentage of payment invested thereafter
1–29	87.1[1,2]	110.6
30–39	85.9	109.4
40–44	84.7	108.2
45–49	83.5	107.1
50–60	82.4–71.8[3]	105.9–95.3
61 and over	72.9–87.1[4]	96.5–110.6

Several points in Table 12.1 require explanation:

1. Commission is earned in the first two years: hence the smaller percentage going into units. The investor should therefore be certain that he wishes to invest for a reasonably long period, at least ten years.

2. The insurance company is able to invest more than 100 per cent because of the tax relief situation. We have seen how a net premium of £85 enables the

company to claim £15 from the Inland Revenue, so that a net premium of £10 per month is actually worth £11.76 in their hands.

3. The life risk increases more rapidly between the ages of 50 and 60.

4. Initially life cover is 15 times the gross annual premium, but this is reduced somewhat for older lives; hence the larger amount invested.

Table 12.2 shows how much a policyholder might expect to receive, given an assumed annual growth of either 6 per cent or 9 per cent per annum.

Table 12.2 Regular savings plan of £20 a month: estimated cash value of units after 10, 15 and 20 years for selected ages

Age at entry	Plan cashed after year	Total net payments over term	Estimated cash value of units assuming annual growth of 6%	9%
		£	£	£
Up to 29	10	2 400	3 239	3 766
	15	3 600	5 799	7 371
	20	4 800	9 224	12 916
45–49	10	2 400	3 128	3 637
	15	3 600	5 606	7 123
	20	4 800	8 919	12 488
60	10	2 400	2 766	3 212
	15	3 600	4 964	6 301
	20	4 800	7 903	11 054

Clearly, age at entry does not make a vast difference to the amount of capital that can be built up. Schemes are limited to a twenty-year maximum, but thereafter the funds can be left invested indefinitely so that a young saver's £4 800, for example, would grow to £16 519 at 6 per cent or £70 581 at 9 per cent if it remained for a further ten-year period. But the fundamental logic of compound interest should not obscure the fact that such returns will bring little comfort in twenty or thirty years' time unless inflation is brought under control.

The selection of a single 'best' linked scheme is virtually impossible, in view of the vast number of schemes and the unpredictability of the underlying funds. The fund to which the policy is linked should come from one of the better management companies and should preferably have a proven record of growth. Not all the so-called capital or growth funds have performed as might have been expected. The most usual link is with a unit trust but many other funds, such as property bonds and managed bonds, are operated by insurance companies.

12.6 Annuities

An *annuity* is really a special form of insurance policy – a sort of life assurance in reverse. Instead of paying regular premiums over a period of years in return for a guaranteed sum payable on death or survival to a stated age, the annuitant pays a capital sum to the insurance company and, in exchange, receives regular annual payments for the remainder of his life or for a fixed period. As with life assurance, the size of the annuity payable for a given premium depends upon the sex and age of the annuitant.

The annual payments received consist partly of capital and partly of income. The earlier payments are mainly income, but over a period of time the income portion decreases. For convenience the Inland Revenue has agreed proportions, based on the life expectancy tables, which remain fixed. The example shows the return a man of 65 would have obtained for £10 000 in late 1979:

Gross annuity:		
Capital	£695	
Interest	£932	
		£1 627
less income tax on £932 at 30%		£ 280
		£1 347

There are many variations on the standard contract, one disadvantage of which is the possibility of the death of the annuitant soon after entering into the contract. All the alternative schemes must be more expensive, however. One of the commonest is the joint annuity paid until the death of a surviving spouse: another makes provision for an increase in the annuity of 5 per cent per annum compound. Annuities for these contracts quoted by another leading company for a premium of £10 000 were as follows:

	Male (age 65)	*Female* (age 60)
Immediate level annuity	£1 619	£1 356 (£1 488 at 65)
Joint and survivor annuity	£1 323	£1 323
Escalating annuity (5%)	£1 194	£950

Annuities provide a high – usually fixed – return; because of inflation, they are only really suitable for elderly people and purchase should be deferred as long as possible. Table 12.3 (page 178) makes this strikingly clear.

Certain kinds of annuity may be used in special circumstances by younger people. Consider, for example, an investor aged 45 years, who has £5 000 available for investment and whose marginal rate of tax is 60 per cent. A

Table 12.3 Annuities and inflation

Years later	Number of survivors Men of 65 (%)	Women of 60 (%)	Value of £100 at yearly inflation rate of 5% (£)	10% (£)	15% (£)
0	100	100	100	100	100
5	87	95	78	62	50
10	69	87	61	39	25
15	47	75	48	24	12
20	25	59	38	15	6
25	9	39	29	9	3
30	2	19	23	6	2
35	0	6	18	4	1

Source: *Money Management*

straightforward investment might produce a gross return of around 12 per cent, but this would amount to only a mere 4.8 per cent net (£600 less tax £360). Instead he can use the £5 000 to acquire a nine-year temporary annuity and pay the first premium on a ten-year qualifying endowment policy.

Proceeds of endowment after 10 years			£9 750
1st premium	£730		
less 15% tax relief	£110	£ 620	
Cost of 9-year annuity		£4 380	£5 000
Tax-free profit			£4 750

The annuity then produces a net annual sum (after tax) of £620 to pay the remaining premiums. The tax-free profit of £4 750 represents an annual net return of 7.2 per cent – a gross equivalent of 18 per cent – on the investment of £5 000.

Home-income plans provide an opportunity to unlock some of the capital tied up in a house while continuing to benefit from its use. These plans usually involve taking a mortgage of 75 to 80 per cent of the value of the property, and using the funds to purchase an annuity. Low-cost 'option' mortgages are available to non-taxpayers and persons unable to use the full tax relief on the interest of a conventional mortgage. But all home-income plans are restricted by law to persons aged 65 years and over. In practice, the companies offering these schemes do not consider them worthwhile until the age of 67 for men, 70 for women and 73 for policies taken out on joint lives.

On the death of the annuitant the loan is redeemed from the sale proceeds of the house (or other investments in the estate), and this factor may deter elderly people who wish to pass on the property and all of their other capital to their heirs. But the loan is not for the full value of the property, and the property itself is likely to appreciate considerably during the period the scheme is in operation.

12.7 Single-premium Assurance Policies

There is a wide variety of what are often called *investment bonds*. These are technically *single-premium assurance policies*. The actuarial element in the policy is usually very small and by far the larger part of the premium is used to purchase units in a fund of one sort or another. For example, a premium of £10 000 might initially give a cover of only £20 000, which could fall to £5 000 by the maturity date. During this period, however, the £9 500 (95 per cent of the premium) invested in the fund is likely to increase substantially in value, so the insurance benefit is only really important in the early years. Income may be converted into additional units and the policy can be surrendered at any time, subject to higher-rate income tax.

Such policies clearly do not normally attract tax relief. Indeed, because they could be used as a vehicle for avoiding higher-rate income tax (the net distributions being reinvested) the Inland Revenue impose additional tax on the proceeds – referred to as *top-slicing* – in the case of higher-rate taxpayers. Because of these tax disadvantages such policies are best avoided by taxpayers who have not used their maximum life assurance relief. They are mainly of interest to investors in the higher tax ranges. Because the insurance company pays tax on dividends at 30 per cent (the basic rate) and on other income at 37½ per cent, this can be a most useful way to accumulate capital. The Inland Revenue also allows modest tax-free withdrawals, up to a cumulative maximum of 5 per cent annually. These policies can also be of use where income fluctuates substantially from year to year, involving considerable changes in tax liability, or where the investor comes into a useful inheritance.

The following example shows how a higher-rate taxpayer can exploit the benefits of a single-premium life policy:

Single-premium life policy acquired for			£10 000
Annual withdrawals:			
Years 1 to 3	£1 500		
Years 4 and 5	nil		
Year 6	£ 700		
Year 7	£1 300	£ 3 500	
Policy cashed after 7 years for		£11 400	£14 900
Overall profit on policy			£ 4 900

Such a profit is not tax-free but is exempt only from the basic tax charge. To ascertain the tax payable we must first deal with the overall profit on an annual basis (£700 per annum). If the investor's marginal rate in the particular financial year is, say, 45 per cent when the £700 is added to his other income, the additional tax is calculated as follows:

£700 × 45 per cent	£315
less basic-rate relief	£210
	£105

The overall tax charge is then £735 (£105 × 7), an average rate of 15 per cent. Of course, the annual profit could also be subject to the investment income surcharge, depending on the extent of investment income.

Single-premium bonds, like unit trusts, can be either general or specialized. There are five principal groupings: managed, property, fixed-interest, money and equity bonds. Included in fixed-interest bonds are gilt funds, and within the equity category are those emphasizing income, growth, take-over situations and so on. Most of them are expressed in units, in the same way as are unit trusts, but they can only be acquired through the medium of a life assurance policy. Thus legal ownership of the units remains vested in the insurance company.

Investment bonds, like unit trusts, are free to set their charges at whatever level they like. In practice, because of competitive pressures, the initial charge is commonly 5 per cent, the same as for most authorized unit trusts. The annual charges vary, however, from as little as $\frac{1}{4}$ per cent to over 1 per cent. In addition there is usually a policy fee, and there may be a further charge on encashment to cover a fund's contingent capital gains tax liability.

The regularly published prices show substantial differences in the bid/offer price spread for investment bonds, some being narrower than the usual 6 to 8 per cent spread for unit trusts and others wider. Taking all the likely charges into account, however, buying investment bonds usually works out marginally more expensive than investing in an authorized unit trust.

12.8 Property Bonds

Several unit trust management companies offer unit trusts specializing in property shares. The authorized unit trust can invest only in securities, not in tangible assets such as property. The investor does however have a suitable alternative in *property bonds*. The attractions of property as an investment have long been recognized and property bonds have been no exception. As with all investments, the timing of the purchase is of crucial importance and the bonds should be regarded as long-term, or at least medium-term, investments. The property market collapsed in 1973–74 but in the boom of 1978–79 property bonds came into their own again.

The two main problems with the property fund are liquidity and valuation.

Property is less readily marketable than are stocks and shares and the managers must therefore maintain a degree of liquidity to enable them to meet withdrawals as they occur. Very large withdrawal demands could be disastrous for the fund, and the investor should therefore buy only those bonds issued by leading companies that have the backing of, say, a large insurance company.

Property is notoriously difficult to value and the only real valuation is the ultimate sale price. Some attempt at valuation must be made for investment and withdrawal purposes, however. A fund will have all its properties independently valued each year, and subsequently update these valuations on a month-to-month basis by reference to an index such as that reflecting the cost of new construction.

The other dangers to investors in property-linked contracts are similar to those involved in equity-linked contracts: the level of charges, and the freedom from supervision of dealings, which are legally permissible between associated companies. Although most property bond companies subscribe to a voluntary code of conduct which forbids deals between associates, a property fund can be used by less scrupulous insurance companies as a 'dump' for their unsuccessful property investments. As with equity funds, the proof of the pudding is in the eating; it is the medium- to long-term performance that counts. The early performance of new funds should be ignored in making comparisons, as this is almost certainly based on other forms of investment. A substantial sum is needed before the first property can be purchased.

12.9 Managed Bonds

These are assurance contracts that are linked on the unit principle to a number of underlying funds, the split between them being determined by the promotors. Also known as a *flexible* or *three-way fund*, the typical *managed bond* consists of elements of equities, fixed-interest stocks and property, but the managers have absolute discretion and some from time to time contain only fixed-interest securities.

In practice these bonds are less flexible than they claim to be. Property, in particular, cannot be acquired or disposed of very quickly. But there is a degree of flexibility in that managers can invest new funds in those areas that currently appear to offer the best prospects for investors. This can be offset should withdrawals for a time exceed new money coming in.

As with most insurance schemes the operation is organized to deal with an expanding fund. There have been occasions when certain linked funds have met a negative cash flow situation, that is, their new money fell short of surrenders and maturities. This always causes problems, particularly with a mix of equity and property funds, where the equity fund must always be resorted to in the shorter term. The claims of the promoters – to be influenced in their investment policy solely by good prospects in different investment areas – assume a growing fund with a successful record. Sheer force of circumstances could, on occasion, make those claims impossible to maintain.

12.10 Income Bonds

Several types of *income bond* are in issue and each is subject to a different type of tax treatment. One type consists of a combination of a *deferred annuity* and an *immediate annuity*. The latter provides an 'income', part of which is a return of capital and so is free of tax. The taxable portion is paid net of basic-rate tax, and the holder must of course pay any higher-rate tax and investment income surcharge. At maturity the investor can receive the deferred annuity, or he can withdraw his investment by taking a cash option instead. The latter course of action is generally preferred, because if he requires an annuity it is usually possible to obtain one on better terms from another company. However, the whole of the gain on the deferred annuity is taxable at the investor's marginal rate of tax, including investment income surcharge.

An example will illustrate how such an income bond works. A 60-year-old man invests £10 000 over a five-year term: £3 400 goes to provide the temporary annuity and £6 600 is deferred. The temporary annuity is £900 gross of which only £193 is taxable, giving the 30 per cent taxpayer a net £842 per annum and the 60 per cent taxpayer not much less at £784. The deferred annuity will produce £11 457 – a profit on £6 600 of £4 857. After basic-rate tax, the amount paid back to the investor will be his original investment of £10 000. Of course, a higher-rate taxpayer must pay the extra tax.

The currently popular type of income bond consists of the purchase of a series of single-premium endowment policies and the initial premium on a qualifying policy. The maturing policies provide not only further premiums but an income as well. The tax subsidy that can be obtained on the qualifying premiums enhances the return on the bond, although there will be some 'clawback' if the bond runs for less than four years.

A third type of bond simply uses a single-premium endowment policy with guaranteed bonus additions which are automatically encashed at the end of each policy year to provide the income. The tax treatment is the same as for the investment bonds discussed in Unit 12.7.

In all cases repayment of the initial sum is guaranteed, but this will of course have lost much of its buying power because of inflation. The great advantage of income bonds is the above-average return they can offer over a range of investment periods.

12.11 Guaranteed Growth Bonds

Some income bonds have what is described as a 'growth option', which simply involves reinvestment of the income during the investment term. In fact, all the specialist guaranteed growth bonds are variants on the schemes discussed for income bonds in Unit 12.10. A deferred annuity contract with a cash option available was once the most popular type of growth bond, but, as mentioned in Unit 12.10, the whole of the gain on such a contract is subject to basic-rate and higher-rate taxation, plus investment income surcharge if the investor is so liable. Consequently a more common scheme nowadays is one written simply as a single-premium endowment policy with guaranteed bonus additions which are not realized until the end of the endowment period. Any gain is then subject to the normal 'top-slicing' arrangement for investment bonds.

12.12 Bond Switching

'Buy low and sell high' is an obvious truism, but few investors can accomplish this regularly. It may be possible to do just this with investment bonds, however. A recent limited study – admittedly a retrospective exercise – showed that investing in the worst-performing rather than the best-performing fund can produce a vastly better investment performance. This is because the worst-performing fund, or rather its underlying investments, has tended to be oversold and there must always come a time when prices are due to recover. It was shown that an investment of £10 000 could have grown in eight years to over £76 000 using this method, whereas following fashion and investing in the previous year's best fund would have produced an overall increase of only about 50 per cent. Other studies have produced similar findings.

Most companies permit bond switching on advantageous terms – ½ per cent being commonly charged – which makes this kind of exercise a very practical possibility.

12.13 Friendly Societies' Bonds

A useful but limited scheme can be operated by friendly societies, which pay no tax whatsoever and thus can write endowment policies that are entirely tax-exempt. Such policies must not be for less than ten years, with the premiums payable throughout the period, but the sum assured is limited to £2 000. Such policies can only be taken out by married people, or single people with at least one dependent child, and then only to the extent of one policy each (thus a married couple can take out two policies). The schemes available are of the managed fund type and performance, not surprisingly in view of the tax benefits, is generally better than other similar or building-society-linked funds.

These bonds must be regarded as a long-term investment, because in cases of surrender before the maturity date the societies are only allowed to repay (subject to clawback provisions) the gross premiums paid.

12.14 Building-society-linked Contracts

In essence these contracts are like any other linked insurance scheme but with the underlying investment being in building society share accounts. Their main attraction lies in the income tax relief available on the premiums. As the value of the underlying fund cannot fall, the guaranteed minimum values are somewhat higher than with equity-linked schemes. The main disadvantage of these schemes is that the total return cannot be guaranteed: all building society rates are flexible and are liable to move up or down during the contract period.

The optimum period for such policies is four years and a day, the minimum period to avoid the clawback provisions referred to in Unit 12.3 and the penalty imposed on surrender within the first year (or two years) of the policy. When building society shares yield $8\frac{3}{4}$ per cent net these bonds offer a net return, depending on age, of up to 14 per cent. Higher-rate taxpayers will find the yields reduced somewhat since they must pay additional tax on the difference between the basic surrender value and the total gross premiums paid.

12.15 Investment in Life Assurance

The extraordinarily wide range of policies available makes it extremely difficult to compare like with like. In the last analysis, it is often the investment performance of the underlying fund that determines the best available contract, performance not only in the next year or two but as much as fifteen or twenty years into the future. Even the best adviser cannot attempt to prophesy investment expertise so far ahead. So there is an element of luck in the selection of any particular scheme.

Fortunately, or perhaps unfortunately, professional advisers in insurance matters are remunerated by commissions paid by the insurance companies. 'Fortunately', because this means that their advice is free to their clients. 'Unfortunately' because rates of commission vary and some advice is thus more valuable than others. A great deal of information on insurance contracts is now available to the public and a prospective investor can make some assessment of the advice he has been given, although with difficulty.

No serious investor enters into any contract recommended to him by a door-to-door salesman without independent advice. No intending investor should enter into an insurance contract advertised in the press, or recommended by advisers of whom he has never heard, without careful evaluation of the proposed contract or independent, impartial advice. Many people sell schemes, contracts or 'plans' for the commission they receive, and are not primarily concerned with their customers' requirements or the real merits of their particular products.

The legal aspects of life assurance are dealt with in Unit 18.11.

12.16 Questions

1. Property bonds have become more popular over the past few years. What are property bonds, and what are the advantages and disadvantages of investing in them?
2. A customer and his wife, both aged 65 and in good health, seek your advice concerning the investment of £10 000 he has received by

commuting part of his pension rights on retirement. They own their house free of mortgage and have about £5 000 invested in various old issues of National Savings Certificates and in a building society share account. They also have about 1 500 Premium Savings Bonds.

(*a*) He says he has been told that he can more than make up the net loss of pension through commutation by the purchase of a joint and survivor annuity from a leading insurance company. He asks if you would recommend the purchase. What reply would you give and for what reasons?

(*b*) They say they have heard of mortgage/annuity schemes. Explain how these operate and list their advantages and disadvantages.

3. As an alternative to unit trusts your customer is considering the purchase of a managed bond. Explain the advantages and disadvantages of this type of investment over a unit trust. What is the investment theory involved in a managed bond and what are the principal criticisms of them in this regard?

Unit Thirteen

Real Assets and Other Investments

Investments in land, buildings and the many types of personal possessions are specialized matters requiring specialized advice. It is not possible here to arm the prospective investor with sufficient knowledge of the various markets to enable him to operate successfully on his own, and this Unit merely reviews the investment areas available under these headings.

13.1 Investment in Property

Direct investment in property can take several forms. The investor, usually an institution, can purchase the freehold or leasehold interest in a number of different types of property – commercial (offices, shops, hotels), industrial (factories, warehouses), residential (houses, flats) or agricultural. There is also investment in freehold or leasehold ground rents and the granting of a mortgage secured on land and buildings. We shall discuss these investments one by one.

13.2 Freehold Property

Ownership of the freehold of a property is the nearest it is possible, in English law, to get to absolute ownership of the property. All land is theoretically leased from the Crown and this enables Parliament to take away certain rights of ownership from freeholders. Thus although ownership of land is deemed to include all the air space above the land and everything below the surface down to the centre of the earth, deposits of coal and petroleum are vested in the Crown irrespective of the ownership of the land above them, while aircraft have the right to fly through air space notwithstanding any objections of freeholders below.

Owners of freehold land own everything attached to the land, although it is customary to refer to 'land and buildings' where the land has been built on. Thus a freeholder may occupy the land (and buildings if any) for his own use, or he may let it. If he lets it for its full value to a tenant, the rent received is called a *rack rent*. Tenancies or leases at rack rents are usually for periods of up to fifty years; where the term of a lease is more than a few years, it usually contains provisions for increases in rent at fixed intervals during the term. Various statutory provisions protect the interests of tenants on the expiry of leases, and possession of the property by the freeholder at that time cannot be relied on.

Where land is suitable for building on, the granting of a building lease of the land, or the granting of a lease of the land and completed buildings, is common. These leases are often for terms of ninety-nine years or even longer, and the rent received is a *ground rent*. This rent usually represents the rental value of the land only. The cost of the buildings is met by the leaseholder, and the freeholder has no right to those buildings until the lease expires, when the occupation of the land reverts to the freeholder, including all buildings erected on the land. The rights of leaseholders have been protected by the Leasehold Reform Act 1967 and the 'reversion' is not now automatic in all cases. Nowadays some provision is usually made for increase of the ground rent during the term of the lease. The value of freehold ground rents lies in the reversion at the end of the term, although the Leasehold Reform Act has made them unattractive as investments even when the reversion date is relatively near.

13.3 Leasehold Property

Leasehold property is land or buildings held on a lease from the freeholder. The term is also used for *underleasehold* properties, where the holder of a lease from the freeholder grants a further lease, or underlease. Further leases can be granted to sub-underlessees and so on. Thus a leaseholder may hold the lease in order to use the property for his own purposes or to grant further leases at a profit. Where the original lease is a building lease, the underlease may be at a rack rent or a further lease of the land only. In the latter case the holder of the first lease owns a leasehold ground rent, sometimes called an improved ground rent, and his income is the difference between the ground rent received and the ground rent paid. Underleases must be for shorter periods than those of the leases immediately above them, even if only one day shorter.

Occupiers of leasehold business premises have a right to the renewal of their lease at a current market rent on expiry, under the Landlord and Tenant Act 1954. Occupiers of leasehold residential property are protected by the Leasehold Reform Act. The law of landlord and tenant is a specialized field and you should refer to standard textbooks on the subject. Should you be confronted by a real-life problem you should consult a solicitor.

13.4 Mortgages

The lending of money to assist with the purchase of property has become almost entirely the province of building societies and other institutions, and the role of the private mortgagee has almost disappeared. This is largely because of the unattractiveness of mortgages as investments. Although money lent on mortgage receives a rate of interest comparable with fixed-interest stocks, and the security should be undoubted, mortgages have all the disadvantages of fixed-interest stocks and the additional one of possible default on the part of

'It just means we address you as sir and madam.'

the borrower, with consequential court action. Private mortgages are now common only as investments in private trusts with the borrower being one of the beneficiaries. This provides help to the beneficiary from the funds with no loss of security to the other interests and no likelihood of default.

13.5 Investment in Freehold Rack Rents

Freehold property is a growth investment. Property values and rents increase with the fall in the value of money. Consequently properties, like equities, have low initial yields, as Table 13.1 shows. At the beginning of 1978 institutions were heavy buyers of property, and initial rental yields fell to only 4 per cent on prime shops, 5 per cent on offices, and only 6½ to 7 per cent in the case of prime industrial property.

The advantages of freehold property to large-scale investors, such as the institutions, are as follows:

(*a*) Property is an excellent hedge against inflation, even of the wage-led variety, which tends to affect equities adversely. Rent is a prior charge on a

Table 13.1 Initial rental yields on property, 1966–76 (%)

	Offices	Shops	Industrial
1966	$6\frac{3}{4}$	7	9
1967	$6\frac{1}{4}$	$6\frac{1}{2}$	9
1968	6	$6\frac{1}{4}$	$8\frac{3}{4}$
1969	$5\frac{3}{4}$	6	8
1970	6	$6\frac{1}{4}$	9
1971	$6\frac{1}{2}$	$5\frac{1}{2}$	$8\frac{1}{2}$
1972	5	$5\frac{1}{4}$	8
1973	$4\frac{1}{2}$	$4\frac{1}{2}$	$7\frac{1}{2}$
1974	7	$7\frac{1}{4}$	$10\frac{1}{2}$
1975	$7\frac{1}{4}$	$7\frac{3}{4}$	$9\frac{1}{2}$
1976	6	$6\frac{1}{4}$	$8\frac{1}{2}$

Source: Pension funds' evidence to the Wilson Committee

company's income; even if there is no profit out of which to pay a dividend, the landlord still has to be paid. Rents do not increase annually as equity dividends can, but there are periodic rent reviews – usually every three or five years on a modern forty-five year lease – and the rent is paid gross (excellent for pension funds) and quarterly in advance (whereas dividends and interest are paid in arrears). Most leases contain 'upward only' rent-review clauses. In the past, initial yields have tended to be higher than on equities, and rent controls are likely to be less frequent than dividend controls because they are less of a political issue.

(*b*) Property is a particularly secure investment. It cannot disappear or become valueless (except in the event of fire, earthquakes or other natural disasters, all of which the investor can insure against). If a company goes into liquidation, the equity-holders may be left with worthless pieces of paper. If a tenant becomes bankrupt, however, the property-owner is left with a building which can be relet.

(*c*) The average size of deal is very large, and this suits bigger pension funds and insurance companies, which can invest perhaps £30mn in a single property but might find it very difficult to invest the same sum in a single company's shares.

(*d*) There are no wider responsibilities attached to property investment as there are with equities. Institutional equity investors have reluctantly but inevitably been drawn into involvement with company management, which is not only time-consuming but may also lead to adverse publicity over matters such as redundancies (see Unit 1.7). Only in residential property is the landlord's responsibility likely to attract attention. Most of the insurance companies that used to own sizeable residential portfolios have reduced them substantially over the past fifteen years, investing the proceeds in commercial property.

Property investment also has its disadvantages:

(*a*) Whereas ordinary shares or gilts can be bought simply and quickly, property, although normally marketable, takes time to buy or sell. Lack of liquidity is not a deterrent to institutions, because of the other assets they hold and their positive investment cash flows. There have been occasions, such as 1974–76, when it has been very difficult to sell at all, but the same then also applied to equities. Equities are only liquid if there is a two-way market. All institutions cannot be simultaneous sellers if there are no personal buyers.

(*b*) The valuation of property is more subjective than that of shares or gilts because no two properties are the same, simply by differences in location. It is impossible to value a large number of properties every day or every week, and there is no authoritative index against which to measure performance. Institutions are generally long-term investors, however, and anything that mitigates the obsession with short-term performance is not all bad.

(*c*) The law of property is complicated and the services of solicitors are frequently required. Apart from the law of landlord and tenant, property-owners may be concerned with compulsory acquisition, planning permissions, the rights of owners of adjacent property, third-party liabilities and so on. The taxation of income from property is also complicated, while looking after a portfolio of property investments requires professional advice from estate agents and surveyors. A fund investing in property normally has a separate property investment team, therefore. The investor then has some control over the investments, and can help to ensure that they are successful.

(*d*) Buildings do not last for ever and extensive repairs, modernization or rebuilding may be necessary. But it is now normal to grant what is called a full repairing lease, so that the tenant is responsible for repairs and decoration. As the property reverts to the landlord at the end of a lease, the lease normally stipulates that dilapidations must be made good so that the property is returned to the landlord in the condition in which it was handed over.

(*e*) There is a risk of loss of rent through lack of a tenant. This arises where a tenant vacates the property on the expiry of the lease and no new tenant can be found. Also the bankruptcy or liquidation of a tenant can make it impossible to enforce his obligations under the lease. Institutional investors used to set great store by the standing or *covenant* of the tenant. A 'good covenant' means that the tenant's agreement to pay the rent is backed by guarantees from the individuals owning the business or from associated or parent companies, and this gives reasonable security that the rent will always be received. Nowadays, with prime property it is less important.

Prime property is property in a first-class location, suitable for a wide variety of tenants and having an existing tenant of first-class financial status. Offices are usually considered the safest or best form of property investment, because they can be let to many different tenants without needing any structural work, or indeed without alterations of any kind. Factories have traditionally had a poor rating as investments because they tend to be single-purpose buildings, as are specialist commercial properties such as garages, petrol stations, multi-storey car parks, cinemas and hotels. Properties like these should be avoided unless their yield is commensurate with their risk, or unless it would be profitable to pull them down and redevelop the site.

(*f*) One type of risk that is largely unavoidable is that of changes in supply and demand for the particular item of property. A hotel has no alternative use, and if demand for hotel accommodation in the area falls off – either through a change in the area itself or by the overprovision of hotels there – the freeholder may find himself with an empty building unsuitable for any other purpose. But even if the property is multi-purpose, such as a town centre shop, a lost tenant may be difficult to replace if demand has declined because of a shift of population, the 'rundown' of the area, or the building of a competing shopping centre or even new out-of-town hypermarkets.

A fall-off in demand may reflect premature obsolescence. The introduction of mechanical handling and pallets has rendered many warehouses considerably less valuable, especially where floor-to-eaves height fails to conform with present-day standards. It is not impossible to imagine that office blocks may become obsolete altogether with the computerization of so much 'white collar' work. The future may well see a return to 'cottage industry' with people working from home, linked to a centre via a television, telephone and computer network.

13.6 Investment in Leasehold Property

Leasehold property is a wasting asset. When the lease comes to an end the rights of the tenant cease. Even if he is entitled to remain in possession, by virtue of statutory protection, there is no investment value in the new lease which may be granted. Investment in leasehold property is practical where the lease is a building lease, and the property can be let at a rack rent. In these circumstances all the points made in Unit 13.5 are relevant, but in the valuation of the property the term of the lease is an additional factor.

13.7 Owner-occupation

Direct investment in property is not usually a suitable investment for the individual of moderate means. Clearly large office blocks, blocks of flats and shopping precincts are available for investment only to the pension funds, insurance companies and property companies. The individual is restricted to the smaller type of property and, unless his means are substantial, he will have a large proportion of his capital invested in a single property, or a small block of properties. Diversification is difficult to achieve in this type of investment and the ownership of a small terrace of houses, or a row of little shops, provides all the problems of property ownership with few of the advantages. Small shop property is more likely to be subject to frequent changes of tenant, and consequently more 'empties', than property let to the large multiple stores.

Residential property is subject to the largest number of statutory restrictions, although with the passing of the Housing Act 1980 a new form of tenancy, the *protected shorthold tenancy*, can arise under lettings of between one and five years. Shortholds apply only to the letting of dwellings to new tenants and are subject to fair rents which must be properly registered. During the period of a protected shorthold tenancy the tenant is fully protected provided that he pays the rent and otherwise keeps his part of the agreement. On expiry of the term the landlord, subject to the giving of three months' written notice, can compel the tenant to vacate the property.

For most personal investors, the owner-occupied house has undoubtedly proved to be the most profitable long-term investment over the last two decades, for the following reasons:

(*a*) House prices have been volatile, but over a long period they have tended to keep ahead of inflation. (In the seven years to 1978, inflation in retail prices averaged 14 per cent, but house prices rose on average by 18 per cent annually.) In fact they are more closely linked to average earnings, and over the long term the average house price is around three and a half times average annual earnings.

(*b*) This is one of the few assets for which it is possible to borrow up to 90 per cent of the purchase price. A high level of personal gearing means that any capital gains on the house are magnified in their impact on the investor's equity.

(*c*) Building society finance, made available under the normal repayment mortgage, is probably the cheapest money available to the investor (between 1972 and 1978, despite high rates of inflation, the building societies' lending rate averaged only 10.5 per cent). One reason is that most of the funds raised are very short-term, although lent by the societies for long periods. Another is that building societies, unlike banks, are not required to hold specified reserve assets, and a third is the effect of Government intervention. Mortgage interest rates are a political hot potato, particularly around election times, and it is almost inevitable that from time to time formal or informal pressure is put upon societies to hold rates below the free market level. This benefits those borrowers who can obtain a mortgage, but inevitably means that allocation is by queue or arbitrary selection rather than by price.

(*d*) Mortgages for house purchase or improvement are the only form of personal borrowing nowadays where tax relief is available. This applies to borrowings up to £25 000 at the time of writing. The higher the investor's marginal tax rate, the greater the tax relief and the lower the net cost of the mortgage.

(*e*) Any capital gain on the owner-occupied house is entirely free from capital gains tax.

(*f*) Also free from tax is the *imputed rent* from the owner-occupied house – what the investor could have received if he had let the house rather than lived in it himself. Until 1963 this was taxed under Schedule A, and tax relief on mortgage interest was restricted to this liability. After 1963, Schedule A liability on owner-occupied houses was abolished and the interest tax relief was extended to other forms of income.

Most people, when questioned about the gains made from house purchase, say that they are no better off because they cannot sell one house without buying another. Building societies frequently insist that most, if not all, of the capital gain on a sale be invested in the equity interest in a purchase, thus preventing spending of the gain on consumption goods. Nonetheless, owner-occupied houses provide appreciable assets that can be passed on to one's heirs. Alternatively, on retirement the owner can move into a smaller property or rented accommodation, and so be able to consume part or all of the capital. Home-income schemes are also available from a few insurance companies whereby the property can be remortgaged or sold to the company in return for an annuity income (see Unit 12.6).

13.8 Indirect Investment in Property

There are two main ways of investing indirectly in property, namely by means of *property shares* and *property bonds*. In addition there are managed bonds, in which property forms only one part (see Unit 12.9) and property unit trusts, which are of restricted use. All have the advantage of generally being more liquid than investment in property itself.

(*a*) Property Shares

Shares in the larger property companies provide a means of participating in a well-diversified portfolio of prime properties, both in the United Kingdom and in Europe as a whole, for a relatively small outlay and without the need for skilled knowledge. Besides the properties themselves, an investor is buying property expertise in the areas of investment, development and trading.

The particular attraction of property shares to many investors is their high level of gearing. This means that any increase in the value of the company's assets leads to a more than proportionate change at the equity level. But such a practice has its drawbacks. Excessive short-term borrowings jeopardized the existence of many companies in 1974–76. High interest rates paid on borrowings used to finance property investment which itself has an initially low yield means that property shares have very low earnings and dividends relative to their assets. Current income is sacrificed for greater future capital growth. The gearing effect is also a contributory factor in the extreme volatility of property shares relative to other share prices because it makes shareholders' net assets more variable. In addition, as with investment trusts, the share price can change independently of the net asset value, depending on the forces of supply and demand for the shares.

It is difficult to see the attraction of property shares to institutions which could undertake direct investment themselves. When property companies pay corporation tax they do so at 52 per cent, whereas insurance companies normally pay 37½ per cent and pension funds no tax at all, and the difference cannot be reclaimed. Shares with low initial yields are not particularly attractive to pension funds because of the low accompanying tax credit. Any premium over asset value paid in order to gain the benefits from gearing would also seem to be an unnecessary expense to these institutions.

(*b*) Property Bonds

At first sight the tax treatment of property bonds (see Unit 12.8) is more favourable than that of property companies. Unfranked income is taxed at the normal insurance company rate of 37½ per cent, as compared with 52 per cent for property companies. But property bonds have no gearing, so they have no interest payments to offset against income before tax is calculated. Although they pay no dividends, the withdrawal schemes available with property bonds provide a higher potential income stream to a bondholder than would dividends from a comparable investment in property shares. It is possible to defer or avoid higher-rate tax by means of the 'top-slicing' arrangements.

Bond values are also more stable than property share prices. This reflects the absence of gearing, and the valuation of the bond on a unit basis, as with a unit trust. It is also due to the fact that the funds are never fully invested in property. Liquid assets are held because of the 'lumpy' nature of property investment, because prospects in the property market may be unfavourable, and in order to meet possible bond redemptions.

Property bonds are less tightly controlled by the Department of Trade than are unit trusts. Valuation methods are not subject to strict regulation. Unlike a share, an individual property is not dealt in daily, so any method of valuation must inevitably be arbitrary, particularly at those times when the market has 'dried up'. Fund valuations are undertaken by independent valuers, but there is a suspicion that prices are 'smoothed' to disguise wide variations in price.

Most property funds are considerably smaller than the leading property companies and therefore lack the latter's diversification. Although maintaining a margin of liquidity, a bond fund may exercise its right to delay repayment in the event of a large number of net redemptions. In these circumstances, they are more illiquid than shares, which are dealt in through the stock market independently of the company. On the other hand, the specialist nature of some bond funds, such as those investing solely in agricultural land, appeals to certain investors.

13.9 Unauthorized Unit Trusts

There are three principal kinds of unauthorized trust (see Unit 11.15): *house funds*, *property unit trusts* and *offshore funds*.

(*a*) House Funds

Many stockbrokers, merchant banks and other institutions run funds on unit trust lines which are designed for their own clients. Some of these are in fact authorized unit trusts, although not advertised or promoted, and their prices do not appear in the newspapers. Many of them, however, are not authorized and the unit principle is used for these funds only because it is a convenient and efficient way of running an open-ended fund, maintaining fairness between incoming, outgoing and continuing investors. Investors whose advisers encourage them to place moneys in an unauthorized trust should realize that they have none of the protection afforded by authorization. The Department of Trade is not involved, the trustee need not be independent of the managers and the investment powers may be unrestricted.

(*b*) Property Unit Trusts

These are special funds designed for tax-exempt investors such as pension funds or charities. They are designed for institutions that are not large enough to buy a diversified portfolio of properties themselves, or that do not have the management or facilities to undertake this form of investment. This special type of unit trust provides a vehicle for indirect investment without the corporation tax levied on property companies and property bonds.

Unit trust practice is governed by the Prevention of Fraud (Investments) Act 1958. The Act defines a unit trust scheme as 'any arrangement . . . for the participation by persons, as beneficiaries under a trust, in profits or income arising from the acquisition, holding, management, or disposal of securities or any other property whatsoever'. This would seem to leave the way open for the formation of property unit trusts, but a separate section dealing with the authorization of unit trust schemes defines 'units' in such a way as to exclude all investments except securities and cash. So property unit trusts can only be constituted as unauthorized, but are allowed to distribute circulars containing an invitation to acquire units, provided they are restricted to pension funds and charities and have specific Department of Trade approval.

Although some of these trusts are modelled closely on authorized unit trusts, with separate trustee and managers, they face the same difficulties as property bonds in the areas of valuation and of large-scale repurchases. All property unit trusts do, however, have a provision enabling them to borrow from banks up to a certain percentage of the value of the fund, usually 20 to 50 per cent. This option can be used to redeem units if the fund is fully invested or to meet investment commitments if money is not immediately available; it is not really looked upon as a means of long-term gearing.

(*c*) Offshore Funds

To the British investor, the term *offshore funds* refers principally to funds established in the Channel Islands and the Isle of Man. The expression originated in the USA, where mutual fund managers attempted to avoid tax and restrictive legislation by setting up funds based in various tax-free areas with good communications both to New York and London, the most favoured sites being Bermuda, the Bahamas and the Cayman Islands. Since most of these new fund centres could be called 'offshore islands' the funds were given this unofficial title.

Offshore funds are free from corporation tax, and so have a decided advantage over authorized unit trusts as regards investing in overseas countries where corporate tax rates are lower. The unfranked income of an authorized trust from this source is subject to corporation tax and any higher-rate tax payable by the investor; that of an offshore fund, on the other hand, would only be taxed at the marginal income tax rate of the investor.

Although most unit trust groups have for some time been able to offer authorized funds investing in all the major stock markets throughout the world they have, for this tax reason, orientated funds towards capital growth rather than high income. Investment trusts have also invested heavily overseas, generally in a more across-the-board fashion than authorized trusts, but they have the advantage of being able to offset their interest charges against unfranked income before tax.

Freedom from control inevitably has its drawbacks. Not being subject to detailed Department of Trade scrutiny means that offshore funds tend to be more risky than mainland ones. They are also generally more expensive, charging against the fund items such as audit fees and custodian and advertising expenses which, in the case of an authorized trust, would be borne by the managers. Short-term investors, however, may be attracted to offshore funds by their smaller initial charge (the 'front-end load'). This is because mainland funds pay stamp duty of 2 per cent on share purchases, plus a commission of around 3 per cent to intermediaries like insurance brokers, contributing to a spread between bid and offer usually between 6 and 8 per cent, compared with 4 to $4\frac{1}{2}$ per cent for an offshore fund.

Because of the risk, the would-be investor is well advised to invest only in a fund run by a well-known institution. These funds are not allowed to send their booklets, leaflets and prospectuses to members of the public directly, but only via a professional adviser such as a bank manager or stockbroker.

Apart from the equity-orientated funds, three kinds of specialist sterling fund are suitable for certain categories of investor resident in the United Kingdom.

(i) **Capital accumulation sterling deposit funds.** These are registered companies which issue and redeem their own participating redeemable preference shares in the same way that authorized unit trusts issue and redeem units in the United Kingdom. The attraction of these funds, which are all identical in concept, is that they effectively allow income to be taxed as capital gain.

Almost always, the assets are invested in readily marketable short-dated sterling money market instruments like certificates of deposit and bank bills. They are sold before reaching maturity, so that the fund receives no income as such, only the capital gain. A United Kingdom resident is liable to income tax on such gains, instead of capital gains tax.

The funds only seek income to pay their expenses and any distributions are, therefore, tiny. On redeeming these shares, personal investors are liable in respect of capital gains tax, while companies are required to pay corporation tax at the reduced rate applicable to chargeable gains. Their appeal is therefore to the higher-rate taxpayer, and to companies with short-term surplus cash.

These funds have attracted considerable publicity, and the feeling that they dress up income in the form of capital gain may lead the Inland Revenue to seek to tax the capital gain as income under the Income and Corporation Taxes Act 1970. Whatever the outcome, it should not affect companies or non-residents.

(ii) **High-yielding sterling funds**. For non-taxpayers, or for investors who pay less than basic-rate tax, these funds are more attractive than building society or bank deposits. Most invest in gilts, short-term deposits and other money market investments where income is paid gross to the fund. The income is then distributed half-yearly or quarterly. Investors may, however, be deterred by the high minimum sums, in some cases £2 500.

Similar schemes are also available in a number of foreign currencies.

(iii) **Sterling commodity funds.** *Commodities*, for investment purposes, are essentially raw materials which can be bought and sold easily in large quantities on organized markets based in the City of London. They fall into two groups, 'hard' and 'soft'. *Hard commodities* are almost all metals (copper, lead, gold, silver, tin, zinc) together with diamonds, while *soft commodities* are mostly foodstuffs – barley, cocoa, coffee, palm oil, soya-bean meal, sugar and wheat – together with rubber and wool.

Investors can buy and sell commodities in two ways: either for delivery straight away, or for delivery on an agreed date in the future. The former is known as buying or selling *physicals* or *actuals* and the price paid is called the *spot price*. Payment has to be made in full at the time of purchase, and charges are made for storage and insurance. A minimum amount must be bought – 25 tonnes of copper, for example. Buying or selling for delivery on an agreed date in the future is known as dealing in *futures*, and the agreement is called a *futures contract*. There are rules about how far in advance deals can be arranged: up to three months with copper, for instance, and up to seventeen months or so with cocoa. The advantages of dealing in 'futures' are the gearing (payment is not required in full on a futures contract, only a deposit of perhaps 10 per cent of its value), and the absence of storage expenses.

The personal investor can buy and sell commodities directly through a commodity broker, or put money into a fund that has been set up specially to invest in commodities. Dealing in physical commodities is not a practical proposition for most people, because of the minimum quantities that must be bought and also because of the risk of the commodity deteriorating in quality before it can be sold. Futures involve smaller stakes, a deposit of perhaps around £1 000, and there are no worries about the product deteriorating in storage. Some commodity brokers run syndicates for investors to pool their funds. Nevertheless, the risk of a large loss remains, and deters many people.

The choice for most investors is a *sterling commodity fund*. Authorized unit trusts are prohibited from investing in anything other than securities, so if the small investor wishes to have an interest in a professionally managed fund he must look offshore. A variety of funds deal in commodities, differing in their areas and degrees of specialization, their permitted levels of gearing and their ability to 'go short'. Most of the funds use at least part of their money to trade in 'futures', so a fund's performance may not exactly correspond to the trend in the spot prices of the underlying commodities. These funds are attractive to an investor who is interested in real assets as a hedge against inflation, and who is also looking more towards capital growth than income. They must not be confused with authorized unit trusts that invest in the shares of companies that produce, deal in or distribute commodities.

13.10 Investment in Chattels

Investment in real assets has appeared to be one of the few ways of protecting the purchasing power of one's money in recent years. Two types of real asset – property (or 'real estate') and commodities – have already been discussed. The third type is *chattels*, or personal possessions. Examples of traditional investments in this field which may appeal to the investor are:

Precious stones and jewellery
Antique silver
Antique furniture
Pictures
Sculpture
Porcelain, china and glass
Books and manuscripts
Postage stamps
Coins and notes
Clocks and watches
Objets d'art of many kinds

New areas to have developed rapidly in recent years have been:

Wine
Tribal art
Musical instruments
Old photographs
'Busted' bonds (see Glossary)

'Alternative investments', as they are commonly called, have attracted the interest of the institutions. In the early 1970s, for example, Allied Breweries pension fund bought bullion and precious metals, the Ciba–Geigy pension fund bought Krugerrands, and British Rail's pension fund invested in paintings, porcelain, tapestries, glass, rare coins and even a score by Wagner! The accumulation of works of art by the pension funds attracted considerable criticism from the art world. But British Rail, for one, decided after five years of investing to 'round out' the collections and then cease such investment altogether. Their reasons were the high insurance and security expenses, particularly when the items were displayed, and also the tax inefficiency of a pension fund – a gross fund – investing in assets that yield no income.

The position of pension funds is in complete contrast to that of the higher-rate taxpayer for whom returns in the form of capital gain are attractive, especially since gains on personal belongings such as furniture, antiques, jewellery and other tangible, movable objects are tax-free, provided the value of each object at the time of disposal is not more than a certain figure fixed annually in the budget.

While each type of investment has its own characteristics, and each requires specialist knowledge, there are several common factors that the potential investor should understand. These are as follows:

(*a*) They yield no income (in this respect 'real estate' differs from all other real assets discussed in this book). This may not deter high-rate taxpayers, but it does mean that there is no rational method of valuation. In any market, price depends on the balance of supply and demand. These in turn are influenced by rational expectations of the future, speculation and fashion. Fashion is a factor in investment in shares, with certain sections of the market being in and out of favour with investors from time to time. Here, though, there is a limit below which prices cannot fall on grounds of fashion alone. The assets, earnings and dividends of a company exist and have value outside the stock market. Dividend and earnings yields therefore never get too far away from the

'How much would a first issue Access card, unused, fetch?'

general market levels. But this is not true of personal possessions. In many areas demand has been constant for years, but in others changes in fashion have markedly affected the demand from collectors, with a consequent effect on prices. There is now even a journal devoted to alternative investments, which attempts to discern such changes in fashion at an early stage.

(*b*) There is the risk of buying forged, faked, doctored or stolen items.

(*c*) Storage presents a problem, in terms of space and conditions of light and temperature, particularly for items such as furniture, books and wine.

(*d*) Valuables need to be insured against hazards such as theft and fire. This might cost, say, £3 to £6 a year for each £1 000 of cover. Extra expense may also be involved in fitting special locks, burglar alarms, floodlighting and so forth. One way of overcoming this and the preceding problem is to pay for the asset to be stored with a dealer, but of course the investor is then denied any immediate enjoyment of his possession.

(*e*) Valuation presents a problem as generally no two items are identical, and prices may well vary considerably between dealers.

(*f*) Dealers' margins and expenses are usually much greater than in the case with financial assets – sometimes as much as 50 per cent, or even more. For this reason alone the investor should be wary of promises of quick returns. He should be sceptical also of promises to buy back at a significantly high price after a fixed period. These guarantees are only as good as the creditworthiness of the dealers who make them.

The relative performance of 'alternative investments' since 1950 has been impressive (see Table 13.2 and Fig. 13.1). These figures should be treated with a little caution, however, since they are based on the auction prices of things that proved to be successful investments. They do not include items that were sold through dealers, or for which the expected price acted as a deterrent to sale.

Table 13.2 Money invested in alternative assets, 1970–78 (average percentage annual increase)

Chinese ceramics	24.7
Gold	24.3
Old master drawings	19.8
Early books	16.2
Old master paintings	15.8
Modern paintings (1900–50)	14.0
Impressionist paintings	11.6
FT All Share Index	9.1
Dow-Jones Index	6.0

Source: Sotheby's

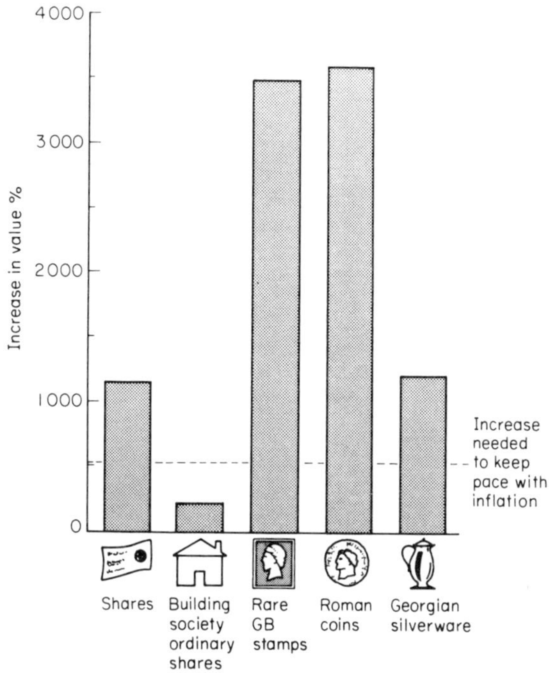

Fig. 13.1 How investing in things has compared with other investments: investments made in 1950 and cashed in 1978, with any income (net of basic-rate tax) reinvested

The investor should be cautious when venturing into these unfamiliar fields. Investment in chattels should perhaps be restricted to items which not only appreciate in value but also give pleasure to the owner, because of either their beauty or their 'hobby' appeal. And yet there is a growing demand for wines as investments, which can only appeal in purely commercial terms since their 'enjoyment', in the only other meaning of the word, plays havoc with their resale potential!

13.11 Gold

Gold has been an excellent investment over the centuries, and always performs well in times of currency turmoil and international crisis. Since the earliest times it has been a traditional investment for savers in the East, and also for continental Europeans. This right was denied to United Kingdom residents for many years, until the removal of exchange controls in October 1979. Previously they were limited to coins (principally Krugerrands and Canadian maples) selling at a relatively small premium over their gold content.

British investors now have complete freedom to invest in gold bullion, either through a bank or directly with a dealer in the London gold market. As many customers do not want to take delivery of the gold personally, London dealers are happy to hold it in *unallocated accounts*, the cheapest and normal method of storage. So many ounces of gold are simply credited to the customer's account, and the question of price fluctuations, as well as the eventual sale, is no more than a book-keeping exercise. Alternatively some banks have offered gold in slivers of as little as five grammes, in the shape of an elongated disc which can be used as jewellery. These sell at a premium of about 6 to 7 per cent for manufacturing and handling charges.

One disadvantage of buying bullion rather than coins is that it is subject to value added tax. Unless the purchaser is registered with the Customs and Excise for VAT purposes he cannot reclaim VAT when the bar is sold. Larger-scale investors can avoid the problem by channelling their gold purchases via foreign centres where no sales tax is applied. Similar treatment applies to *gold certificates* issued by several leading American banks. A further problem is that an investor who sells his coins and bars at a profit may be liable to income tax rather than capital gains tax on the benefit, if the Inland Revenue judges him to be behaving as a trader. This could happen if bars are regularly cashed in for a short-term profit (post-1836 British gold sovereigns are free of capital gains tax).

Indirect investment in gold includes the gold certificates already mentioned, gold shares, offshore trusts, gold futures and gold options. The last two involve considerable gearing and are best suited to the professional investor.

13.12 Questions

1. Discuss the relative attractions of property and equities as a hedge against inflation.

2. From the viewpoint of the personal investor discuss the relative merits and demerits of (*a*) direct investment in property, including owner-occupation, (*b*) property bonds, and (*c*) property company shares.

3. What is meant by the term *alternative investments*? What are the risks involved?

Unit Fourteen

Portfolio Planning

14.1 The Tax Environment

The most important of an individual's circumstances, where investment matters are concerned, is the incidence of taxation, since tax reliefs and liabilities influence investment decisions made in respect of all portfolios except those of registered charities and exempt pension funds. Before dealing directly with portfolio planning, we shall therefore examine the various taxes on investments.

Every investor needs to know his effective highest rate of tax in order to compare the net-of-tax returns from different investments, and to be able to calculate his total net income. Because of the differential impact of taxes it can make sense for some investors to make what might otherwise be regarded as poor investments. A classic example is the low-coupon short-dated Government security which produces low 'flat' and redemption yields (see Unit 4). However, to the higher-rate taxpayer such an investment makes a considerable appeal for there is comparatively little income to be taxed, but the capital gain (provided the stock is held for more than one year) is absolutely free of tax.

In the first part of this Unit we shall look at the broad principles of income tax, capital gains tax and capital transfer tax. *The rates are likely to change every year, so the figures quoted are illustrative only.* Up-to-date rates and allowances can be obtained from your local tax office, or in one of the excellent guides published by *Hambros*, the *Daily Mail*, or *Money Which?* (March each year).

14.2 Income Tax

Income tax in the United Kingdom is based on income for a twelve-month period ending on 5 April each year. It is imposed on earnings, pensions and investment income. But you are unlikely to pay tax on the whole of your income. All the moneys you receive are added together to arrive at your *gross income*. From this are deducted *outgoings* (certain eligible payments you have to make, such as interest on a mortgage). This leaves what the tax inspector refers to as *total income*. In turn from this figure you deduct *allowances* to leave you with *taxable income*, on which tax is charged. A married couple's income is combined for tax purposes, unless they opt to be taxed separately, each then receiving only the single person's allowance. Children's investment income is also aggregated if it is derived from capital contributed by the parents.

The principal allowances for 1981–82 are as follows:

Single man's or woman's personal allowance	£1 375
Married man's personal allowance	£2 145
Wife's earned income allowance	£1 375
Single parent	£2 145
Age allowance: single	£1 820
married	£2 895

Age allowance is in place of the personal allowance for persons aged 65 or over or for married couples of whom one is 65 or over, but it is reduced by £2 for every £3 by which 'total income' exceeds £5 900, and is thus extinguished at

'Are you sure this is what it said in the guidance notes?'

£6 567 for a single person or £7 025 for a married couple, at which point the normal personal allowance applies.

In addition there are allowances for a housekeeper or a person looking after children; there are also allowances for a dependent relative and for a son's or daughter's services. Blind people are eligible for a special allowance.

As mentioned in Unit 12.3, life assurance 'qualifying' premiums are paid net and the insurance company claims the tax relief on its client's behalf. Gross premiums are reduced by 15 per cent (at the time of writing) – that is, an effective subsidy on net premiums of 17.65 per cent, provided that total premiums do not exceed £1 500 or one-sixth of 'total income' (gross income minus 'outgoings'), whichever is the greater.

After deduction of 'outgoings' and allowances, income is subject to a progressive scale of taxation. For 1981–82 the first £11 250 of taxable income is taxed at 30 per cent and successive bands of income are subject to increased rates up to £27 750. Any taxable income above this is taxed at 60 per cent. Investors having more than a certain amount of investment income (£5 500 in 1981–82) pay an additional tax called an *investment income surcharge*. Investment income is assessed after deducting certain 'outgoings', but not normally any allowances. The rate for 1981–82 was 15 per cent. So should your taxable income exceed £27 750, including more than £5 500 of investment income, you will pay 75 per cent on your marginal investment income.

14.3 Capital Gains Tax

Capital gains tax in its present form was introduced in 1965. Briefly, it is a tax payable on the profit made on the disposal of an asset. Anything you own (whether in the United Kingdom or not) counts as an asset. You are held to 'dispose' of an asset not only if you sell it, but also if you give it away, exchange it or lose it. On the other hand, a transfer between a husband and wife who are not separated does not count as a disposal, nor does a transfer on death. In the latter case, persons inheriting assets under a will or intestacy acquire them at their value on the date of death. In addition, for lifetime gifts made on or after 6 April 1980, a special concession called *roll-over relief* is available, whereby the capital gains tax is deferred until the donee ultimately disposes of the asset (see Unit 14.3(*d*)(v)).

(*a*) Exempted Investors and Assets

Certain types of investor and asset are exempt from the tax. Charities, pension funds, friendly societies, registered trade unions and non-residents of the United Kingdom pay no capital gains tax, and the following are some of the assets on which gains are exempt:

(i) The principal place of residence. Disposal of a house or other residence occupied as the sole or main place of residence of a taxpayer is exempt unless (1) only part of the house is the residence, in which case there may be a liability on part of the proceeds, or (2) the area of land sold with the residence exceeds the normal accommodation land area.

(ii) A residence occupied rent-free by a dependent relative. Only one property can qualify for exemption on this ground.

(iii) All chattels that are wasting assets (assets with a predictable life of fifty years or less), such as animals, boats, wine and private cars.

(iv) Household goods, personal belongings and other chattels, provided the value of each object at the time of disposal is no more than a given sum (£2 000 in 1981–82). A 'set' or 'collection' of articles is usually treated as one asset.

(v) British money, including post-1836 gold sovereigns.

(vi) British Government stocks held for more than a year, or which have been inherited.

(vii) National Savings Certificates and SAYE.

(viii) Life assurance policies, although these may be liable for income tax if held by a higher-rate taxpayer and the policy does not qualify for tax relief (such as a single-premium bond), or if cashed in early.

(ix) Betting winnings, including football pool dividends and premium bond prizes.

(x) Gifts of assets liable for capital gains tax which are made during the tax year, provided their total market value is not more than a certain amount (£100 in 1981–82).

(*b*) Basis of Assessment

The current tax was introduced on 6 April 1965 and was not made retrospective, so it only applies to gains made since then. With assets acquired after this date tax is chargeable on the difference between the total cost of acquisition and the net proceeds of sale. Where the disposal of an asset at a profit would produce a liability to tax, its disposal at a loss produces an allowable loss which can be set against other profits to reduce the total liability. A net loss in any year can be carried forward indefinitely, but it cannot be carried back to be set off against profits made in earlier years.

(*c*) Tax Rates

Capital gains tax is worked out on the net capital gains for the tax year. It is payable at a rate of 30 per cent, but this only applies to net capital gains in excess of £3 000 (the 1981–82 figure), that is, the first £3 000 of net gains in the tax year are free of capital gains tax.

(*d*) Special Cases

(i) **Pre-1965 purchases.** With assets acquired before 6 April 1965, there are two methods of calculating the gain. For assets other than quoted securities, where the acquisition price is taken, the resulting profit or loss is *apportioned* over the period the asset has been held, and only the profit or loss made since 6 April 1965 is chargeable or allowable. Alternatively, the value on 6 April 1965 may be substituted for the cost of acquisition.

In the case of quoted securities purchased before 6 April 1965, the normal basis of assessment is that the taxable gain is deemed to be the *lesser* of either the gain since acquisition or the gain since 6 April 1965; the allowable loss is similarly deemed to be the *lesser* of the loss since acquisition or the loss since 6 April 1965. There is no time apportionment. If one calculation shows a gain and the other a loss, the share is said to be within its *neutral zone*, and there is no chargeable gain and no allowable loss.

(ii) **Matching bargains**. In cases of share dealing where there is more than one purchase and one sale, there are capital gains tax rules for matching bargains. Sales are first matched with any purchases made on the same day. Otherwise purchases are added to a pool of shares bought on or after 6 April 1965, and their average cost is calculated.

These rules apply to shares and all other securities except gilts. For these, sales are again matched with purchases made on the same day, where applicable, but otherwise sales are matched against purchases made in the preceding twelve months, on a first in, first out basis. Anything earlier than that is of course exempt from capital gains tax.

(iii) **Scrip issues and rights issues.** When a company makes scrip issues ('bonus issues') this alters the acquisition cost per share, but not the total cost of the holding, as no payment is involved. For example, suppose that 1 000 25p shares are held at a cost of £3 000, or £3 a share. A scrip issue of one new share for each one held is made. The holding becomes 2 000 shares, still at a cost of £3 000, but an average price of £1.50.

Rights issues are treated similarly, except that the cost of the rights taken up is added to the original acquisition figure. Imagine, for example, as before, the investor has a holding of 1 000 shares at a cost of £3 per share, but this time the company makes a rights issue (instead of a scrip issue) of one new share for each existing share at £1. If the rights are taken up the holding becomes 2 000 shares at a cost of £4 000 (£3 000 + £1 000), or £2 a share.

(iv) **Take-overs and mergers.** Where take-overs and mergers occur, the liability for capital gains tax depends on what is received in exchange for the shares disposed of. If cash only is received, the position is identical to that of a sale. If one class of share or stock only is received, the previous acquisition details are applied to the new holding and no liability arises at that time. If the offer is part cash and part shares, this represents a part disposal and the acquisition cost is apportioned over the cash and new securities on the basis of the amount of cash received and the value of the new securities. Where more than one type of security is received, again the original cost is apportioned over the new holdings on the basis of their values at the time of the acceptance of the offer, to form the basis of a charge on eventual disposal. Some of the calculations arising from the take-over of a company's shares can be extremely complicated, especially when the bid contains a combined offer of cash, loan stock and ordinary shares.

(v) **Roll-over relief**. For gifts made on or after 6 April 1980 the donor and donee can jointly claim this special form of relief from capital gains tax. The effect of this concession is to reduce the donor's taxable capital gain to zero. When the donee eventually disposes of the asset, however, he must take as its acquisition value its market value when received less the donor's capital gain. In effect, the donor's original acquisition price becomes that of the donee. But any capital transfer tax paid on the transfer, by either party, can be deducted by the donee before calculating the capital gain, to the extent that it reduces the capital gain to zero. This concession eliminates the previous double capital taxation of lifetime gifts.

(*e*) Tax Strategy

Capital gains tax considerations should not dominate portfolio decisions, but attention to tax details can enhance the net-of-tax returns.

First, the investor must be aware of the potential tax liability on his investments; he must accordingly keep accurate and up-to-date records, and scrutinize them well before the end of the tax year.

If the investor is likely to realize substantial capital gains over a period of years, then he should ensure that in every one of those years at least the tax-free maximum net gain of £3 000 is realized. If capital losses are to be established purely for tax purposes, they need only be sufficient to reduce the net capital gain to £3 000, because if the net gain falls between zero and £3 000 he cannot carry forward any of the year's allowable losses. Any losses brought forward from previous years only have to be used up to the point where the net capital gain is reduced to £3 000, however; any excess can be carried forward again.

Whenever an asset is sold to establish a gain or loss purely for tax purposes, the investor should take the opportunity to consider the merits of the asset in the overall portfolio, and whether it should be immediately repurchased or perhaps replaced. If a share is repurchased the normal procedure is a *bed and breakfast* transaction. The investment is sold and repurchased the following day – that is, it is sold before 3.30 p.m. on one day and bought back after 9.30 a.m. the following morning. Concessions in the form of reduced 'jobber's turn', broker's commission on only one bargain, and freedom from transfer stamp duty ease the cost of such an operation.

The rules on the 'bed-and-breakfasting' of gilt-edged securities are stricter in order to prevent an investor from establishing a loss in a stock which he continues to hold, yet being exempt from tax on the capital appreciation after one year. If a loss occurs on the disposal of gilt-edged securities and the same securities are reacquired within one month (six months if not through a Stock Exchange), the loss may only be deducted from the chargeable gain on a *subsequent* disposal of those securities.

For disposals where a person who owns gilt-edged securities acquires an additional holding of securities of the same kind and disposes of securities of that kind at a loss within one month of acquiring the additional holding (six months if not through a Stock Exchange), he is treated as if he had sold and reacquired the securities, so that the loss may only be deducted from a gain on a later disposal of the same securities.

14.4 Capital Transfer Tax

Capital transfer tax replaced estate duty in 1975. It is a much more comprehensive method of taxation because it applies to gifts made during a lifetime as well as possessions left on death. Estate duty used to be referred to as a 'voluntary' tax because of the many loopholes in the system, the most important of which was the complete exemption of all gifts made seven years prior to death.

The scope of capital transfer tax includes all financial assets, property and chattels owned by a person. Anything you own can in theory be counted as a taxable gift if you give it away. On death, you are considered to give away everything you own at that time, and your estate is assessed for capital transfer tax, instead of capital gains tax, on these disposals. There are two tax tables: one for the cumulative total of gifts made during the previous ten years (or since March 1974 if less) up to three years before death, and the other for gifts on death, or made within the three years prior to death. On both scales the first £50 000 of assets is exempt. Above this figure the lifetime rate begins at 15 per cent and reaches a maximum of 50 per cent on sums over £2.01mn. The comparable rates on the death scale are 30 per cent and 75 per cent. The more penal death scale, and the aggregation of lifetime gifts over a ten-year period, together encourage lifetime distribution of assets, over the maximum period possible.

Certain gifts are tax-free (see below), but any other gift counts as a taxable gift, and the Inland Revenue continually update the cumulative total of all the taxable gifts the investor has made and declared since 26 March 1974. Each person has only one running total, which covers both gifts made in life and those made on death. A husband and wife are treated separately, however, which means that they can each make their own tax-free gifts, and can each make £50 000 of taxable gifts before they have to pay any capital transfer tax.

Tax-free Gifts

Certain gifts are tax-free and are therefore not included in the running total. They fall into three groups:

(i) those that are tax-free irrespective of when they are made;
(ii) those that are tax-free during lifetime;
(iii) those that are tax-free on death.

(i) **Tax-free at all times**. The most important item in this group for the personal investor is gifts between husband and wife.

(ii) **Tax-free during life**. These include (with 1981–82 figures):

1. gifts made out of income (but not by drawing on capital) which are part of

normal spending – the donor must be able to maintain his standard of living from the remaining income if the gift is to be tax-free;

2. gifts of up to £250 each to any number of different people in each tax year;

3. gifts to support an infirm or elderly relative or widowed, separated or divorced mother or mother-in-law;

4. gifts to maintain an ex-wife or ex-husband, and the maintenance and education of children;

5. wedding gifts of up to £5 000 from a parent of the bride or groom, up to £2 500 from grandparents and up to £1 000 from anyone else;

6. gifts of up to £3 000 during any tax year in addition to the above. This tax-free allowance, or part of it, can be carried forward one year only.

(iii) **Tax-free on death**. These include lump sums paid to dependants from an employer's pension scheme, and reasonable funeral expenses.

Here we have only sketched the main features of capital transfer tax; for a detailed understanding and exploitation of all its provisions one requires the services of an experienced professional adviser, such as an accountant or solicitor, especially in the case of complicated areas such as the taxation of trust funds and settlements. Nevertheless, this tax is not just a problem for the very rich. Because of the non-exemption of owner-occupied property, many less-wealthy families may, perhaps to their surprise, find themselves subject to it. This liability can be reduced by taking advantage of the lifetime gifts allowances outlined above.

One approach might be to use the £3 000 a year allowance (plus £250 per person) to pay the premiums on a life assurance policy, preferably a 'qualifying' one. A policyholder is eligible for the tax credit on the premium payments irrespective of whether or not he pays tax. This, however, does not apply to policies taken out on children under twelve, though the Inland Revenue will allow the tax credit once the child reaches the age of twelve. When one of the parents is giving money regularly in this way, a way of overcoming the problem is for the policy to be written on his or her own life, in favour of the child or children. In this way the premiums are eligible for tax relief up to the normal limits, and should the parent die the policy will mature. There may be advantages in having the policy written in trust form for the absolute benefit of the child (or children) and this can be arranged with the insurance company.

It is often more tax-efficient if capital jumps a generation, from grandparents to grandchildren. Again life assurance is ideal for regular gifts, and where there is no direct parent–child relationship a *deed of covenant* can be used. This is a legally binding agreement under which one person promises to make a series of payments to another for more than six years. By this means a child can recoup basic-rate tax paid by a grandparent and if this is combined with the 17.65 per cent subsidy (1981–82 figures) on the 'net' premiums of a qualifying policy on the child's life, £70 paid by the grandparent becomes £117.65 ($£70 \times \frac{100}{70} \times \frac{100}{85}$) invested on behalf of the grandchild. For such a scheme the beneficiary should be aged at least twelve but not earning and paying tax, as otherwise the tax advantage of the covenant is lost. The covenant can usually be cancelled at any stage by mutual consent once the child reaches eighteen, and it normally ceases if either party dies. The flexibility and high returns on a building-society-linked insurance policy make it a very suitable adjunct to a covenant.

If a husband and wife have a stable marriage it is worth considering the division of assets between them. There will be no tax on the transfer of gifts between them and, by sharing possessions, they can each take full advantage of the tax-free ways of making gifts. In addition, they are each allowed to make £50 000 worth of taxable gifts before any tax is charged. They will also pay less tax in the long run if they each leave their assets to the children, or anyone else but each other.

14.5 Identifying the Investor

No investment policy is right for every investor in every circumstance. Investment strategies of institutional investors, for example, are to a large extent dictated by the nature of their liabilities, and the restrictions of law or trust deed. They nevertheless retain some discretion to decide on the relative weightings of assets in their portfolios, and to adjust them when their 'reading' of economic trends deems this to be necessary. However, for a large insurance company or pension fund to try suddenly to switch all its investments out of one area and into another is rather like asking a huge oil tanker, travelling at full speed, to turn about on the spot! It cannot be done. It is usual to adopt a gradualist approach by redirecting the new moneys coming in, rather than turning over the fund itself. This makes it all the more imperative that the correct long-term strategy is adopted, and that it is not influenced too strongly by short-term events and trends in performance.

The personal investor is obviously much more flexible in portfolio planning, but, in many ways, the task is more complicated because of the need to take cognizance of so many factors relevant to the individual. No two people are the same; neither are their investment needs. An investment adviser needs to know certain personal details before beginning to give advice on particular investments. These details fall under three headings:

(i) income and tax position (see Unit 14.6);
(ii) responsibilities and commitments (see Unit 14.7);
(iii) personal feelings (see Unit 14.8).

14.6 Income and Tax Position

Income available and spending needs vary over a lifetime. In the case of 'white collar' workers, income, in real terms, may be at its lowest level when they are students or pensioners, and at its peak somewhere between middle age and retirement. The income of manual workers is more evenly spread. The demands on income for spending needs are usually greatest when one is still fairly young, having invested in a house and started a family. The surplus of income over spending needs is probably greatest when, in the typical family, the children have grown up and perhaps left home, while the husband is reaching the peak of his earning power and the wife is back at work.

The size of income (relative to spending needs) determines how much an individual can afford to invest. It also determines his tax position, and therefore the type of investments most suitable. High-rate taxpayers prefer capital growth to income which is to be taxed. Capital growth can be guaranteed with some investments; with others, such as equities, it is more suspect and the investor obviously should not rely on it as an important source of funds for day-to-day living expenses. In addition, the higher, the more secure and the more liquid the returns, the greater the amount the investor can commit without sacrificing his immediate standard of living. Finally, the greater the stability and certainty of income and consumption, the larger the proportion that can be invested in a regular or long-term form.

To make such judgements, the sort of questions the investor or adviser should bear in mind are:

(*a*) **Earnings**

(i) What are net earnings after tax?

(ii) How secure is that level of earnings?

(iii) How would illness or injury affect them in the short term?

(iv) How secure is the investor's employment?

(*b*) **Pension**

(i) How long is it to retirement?

(ii) What level of pension (both state and private), in real terms, is likely to be received?

(*c*) **Income from Trust Funds and Other Sources**

(i) What is the net income, after tax deduction, from these sources?

(ii) What investment policy is being pursued by the trustees?

(iii) What events terminate the interest in the funds?

(iv) Is there any other factor likely to cause a major change at some stage in the investor's life, such as a large inheritance?

(*d*) **The Investor's Tax Position**

(i) What is the investor's marginal (highest) rate of income tax?

(ii) Is the investment capital such that the investor incurs, or could incur, the investment income surcharge?

(iii) Are there any accrued losses for capital gains tax purposes?

(iv) Is the investor's wealth such that consideration should be given to avoidance of capital transfer tax?

14.7 Responsibilities and Commitments

Spending needs have already been touched upon, and these reflect the responsibilities and commitments of the investor at different stages of his life.

(*a*) **Age**
At fifty, for example, the investor is more likely to be concerned with building a nest-egg for retirement than with saving up for the deposit for a first home. The children are probably off his hands by now (or soon will be).

(*b*) **Dependent Spouse and Children**
(i) What is the investor's state of health? Is there likely to be any difficulty obtaining the right sort and amount of life assurance?
(ii) Are the dependants adequately provided for in the event of his early death?
(iii) Have precautions been taken to reduce the liability for capital transfer tax on death?
(iv) Does the investor want to leave money for the family to inherit?
(v) Is money required, or likely to be required, in order to send the children to fee-paying schools, or to provide assistance at university or college?

(*c*) **Housing**
(i) Is cash likely to be required in the foreseeable future to buy a house, or a different house?
(ii) Is there any prospect of being able to increase the mortgage?
(iii) Is the mortgage covered by life assurance?

(*d*) **Other Commitments**
(i) Is the investor likely to have to assist any other relatives?
(ii) Is cash likely to be required for any other specific purpose in the foreseeable future (house repairs, for example, or buying new furniture or a washing machine or going on holiday)?

These questions should naturally lead to the question of sickness, accident and life assurance cover. Special insurance schemes are also available to assist in such matters as school fees.

It is often remarked that comparatively few people have made anything like adequate provision for their dependants. The primary purpose of life assurance is to provide for death. Yet most people seem to prefer an endowment-type policy with a guaranteed minimum return on survival to a stated age, whereas term assurance gives considerably more cover for the same outlay.

14.8 Personal Feelings

(*a*) Temperament

Some investors are inherently nervous; they cannot help worrying about their investments. There are people who are frightened by equity investment, since they feel that unless their money is invested in something where the value cannot fall (in money terms), they are likely to lose their wealth. Diversification can reduce risk, but, at the end of the day, the question must be asked: 'Are you prepared to risk losing some money for the chance of a greater gain?' This inevitable trade-off between risk and return must be clearly understood.

Investors who are risk-averse in the extreme are best advised to avoid volatile securities (shares, gilts except short-dated) and to concentrate on cash investments and non-marketable Government borrowing, such as National Savings Certificates and SAYE.

(*b*) Sentiment

Certain investors will not purchase shares in particular sectors of the market such as breweries, tobacco companies, distilleries or gaming organizations. Other investors find a company objectionable if it operates in a country whose government they see as politically unacceptable.

Others will wish to hold shares in certain companies irrespective of investment merit in the usual sense, often because of the gifts or special concessions offered to holders of a stipulated number of shares. One of the most widely publicized is European Ferries' discount to shareholders on cross-Channel voyages.

'Bearing in mind your liquidity position I can wish you a Merry Christmas but not a Prosperous New Year.'

14.9 Liquidity

Part of any investment fund should be in liquid form, that is, as cash investments. The proportion is not a constant, but depends on the investor's security of income and employment, his time horizon and immediate commitments, and his view of the state of the markets for different types of longer-term asset.

At certain times, as when the yield curve was downward-sloping in late 1979, cash investments provide a high return compared with other assets. If neither the equity nor the fixed-interest markets appear attractive, the personal investor might seriously consider 'going liquid' to a large degree. (This is something institutional investors are constrained from doing to anything like the same extent.) The danger of such a policy is that income is uncertain, and it is difficult to predict when interest rates have reached a peak. This is the time when the investor should be fully invested to benefit, long-term, from the high yields and the capital gains that will be made on both equities and fixed-interest securities as interest rates begin to fall, the gilts' rise usually preceding that of equities.

14.10 Diversification

The old adage about avoiding putting all your eggs in one basket is highly relevant to investment theory. The investor's objective is to obtain the highest return for a given level of risk, and the lowest level of risk for a given return.

Much risk is unnecessary and easily avoidable. This is *independent* (or *unsystematic*) risk, which can be eliminated by holding a reasonably diversified portfolio. An extreme example will illustrate the principle.

Suppose two shares, A and B, both offer a 50 : 50 chance in a particular year of earning either 20 per cent or nothing, the outcome depending on certain unpredictable economic events. These are obviously risky investments, each with a mean expected return of 10 per cent.

But what if they were shares in an ice-cream company and an umbrella manufacturer? When one prospers, the other does badly: when one earned 20 per cent, the other earned zero. In this case, although both securities are risky if held independently, if held together they are risk-free because they always yield 10 per cent (20 per cent + 0 per cent, or 0 per cent + 20 per cent).

This is admittedly an idealized example, but the principle is nevertheless sound. Provided the returns on any two securities are not perfectly correlated (that is, they do not move perfectly together in the same direction), their combined risk is less than a weighted average of their individual risks. In fact, the riskiness of a portfolio depends on three factors: the riskiness of the individual investments, the proportion of the portfolio invested in each asset and the correlation of returns between assets. The smaller the positive, or the greater the negative, correlation of returns, the greater the risk reduction through diversification.

The scope for diversification within a fairly homogeneous sector of the market – such as banking, insurance or brewing – is strictly limited, because most shares within these sectors move up and down very much in line with the sector as a whole. Research has shown, however, that by far the greater part of independent risk can be eliminated by holding about fifteen to twenty shares selected fairly randomly. This gives a level of risk broadly similar to that of the stock market as a whole.

A personal investor does not need to worry about adequate diversification if he opts for indirect investment via a broad-based unit trust or insurance scheme. Specialist unit trusts, concentrating on certain sectors of the market or geographical areas, should not dominate his portfolio, and should only be purchased after adequate diversification has been achieved. Many of these specialist funds have a far more volatile performance record than that of the general trusts, but much of this risk can be diversified away if they are held in conjunction with the latter. Held in isolation, their risk/reward ratio tends to be poor, appealing only to those largely indifferent to risk.

The degree of diversification in an insurance policy depends on the policy itself. The funds of traditional with-profits endowment policies, for example, are spread across equities, gilts, property and cash. The overall returns above the guaranteed level are passed on to the policyholder in the form of bonuses, abrupt changes in which are prevented by the actuarial 'smoothing-out' process. Unit-linked policies are more risky, being far more dependent on capital values at the time the policy is encashed and the degree of diversification in the chosen unit fund.

14.11 Net-of-tax Returns

Taxation has already been mentioned as one of the most important considerations for both personal and institutional investors. The investor should aim to hold a 'tax-efficient' portfolio, that is, one that offers the highest net-of-tax return for a given amount of risk. The nil taxpayer can compare investments on the basis of their gross yields, but all others should look at the yield net of their own marginal rate of tax.

The nil taxpayer is penalized when investing in a building society because the tax paid by the society is not recoverable; for such a person the National Savings Bank Investment Account or a bank deposit account would be worth examining. Some nil- or low-rate taxpaying investors, such as unemployed, disabled and retired people, need to ensure that any income or capital gain is not more than outweighed by the withdrawal of any means-tested state benefits they may receive.

Higher-rate taxpayers, particularly those paying 75 per cent on marginal investment income, are restricted as to their choice of tax-efficient outlets for funds. To some extent their choice must depend on their attitude to risk-taking, and their need for liquidity (see Table 14.1; note that in some cases the time-scale is flexible).

Table 14.1 Investments for high-rate taxpayers

Low risk	Higher risk
Short term	
National Savings Bank ordinary account (up to £1 400) Low-coupon, short-dated gilts Offshore deposit funds	Options
Medium term	
National Savings Certificates, particularly 2nd index-linked issue Index-linked SAYE Building-society-linked life assurance	High-PE/low-income equities Warrants Capital shares of a split-level investment trust Offshore commodity funds Chattels, including gold, diamonds etc. Premium bonds
Longer term	
Property, particularly owner-occupied Traditional life assurance Pension schemes	Unit-linked life assurance – regular savings or single-premium investment bonds

14.12 Investing for Income

Income may be an important consideration for certain investors, such as those investing immediately prior to retirement. Income may be obtained directly, in the form of interest and dividends, or 'manufactured' by the realization, in whole or part, of any capital appreciation. The latter policy is frequently adopted by higher-rate taxpayers holding low-coupon short-dated gilts, and can also be applied to index-linked National Savings Certificates after one year. Unfortunately, with regard to equities, these 'home-made dividends' are not perfect substitutes for the real thing. Gains may be costly to realize on small share stakes and, more importantly, capital growth is not guaranteed, even over a period as long as ten years.

Equities should not be bought for their immediate income, as their initial yields are generally low compared with those obtainable on fixed-interest securities (the 'reverse yield gap') and cash investments. Nevertheless they do provide a growing income stream (growth in income is more reliable than growth in capital values), which is attractive for someone wishing to maintain at least a constant level of purchasing power. Some individual equities or unit trusts offer high yields but this is only commensurate with their higher levels of risk and poorer long-term growth prospects. An alternative might be *income shares of a split-level investment trust*. These provide a growing stream of income until their redemption date.

For investors of beyond retirement age, *annuities* provide a high level of income per pound invested – more than could be obtained on a fixed-interest security. This is because the interest is boosted by an annual return of capital. The initial return is less if a growth rate is built into the return, or if the annuity is on joint rather than single lives. The annuity might be financed by a mortgage in the form of a home-income plan (see Unit 12.6).

The income solution for most investors is the inclusion of some *fixed-interest securities* in their portfolios to boost the initial return. The exact proportion should depend on the minimum yield required on the portfolio relative to the interest and dividend yields currently available on debt and equity capital respectively, and must also take into account the yield from the cash investments, together with the investor's assessment of the relative prospects for the bond and share markets.

When seeking income the investor must decide on the relative merits of *gilts*, company *debentures* and *unsecured loan stock*, *preference shares* and *non-marketable* and *cash investments*. Corporate debt offers higher yields than Government borrowing (but also higher risk), no exemption from capital gains tax after a holding period of one year and no facility for purchase through the Post Office. Moreover, it is harder to find a stock with adequate interest and asset cover and a redemption date coinciding with that at which the investor is looking for full and certain recovery of capital. Local authority debt offers higher returns than British funds, with very little additional risk. Preference shares are not attractive to the personal investor (see Unit 7.1(*b*)).

Finally, mention must be made of the income attractions of certain insurance-based schemes. Guaranteed-income bonds offer attractive rates to basic-rate taxpayers. For higher-rate taxpayers, the 5 per cent withdrawal facility available with single-premium investment bonds is worth considering (see Unit 12.7).

14.13 Protection Against Inflation

For investors who place a high priority on maintaining the real value of their capital the two *index-linked investments* (National Savings Certificates Second Index-linked Issue and SAYE Third Issue) are very attractive as they are the only forms of direct personal investment where real capital maintenance is 100 per cent guaranteed. The index-linked National Savings Certificates have the added benefit that they can be encashed after the first year with the appropriate indexation. But unless they are held for the maximum period they provide no real return above that needed to maintain the purchasing power of the original investment.

It is to be hoped that *equities, property* and other *real assets* will, in the long run, provide a real increase in capital. At the time of writing, the share of profits and dividends in the national income has been falling, but there is a point at which this decline must cease if the mixed economy is to survive. If that point has been reached, or temporarily passed, the earnings, dividends and market value of shares should grow in line with money incomes generally. Personal property investment still offers the best opportunity because of the gearing and special concessions attached to owner-occupation.

14.14 Case Studies

To illustrate the ways in which investors can be helped to plan their portfolios, we shall look in some detail at two fairly simple examples.

(*a*) **The Middle-aged Family Man**

George Smith is 40 years old and married, with three children aged 17, 14 and 11. The family have no health problems, and Smith has adequate life assurance cover arranged through traditional types of endowment policies. He also holds educational policies to cover his children's education. He is a finance director of a medium-sized industrial company, with a current salary of £20 000. The position is pensionable in due course. There are no other sources of income. His assets consist of a £40 000 house with a £10 000 mortgage outstanding. With much effort he saves about £1 000 a year. Smith has recently received an inheritance of £100 000, which is on bank deposit account for the time being.

(i) Suggest appropriate investment objectives for Smith.

(ii) Indicate the types of investment which could best achieve those objectives.

(i) Mr Smith has no pressing problems at the moment, with adequate life assurance, educational schemes for the children and the prospect of a growing and secure income until retirement. The obvious investment objective is to minimize tax. Liquidity is not paramount, and he can be assumed to be willing to accept a reasonable degree of risk. Income needs will probably be greatest over the next ten years (until the youngest child has finished any higher education) and after twenty-five years (retirement).

(ii) The types of securities and other assets appropriate for Mr Smith are outlined in Table 14.1. There is the possibility of moving to a larger or more expensive property, and/or paying off the mortgage. It is probably worth retaining the mortgage because, with an appropriate choice of investments, he can earn a higher net-of-tax return than the net cost of the mortgage. He would certainly be wise to increase his regular life assurance premiums to one-sixth of his total income. A possible portfolio might look like this:

	£
National Savings Bank ordinary account	2 800
National Savings Certificates	
index-linked issue (maximum £3 000 × 5)	15 000
21st issue yielding 9 per cent over 5 years	
(Maximum tax-free holdings for a husband and wife)	10 000
Low-coupon gilts, such as	
Exchequer 3 per cent 1984	5 000
Transport 3 per cent 78–88	5 000
Single-premium investment bonds:	
property	10 000
fixed-interest	2 200
managed	10 000
Growth-orientated unit trusts	
(with some overseas content)	20 000
Offshore commodity funds	5 000
Offshore deposit fund	5 000
Warrants	2 000
Capital shares of a split-level investment trust	2 000
Gold	3 500
Temporary annuity	2 500
	100 000

For an outlay of £2 500 a temporary annuity could be purchased to pay the subscription to SAYE (maximum £50 per month) for five years. Investment income received, the withdrawal facility on single-premium investment bonds or a further temporary annuity could be used to pay the premiums on a unit-linked savings plan (regular-premium life assurance linked to a number of funds, such as property or managed).

Premiums for qualifying life policies might now exceed one-sixth of total income. But this need not concern Mr Smith. Although the excess premiums do not qualify for a tax subsidy, the main tax planning feature is that the sums received on cashing in the policy are free of all taxes (basic-rate and higher-rate income tax, investment income surcharge and capital gains tax) provided the cash-in takes place after a given period. The main feature of all these plans is that the investor pays his premiums for ten years. With many such plans, the investor can stop paying premiums after ten years and cash in when he likes. The value of the investments will continue to grow. He can cash in a few policies at a time, providing himself with a tax-free income. Alternatively he can continue paying the premiums to build up his capital even more rapidly (hence the nickname 'greenhouse' schemes). Lump-sum investments are less attractive than these regular savings schemes because of the absence of tax subsidy and the 'top-slicing' applied to total gains. They do, however, have advantages in terms of flexibility and the withdrawal facility.

(*b*) **Retirement Pensioners**

Mr and Mrs Dudley come to you for investment advice. Both are in their sixties, Mr Dudley having retired a few years ago on a fixed pension which they feel is becoming inadequate. Neither has anything more than a cursory knowledge of investment, although they seem aware of the general principles. Their capital amounts to £35 000, all of which has been deposited with three building societies since Mr Dudley retired. They own their house, and have two children who are not dependent upon them. Mrs Dudley speaks with anxiety of rising prices, and how difficult it is to manage in these present inflationary conditions. As a result of reading newspaper comment and listening to friends, they have become increasingly nervous and wonder whether they should deploy their savings to better purpose.

(i) State with reasons the advice you would give these customers.

(ii) If appropriate, give an indication of the portfolio you would recommend.

(i) The position of the Dudleys was discussed to some extent in Units 14.12 and 14.13. Clearly they need to boost their initial income, but they have to balance this against the need for future purchasing power. They have capital tied up in the house, and this money could be released by moving to a smaller property, but they are not old enough to use any form of home-income plan. Conventional annuities are possible, but satisfactory returns will not be obtained until they are well into their seventies. *Property-linked annuities* overcome some of these disadvantages; the payments increase in line with property values, and the annuity can be cashed at any time, at rates set by the insurance company's actuary. *Building society deposits* are suitable because the Dudleys are paying basic-rate tax, although a higher return could be obtained from a term share or, better still, one of the more flexible 'escalator'-style bonds. High immediate income can be obtained from *local authority loans*. Capital growth could come from the maximum allocation of index-linked *National Savings Certificates*. If kept for the full five years these could be used to purchase an annuity; if funds were urgently needed in the meantime they could be partially or wholly cashed after one year without sacrifice of the indexation. A *high-yield unit trust* would provide additional income growth, and the building society ordinary share account and the *National Savings Bank Investment Account* would cover immediate liquidity needs.

(ii)

	£
Building society	
ordinary share account	700
bonus shares, escalator bonds, build-up bonds	4 500
National Savings Bank Investment Account	800
National Savings Certificates (Index-linked)	6 000
Local authority loans for, say 3, 5, 10 years	10 000
Income shares of a split-level investment trust	3 000
High-yield unit trusts	7 000
Property-linked annuity	3 000
	35 000

14.15 Investment Policies of the Institutional Investors: Principles

In 1978 the pension funds and the life assurance companies had a net cash inflow of £7.73bn, amounting to nearly 50 per cent of Britain's gross personal savings (£16.14bn) and almost 80 per cent of the personal sector's net acquisition of financial assets (£9.76bn). Although during the 1970s life assurance companies remained the largest institutional investors in terms of funds invested, the pension funds were the faster growing, and by the end of the decade had more 'new money' coming in. This was because of the rise in the number of workers covered by occupational pension schemes, the automatic increase in pension contributions in line with wages and salaries (as compared with fixed, or periodically revised, contributions into life assurance schemes), and additional payments by employers into pension funds to cover actuarial deficiencies resulting from increases in expected pension payments.

The enormous sums of money going into institutional coffers pose immense investment problems. It has been said that if the insurance companies and pension funds continue to expand at their present rate it will be they, rather than the meek, who shall inherit the earth! At the end of 1979 the Post Office pension fund had estimated assets in excess of £2bn. The National Coal Board, British Rail and the electricity supply industry are also pension fund billionaires. What principles govern the direction of these funds?

Although long-term investment tends to be more profitable than short-term, dangers can arise if the investment assets are of a considerably longer maturity than the liabilities which financed them. In any fund, therefore, risk is lessened by *matching* the maturity structures of assets and liabilities. Both life assurance companies and pension funds have long-term liabilities. Life assurance policies may not mature for thirty years or even more; still longer periods can be involved before a pension contributor retires. The difference is that life assurance contracts are essentially fixed in money terms (or at least the guaranteed element is), whereas pensions are based on earning power in the final years before retirement, and therefore these are fixed more in real terms. Pension funds therefore have the greatest need to find assets that will provide a rising stream of income in line with earnings. On the other hand, being gross funds, they should only be concerned with comparing the gross yields of one type of investment with another.

Unit trusts and investment trusts principally invest in quoted company securities. They have less discretion in their choice of investment outlets, being restricted by trust deed and articles of association and by the need for Department of Trade approval before receiving certain tax concessions. Their investment policies were examined in more detail in Unit 11.

14.16 Investment Policies of the Institutional Investors: Practice

After the Second World War, insurance companies and pension funds principally invested in gilt-edged securities. Inflation was low, and so were interest rates. Typical interest yields for Treasury bills were ½ per cent and for Consols (undated Government securities) 2 or 3 per cent, while equities had dividend yields of 4–5 per cent and earnings yields of 12–13 per cent. There seemed little risk of capital loss if one invested in gilts, and in fact prospects of capital appreciation if interest rates were to fall in the recession expected by many, as after the First World War. Equities on the other hand were risky; memories were fresh of the liquidations and dividend cuts experienced in the 1930s.

The 'cheap money' policy was abandoned by the Conservative administration of 1951, when Bank Rate (now Minimum Lending Rate) was increased to 2½ per cent, having been held at 2 per cent for no less than twelve years. But the change had been apparent before then. War Loan reached its post-war peak of 108 in October 1946. From then on it fell precipitately, to 50 by mid-1961, and to less than half of that in the 1970s.

During the mid-1950s many insurance companies and pension funds diversified into equities, and to a lesser extent into property: the 'cult of the equity' was born. The main reason for this switch was a recognition that inflation and higher interest rates were likely to be persistent features of a full employment policy, although admittedly at a much lower level than today. Given the 'demand-pull' type of inflation then largely prevalent, dividend income could be expected to rise with money incomes, and this was particularly attractive to pension funds and insurance companies offering with-profits policies. Equities offered higher yields than gilts, together with a prospect of capital appreciation, whereas gilts had begun to fall in value as interest rates rose. In addition, a diversified portfolio of equities came to be seen as less risky than previously imagined; there seemed little likelihood of a repeat of the slump of the 1930s.

A reorientation of institutional investment policy accordingly took place, mainly by directing the new funds into equities, but also partly by selling substantial amounts of gilts for reinvestment in equities. Between 1954 and 1957 insurance companies' holdings of gilts were reduced by over £50mn, while their ordinary share investments increased by £300mn and their property investments by £120mn. The Trustee Investments Act 1961 gave trustees power to invest in ordinary shares up to 50 per cent of the funds for which they were responsible, if they so wished. Very substantial sales of gilts took place, some of it in anticipation of the passing of the Act. With the clearing banks also reducing their holdings of gilts to make room for advances to industrial borrowers, the gilts market of 1954–61 was characterized by institutional selling.

By October 1959 the persistent rise in share prices had driven the average dividend yield calculated for major representative companies below the yield on 2½ per cent Consols for the first time since records had been kept. This was the beginning of the so-called 'reverse yield gap'.

By the mid-1970s disillusionment with equities had set in with investors. The FT 30 Share Index (see Unit 16.1), 521 in 1968 and 543 in May 1972, had fallen to 146 in January 1975, lower in real terms than during the 1940 London blitz. (Although long-term investors would say they are more interested in the growth trend in dividends than in capital changes, and dividends still increased during this period.) Profits had been a shrinking part of national income, there was continuing price and dividend control, and equities were no longer seen as a hedge against inflation. This was because the main type of inflation now seemed to be 'cost-push', which eroded profit margins.

By the late 1960s, property had become an attractive alternative to equities. Like equities, it offered a prospect of a rising stream of income, but it appeared more secure. It seemed to be a better hedge against 'cost-push' inflation, because rents are a prior charge on a business, and less susceptible to continuing government control than would be the case with dividends.

Table 14.2 illustrates the recent pattern of investment by the main groups of institutional investors.

Table 14.2 Pattern of asset holdings of institional investors at end 1978 (per cent of total assets at market values)

	Insurance companies		Pension funds	Investment trusts	Unit trusts
	Long-term	General			
Cash and other short-term assets	4	17	5	5	10
Public-sector securities	27	28	22	4	1
Company securities	38	36	53	91	89
Mortgages and loans	8	3	3	–	–
Property	22	11	17	–	–
Other investments	1	5	1	1	–
Total assets	100	100	100	100	100
£ bn	37.8	7.1	31.3	6.7	3.9

Source: *Wilson Report*, p. 47. All figures rounded

Table 14.2 shows that long-term and general insurance hold surprisingly similar proportions of their funds in public-sector securities and company securities. But a greater proportion of the general insurance public-sector securities are short-dated, and they also hold more short-term assets. Company securities for both general and long-term business are primarily ordinary shares. The pension fund figures are an amalgam of the three types of pension fund (local authority, other public-sector and private, of which the last-named is by far the largest), but it is clear that overall pension funds hold fewer public-sector securities and more company securities, again primarily ordinary shares.

Public-sector securities have been the dominant outlet for insurance company funds in recent years, and pension funds have invested almost as much in them as they have in company securities. In fact, of the total net official sales of gilt-edged stock between 1972 and 1978 (nearly £25bn) over half (nearly £14bn) were bought by the insurance companies and pension funds.

Insurance companies and pension funds are the growth sectors, compared with unit and investment trusts, and they are mainly responsible for the institutions acquiring about 2 per cent of the United Kingdom equity market each year. In the case of insurance companies and private pension funds since the late 1960s, however, it is the increase in *total* assets which is responsible for this persistent acquisition, rather than an increasing proportion of the funds being devoted to equities. Only the local authority and other public pension funds exhibited any increased concentration in equities. Local authority funds also appear to be much higher in public-sector securities and much lower in property than are the other pension funds.

14.17 Questions

1. In the review of a customer's personal portfolio, what information would you require and what investment considerations would you bear in mind?

2. A married customer, aged 30 with three children aged 3, 5 and 8, seeks your advice on the investment of £20 000, which he has inherited on the death of his mother. He has a steady job with a salary of £6 000 per annum, but neither he nor his wife has other sources of income. He is not averse to risk, but would not wish to take more risk than is necessary to try to maintain the real value of his capital. He would also like to supplement his income. He owns his house subject to a mortgage, the balance of which is about £10 000, and says he is thinking of paying this off. He has been asked to invest some money in the private company for which he works.
   (*a*) Detail the advice you would give this customer concerning the investment of the inherited sum, and suggest a suitable portfolio structure (you are not required to suggest individual holdings).
   (*b*) State the advice you would give him in connection with the proposals (i) to pay off the mortgage, and (ii) to invest in the shares of his employer.
   (*c*) If your customer wished to give £1 000 to each of his three children, how would you suggest these sums were invested?

3. A customer and his wife, both in their early thirties, consult you for investment advice. They have no children and do not expect this situation to change. Their combined earnings amount to £12 000 gross per annum,

out of which they are able to save £100 net per month. They hold the maximum amount of the current issue of National Savings Certificates, they own their house subject to a small mortgage, and have £10 000 invested in building society share accounts.

(*a*) How would you advise them to invest their monthly savings?

(*b*) Would you recommend any changes in their existing investments?

Unit Fifteen

Selection and Review of Investments

15.1 Techniques of Investment Analysis

The objectives of investment analysis are twofold: first, to determine the characteristics of an investment – its degree of risk, its yield, its tax position – and its suitability in the portfolios of different types of investor, and, secondly, to suggest whether the security is cheap or dear relative to other investments, taking into account differences in risk. With regard to equity investment, the second purpose is usually over-emphasized, and the analyst is seen merely as a purveyor of 'buy' or 'sell' recommendations. In this role, most analysts belong to the mainstream of *fundamentalists*, although there is also a minority group (or 'cult') called the *technicians*.

The fundamentalist tends to look forward. He is concerned with future earnings and dividends, and the risk attached to them. The technician tends to be backward-looking, as his sole preoccupation is with the action of the market itself, particularly price and volume changes; he believes that past price data hold the key to the future.

15.2 The Fundamental Approach

(*a*) Discounted Future Dividends

Fundamentalists are strong believers in the *intrinsic* (or 'true') value of a share. This is the present value of the future dividend stream expected from the share; which can be expressed in the following formula:

$$V_0 = \frac{D_1}{(1+r)} + \frac{D_2}{(1+r)^2} + \frac{D_3}{(1+r)^3} + \frac{D_4}{(1+r)^4} + \cdots\cdots + \frac{D_n}{(1+r)^n}$$

where V_0 is the intrinsic value of the share today, time 0.)

The obvious disadvantage of this approach is its requirement to forecast individual dividends (D_1, D_2 and so on) to time n, and as n is in theory infinite this is virtually impossible. In addition, the discount rate r, the required rate of return on the share, may also change over time. To make this method manageable, one is forced to compromise by assuming that dividends either grow at some constant rate for ever, or grow at different rates for specified future time periods.

To take the simpler case, let us assume that the next expected dividend D_1 is 10p per share, that dividends are expected to grow at a rate g of 12 per cent a year for ever, and that the required rate of return r is 16 per cent. Given these assumptions, the formula becomes:

$$
\begin{aligned}
V_0 &= \frac{D_1}{r-g} \\
&= \frac{10\text{p}}{0.16-0.12} \\
&= \frac{10\text{p}}{0.04} \\
&= £2.50
\end{aligned}
$$

If the actual share price was, say, £3, the analyst would recommend a 'sell', if £2 a 'buy'. Incorporating different growth rates (to correspond, for example, to the life cycle of the product and the company) makes the arithmetic more

complicated, but the principle is the same. Dividends are usually forecast, apart from perhaps the immediate term, by predicting earnings, and multiplying these by a target *payout ratio* (the proportion of earnings paid out as dividends).

In predicting future earnings one should beware of simply extrapolating past earnings figures. There is a theory, that of 'higgledy-piggledy growth', which says that, with a few notable exceptions, there is little correlation between past and future earnings growth. Companies which have done badly in the past may be reorganized or taken over; those that have done well may suffer from a slowdown in market growth or from the inroads made by new competitors.

Analysts place great emphasis on the *quality* of earnings, by which they mean their stability and security. For each major product area the analyst must pay attention to the nature and prospects of demand for the products or services, the structure and state of competition in the industry, cost conditions and profitability, and the importance of research and development.

One problem is that it may be a long time before the share price reaches its 'true' value, appearing almost permanently under- or overvalued. The 'intrinsic' value may be swamped in the short or medium term by speculative factors, and before these have been overcome the fundamentals themselves may have changed. This approach requires a strong nerve, for frequently the long-term investor is going against the trend, selling when share prices are high and rising, while buying when they are low and falling. In this respect, as Keynes remarked, he may appear 'eccentric' and 'unconventional', and need the support of a long-term contract!

(*b*) Market Yield

Rather than using the formal dividend valuation model outlined in (*a*), many analysts and fund managers prefer to estimate an appropriate *dividend yield* or *PE (price–earnings) ratio* for the share. These can then be applied to the 'normalized' dividend and earnings per share respectively.

The three main factors affecting the 'true' prospective PE ratio are growth expectations, the payout ratio and the discount rate (incorporating the risk-free rate of interest and a risk premium).

Most analysts who use this approach do so fairly loosely. Generally, they take the average PE ratio for the sector as a whole and, in an ad hoc fashion, add on the odd percentage point or two for above-average growth or payout, and knock off points for excessive risk in the form of greater instability of sales or financial gearing.

Another very straightforward method of using PE ratios is to establish a 'norm' based on average past levels, either for the share or for the stock market. In a similar way, some analysts calculate PE ratio relativities (traditional PE ratio differentials between the share and others in the industry, sector or the stock market as a whole). Significant deviation from this premium or discount would warrant investigation of the fundamentals of the company. The investor should beware, however, of mechanical trading systems, signalling when to buy and sell. PE ratio differentials cannot remain inviolable, independent of economic changes in demand and supply in the industry and company.

(*c*) Leading Indicators

A *leading indicator* is an economic variable which changes in advance of ('leads') another economic variable. It may be a causal relationship, changes in one leading to changes in the other, or both may be reacting to a third factor, but with different reaction times.

A number of leading indicators for the economy are regularly published in *Economic Trends*. The money supply and bank advances have featured in several studies, both because of their direct impact on the financial markets, and the widespread belief that they affect the economy generally after a time lag of six to eighteen months. At one time, increases in the money supply were thought to be good for gilts and equities in the short run because of the expected consequential fall in interest rates. Nowadays, brokers are more concerned about the inflationary effect of such increases and the Government's likely response in the form of tighter credit and higher interest rates.

There is considerable dispute as to whether the money supply is a leading or coincident indicator. In the United Kingdom, most of the evidence supports the latter view. But even if a significant leading indicator was found, it would probably not remain one for long. If such an indicator became widely recognized among brokers, the market would react to, if not anticipate, changes in its value, thus reducing or eliminating the lead time altogether.

(*d*) Profit Forecasts

Rather than using a formal model to predict the exact level of a share price, a popular method among analysts is simply to compare their personal dividend and earnings estimates for a particular company with those being made by other analysts. The presumption is that the share price is a reflection of consensus opinion. If one analyst's estimates are on the high side compared with market opinion, that analyst will consider the share an attractive investment. He expects the announcement of the results to provide a pleasant surprise for the market, and hopes that this will be quickly reflected in the share price itself.

At the aggregate level, movements in corporate profits are correlated closely with the stock market indices – but unfortunately for analysts the market appears to lead the disclosure of company profits. Profits are themselves dependent on the level of economic activity. So here again the analyst and fund manager can compare their own forecasts of the business cycle with those of other investors, and take a view on the market. This area has been studied in detail by leading brokers such as Phillips and Drew and Hoare, Govett, whose forecasts are regularly published in the financial press after having been communicated to their own clients. In addition a mass of information is published regularly by such authoritative bodies as the NIESR, the London Business School, the Bank of England, the Henley Centre for Forecasting and others.

Any general view of the market can be converted into a view on individual shares by the use of 'beta coefficients', mentioned in Unit 6.10. If one is *bullish* about the market as a whole, one should buy shares with high betas (those which are highly responsive to movements in the market). If one is *bearish*, one should sell, again especially those with high betas.

15.3 Technical Analysis

A trend is a trend is a trend
But the question is, will it bend?
Will it alter its course
Through some unforeseen force
And come to a premature end?

Technical analysis is the study of stock exchange information principally in the form of price and volume data. The word 'technical' implies a study of the market itself, and not of those external economic factors that are reflected in the market. Many technical analysts would claim that a knowledge of the company and industry is a positive disadvantage. Some would prefer not to know the nature of the underlying asset, claiming it is immaterial whether they are predicting the price of ICI shares, gold or postage stamps!

Technical analysis is essentially based on trends and patterns. Mechanical trading rules in the main are concerned with deciphering major turning points, but they are based on the belief that there is a certain momentum in share prices both upwards and downwards.

(*a*) Relative Strength

This approach is based on the belief that a share or sector which is outperforming the market will probably continue to do so; it embodies the 'momentum idea' or 'bandwagon effect'. It may also reflect the gradual dissemination of good or bad news to a progressively wider investing public. In one study, relative strengths were determined by dividing the current market price by the average of the previous twenty-six weeks; these ratios were computed weekly, and the highest 10 per cent were bought and the lowest 10 per cent sold. Success was claimed for such a policy.

(*b*) Filter Rules

Filters are designed to isolate the primary trends from minor price changes arising from random factors. Fig. 15.1 illustrates their use: if the price of a share moves up at least x per cent from a low point, it should be bought and held until its price moves down at least x per cent from a subsequent high, at which time it should be sold. The share is not repurchased until it moves up again at least x per cent from the subsequent low point.

The problem with using this technique is deciding on the size of the filter. If x is small (3 to 5 per cent, say) the investor is constantly buying and selling, and thus spending heavily on broker's commission and stamp duty. If x is large (perhaps 20 to 25 per cent) much of the price movement has taken place before the investor acts.

(*c*) Chartism

Most analysts use charts at times as a method of keeping track of the price movements of particular shares, or of the market as a whole. In the case of individual shares, charts can alert the analyst to any sharp upwards or downwards movement or any persistent trend relative to the market and he may then decide to investigate the fundamentals of the company.

Chartists are a special breed, however, in that they rely on charts alone, and have their own ways of plotting share prices. The essence of chartism is the belief that share prices trace out patterns over time. These are a reflection of investor behaviour and, if it can be assumed that history tends to repeat itself in the stock market, a certain pattern of activity that in the past produced certain results is likely to give rise to the same outcome should it reappear in the future.

There are three principal forms of chart that plot the movement of the prices of individual shares and of market indices.

(i) The simplest form of chart is a *line* chart (see Fig. 15.2). This consists of a line connecting the closing prices of the share, or average prices over a period of perhaps a week, to show the price movements over a period of months or, more probably, years. Those analysts who use line charts usually plot other lines on the same chart. These may show the movement of the share price relative to index for the appropriate market sector or for the market as a whole. They may also show the price movement relative to earnings or, with investment trusts, the price as a percentage of asset value.

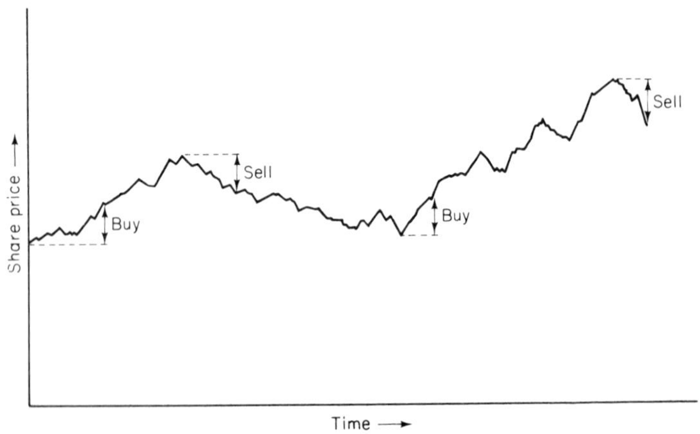

Fig. 15.1 Filter method

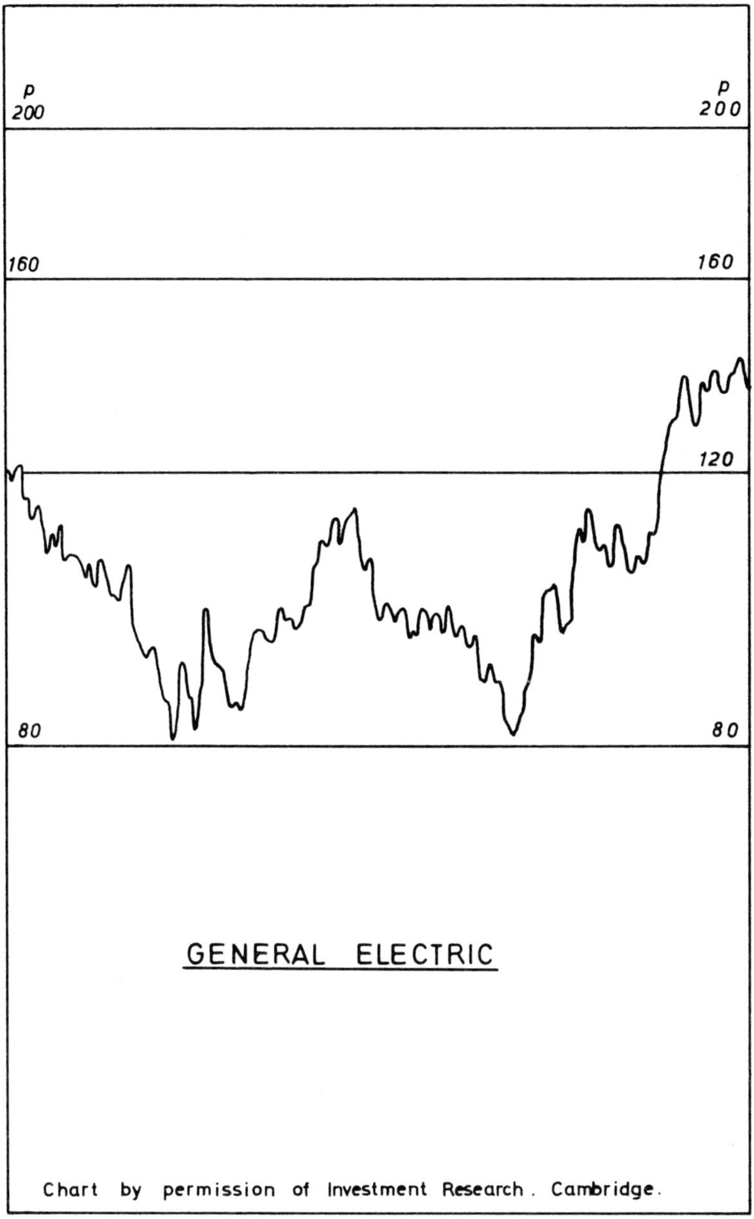

Fig. 15.2 Line chart showing 'double bottom'

Fig. 15.3 Bar chart showing 'head and shoulders' top

(ii) Another form of chart is the *bar* chart (see Fig. 15.3). This shows the highest and lowest prices a share reaches each week, joined by a vertical line or bar. Bar charts usually attempt to indicate the volume of business each week in the share. Volume figures for individual shares are not released on the British market, however. Full turnover figures are available on Wall Street, where bar charts are popular.

(iii) The third form of chart in common use is the *point-and-figure* chart (see Fig. 15.4). In this type there is no time scale and only price movements are plotted. As a share price rises a vertical column of crosses is plotted. When it falls a circle is plotted in the next column, and this is continued downwards while the price continues to fall. When it rises again a new vertical line of crosses is plotted in the next column, and so on. A point-and-figure chart that changes column on every price reversal is cumbersome and many show a reversal only for price changes of three units or more (a unit of plot may be a price change of, say, one penny).

In all charts, different patterns are produced by use of arithmetic or logarithmic scales. An arithmetic scale is calibrated in equal sections for equal absolute changes, whereas the calibration in a logarithmic scale gives equal sections for equal percentage changes.

Virtually all chartists employ colourful, and sometimes almost mystical, terminology. For example, if the share price persistently fails to rise above a certain level this is known as a *resistance level* (Fig. 15.5). This is perhaps because at this price people who bought previously, but then saw the share price fall, took the opportunity to sell at the price they previously paid. Likewise, a *support level* is a price at which buyers constantly seem to come forward to prevent the share price dropping any lower.

A *line* (Fig. 15.6) is a period of consolidation, when the share price moves sideways within a range of about 5 per cent of the share price. Eventually a *break-out* will occur, and it is often suggested that the longer the period of consolidation the greater will be the extent of the ultimate rise or fall.

A *trend line* is a line joining at least two points (often three or more). Advances or declines sometimes appear to be composed of a series of ripples around a straight line. Chartists reckon that in a rising market the trend line is likely to be the one connecting the minor bottoms (Fig. 15.7), and in a declining market the one connecting the tops of the minor rallies. If another line is drawn in parallel, a *channel* is created which can supposedly be used for predicting the extent of the minor rallies and falls.

Probably the best-known pattern is the *head and shoulders* pattern shown in Fig. 15.3. Here the share price rises on buying pressure from investors who have specialist knowledge of the company, and this is later reinforced by other investors 'jumping on the bandwagon'. A major top is formed at A. A reaction sets in as some investors decide to take their profits. Another upsurge then takes place, as the share is still very much in the limelight and no doubt the subject of press comment. A new high top is formed at C. Again buying support is exhausted, as some investors believe the upward trend has been overdone. A reaction takes place back to D; although there is a further rise to E it is based on very little volume of deals, and fails to reach C. The crucial point is reached when the third reaction takes place from E, and if this penetrates the *neckline* it signals, according to the chartists, a significant change in sentiment for the share and the beginning of major decline in price. Another pattern, the *double bottom*, is illustrated in Fig. 15.2. This is very much like the 'head and shoulders' in reverse!

Pure chartists have frequently been the object of ridicule by fundamentalists, who have compared them to astrologers, palmists and readers of tealeaves. Jim Slater of Slater, Walker Securities, when at the height of his fame, referred to them as a bunch of 'long-haired men in ragged overcoats with big overdrafts'.

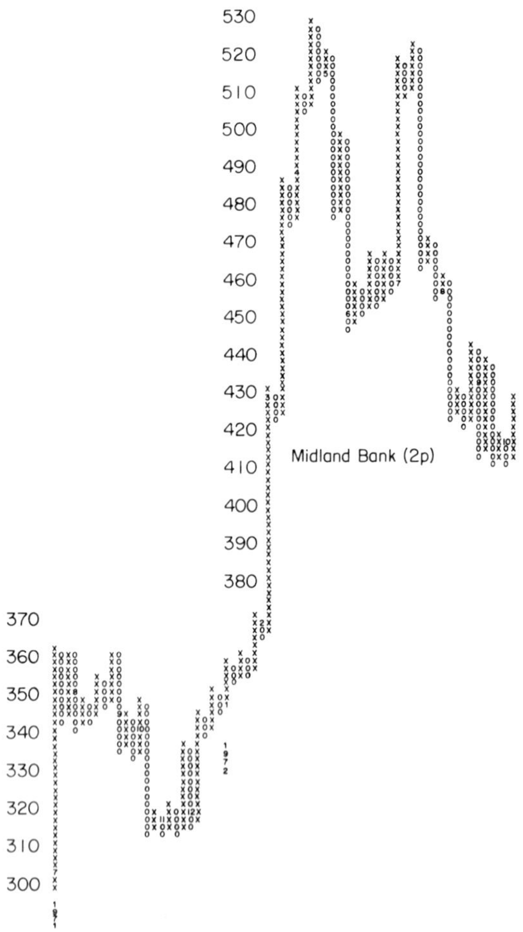

Fig. 15.4 Point-and-figure chart showing 'double top'

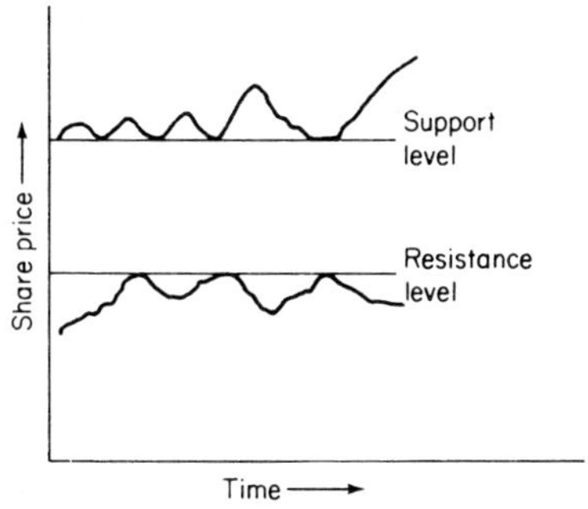

Fig. 15.5 Chart patterns: support level and resistance level

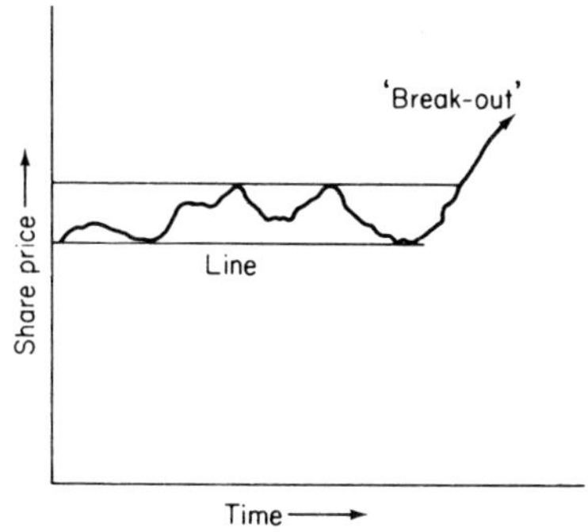

Fig. 15.6 Chart patterns: line and break-out

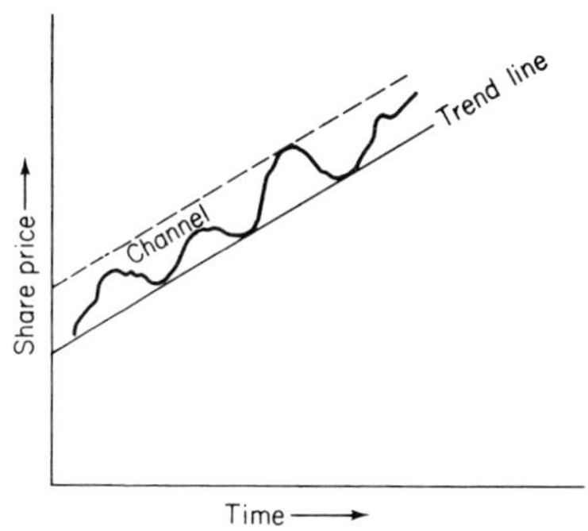

Fig. 15.7 Chart patterns: trend line and channel

The scepticism of the mainstream analysts is due to the absence of any economic foundation to the chartist methodology. Chartism seems to imply that there is no learning process, that there are always 'leaders' and 'followers', and that information about a company is only slowly disseminated through the market. Attempts to measure chartist performances have been inconclusive, as the chartists consistently maintain that their role is not simply a mechanistic one, but rather that it is interpretative. Unfortunately, chartists frequently receive different messages from the same chart!

15.4 Interpretation of the Annual Report and Accounts

To the average investor, the annual report and accounts are the major, if not the only, source of primary information on a public company. They contain, at the very least, a *profit and loss account,* a *balance sheet, notes to the accounts,* the *auditors' report* and a *directors' report*. In addition, most company chairmen issue an annual statement to shareholders, discussing the company's operations during the year, together with some comments about future prospects and often with a few general economic and political remarks thrown in for good

'Hold everything . . . the chairman's daughter has done a drawing for the cover of the annual report.'

measure. In addition to the annual report and accounts, the Stock Exchange requires that listed companies publish half-yearly financial statements. These interim statements are usually unaudited.

The content of the annual report and accounts is governed by the Companies Acts of 1948 and 1967, the accounting bodies and the Stock Exchange. The accounting bodies have attempted to standardize accounting practice by issuing *statements of standard accounting practice* (SSAP). Listed companies in particular are required to follow such standards, violating them only in very exceptional circumstances. They risk the suspension of their quotation if they do not concur, although so far the Stock Exchange has been reluctant to enforce such a penalty.

The report and accounts provide some basis for understanding the business activities and the past financial performance of a company. They indicate to some extent the breakdown of profitability between different areas, and the variability of profits, particularly where this is due to such factors as financial gearing. Experienced analysts, however, build up a picture of a company from a variety of sources, such as trade journals and information received from customers, suppliers and competitors. The 'accounts' are only a starting point. Much of the information contained in the latest set will have been anticipated from other sources, the 'accounts' thus performing a largely confirmatory role.

Some investors naively believe that studying the 'accounts' is all one has to do in order to determine whether or not the shares are 'a good buy'. In fact, the analysis of the report and accounts must be supplemented by a considerable knowledge of the industry, the sector, even the economy as a whole. Different companies have different accounting practices, despite the attempts at standardization. This is not too important if the latest results are seen as part of a series beginning five or ten years before and stretching for the same period into the future. The analyst looks at how the latest results fit into that pattern, and how far they may alter it. The greatest influence on the share price rating in the long term is any evidence of a change in the growth rate. But the hardest part of the job is deciding how far any information revealed by the 'accounts' is already discounted in the share price. The purpose, after all, of fundamental analysis is to discover which shares are 'cheap' or 'dear', not which companies are 'good' or 'bad'.

15.5 Income Statement

Bankers traditionally pay most attention to the balance sheet, because of their interest in security, but equity investors are likely to be far more interested in the *profit and loss account*, an example of which is shown in Table 15.1. This shows the breakdown of sales and profits for a hypothetical company, C W Ltd. It is a *consolidated* profit and loss account, since it relates to a group of companies in the United Kingdom – the parent company and its subsidiary and associated companies.

Table 15.1 Consolidated profit and loss account for C W Ltd for the year ended 31 March 19 . .

		£mn
(i)	Sales outside the group	1 625
(ii)	Trading profit	118
(iii)	Share of profits of associated companies	17
		135
(iv)	Investment income received	5
	Profit before interest and tax	140
	Interest payable	40
	Profit before taxation	100
(v)	Taxation	52
	Profit after taxation	48
(vi)	Net dividends	35
	Retained profit	13

(i) This figure represents sales other than between companies within the group or between units within the one company. Strictly speaking, this item belongs in the *trading account* and is not part of the profit and loss account. The Companies Acts do not impose an obligation to disclose separately the cost of goods sold, wages and salaries, or rents and other expenses.

(ii) This represents the trading profit after deducting various items, including depreciation, audit fees, directors' emoluments, and hire of plant and machinery; the amount of each must be shown, either in the account or in a separate note.

(iii) An *associated* company is one in which the parent company generally has control over from 20 to 50 per cent of the voting capital and influence in the management. In such cases a share of the associate's profit or loss, in proportion to the equity interest, is taken into the consolidated profit and loss account, instead of the dividend income received.

(iv) Other income, not derived from the trading of the company, must be shown separately, and will be detailed in a note to the account.

(v) Taxation is shown here at 52 per cent, but in practice the actual amount is unlikely to be a straight percentage of the profit figure at the prevailing corporation tax rate. A company's liability will in practice be affected by rates of tax paid on overseas income and by various allowances for investment in fixed assets and stocks.

(vi) Net dividends comprise both the preference and the ordinary share dividends net of advance corporation tax. Separately published notes to these accounts would show that there are £4mn and £31mn respectively.

Under the imputation system of corporation tax, in operation since 1973, companies pay dividends to shareholders net of basic-rate income tax, but at the same time make a payment of *advance corporation tax* (ACT) to the Inland Revenue. ACT has always been set at the same rate as the basic rate of income tax. Thus, in 1980, companies made payments of three-sevenths of their 'net' dividends (= 30 per cent of the 'grossed-up' dividends) to the Inland Revenue as ACT. Companies can offset this ACT against their total corporation tax liability, however, reducing the latter by a factor of up to $^{30}/_{52}$. The resultant net liability is known as the *mainstream corporation tax*. The shareholders receive tax (or imputation) credits equal to the ACT paid on their behalf. Gross funds, such as pension funds, and non-taxpayers generally can reclaim them, basic-rate taxpayers have no further liability, and higher-rate taxpayers have to pay the difference between the appropriate higher rate and basic rate, assessed on the 'grossed-up' dividend.

At the time of writing there are three bases for calculating 'earnings' – *nil, net* and *full*; they will be explained by reference to C W Ltd, whose income arises solely in the United Kingdom.

	£mn	
Pretax profits	100	
Corporation tax at 52 per cent	52	
Net profit after tax	48	
Less preference dividend (net)	4	(ACT = 1.71)
Available for ordinary shareholders	44	
Less ordinary dividend (net)	31	(ACT = 13.29)
Retained earnings	13	
Maximum grossed-up ordinary share dividend	62.86	(ACT = 18.86)
Cover	1.42	

Nil basis. This method bases earnings on the assumption that the company pays no ordinary share dividend (even though, as in this case, it does). In our example, the earnings figure will therefore be £44mn (net profit after tax less net preference dividend).

Net basis. This method uses the actual net dividend paid on ordinary shares, plus retentions, to define earnings. Although a total of £15mn in ACT is incurred (three-sevenths of £35mn) it can be entirely offset against the £52mn total corporation tax liability, producing a mainstream corporation tax liability of £37mn (£52mn – £15mn). Thus, because no additional tax is incurred in total, the sum of the net ordinary dividend, £31mn, and the retentions, £13mn, is identical to the 'nil' basis figure of £44mn.

Full (maximum) basis. Earnings under this definition represent the maximum grossed-up dividend that could theoretically be paid from the profits of the year, that is, £62.86mn (£44mn × $^{100}/_{70}$). The actual grossed-up dividend is £44.29mn (£31mn × $^{100}/_{70}$), so the dividend is covered by earnings 1.42 times (£62.86mn divided by £44.29mn).

PE ratios quoted in the *Financial Times* are calculated on the basis of 'net' earnings, while 'full' (maximum) distribution earnings are used in the calculations of dividend cover and earnings yields. *Earnings per share* (EPS) are profits after deduction of interest, tax and preference dividends divided by the number of issued ordinary shares. *Dividends per share* (DPS) are ordinary share dividends divided by the number of issued ordinary shares.

For C W Ltd, whose 2mn ordinary shares were trading at this time for £2.50 each, the appropriate figures and investment ratios are:

$$\text{EPS (net)} = \frac{\text{£44mn}}{\text{200mn}} = 22\text{p} \qquad \text{EPS (full)} = \frac{\text{£62.86mn}}{\text{200mn}} = 31\tfrac{1}{2}\text{p}$$

$$\text{DPS (net)} = \frac{\text{£30mn}}{\text{200mn}} = 15\tfrac{1}{2}\text{p} \qquad \text{DPS (grossed-up)} = 15\tfrac{1}{2}\text{p} \times \frac{100}{100 - 30}$$

$$= 22.1\text{p}$$

$$\text{PE ratio} = \frac{\text{£2.50}}{\text{22p}} = 11.4$$

$$\text{Gross dividend yield} = \frac{22.1}{\text{£2.50}} = 8.8 \text{ per cent}$$

$$\text{Earnings yield} = \frac{31.5\text{p}}{\text{£2.50}} = 12.6 \text{ per cent}$$

So far we have dealt only with the simple case like C W Ltd. Difficulties arise when we introduce unrelieved ACT. This occurs when the ACT charge exceeds $^{30}/_{52}$ of the United Kingdom total corporation tax liability. This can arise as a result of low taxable profits due to capital allowances or stock relief, or simply because a company wishes to pay a dividend out of revenue reserves. The 'excess' ACT can be carried back for two accounting periods and forward indefinitely. Another reason for excess ACT may be that a high proportion of profits is earned overseas. These overseas profits may be used to pay dividends in the United Kingdom but there may be little or no British corporation tax (CT) against which to offset the accompanying ACT. Double taxation agreements exist to prevent foreign earnings being taxed in the United Kingdom without recognition of overseas taxes already paid. The normal rule is to allow overseas corporation taxes paid to be offset against a potential British CT liability. However, any ACT to be paid on a dividend has to be set off against the British CT liability in priority to the application of double taxation relief. This type of excess ACT is known as *unrelieved foreign tax*, and cannot be carried forward. The following example shows the application of the different earnings bases when unrelieved foreign tax arises. It is assumed 70 per cent of profits arise overseas, and that the overseas CT rate is 52 per cent.

	£mn	£mn	
Profit before tax			
Overseas	70		
United Kingdom	30		
		100	
CT at 52 per cent			
Overseas	36.4		
United Kingdom	15.6		
		52	
		48	
Less excess ACT (=unrelieved foreign tax)		6	
		42	
Less dividend payable		35	net (ACT 15)
Retained		7	

'Nil' earnings, representing the maximum that could possibly be retained if the company paid no dividend, are again £44mn. But 'net' earnings, the sum of net ordinary dividends and retentions, are only £38mn (£31mn + £7mn). The difference is the £6mn unrelieved foreign tax. This arises because the ACT of £15mn cannot be totally set off against the total United Kingdom CT liability of £15.6mn. The latter can be reduced by a factor of up to $^{30}/_{52}$, that is, by £9mn to a minimum figure of £6.6mn. This leaves £6mn of surplus ACT. It is unrelieved foreign tax, as illustrated by a reworking of the figures.

	£mn	£mn
Profit before tax		
Overseas	70	
United Kingdom	30	
		100
Overseas CT (52 per cent)		36.4
		63.6
UK CT (52 per cent) on UK income	15.6	
Less ACT relievable against UK income	9	
	6.6	6.6
UK CT on overseas income	36.4	
Less ACT not relievable against UK income	6	
	30.4	
Double taxation relief	30.4	
		57
Net dividend	35	
ACT	15	50
Retentions		7

The 'nil' earnings approach treats the unrelieved foreign tax (and any excess ACT) as simply part of the cost of distribution; under the 'net' approach it is part of the overall tax charge, and thus reduces earnings.

When a company is experiencing unrelieved ACT or unrelieved foreign tax full distribution earnings can be calculated by summing the grossed-up ordinary dividend and the retained earnings. In our example this gives us a figure of £51.29mn (£31mn × $^{100}/_{70}$ + £7mn). Therefore:

$$\text{Dividend cover} = \frac{\text{'Maximum' earnings}}{\text{Grossed-up net ordinary dividend}}$$

$$= \frac{\text{£51.29mn}}{\text{£44.29mn}} = 1.16 \text{ times}$$

If a company is not currently experiencing 'excess' ACT but would do so at some higher rate of distribution of profit, the above definition of 'maximum' earnings can no longer be used. In these circumstances 'maximum' earnings are better defined as the sum of 'nil' earnings and the maximum possible amount of recoverable ACT payable on an ordinary share dividend. In our example this gives a figure of £51.29mn (£44mn 'nil' earnings plus £9mn ACT relievable against United Kingdom income minus £1.7mn ACT payable on the preference dividend). Note that because we are already in a position of 'excess' ACT the two approaches give the same answer for 'maximum' earnings; where there is simply a problem of 'potential' unrelieved ACT the second approach gives a lower figure.

15.6 The Balance Sheet and Other Items

One of the requirements of the Companies Acts is that a balance sheet be sent out to each shareholder and stockholder annually. Where the company has subsidiaries, a consolidated balance sheet must be submitted *in addition to* the balance sheet of the parent company. (The consolidated profit and loss account normally *displaces* the holding company's account.) As with all balance sheets, that of a company shows the position on the day on which it was drawn up. It therefore gives a picture that is already out of date, but nevertheless the information contained can be of interest to the shareholder and, still more so, to the creditor.

Accounts must contain the specific information required by the Companies Acts to be disclosed, and must also show a 'true and fair view' of the state of the company's affairs at the balance sheet date and of the profit or loss for the accounting period covered. A 'true and fair view' means nothing more than an appropriate classification and grouping of the items and therefore the balance sheet needs to show in summary form the amounts of the share capital, reserves and liabilities as on the balance sheet date, and the amounts of the assets representing them, together with sufficient information to indicate the general nature of the items. A 'true and fair view' also implies the consistent application of generally accepted principles.

It is essential to understand that the phrase 'true and fair view' has the technical meaning outlined above, and is not synonymous with 'true worth'. Figures shown in the balance sheet for both fixed and current assets are not the amounts expected to be realized if the company were wound up ('liquidated'). They do not disclose the 'break-up' value of the company's business, but are based on the assumption that the company will continue as a 'going concern'. Except for possible revaluation of land and buildings, fixed assets are generally shown in the accounts at historical cost less an allowance for depreciation. Current assets, including stocks of finished goods and work-in-progress, are also shown in the balance sheet at cost, unless their net realizable value is estimated to be lower than their cost.

The balance sheet in Table 15.2 is presented in the 'net asset' format. *Capital employed* represents the permanent capital tied up in the business, used to finance longer-term assets and also short-term assets not financed from short-term sources.

(i) *Fixed assets* are resources which have a relatively long economic life and are acquired not for resale in the normal course of business, but rather for use in producing other goods and services. They can be subdivided into land and buildings, plant and machinery, and vehicles.

'Convenient it may be to hide our profit in good years as deferred taxation – but when we start hiding our losses too . . .!'

Table 15.2 Consolidated balance sheet for C W Ltd at 31 March 19 . .

		£mn	£mn
(i)	Fixed assets		500
(ii)	Goodwill		100
(iii)	Investments		40
(iv)	Long-term debtors		10
			650
(v)	Current assets:		
	Stock and work-in-progress	400	
	Debtors	250	
	Cash	75	
		725	
	Less:		
(vi)	Current liabilities:		
	Creditors	300	
	Current taxation	40	
	Proposed final dividends	25	
	Bank overdraft	75	
		440	
(vii)	Net current assets		285
(viii)	Net assets		935
Financed by:			
	200mn Ordinary £1 shares issued fully paid	200	
(ix)	Share premium account	50	
	Other reserves	410	
	Ordinary shareholders' interest		660
	50mn 8% cumulative preference shares issued fully paid		50
(x)	Medium and long-term borrowings		225
	Capital employed		935

(ii) *Goodwill* is the excess of the purchase price paid by a parent company for its investment in a subsidiary over the net book value of the subsidiary's assets less its liabilities at the time of its acquisition. It is considered as an 'intangible' asset.

(iii) *Investments* are usually trade investments, which represent holdings of shares (or other securities) in other companies; they are investments made for the purposes of the business and therefore not readily realizable. Interests in customers, suppliers or even competitors are included under this heading.

(iv) *Long-term debtors* are defined as amounts which are receivable more than twelve months from the balance sheet date.

(v) *Current assets* generally include cash in hand and at the bank, together with assets expected to be converted into cash (such as debtors) or consumed in the business (such as stocks of raw materials) within twelve months from the balance sheet date.

(vi) *Current liabilities* are liabilities due to be paid within twelve months from the balance sheet date. Strictly speaking, that part of the tax liability which is payable more than a year hence should be shown as a separate item. Bank overdrafts are included because in theory they are recallable on demand, but in practice they are frequently 'rolled over' from year to year.

(vii) *Net current assets* represent 'net working capital', that part of current assets which must be financed from longer-term funds.

(viii) *Net assets* represent those assets financed by longer-term funds.

(ix) *Share premium account* is the excess of the actual proceeds of share issues over their nominal ('par') value. It is treated in the accounts as a capital reserve which, in contrast to a revenue reserve, is not available for distribution as dividends.

(x) *Medium- and long-term borrowings* are loans repayable more than twelve months from the balance sheet date. In the case of C W Ltd these consist of

£50mn 10% mortgage debenture 1987
£100mn secured medium-term bank loan – variable-rate 1990
£75mn 12% unsecured loan stock 1992

(*a*) **Sources and Application of Funds Statement**

All listed companies are now required to provide a consolidated sources and application of funds statement. The actual format of the table tends to vary from one company to another, but all show the internal and external sources of funds and where they have been invested. The statements are useful, taking several years together, for predicting external fund-raising operations dictated by the inability of internal funds alone to sustain the company's planned investment programme.

One important internal 'source' of funds is *depreciation*, which is a deduction from profit but which does not represent an actual outflow of cash. Cash is only expended when an asset is bought; depreciation is part of the accrual system of matching revenue and expenditure period by period. Analysts frequently use retained earnings and depreciation allowances as a proxy for *cash flow*, and this figure can then be compared with future capital commitments, whether contracted yet or not. Unfortunately, the notes to the accounts normally only give details of fixed-capital expenditure intentions, so some forecast needs to be made of likely changes in net working capital. Changes in tax liabilities will also affect the cash flow position.

(*b*) Inflation Accounting

During the 1970s, with inflation seemingly endemic in the British economy, accountants and investors became increasingly aware of the need to introduce some form of inflation accounting. The method eventually adopted, and issued as *Statement of Standard Accounting Practice 16* (SSAP 16), is a form of current cost accounting based largely on specific replacement costs of assets, rather than a system adjusting for changes in the purchasing power of money.

SSAP 16 is mandatory for all listed companies and also for large unquoted companies. It applies to published accounts for periods beginning after 1 January 1980. It requires these companies to show the impact of inflation by means of an adjusted profit and loss account and balance sheet, which can supplement or take precedence over the historical accounts. The essence of any system of current cost accounting is the distinction between the gains from 'making' and 'selling', and the gains through simply holding real assets during a time of inflation. The former are termed *operating gains* (operating profit); the latter are *holding gains*, whether realized or unrealized.

Operating profit is often equated with 'real' profit, that is, the maximum that might be prudently distributed without jeopardizing the scale of the existing business. It therefore differs from historic cost profit in that there is a deduction for extra depreciation (the excess of replacement over historic cost depreciation) and also a *cost of sales adjustment* (COSA) to reflect the difference between the replacement cost and the original purchase price of stock used.

Some businesses have the additional difficulty of financing trade debtors, a problem that increases with inflation, while other companies, such as stores, find that trade debtors and all or part of stock appreciation can be financed by an increase in trade creditors. SSAP 16 provides for these differences by means of a *monetary working capital adjustment* (MWCA). Monetary working capital is defined as trade debtors minus trade creditors. When this figure is positive, the MWCA supplements the COSA, but when it is negative it offsets some of the impact of the COSA. These three adjustments to historic cost profit produce *current cost operating profit*.

In order to arrive at the *current cost profit attributable to the shareholders* SSAP 16 introduces a *gearing adjustment* to be applied to the operating profit. This is to allow for the fact that part of the inflationary increase in fixed and working capital could be financed by increased borrowing, excluding trade creditors, without upsetting traditional balance sheet gearing ratios. The proportion of the net operating assets, at current cost, financed by net borrowing represents the proportion of the deductions for additional depreciation, COSA, and any MWCA that can be added back to profit because they can be debt-financed (see Table 15.3).

The impact of SSAP 16 on companies' ability to pay dividends appears to be adverse. Phillips and Drew estimated an average fall in pretax profits of 36 per cent in 1979, and 40 to 45 per cent in 1980, where the 'standard' is used instead of traditional historic cost accounting. As a consequence, average CCA dividend cover fell to 1.1 times in 1980, almost half their sample of 150 major

Table 15.3 The calculation of current cost profit

	Historic cost profit
−	(a) (replacement cost − historic cost depreciation)
−	(b) (cost of sales adjustment)
−	(c) (monetary working capital adjustment)
=	current cost operating profit
+/−	net interest
+	$(a + b + c) \times \dfrac{\text{net borrowed funds}}{\text{net operating assets}}$
−	taxation
=	current cost profit attributable to shareholders

quoted companies paying dividends not fully covered by CCA earnings, on the basis of unchanged policies. According to another broker, W. Greenwell, the sectors to suffer the greatest diminution in earnings under inflation accounting are textiles, motors and distributors, metals, chemicals, oil (BP), mechanical engineering, packaging and paper, banks and pharmaceuticals. The service sector is relatively unaffected.

To a considerable degree the stock market had anticipated the introduction of inflation accounting in its relative rating of different sectors, and companies had increased their historic cost dividend cover during the 1970s. The latter was partly because of the statutory limitation of dividends, but also no doubt due to a recognition of the need to preserve capital.

In 1950 the payout ratio for larger quoted companies in manufacturing, distribution and other services was 31 per cent. This increased fairly consistently to 66 per cent by 1962 and remained above 50 per cent for most of the 1960s, but dropped to 26 per cent in 1972. At the end of 1979 the payout ratio of the FT Industrial Group (493 companies) Actuaries Index was still only 38 per cent.

(*c*) The Directors' Report

This gives certain factual information relating to the year under review, which has to be disclosed by law. The most interesting points are the recommended final dividend, the directors and any change in their shareholdings, the current valuations of properties relative to their book value, details of any interests of over 5 per cent in the company, and any breakdown of the profit figures.

(*d*) Report of the Auditors

One of the first tasks of any user of accounts is to check to see that the auditors have not 'qualified' their approval in any way. But even this does not guarantee the best method of presentation. The survey of published accounts in 1977–78, for example, shows that only six from three hundred companies had their accounts qualified for non-compliance with an accounting standard. Any proposed change of auditors should be noted in the directors' report.

15.7 Ratio Analysis

Ratio analysis is an important tool in investment, enabling the analyst to highlight the salient figures in the accounts and to make comparisons with previous years (to establish trends) or with rival companies or some industrial average, although ratios rarely tell the user much when considered in isolation. They are usually grouped into four main categories: *liquidity*, *gearing*, *activity* and *profitability*.

15.8 Liquidity Ratios

Generally the investment analyst's first concern is liquidity: has the company sufficient cash to meet its immediate trading needs? Although on the 'accruals' system of accounting income and expenditure may appear stable, actual payments and receipts of cash are frequently more irregular, and differ in their actual timing. The bank overdraft is ideally suited to accommodate fluctuations in financial flows, enabling the company to meet its bills as they fall due.

Most companies make use to some degree of short-term sources of finance, principally trade creditors and the banks. Normally, both of these are willing to continue such lending on a 'revolving' basis, providing the company is trading profitably. If there is any suspicion about the company's ability to meet its debts, however, suppliers might refuse to continue to trade with it except on a cash basis, and the bank might refuse to extend further overdraft facilities. It is therefore essential that a company retains the confidence of its trade creditors and bankers. One way of doing this is by demonstrating that it could repay their lending if necessary. The two most commonly used measures of liquidity are the *current ratio* and the *quick assets ratio*.

(*a*) Current Ratio

The *current ratio* or *working capital ratio* is computed by dividing current assets by current liabilities. It indicates the extent to which the claims of short-term creditors are covered by assets that are expected to be converted to cash during the next year. For C W Ltd (see Table 15.2):

$$\frac{\text{Current assets}}{\text{Current liabilities}} = \frac{£725\text{mn}}{£440\text{mn}} = 1.65{:}1$$

(*b*) Quick Assets Ratio

The disadvantage of the current ratio is that it treats all current assets as being equally liquid. The *quick assets ratio* (sometimes called the *liquid* or *'acid test' ratio*) excludes stock. The reasons for this omission are (i) that stock is at once the least liquid of the current assets, and the current asset on which losses are most likely to occur in the event of a disposal, and (ii) that the company could not continue to trade effectively with stocks below a certain minimum level. For C W Ltd,

$$\text{Quick assets ratio} = \frac{\text{Current assets} - \text{Stock}}{\text{Current liabilities}}$$

$$= \frac{\pounds725\text{mn} - \pounds400\text{mn}}{\pounds440\text{mn}} = 0.74{:}1$$

The traditionally acceptable minimum values for current and quick assets ratios are 2:1 and 1:1 respectively. By present-day standards, however, these appear rather high.

15.9 Gearing Ratios

Gearing (or leverage, as the Americans refer to it) shows the relationship between a company's creditors and its shareholders. There are two main types of gearing ratio – *capital* and *income*. Capital ratios show the proportion of funds supplied by the creditors as compared with those from the owners. The higher the proportion of borrowings, the higher the capital gearing. This ratio can be expressed in *book value* (balance sheet) terms, or using *market values* if the securities are quoted.

Income gearing shows the distribution of income among the holders of the different classes of capital. If a company has a high proportion of interest payments relative to shareholders' earnings, it again is said to be highly geared. There are no agreed definitions of gearing, however, and within each of the two main categories there are several different ratios. The main difficulty lies in deciding what types of prior charge capital to include.

(*a*) Capital Gearing

(i) **Capital gearing ratio.** This is designed to give lenders some indication of the protection for their loans. If the company were to go into liquidation would the assets be sufficient to repay the creditors in full, given that some items, such as plant and machinery, are unlikely to realize their book values? Goodwill is deducted, as it is an intangible asset. The ratio is defined as:

$$\text{Capital gearing ratio} = \frac{\text{Borrowed funds}}{\text{Total funds} - \text{Intangibles}}$$

The difficulty lies in deciding what items to include in the numerator and denominator. One view is that capital gearing should measure simply the capital structure – that is, it should be restricted to the long-term financing of the company represented by long-term debt, preference shares and net worth (ordinary shareholders' funds). In this way, 'capital structure' is distinguished from 'financial structure', which also includes all forms of short-term debt.

Most analysts include preference shares as part of borrowed funds because they are fixed-return securities, although unlike loan capital interest, preference share dividends can be 'passed' with relative impunity. Bank borrowings are generally more important than preference shares. Often medium-term bank loans have replaced debentures and loan stocks, and there is no case for omitting them from 'borrowed funds'. Likewise, there is a very strong argument for including bank overdrafts, especially if in practice they are of a semi-permanent nature. Indeed, any contractual obligation, such as leasing, should be capitalized and included. The inclusion of short-term liabilities (such as taxation, trade creditors and accruals) is more debatable, particularly if they fluctuate a great deal.

Difficulties arise not only from having to decide what items to include in the ratio, but also how to value them. For example, should shares and loans be included at balance sheet or stock market values? Shareholders' funds in the balance sheet can now be expressed in terms of either historic or current (inflation-adjusted) costs. There are arguments for and against each approach, but traditionally the ratio has been restricted to permanent sources of funds, shown at historic cost balance sheet valuations. For C W Ltd,

$$\text{Capital gearing ratio} = \frac{\pounds 275\text{mn}}{\pounds 935\text{mn} - \pounds 100\text{mn}}$$
$$= 0.33$$

(Preference shares are included in the 'borrowed funds' in the numerator, but short-term bank borrowings have been excluded.)

(ii) **Capital cover and priority percentages**. Debt-holders and other lenders may be more interested in the security of their particular loan, rather than in the indebtedness of the company as a whole. It is possible to calculate capital cover for each type of loan, but this should be done on a cumulative basis. In this way it is never possible for a lower-ranking security to have a greater cover than a higher-ranking one. For C W Ltd, we can list the prior charge capital in descending order of priority and calculate capital cover for each:

	Amount	*Capital cover*
10% mortgage debenture	£50mn	$\frac{\pounds 835\text{mn}}{\pounds 50\text{mn}} = 16.7$ times
Medium-term bank loan	£100mn	$\frac{\pounds 835\text{mn}}{\pounds 150\text{mn}} = 5.57$
12% unsecured loan stock	£75mn	$\frac{\pounds 835\text{mn}}{\pounds 225\text{mn}} = 3.71$
8% cumulative preference shares	£50mn	$\frac{\pounds 835\text{mn}}{\pounds 275\text{mn}} = 3.04$

Note that for reasons of simplicity current liabilities and their equivalent assets have been ignored in the calculation.

An alternative way of presenting the same information is in terms of *capital priority percentages*. These tables show what proportion of assets belong to different types of capital, again in descending order of priority. Thus:

	Percentage of assets	*Priority percentage*
10% mortgage debenture	$\frac{£50mn}{£835mn} \times 100 = 6$	0–6
Medium-term bank loan	$\frac{£100mn}{£835mn} \times 100 = 12$	6–18
12% unsecured loan stock	$\frac{£75mn}{£835mn} \times 100 = 9$	18–27
8% cumulative preference shares	$\frac{£50mn}{£835mn} \times 100 = 6$	27–33

(iii) **Proprietary ratio.** The converse of the capital gearing ratio is the proprietary ratio, which is defined as:

$$\text{Proprietary ratio} = \frac{\text{Shareholders' funds}}{\text{Total funds} - \text{Intangibles}}$$

If preference shares are included in the numerator, and intangibles are deducted from both the numerator and the denominator, the resulting figure is the proportion of the total book amounts of the tangible assets which would be lost on a forced realization before the investments of unsecured creditors were jeopardized. For C W Ltd,

$$\text{Proprietary ratio} = \frac{£660\text{mn} + £50\text{mn} - £100\text{mn}}{£935\text{mn} - £100\text{mn}}$$

$$= 0.73$$

(*b*) **Income Gearing**

While capital ratios are very much akin to 'shutting the stable door after the horse has bolted', in that they are concerned with the ability to repay loans in the event of a liquidation, income ratios have the merit of measuring directly the ability of a company to service the interest on borrowed funds. The two most popular types of income ratio are *interest times covered* and *income priority percentages*.

(i) **Interest times covered.** This is defined as:

$$\text{Interest times covered} = \frac{\text{Profit before interest and tax}}{\text{Gross interest payments}}$$

This measures the extent to which profits can decline without resulting in financial embarrassment to the company because of an inability to meet annual interest costs. For C W Ltd,

$$\text{Interest cover} = \frac{\pounds 140\text{mn}}{\pounds 40\text{mn}} = 3.5 \text{ times}$$

With high rates of interest, it is usually the interest cover constraint that limits further borrowing, rather than asset cover.

(ii) **Income cover and priority percentages.** Income priority percentage tables are similar to the capital version introduced in Unit 15.9(*a*)(ii), except that they show the particular slice of the total profits that is used to remunerate a specific stock, rather than the percentage of assets relating to that stock. For C W Ltd, we can list the income priority percentages and income cover as follows:

	Available profits	*Net income required for charge*	*Cumulative total*	*Percentage of profit taken (rounded)*	*Priority percentage (rounded)*	*Income cover*
	£mn	£mn	£mn			
£50mn 10% mortgage debenture	67.2	2.4	2.4	4	0–4	25 times
£100mn medium-term bank loan (15% gross)	64.8	7.2	9.6	11	4–14	7 times
£75mn bank overdraft (14¾ gross)	57.6	5.3	14.9	8	14–22	4½ times
£75mn 12% unsecured loan stock	52.3	4.3	19.2	6	22–29	3½ times
£50mn 8% cumulative preference share	48	4	23.2	6	29–35	3 times
Ordinary dividend	44	31	54.2	46	35–81	1¼ times
Retentions	13	13	67.2	19	81–100	

Profits and interest on borrowings are taken net of tax at 52 per cent. The net-of-tax cost of servicing the interest, £19.2mn (£40mn × (1 − 0.52)), is added to the net-of-tax profit figure, £48mn, to determine the available profits of £67.2mn.

Taking the reciprocal of the priority percentages gives a much sounder indication of cover than that obtained by comparing the profits available for a particular item of capital with its individual income requirement. If we take C W Ltd's ordinary shares, for example, a 'naive' comparison of 'available profits' (£44mn) with 'income required' (£31mn) suggests a cover of 1.42. Indeed this is the figure mentioned in Unit 15.5, and would be the figure quoted in the press. But dividend cover calculated on a cumulative basis (total available profits of £67.2mn divided by total charges of £54.2mn) is only 1.24. This tells the investor more about the security of the dividend – that total profits are currently only 24 per cent more than is required to cover the present distribution and prior claims.

15.10 Activity Ratios

Activity ratios measure how effectively the company employs the resources at its command. These ratios all involve dividing the sales figure by the level of investment in various categories of asset. A ratio that is low compared to the average from the past, or to that of rival companies, suggests that there is an underemployment of assets and usually reflects poor management. A high ratio may indicate that the company's asset base is too narrow, that recent investment has been inadequate, and that further capital may be required to finance sales. Overhasty conclusions should not be drawn, however, as changes may simply reflect shifts in company policy in accounting practice, factoring of debtors, leasing of assets or revaluations.

(*a*) **Total Assets Turnover**
This ratio is defined thus:

$$\text{Total assets turnover} = \frac{\text{Sales}}{\text{Net tangible assets}}$$

For C W Ltd,

$$\text{Total assets turnover} = \frac{£1\ 625\text{mn}}{£835\text{mn}} = 1.95 \text{ times}$$

(*b*) **Stock Turnover**
For C W Ltd, this ratio is given by:

$$\text{Stock turnover} = \frac{\text{Sales}}{\text{Stocks}}$$

$$= \frac{£1\ 625\text{mn}}{£400\text{mn}} = 4.06 \text{ times}$$

(*c*) **Credit Granted to Debtors**
The relationship between trade debtors and sales can be expressed in terms of *either* the number of times debtors are turned over in a year, *or* the average number of days a debt is outstanding. For C W Ltd the ratios are:

$$\text{Trade debtor turnover} = \frac{\text{Sales}}{\text{Trade debtors}}$$

$$= \frac{£1\ 625\text{mn}}{£250\text{mn}} = 6.5 \text{ times}$$

$$\text{Average collection period} = \frac{\text{Trade debtors}}{\text{Sales}} \times 365$$

$$= \frac{\pounds 250\text{mn}}{\pounds 1\ 625\text{mn}} \times 365 = 56 \text{ days}$$

(Long-term debtors have been excluded.)

A reduction in debtor turnover (increase in the average collection period) may be indicative of inefficiency in credit control, and may lead an analyst to suspect an increase in the proportion of bad debts.

15.11 Profitability Ratios

(*a*) Return on Capital Employed

This is the prime measure of profitability, and one of the key ratios overall. It is defined as:

$$\text{Return on capital employed (ROCE)} = \frac{\text{Profit before interest and tax}}{\text{Capital employed} - \text{Intangibles}}$$

For C W Ltd,

$$\text{Percentage ROCE} = \frac{\pounds 140\text{mn}}{\pounds 835\text{mn}} \times 100 = 16.8 \text{ per cent}$$

To be precise, bank overdraft interest (£11mn) should be deducted from the profit figure, as the bank overdraft is not included in the figure for capital employed.

(*b*) Profit Margin

The profit margin is the profit expressed as a percentage of sales. Using the same profit figure as before, for C W Ltd:

$$\text{Percentage profit margin} = \frac{\text{Profit}}{\text{Sales}} \times 100$$

$$= \frac{\pounds 140\text{mn}}{\pounds 1\ 625\text{mn}} = 8.6 \text{ per cent}$$

Some analysts would argue that 'profit' should be trading profit, before deducting such items as depreciation, auditors' remuneration and directors' emoluments, and adding investment income. Sales of associated companies are not normally consolidated, so there is a strong case for omitting 'share of results of associated companies'. But the case for adopting the simple approach is that it illustrates the fundamental relationship determining return on capital employed (ROCE), that is:

$$\text{ROCE} = \frac{\text{Profit}}{\text{Assets}} = \frac{\text{Profit}}{\text{Sales}} \times \frac{\text{Sales}}{\text{Assets}}$$

Provided that these three ratios are defined consistently it should be possible to diagnose the causes of changes in the return on capital employed.

The relationship between the profit margin and the asset turnover demonstrates that no one ratio should be considered in isolation. In retailing, for example, discount warehouses tend to have a much higher asset turnover than traditional department stores, but their 'stack 'em high, sell 'em cheap' philosophy means a lower profit margin. It is the overall impact in terms of return on capital that matters.

(*c*) Return on Ordinary Shareholders' Funds

This will differ from ROCE because of the effect of gearing, and also because it is usually expressed net of the total corporation tax charge. For C W Ltd it is calculated as follows:

Return on ordinary shareholders' funds

$$= \frac{\text{Earnings attributable to ordinary shareholders}}{\text{Ordinary shareholders' funds} - \text{Intangibles}}$$

$$= \frac{\pounds 44\text{mn}}{\pounds 660\text{mn} - \pounds 100\text{mn}} = 7.9 \text{ per cent}$$

(*d*) Net Asset Value per Share

The *net asset value per share* is the value of shareholders' assets (minus intangibles) divided by the number of shares outstanding. For C W Ltd the values are:

$$\text{Net asset value per share} = \frac{\pounds 660\text{mn} - \pounds 100\text{mn}}{200\text{mn}} = \pounds 2.80$$

That part of the proposed final dividends relating to the ordinary shares could also be added to the numerator.

A share would normally be expected to sell at a premium to its net asset value, as investors would be willing to pay something for 'goodwill' – the company's management, expertise and reputation. But during the 1970s, because of low returns on capital, many companies had share values significantly below their net asset values per share, especially in current cost terms. Under such circumstances the asset backing may give an underpinning to the share price, as the share is valued on the basis of its assets rather than its earnings.

Attention to the net asset value per share presumes either that sooner or later the company will earn an acceptable return on capital, or that it will be taken over, or that the assets will be liquidated. The *equity valuation ratio* (the market value of the share divided by its net asset value) can be a good indicator of a take-over 'victim'; if so, the bid price will be influenced by the net asset value per share, and will usually exceed the historical cost value. For C W Ltd,

$$\text{Equity valuation ratio} = \frac{£2.50}{£2.80} = 0.89$$

Many companies manage to remain independent, however, despite a persistently low valuation ratio. The extent of directors' shareholdings may give some indication of their ability to frustrate any approach. They are unlikely to liquidate the company voluntarily, for reasons of self interest or concern for their workers, or because of heavy redundancy and other closure costs. Moreover, both historical cost and current cost valuations are based on the 'going concern' assumption. One would need to examine the constituents of the shareholders' assets to make an estimate of possible liquidation values.

15.12 Sources of Information

It is not necessary to send for copies of the accounts in order to obtain the required information. It is published in the card services of the Exchange Telegraph Company. These *Extel cards* and fact sheets are produced for every company listed on the Stock Exchange, and also for a large number of unquoted companies and North American and Australian companies. Most brokers subscribe to one of these services and they will make cards available to their clients. Many of the large bank branches also subscribe, and a customer requiring a card of a particular company can always ask his branch to obtain it from their brokers if they do not hold it themselves.

The information shown on annual cards includes:

(i) profit and loss accounts;
(ii) balance sheets;
(iii) details of recent statements regarding acquisitions, trading prospects, interim dividends, capital issues and so on;
(iv) capital history;
(v) names of directors;
(vi) market price high and low points;
(vii) net asset value;
(viii) useful tables such as sources and uses and income priority percentages.

The news cards provide more up-to-date information, but they are obviously less detailed.

Those investors who deal directly with a stockbroker should receive regular circulars and company studies, which are restricted to stockbrokers' clients. In addition, the *Financial Times* and the financial pages of other quality newspapers are important sources of information, together with weekly publications such as the *Investor's Chronicle*, the *Financial Weekly* and, in more general terms, the *Economist*. A press cuttings service is provided by McCarthy Information Services, which keeps a constant watch for news and comment on listed companies in the leading newspapers and magazines. This service is taken by major libraries.

For the investor who is determined to be closely involved, the *Stock Exchange Fact Book*, published quarterly, deals with securities generally, and the *Stock Exchange Official Year Book* gives details of individual listed companies. Copies of the latter are available in the reference section of most public libraries. It is extremely useful because it summarizes the mass of information recorded in a company's file at Companies House, with the exception of the list of members and the annual report and accounts.

At Companies House, in Cardiff and London, a separate file is kept for every registered company (the London ones are on microfilm). A file may be inspected by any member of the public for the payment of a small fee. The file contains the memorandum and articles of association, the prospectus, mortgages and charges, the annual return and the annual report and accounts. If an analyst feels the consolidated accounts are inadequate, he can extract the names of the subsidiaries from the annual report and investigate the subsidiary accounts at Companies House if they are companies registered in the United Kingdom (in Edinburgh for Scottish registered companies). The accounts of limited liability subsidiaries must comply with company law in the same way as those of the parent company.

A company must also maintain at its registered office certain registers which again may be inspected by the general public, for a small fee for each register inspected. All of them are included in the annual return at Companies House, but those at the registered office will be more up to date, especially the register of shareholdings.

15.13 Conclusion

For anyone other than the specialist analyst concentrating on only a handful of companies, there is a danger of being overwhelmed by accounting information. Ratio analysis makes it possible to extract the key points in the report and accounts. But ratios are not an end in themselves; they simply provide a means of judging the present and future risk and return prospects of a company generally, and of its equity capital in particular.

The hardest task in fundamental analysis is not analysing the accounts, but rather deciding how far your assessment of them, and other sources of information, is already reflected in the current share price. Supporters of the *efficient market hypothesis* (discussed in Unit 16.4) believe that share prices fully 'discount' most, if not all, published information almost as soon as it becomes available.

15.14 Questions

1. (*a*) Distinguish between fundamental analysis and technical analysis as methods of investment analysis.
   (*b*) Is investment a matter of 'what' to buy or sell, or 'when' to buy or sell?

2. What are the implications for investors of the adoption of the current cost system of inflation accounting?

3. **XYZ Co Ltd: balance sheet as at 31 December 19 . .**

	£	£	£
Fixed assets			
Land and buildings	300 000		
Plant, machinery, vehicles	190 000		
Fixtures and fittings	20 000		
			510 000
Quoted investments			90 000
Current assets			
Stock, work in progress	350 000		
Debtors	500 000		
Cash at bank and in hand	138 000		
		988 000	
Current liabilities			
Creditors	418 000		
Taxation	74 000		
Proposed dividend	50 000		
		542 000	
Net current assets			446 000
Goodwill			170 000
			£1 216 000
Represented by:			
500 000 ordinary £1 shares fully paid			500 000
Share premium account			36 000
Revenue reserves			230 000
			766 000
300 000 7% cumulative preference £1 shares fully paid			300 000
150 000 8% debenture stock, 1983–89			150 000
			£1 216 000

(*a*) From the foregoing balance sheet of XYZ Co Ltd, calculate (i) the capital priority percentages and overall cover, (ii) the current ratio and (iii) the liquidity ratio.
(*b*) What do the resultant figures mean and to whom are they important?
(*c*) From the balance sheet figures, calculate the break-up value of the ordinary shares.
(*d*) Why should an investor be cautious about comparisons between the net asset value of a share and the market value?

(*e*) In the case of XYZ Co Ltd, if the market price of the ordinary shares was, say, 250p per share, what might this indicate to you? Supposing the market price was substantially below the net asset value of the share, what could this mean?

Unit Sixteen

Portfolio Management and Review

16.1 The Stock Market Indices

Stock market indices show the movement over time in aggregate share prices, or the prices of other securities. In the United Kingdom the best known and the most widely used are those published by the *Financial Times*. The share price indices are of two types – the *FT Industrial Ordinary* (or *30 Share*) *Index* and the *FT-Actuaries Indices*. Their functions and methods of calculation are fundamentally different.

(*a*) FT Industrial Ordinary (30 Share) Index

This is the 'original' *Financial Times* index, begun in 1935, and the one which receives most publicity. It is a price index of the equities of thirty leading industrial and commercial companies in Britain. The thirty are chosen to give a wide range of industry and distribution, each being a leader in its field, and together they have always represented a relatively large part of the equity market as a whole (in May 1975 it was approximately one-quarter). In January 1981 the constituents of the Index were:

Allied Breweries
Beecham Group
Blue Circle Group
Boots
Bowater
John Brown
British Oxygen
British Petroleum
Cadbury Schweppes
Courtaulds*
Distillers*
Dunlop*
GEC*
Glaxo Group
Grand Metropolitan
GKN*
Hawker Siddeley Group*
ICI*
Imperial Group*
London Brick*
Lucas Industries
Marks and Spencer
P & O Navigation
Plessey
Tate and Lyle*
Thorn
Tube Investments
Turner and Newall*
UDS Group
Vickers*

Companies marked * have been in the Index since its compilation began. Until fairly recently no oil companies were included, but British Petroleum replaced

Cavenham in April 1975, being considered acceptable because of its domestic interests in the North Sea. All financial companies are still excluded, however.

From its inception the purpose of the Index has always been to show the 'mood' of the equity market – whether it is 'bullish', 'bearish' or 'flat' – and the strength of these moods. Thirty was considered the optimal number because index readings on a few shares had little stability, but as the number was increased beyond thirty the readings flattened out because of the inactivity in dealing in many second-line shares (the New York Dow-Jones Index uses the same number). This factor, together with the tendency of these shares to 'follow' the leading industrials, meant that with their inclusion the desired sensitivity of the Index to changes in sentiment would have been lost.

The FT 30 Share Index is an *unweighted geometric mean* of the price-relatives of the individual constituents. (The *price-relative* of a share is the current share price divided by the price at a base date.) The geometric mean is obtained by multiplying these thirty values together, and taking the thirtieth root of the result; in practice, it is only necessary to multiply the thirty current prices together and then divide by a constant, before taking the thirtieth root. Because of its construction, the FT 30 Share Index places equal weight on each fractional price change, irrespective of the market capitalization of the company. The value of the Index on the base date, 1 July 1935, is taken as 100.

Except where all the numbers have equal values, a geometric mean always understates an arithmetic one. The difference between the two averages is larger the wider the distribution of numbers. The FT 30 Share Index is less affected than an arithmetic index would be by exceptionally large price increases for a small number of shares, but more so should they show abnormal falls in price. In the extreme case, one share price falling to zero would reduce the Index to zero, but in practice such a share would be replaced well before that point was reached. Some shares have been replaced because of take-over, either by another company or through nationalization. A new share is then introduced at a base price that leaves the Index unchanged.

Another advantage of having only thirty shares in the Index is that it can be calculated frequently, in practice seven times a day, every hour on the hour from 10 a.m. to 3 p.m. inclusive, and at the 'close'. The prices for the Index are telephoned from the floor of the Stock Exchange by *Financial Times* representatives. The 'close' Index represents the position at the end of the day's trading and is based on the final prices obtained from the jobbers' offices, usually by 5.15 p.m.

The Index reflects movements in the stock market as a whole reasonably well. As illustrated in Fig. 16.1, it reached low points in June 1940, with an all-time low of 49.4, and in January 1975 with a fall to 146; a then record high was 558.6, reached on the day following the Conservative election victory of May 1979. In recent years its performance has been less impressive than those of more widely based indices because of its heavy emphasis on manufacturing companies at the expense of the service sector.

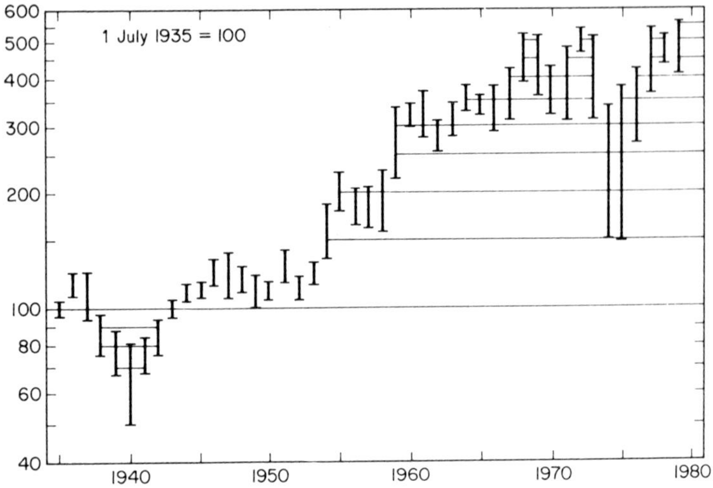

Fig. 16.1 FT Industrial Ordinary Index, 1935–80: annual highs and lows

(*b*) **The FT-Actuaries Share Indices**

The FT-Actuaries Share Indices are designed specifically to measure portfolio performance and so named because they are jointly compiled by the *Financial Times*, the Institute of Actuaries and the Faculty of Actuaries. A large number of these indices are published in the *Financial Times* every day except Mondays. Thirty-six are subsections and seven are major equity groupings. Each index shows in parentheses the number of companies included in it. They can be summarized as follows:

Indices		*Number of shares*
Capital goods		211
Consumer group		199
Other groups		78
	Industrial group	488
Oils		12
	500 Share Index	500
Financial group		118
Investment trusts		109
Mining finance		3
Overseas traders		20
	All Share Index	750

The indices were designed to cover a sufficiently large number of shares to enable their subdivision into groups and subsections having adequate representation in each. In the 'Other groups' category, however, the 'Chemicals' (15 companies) subsection is dominated by ICI, and that for 'Office Equipment' (6) by the Rank Organisation.

The FT-Actuaries Share Indices' principal function is to serve as a reliable measure of portfolio performance. They are *weighted arithmetic means*, in which a price-relative is calculated for each share in an index and then *weighted* by multiplying it by the equity market capitalization (the total market value of the ordinary shares) of the company at the base date. These figures are then added together for all the shares in an index, and the sum is divided by their total equity market capitalization at the base date. The resulting quotient is then expressed in terms of the base date value of 100.

From time to time the weights are modified to take account of capital or constituent changes. For this purpose a 'chain-index' procedure is used, the first 'link' in the chain being the movement in the index from the base date, usually 10 April 1962, to the date of the first capital change. The index is restarted at 100 with new weights, reflecting the new market capitalizations after the change, but this 'new' index is adjusted by a constant factor reflecting the value of the 'old' index at the change-over date, thus preserving continuity.

The indices reproduce the performance of 'model' portfolios in which the holding of each constituent is always proportional to the total market value of its ordinary shares. The model portfolio will 'take up' any 'rights', increasing its holding of that particular constituent and reducing those of all the others, so that the resulting holding of each constituent is still proportional to the new equity market valuations (the implication is that no dividend income is re-invested).

The *All Share Index* (Fig. 16.2) is usually regarded as the yardstick by which to measure the performance of an equity fund. It represents over three-quarters of the total market value of equities on the Stock Exchange. Certainly

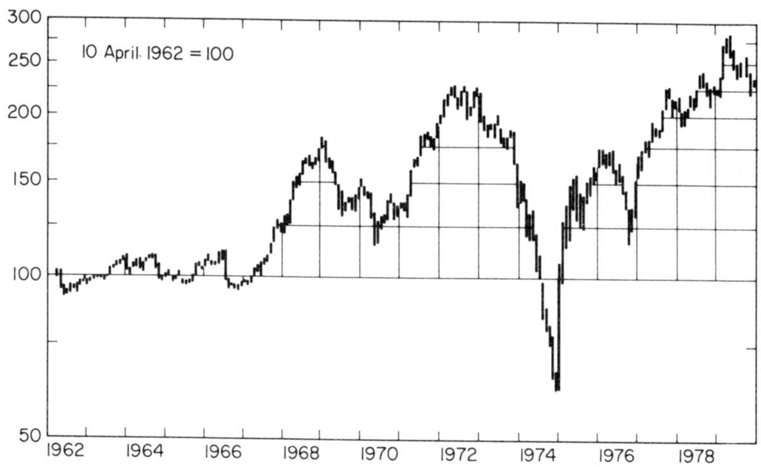

Fig. 16.2 FT-Actuaries All Share Index, 1962–79: monthly highs and lows

it provides a much better measure than the FT 30 Share Index, comparisons with which are grossly misleading because of the latter's geometric construction. Any fund simply investing in the same proportions as those in the All Share Index should always 'beat' the FT 30 Share Index.

One disadvantage of the All Share Index is its restriction to the United Kingdom market. With the removal of exchange controls in 1979, and the freedom to invest in equity markets worldwide, a better yardstick for a large fund might be a world index, a weighted arithmetic mean based on the major shares, or indices, of stock exchanges in the USA, Japan, Australia, Canada, the European Community and so on.

(*c*) Other FT-Actuaries Indices

In addition to the share indices there are five British Government Fixed-Interest Price Indices, ten British Government Fixed-Interest Yield Indices, and two similar sets of indices for debenture and preference shares respectively.

The *British Government Indices* were introduced in May 1977 to provide a comparison measure for the gilts market, equivalent to that provided by the FT-Actuaries Share Indices in the equity market. The gilts market is not homogeneous, but has separate sectors requiring separate analysis. The price indices subdivide the market by maturity period (0 to 5, 5 to 15, 15-plus years, irredeemables, all stocks). The yield indices have a two-way division, being separated by maturity period (0 to 5, 5 to 15, 15 to 25 years, and irredeemables) and coupon (low, medium or high). The various sectors are of interest to different investors, depending on their tax status.

Since the number of gilt-edged stocks on the market is comparatively small, the price indices represent the complete market value of all stocks in each sector expressed in the form of an index the base for which was 100 on 31 December 1975. The irredeemable sector price index, for instance, reflects the movement in the six undated gilts.

The gilts market is more complicated to deal with than that in equities because of the problem of accrued interest. The prices used are middle-market prices, which include an allowance for accrued interest to date. The change in the interest content is not separated from the total price change of an index over a short period of time. The *xd adj* column represents the amount of gross interest received to date from the beginning of the calendar year. This is included so that the performance of a fund rolling-up (reinvesting) interest can be assessed: the increase in interest has to be added to the final index price before dividing by the initial index level to measure change.

(*d*) Other Indices

The *Financial Times* also publishes a *Government Securities Index* and *Fixed Interest, Gold Mines* and *Stock Exchange Activity* indices. Other indices are published by newspapers such as *The Times*, which has separate indices for largest companies, smaller companies, capital goods, consumer goods and stores shares. All of these use a fixed weighted arithmetical mean method of construction.

Details of world bourses, showing changes over varying time periods, can be found in weeklies such as the *Investor's Chronicle*, the *Economist*, and the *Financial Weekly* as well as in the *Financial Times*, which also includes a world index. This *Capital World Index* is a weighted arithmetic mean based on 1 100 shares which account for approximately 60 per cent of the aggregate market value of all shares listed on the national exchanges of the countries represented.

Overseas indices need to be treated with caution because they are not all of the same type. The best known, the *Dow-Jones Industrial Average*, is an unweighted arithmetic mean of thirty leading shares on the New York Stock Exchange. It includes oil and commodity companies and even a public utility, American Telegraph and Telephone. Because of its method of construction the performance of the index corresponds to that of a portfolio in which the relative value of each holding is proportional to share price rather than market capitalization. There are Dow-Jones averages for transportation and utilities as well as industrials. (Chartists pay particular attention to the relationship between the transportation and industrial indices.) A more useful measure for portfolio comparison purposes are the *Standard and Poors* indices, which are weighted arithmetic indices similar to the FT-Actuaries Indices. There are indices for 400 industrials, 20 transportation, 40 public utility and 40 financial shares, which together make up the *Composite 500 Stock Index*.

16.2 Equity Switching

An investor in equities can adopt a simple 'buy-and-hold' policy, preferably with a well-diversified portfolio, or attempt to 'buy-and-sell' according to changing economic circumstances, hoping to outperform the indices. Institutional investors are more restricted than are individuals, because of the size of their existing funds. Unit trusts are the most active dealers generally, but British funds have rarely 'churned' their portfolios to the same extent as did certain mutual funds in the USA in the 1960s. These were nicknamed 'go-go' funds because of their active dealing policy, based on a subsequently discredited belief that frequent purchases and sales would always produce larger capital gains than a more conservative 'buy-and-hold' policy.

One common approach to the active management of an equity portfolio is to buy and sell *sectors*. These can be either the full list of Actuaries' Securities groups (approximately 100) published by the Stock Exchange or, more usually, the aggregate version published by the *Financial Times* in their Actuaries tables. Some large investors may concentrate only on those sectors with the greatest capitalization, such as engineering, electricals, food, drink and tobacco, chemicals, stores, oils, banks, insurance and investment trusts.

The basis of this approach is to buy sectors that are expected to perform well against the FT All Share Index, and to sell those that are expected to do badly.

A variety of techniques can be used. Technical analysis can be employed to determine which sectors have shown relative strength and weakness over some past period, such as the last six months. Some investors would argue that such trends can be expected to continue; others would advocate a policy of 'contrary thinking', on the basis that the worst-performing sectors are likely to show the most recovery in the longer term. Fundamental analysis involves choosing sectors according to the state of the economy, particularly the course of the business cycle.

Some words of warning are apposite at this juncture, however. First, not all sectors are homogeneous, particularly as companies increasingly diversify. Most of the variation in an individual share price is either specific to that company or general to the stock market, rather than being attributable to the industry or sector. Secondly, it is easy to be beguiled by stockbrokers' short-term enthusiasm for a sector but fail to realize any subsequent profits at the appropriate time. This is particularly a danger for the insurance companies and pension funds, where the shares become 'locked' in the funds.

For the investor with a shorter-term perspective, the fundamental approach suggests that the leading sectors at the start of a potential bull market are those benefiting most from the fall in interest rates and easing of credit that usually precede the upturn in the economic cycle. Lower interest rates give a boost to discount houses and hire purchase companies, both of which usually lend longer-term than they borrow. Hire purchase firms, too, benefit from the new business generated by consumer durable sales (television sets, washing machines, hi-fi, cars), which are heavily influenced by the availability of credit. This improvement in business also provides a direct benefit to the stores sector. Other beneficiaries will be contracting and construction (in the form of house-building, which is sensitive to the cost and availability of mortgage finance), building materials and property, which like contracting and construction tends to have high levels of borrowing, although less short-term than it was in the early 1970s.

Banks traditionally suffered when interest rates fell because of the so-called 'endowment element' in their borrowed funds. This is interest-free money obtained from current accounts. A fall in interest rates lowers the margin between the rate the banks can charge for such money and its zero cost. In recent years this effect has become less noticeable, however, because of the greater proportion of funds obtained from the wholesale money markets, the interest imputed on current accounts to be offset against bank charges and the diversification into areas such as hire purchase.

Increased economic activity at the retail level may initially largely be met by a rundown in stocks, but the impetus will soon be felt by manufacturing industry, especially industries with high operating gearing, such as chemicals. Eventually the capital goods sector, with items such as machine tools, will have increased business with the need to expand and re-equip industry. Investment expenditure is much more unstable than consumer expenditure, and capital goods industries tend to oscillate from relative prosperity to depression.

Short-term speculation 'in and out' of different sectors of the market is a very hazardous business, involving frequent and unpredictable changes in sentiment that do not necessarily coincide with changes in fundamentals. The average investor who adopts an active dealing policy is more than likely to fare worse than by following a 'buy-and-hold' policy, taking into account dealing expenses including the jobbers' turn.

16.3 Gilt-edged Switching

When investing in gilts, as in equities, the investor has to decide whether to adopt an active or a passive investment policy: whether to move 'in and out' of different Government securities, or simply to 'buy and hold' until redemption. Low dealing costs, including freedom from stamp duty and the favourable capital gains tax treatment if stocks are held for more than one year, make switching gilts a cheaper proposition than switching equities. Many personal investors, by investing via some form of gilt or managed fund, transfer the responsibility to the institutional fund manager.

Switching can broadly be divided into three categories: *tax switching, anomaly switching* and *policy switching*.

(*a*) Tax Switching

For most United Kingdom investors capital gains are taxed more leniently than is income. Net gains for the tax year of up to £3 000 are free of tax and, moreover, capital gains on British Government funds held for more than one year are free from capital gains tax, irrespective of the size of the gain. This exemption does not apply to banks, discount houses, general insurance companies and general annuity funds, however; these are regarded as dealers in securities and are therefore taxed at the same rate on income and capital gain.

Individuals often find it advantageous to sell a stock cum dividend and buy again later ex dividend, or 'specially ex dividend'. Whether such an operation is worth while depends on whether the difference in the net proceeds from the sale and subsequent purchase exceeds the interest the investor would have received, net of his marginal rate of tax, on investment income. The advantage of buying 'specially xd', in advance of the normal xd period, is that the stock can be sold 'cum dividend' during the same three-week period the following year, but at least one day later, to enable the gain to be tax-free, with the only taxable income being one half-year's interest payment received during the holding period. The investor should beware that if he persistently 'buys' and 'sells' interest excessively, the Inland Revenue may take action to tax him as a dealer.

(*b*) Anomaly Switching

The yield on a stock is described as an *anomaly* if it is out of line with those of neighbouring stocks. The commonest cause of an anomaly is Government sales of 'tap' stocks, which are frequently cheap compared with stocks of a similar maturity, because of the effect of heavy Government sales. This anomaly is usually corrected when the Government raises the tap price, for tactical reasons, or when the tap runs out. Some gilt-edged stocks with sinking funds, on the other hand may appear anomalously dear, either because the fund buys in stock through the market, or because of a possibility of redemption at par.

Anomalies can be detected by examining relative prices and yields. Some brokers keep price records for pairs of stocks, net of accrued interest. These show, usually in chart form, how price differences or relative prices of pairs of stocks change over time, but they are really only appropriate for stocks of similar life and coupon. It is probably more useful to look at the redemption yields of two stocks. If, for example, Stock A yields $\frac{3}{4}$ per cent more than Stock B, and the differential has previously ranged between 0 and $\frac{1}{2}$ per cent, Stock A appears to be anomalously cheap.

Alternatively, yield curves can be used. Such curves can be based on gross yields (see Fig. 16.3) or net yields, but the gross redemption yields fall closer along such a curve than yields net of tax. It is then possible to identify clearly deviations of actual gross redemption yields for individual stocks from those predicted by the curve. The investor may decide to sell those that appear 'dear' and buy those that appear 'cheap' for his particular maturity period, bearing in mind, however, that when the yield curve is calculated in gross terms, high-coupon stocks (particularly at the short end of the market) always look cheap relative to low-coupon ones because of the differences in tax treatment. The net-of-tax yields should be calculated, or a yield curve drawn showing yields net of the investor's marginal rate of tax, before a permanent switch is made.

Some stocks appear to have permanent anomalous positions, for reasons

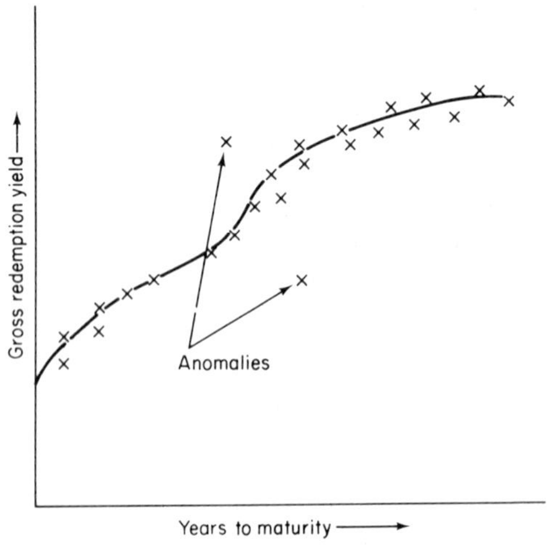

Fig. 16.3 The yield curve and anomaly stocks

other than their size of coupon. This is particularly noticeable with undated stocks, where there are substantial differences in yield despite very similar coupons. For example, War Loan 3½% appears relatively expensive. This is probably because the interest is paid gross, and this appeals to overseas investors who are saved the necessity of applying to the Inspector of Foreign Dividends for exemption from tax. Similarly, 2½% Consols almost invariably appears dear if compared with 2½% Treasury, perhaps because interest on the former is paid quarterly, as against half-yearly for other stocks, but also apparently because the ownership of the two stocks differs. Consols is held more by private individuals, while Treasury is held more by institutions.

If an investor intends to reverse an anomaly switch it is advantageous to do so within twenty-eight days, since the reversal is then free of commission as a 'closing' bargain.

(*c*) **Policy Switching**

If a fund having long-term liabilities invests in long-dated gilts, on a change of interest rate both its assets and its liabilities will move up or down together. But where the liabilities are long-term and the fund invests in short-dated gilts, if interest rates should fall serious problems could arise. This is because there will be an increase in the present value of the future liabilities, but little scope for an increase in the value of the assets already standing near their redemption values. This is known as *income risk*, because the danger of investing short-term is a reduction in income if interest rates fall. The opposite problem is faced by a financial institution such as a bank, with essentially short-term liabilities. If it invests long-term, and interest rates subsequently rise, the assets fall in value while the liabilities remain largely unchanged. This is known as *capital risk*.

Clearly, investors should not adopt investment policies that are wildly inappropriate to their liabilities. If they do so, they should have sufficient reserves to cover themselves against the risks. The perfect matching of liabilities and assets is known as *immunization*; it implies that a change in the interest rate has an identical effect on both.

In order to improve profit, a fund may decide to move away from a matched position, but usually the intention is to return to it as soon as an expected profit has been made. The reason for the change is the expectation of a change in overall interest rates, or in the shape of the yield curve.

The shape of the yield curve varies according to investors' expectations of future interest rates. According to the *expectations theory*, a yield curve that slopes steeply upwards from left to right (see Fig. 16.4) indicates that interest rates are expected to rise. Investors are willing to hold relatively low-yielding short-term assets on the assumption that they can reinvest at higher short-term rates in the future. Conversely, a falling yield curve (Fig. 16.5) implies that interest rates are expected to fall. High short-term rates may be short-lived, and investors may prefer the certainty of income provided by longer-term stocks. A flat yield curve (Fig. 16.6) indicates neutral expectations (that interest rates are not expected to change).

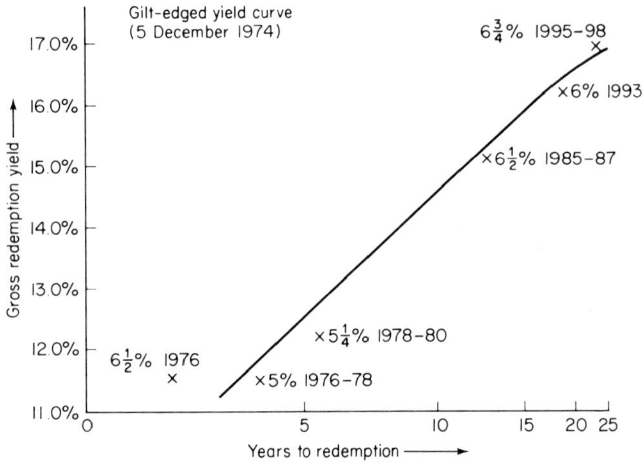

Fig. 16.4 A rising yield curve

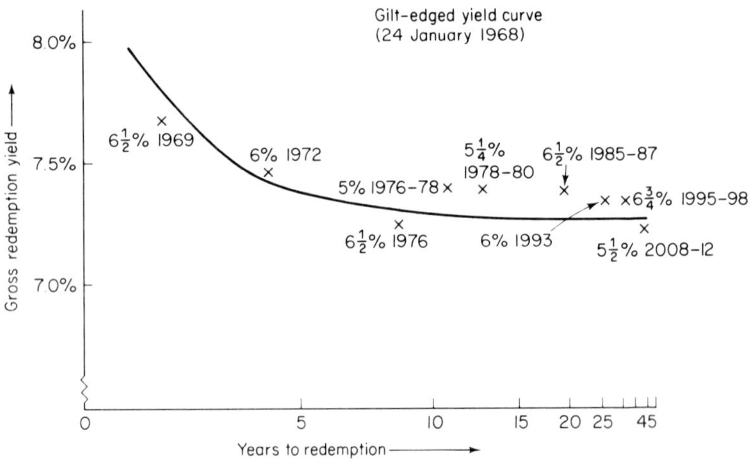

Fig. 16.5 A falling yield curve

The yield curve seems to exhibit an upward bias, which means that with 'neutral' expectations there is still a moderate upward slope. This may be because investors as a whole place greater importance on capital certainty than income certainty. It also could reflect a greater demand, particularly by the Government, for funds at the long end of the market, relative to supply, rather than at the short end. With the growth in long-term investment by the pension funds and insurance companies and the commitment to cut Government borrowing that are both marked at the time of writing, however, these influences may be less important in the future.

If interest rates, for all maturity periods, are expected to increase a fund may decide to 'shorten' its assets, and thus reduce the risk of capital loss. In an extreme case it might 'go liquid', although this would be unacceptable for a life assurance or pension fund. On the other hand, if interest rates were expected to fall it could increase the maturity of its assets.

Longer-term assets are generally more volatile than shorter-term ones, that is, they show a larger percentage price change for a given change in their rate of interest. Obviously very short-dated stocks, near to redemption, cannot deviate far from par. Volatility depends on coupon as well as redemption date, however – the lower the coupon, the greater the volatility. The *duration* of a stock is defined as the average period of time during which inflows of interest and capital are received. It is calculated by discounting these by the gross redemption yield on the stock, and finding the date by which half of the present value is received. The longer the 'duration', the greater the volatility of the stock. 'Immunization' is achieved by matching the volatility (duration) of assets and liabilities.

It is perhaps surprising at first sight that low-coupon undated stocks, such as 2½% Consols, are not the most volatile of all. In fact, at the end of 1972, when gross redemption yields were slightly less than 10 per cent, 2½% Consols had a *volatility rating* of 10.1 (that is, a 1 per cent change in yield would lead to a 10.1 per cent change in price), while those for 3% Gas 1990–95 and 3% Redemption 1986–96 were 12.7 and 13.6 respectively.

The greater volatility of certain long-dated stocks as compared with undated ones may explain why they frequently have higher yields. On occasions, interest rates in certain parts of the yield curve change significantly more than in others. The usual shape of the yield curve is upward-sloping, with short-term

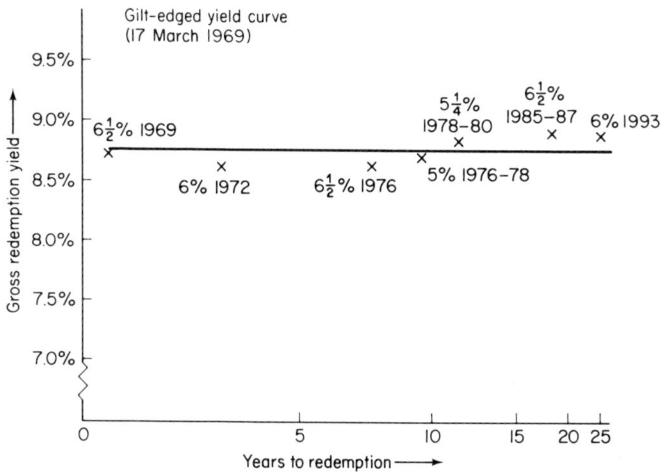

Fig. 16.6 A flat yield curve

interest rates lower than those in the medium term, which in turn are lower than those in the long-term and undated segment. The curve can take on every conceivable shape, however. Short-term interest rates are most affected by Government credit policy, the balance of payments and interest rates abroad. Long-term rates reflect expectations about inflation and the size of long-term public sector debt sales. If a credit squeeze is expected to be relaxed, for example, short-term interest rates may be expected to fall, while long-term rates may remain the same, or even rise on inflationary fears. At such a time a fund might consider moving nearer the short end of the yield curve to benefit from capital gains resulting from the fall in the interest rate.

The volatility indices can still be used to analyse differential interest rate changes. For example, if short-term rates are expected to fall by 4 per cent and long-term rates by 1 per cent, the relative effects on capital values can be ascertained by multiplying the index for the former by four, and taking the index for the latter as it stands.

The aim of any fund manager is to demonstrate that his switching policy has produced a higher rate of return than that shown by the indices that represent a static investment in all available stocks. For long-term institutions, the rates of return on the twenty-five-year indices are the main yardsticks of success.

16.4 The Efficient Market Hypothesis

The *Efficient Market Hypothesis* (EMH) is a theory that capital markets operate to a high degree of perfection. Its roots lie in the *Random Walk Hypothesis* (RWH), which postulates that share price changes are of a random, rather than correlated, nature.

Technical analysis, whether using chartism or mechanical trading rules, is essentially based on the premise that past share prices can, in some way, be used to predict future share prices. This is categorically denied by the 'random walkers', who have subjected the evidence to very extensive statistical tests both in the United Kingdom and, primarily, in the USA. Serial correlation (the connection between price changes in successive periods, or after a time lag) was found to be insignificant, and the numbers of successive positive and negative price changes were close to those that could be expected from chance. After all, if you toss a fair coin, you may experience a run of 'heads' or 'tails' purely by chance. If 'red' comes up six times in a row at roulette the outcome of the next spin of the wheel is no more likely to be red than black, provided the wheel is unbiased. Similarly with share prices: stock market cycles, showing both 'bull' and 'bear' markets, can be simulated purely by using a random number machine.

The RWH has been summarized by one American writer as: 'Prices have no memory, and yesterday has nothing to do with tomorrow. Every day starts out fifty–fifty. Yesterday's price discounted everything yesterday.' In other words, the best 'guesstimate' of the share price tomorrow, or next week, is the share price today. In the longer run, there will be random movements about an upward trend.

Advocates of technical analysis have argued that the type of tests conducted were unfair because they were too rigid; they simply extrapolated price trends, and did not allow for the subtlety of chartism. But whenever trading rules, such as relative strength and filters (see Unit 15.3), were tested they almost invariably failed to generate sufficient profit to cover expenses. The EMH was developed to explain these statistical results. In its 'weak form' it says that any information conveyed by the series of past prices of a share is recognized by investors and is discounted in the current share price.

The 'semi-strong form' of the EMH is a much more serious challenge to conventional beliefs in investment analysis. It asserts that current prices fully reflect not only past prices but all publicly available information about companies, and that efforts to acquire and analyse this knowledge cannot be expected to produce superior investment results. It suggests that the analysis of the annual report and accounts, for example, is largely a waste of time, and is based on the belief not that analysts are no good but that they are too good. All leading companies are under the constant examination of a large number of highly skilled analysts. They peruse and constantly reassess all the available information, and this is reflected in their investment recommendations. The share price is a consensus of their advice to investors, particularly fund managers. Greater weight is given to analysts with the best track records in each sector. Consequently, at any time, the actual share price approximates to its 'intrinsic' (or true) value.

One of the basis of fundamental analysis is the search for shares that are significantly under- or over-valued. But according to the EMH, competition between expert analysts and rational profit-seeking investors ensures that such discrepancies are insignificant. The marginal analyst is, in effect, redundant. The degree of efficiency is greater in the USA than in the United Kingdom because

'. . . and we are fortunate in having with us two experts on credit management.'

of the larger number of analysts and the fuller disclosure of information, both by companies and the stock exchanges. Academic ideas tend to be better received by the financial community in the USA than in the United Kingdom: Even in the USA, however, although some were willing to assent to the weaker assertion and seriously question technical analysis, very few indeed could accept the implications of the stronger form, and thereby abandon fundamental analysis. The irony is that if they did so to any substantial degree, the market would cease to be efficient.

The 'semi-strong' approach supposes that the share reflects and impounds all that is publicly ascertainable about a company, and that its price instantaneously adjusts to any new economic information that becomes available. Technical analysis, on the other hand, generally assumes that information is only gradually disclosed, filtering from one group of investors to another.

The 'strong form' of the EMH is the hypothesis that share prices fully reflect not only what is generally known through public information, but also private information. It seems almost to suggest that 'insider knowledge' is of no use, which could be the case if that information could have been anticipated from other sources. Appropriate tests have consisted of analyses of the performances of portfolios managed by groups that might have special information, and logging the share predictions of investment analysts.

The conclusion, from numerous studies of unit trusts in the United Kingdom and mutual funds in the USA, is that, allowing for differences in risk, no fund does consistently better than average. If any fund could do so, it would indicate an element of inefficiency in the price-making process. This conclusion has been confirmed, less rigorously but more vividly, by commentators picking shares from the *Financial Times* or the *Wall Street Journal* with the aid of a pin or a dart: on average the portfolios thus selected performed no better and no worse than professionally managed funds.

What are the implications of the EMH in its stronger forms? First, it emphasizes the incompleteness of fundamental analysis that fails to consider whether the share price already reflects the substance of the analysis. A very optimistic forecast of a company's future earnings is no justification in itself for buying a share; it is necessary that the analyst's forecasts be significantly more optimistic than other forecasts. In which case, is it credible?

The investor is best advised to split his equity portfolio into two – one part 'active', the other 'passive'. The exact proportions will depend on his attitude to risk, but the 'passive' one should normally be the larger. The 'passive' part is a recognition of the futility of scrutinizing leading shares. It accepts that they are fairly valued. These funds will be essentially invested 'in the Index'. The largest hundred companies in terms of market capitalization account for around 70 per cent of the FT-Actuaries All Share Index. If these are reasonably efficiently valued, it is almost impossible to 'beat the Index' by partial selection from them. It is far better to gain the full benefits of diversification by investing 'across the board' in a broad-based unit trust, investment trust or insurance fund. This is already widely accepted in the USA with the growth of *index funds*

(funds which reproduce index constituents and weightings almost exactly).

The 'active' element of the portfolio can be devoted to second-line shares. Small companies in particular are likely to be of less interest to institutions and subject to less close analysis, and offer a chance of discovering valuation discrepancies. 'Recovery stocks' are another type of share that may be partly overlooked because of their high risk and low capitalization. Certainly the performance of unit trusts investing in these specialized areas seem to suggest that the United Kingdom market may not be completely efficient (in the 'strong' sense) across its whole range. Some unlisted shares may offer opportunities for discovering inefficiencies in the pricing mechanism if they are quoted on the Unlisted Securities Market or on Nightingale's over-the-counter market, particularly fast-growing companies that have not yet reached the necessary size for a full listing.

16.5 Pound Cost Averaging

If the Efficient Market Hypothesis is correct it is just as difficult to decide *when* as *what* to buy and sell. Pound cost averaging (see Unit 11.9) abandons any attempt at optimal timing. It involves investing the same money sum per period, irrespective of the state of the market. Consequently more shares or units are bought when share prices are low, and fewer when they are high. The average price paid is less than the mean price over the same periods, a fact often used as a recommendation for unit-linked savings schemes.

The advantage of pound cost averaging over investing in the same *number* of shares or units per month, or year, results from the difference between the *harmonic mean* and the *arithmetic mean*. The harmonic mean is the reciprocal of the average of the reciprocals of a series of numbers. For example, the harmonic mean of 2 and 4 is the reciprocal of the arithmetic average of $\frac{1}{2}$ and $\frac{1}{4}$, which is 2.67 ($1/\frac{3}{8} = \frac{8}{3} = 2.67$). The arithmetic mean is, of course, 3.

If £240 is invested at each of two dates in shares costing £4 on the first date and £2 on the second, 60 shares are acquired the first time, 120 the second, and therefore 180 in total. The average price paid is thus £2.67 (£480 ÷ 180), the harmonic mean. If the same £480 had been spent at the arithmetic mean price of £3, only 160 shares could have been acquired. The greatest advantage is obtained when share prices are volatile, assuming that there is no persistent downward trend; if such a trend was predictable it would be preferable to stay out of the market altogether. But the EMH suggests valid predictions are likely to be difficult, if not impossible.

16.6 Performance Measurement

We have already referred to the difficulties of consistently 'beating the Index', and outperforming other investors. But the question remains: 'How do you measure performance?'. The answer is that it depends on the purpose for which the exercise is being undertaken. If it is to see what is the overall return on capital invested over a specified period, we use the *money-weighted* rate of return. On the other hand, for comparing the performance of one fund manager with another the *time-weighted* rate of return is more satisfactory. In both cases we calculate the total return on the fund in terms of increase in capital value plus income received. The total return is negative at times when the capital value decreases by an amount greater than the income received.

(*a*) Money-weighted Rate of Return

The simplest method of measuring the return on a portfolio is to value the investments on the two days between which the performance is to be compared, and adjust for items such as sales and purchases, including rights issues, capital gains tax and income received. To take a simple example, suppose that an equity fund was worth £10 000 at the beginning of the year. Dividend income of £600 was received at the end of the year and immediately reinvested in the fund, which was then worth £12 000. The portfolio thus achieved a return of £2 000, and the 'total' rate of return was 20 per cent (6 per cent dividend yield plus 14 per cent capital growth).

The example would have been more complicated if additional capital had been invested or withdrawn during the course of the year. Imagine the following timetable:

	Invested	*Withdrawn*
End of February	£1 000	
End of June		£2 000
End of September	£1 500	

During the year there has been a 'net' investment of £500. If this is deducted from the closing valuation, the rate of return is reduced to 15 per cent (total return = £12 000 − £10 000 − £500 = £1 500).

If greater accuracy is required, the calculation could be modified to allow for differences in timing of capital injections and withdrawals, weighting each by the number of months of the year remaining at the time they are effected:

$$\text{Total rate of return} = \frac{£12\,000 - £10\,000 - £500}{£10\,000 + (^5/_6 \times £1\,000) - (\frac{1}{2} \times £2\,000) + (\frac{1}{4} \times £1\,500)}$$

$$= \frac{£1\,500}{£10\,208} = 14.7 \text{ per cent}$$

Where a personal investor withdraws his capital for spending purposes, any capital gains tax should not be counted as a charge on the portfolio, but effectively paid out of the sum withdrawn. But when the liability results from a 'switching' operation only the 'net' sum (that is, net of any capital gains tax) counts as a withdrawal. The argument in favour of a switch must be that, notwithstanding the tax that will be payable, the shares purchased will show better prospects than the shares sold. The tax payable is a penalty for the ability to manage the portfolio, as any Actuaries index is equivalent to an unmanaged portfolio. The All-Share Index suffers the 'penalty' of having to remain in unsuccessful sectors and companies. If a sale gives rise to an allowable loss against capital gains tax this is ignored until it is used to reduce tax payable when only the net amount of any tax will need to be allowed for in the calculations. If income is received throughout the year and immediately re-invested it can be ignored in simply calculating the total return on the portfolio, but it should be treated in the same way as any other capital injection if comparison is to be made with the Actuaries indices which, of course, do not reinvest income.

The rate of return produced by this method is the actual return on the fund and can be thought of as the rate of interest which the initial portfolio, plus net new money, would have had to earn in a deposit account in order to accumulate to the actual value of the portfolio at the end of the year. This is useful for the individual but is inadequate, and sometimes misleading, for institutional investors.

(*b*) **Time-weighted Rate of Return**

Pension funds and insurance companies need to pay attention to the performance of their assets relative to any change in their liabilities. Thus they generally emphasize growth in investment income more than possible short-term changes in capital values. As long-term investors, with growing funds, capital values can appear largely irrelevant if assets are never likely to be sold on any substantial scale. It is nonetheless sometimes necessary to measure the performance of fund managers, particularly those of unit trusts and investment trusts.

In making such an assessment, the effect of new money must be eliminated; otherwise it cannot be clear whether the overall return was the sole responsibility of the investment manager or whether it was affected by the timing of the new money over which he had no control. A unit trust fund manager, for instance, may be faced with the problem of the greatest inflow of cash when the market is near its peak, and may be under great pressure to invest when he may not wish to do so; the equity fund manager in an insurance company may find that the amount of 'new money' to be invested has been determined by an investment committee. The advantage of the time-weighted rate of return is that it eliminates this effect.

Suppose the FT-Actuaries Index has the following values:

1 January	100
30 June	80
31 December	130

The return over the year is obviously 30 per cent (ignoring dividend income). If an institutional investor had invested £10mn at the beginning of the year and then invested a further £10mn on 30 June, the value at the end of the year would have been £29.25mn (£10mn × $^{130}/_{80}$ + £10mn × $^{130}/_{80}$). Then:

$$\text{Money-weighted return} = \frac{£29.25\text{mn} - £10\text{mn} - £10\text{mn}}{£10\text{mn} + (\frac{1}{2} \times £10\text{mn})}$$

$$= \frac{£9.25\text{mn}}{£15\text{mn}} = 61^2/_3 \text{ per cent}$$

The reason why the portfolio so dramatically outperformed the index ($61^2/_3$ per cent as compared with 30 per cent) is that the 'new money' invested on 30 June achieved a much higher return than the initial fund. Thus the apparent good performance relative to the index had nothing to do with the shares selected, but was solely due to the 'accident' of the timing of the new money.

The problem is partly resolved by breaking down the return for a particular period into subperiods, with a separate subperiod for every injection or withdrawal of capital. In our example the new money was received halfway through the year, so the year can be simply divided into two six-month subperiods. The return for the first half-year was −20 per cent, as the value of the investment, ignoring dividend income, fell to 80 from 100 – a price-relative of $^{80}/_{100}$ – but in the second part of the year the investment rose from 80 to 130 – a price-relative of $^{130}/_{80}$. The time-weighted rate of return is derived from the product of the price-relatives: $(^{80}/_{100} \times {}^{130}/_{80}) - 1 = 0.3 = 30$ per cent. Obviously, this is the same annual return as that on the 'index', despite the timing of the cash inflows. If the investor had not modelled his portfolio on the constituents of the index, but had bought different shares, or given different weightings to the shares, success or failure relative to the 'index' could be identified using this method, without timing distortions.

There are two drawbacks to this method. First, by eliminating the effect of the new money fund managers are no longer penalized by factors beyond their control. But where they have discretion over timing, this approach deprives them of any credit for successfully predicting 'bull' and 'bear' markets; equally they are not 'punished' for getting the market wrong. Secondly, a precise calculation of the time-weighted rate of return requires a valuation of the fund, to measure capital change, every time new money is introduced. One approximation is to calculate the money-weighted rates of return quarterly rather than annually and then combine these returns together to give a fairly good approximation of the time-weighted rate of return for the year.

Alternatively, we may use the *unitization* approach. A unitized fund is revalued every time there is a flow of money into or out of the fund, in order to calculate the unit price. The change in the unit price over a particular period automatically gives the precise time-weighted rate of return.

For funds not unit-linked, the easiest solution to the problem of timing is to calculate the money-weighted rates of return for both the fund and the chosen index – that is, to assume funds were invested in the index in exactly the same amounts and at exactly the same time. A notional fund can be established with the same opening value as the actual fund. Every time cash is added to or withdrawn from the actual fund, the notional fund can be revalued in line with the index, and the appropriate addition or deduction made. A 'chain index' can be used to provide continuity when alterations are made. For example, if the fund commences with £10mn when the index is 200, and at the end of the first month the index is 210, the value of the notional fund will be £10mn × $^{210}/_{200}$ = £10.5mn. If £500 000 is now invested the fund is worth £11mn. At the end of the second month the index stands at 220, and the fund is now worth £11mn × $^{220}/_{210}$ = £11.52mn. If £500 000 is again invested the fund is worth £12.02mn. With each injection or withdrawal of funds, the closing index level becomes the base for the next period. Every time the actual fund is revalued, it can be compared with the notional fund.

(*c*) Base Portfolios

The notional fund outlined above is an example of a 'base portfolio'. The term refers to an unmanaged fund, against which the performance of the managed fund can be compared. It can be used for equities, gilts, property or any other type of asset, or any combination of them.

The base portfolio might be the existing fund, taken in order to see the outcome of an inactive, non-switching policy. It could be an 'index fund'; or it could be constructed independently where no existing index is felt to reflect the requirements of the fund as dictated by the nature of its business, the investment committee or the trustees.

(*d*) Risk

So far we have discussed portfolio performance measurement without mentioning risk. This is not unacceptable in the case of long-term investors, such as life assurance and pension funds, for whom all that really matters is the overall rate of return; year-to-year fluctuations in returns can be ignored. This is not true of most other managed funds, particularly unit and investment trusts; where the investor may hold the portfolio for no more than a few years, the *volatility* of the annual returns needs to be considered. The greater the volatility the less the reliance that can be placed on the mean expected return, particularly over the short-to-medium term. Most 'league-tables' of unit trusts and other unit-linked investments simply offer a crude ranking of fund performance by rate of return alone. More sophisticated techniques have been developed in the USA to measure mutual fund performance, and most of these incorporate risk and return into a single performance measure.

For instance, a leading authority on investment, W.F. Sharpe, calculates the average return and the variability of returns on a wide range of funds over a given number of years. Risk can be plotted against return for all funds on a single graph (as in Fig. 16.7). Clearly, a good fund offers a lot of extra return for a given amount of risk, whereas a poor fund offers much less extra return for the same amount of risk, or offers the same extra return for a much greater degree of risk.

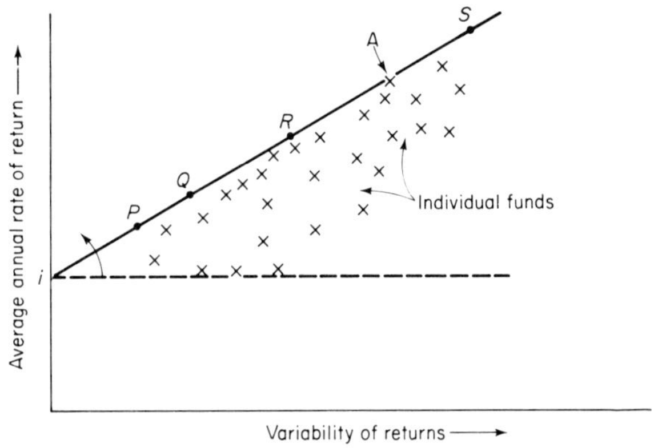

Fig. 16.7 The Sharpe model

The 'best' fund is fund A. This is because it offers a steeper line from i, the risk-free rate (such as a one-year Government bond) than any other fund plotted on the graph. The risk/return combinations shown by points P, Q, and R could have been obtained by holding a combination of risk-free asset and fund A and varying the weights. Point S could have been achieved if it had been possible to *borrow*, rather than invest, at the risk-free rate, i, and invest one's own proceeds plus the borrowed funds in fund A. Therefore any other fund can be shown to be inferior, no matter what its risk level.

Sharpe's method can be adopted to establish relative rankings for unit trusts and similar funds, or to see whether a particular fund has 'beaten the market' (by plotting the FT-Actuaries All Share Index, or a similar index, as a notional fund).

It would be rash to presume that past performance can be used to identify the best-performing funds for the future. The EMH, in particular the 'strong form', casts doubt on continuity of performance. Often the worst-performing trust in one period is the best performer in the next and vice versa, especially when the fund is concentrated heavily in one sector of the market.

16.7 Questions

1. Describe the main features of the *Financial Times* Industrial Ordinary Share Index and compare it with the *Financial Times*-Actuaries All-Share Index. What is the value of these indices to the investor?

2. (*a*) What do you understand by *policy switching* in connection with gilt-edged securities?
   (*b*) What are the implications of a downward-sloping yield curve?

3. What are the implications of the Efficient Market Hypothesis for investment fund management?

Unit Seventeen

The Business of Shareholders' Meetings

The greatest rewards, as well as the greatest losses, come from those investments that contain elements of risk and require therefore the greatest skill in selection. We have seen already that although the preference shareholders' interest is in the risk capital of the business, it is the ordinary shareholders, who hold the equity, who run the greatest risk. For this reason shareholders need to know what rights they have and how they can be exercised, and it is important, therefore, to know something about the nature and conduct of shareholders' meetings. Before dealing with meetings, however, it is necessary to consider the structure of a modern public limited company.

17.1 Legal Personality and Limited Liability

When a company is incorporated it becomes a distinct legal entity, quite separate from its members, even though there may be only two of them and one of these owns 99 per cent of the shares. It follows from this that anyone dealing with the company is not dealing with its members as such. Consequently, the company's rights and duties must be quite distinct from those of its members, although where such members are also directors the separation of powers is not as clear-cut.

From this concept of *separate entity* that of *limited liability* naturally follows. Since members *per se* are not responsible for the actions of the company their liability must be limited. Thus anyone purchasing shares in a company will find that the share certificate states the extent, if any, of any remaining liability. Most shares in quoted companies are fully paid so that whether the investor buys them on the market at above or below the nominal price the company cannot require him to provide further capital. If, however, shares are in partly paid form, there is a real liability. If the company is sound, this is not perhaps a serious matter, but no investor wants to throw good money after bad. Where a company becomes insolvent and has to be wound up, the shareholders only receive something after all the creditors have been satisfied in full. Often, however, they lose everything. If their shares are only partly paid the liquidator can require them to repay the outstanding amount.

17.2 Formation of a Company

The Companies Act 1980 provides for the formation of two kinds of company: *public limited companies*, which are specifically defined, and *private companies* which form the residuary category. A public company is a company limited by shares:

(*a*) The memorandum of which states that the company is to be a public company;
(*b*) which is registered as such;
(*c*) the name of which ends with the words 'public limited company' or 'p.l.c.' (or its Welsh equivalent);
(*d*) which has no fewer than two members; and
(*e*) which has a minimum issued share capital of £50 000.

A company is formed after certain important documents – the memorandum of association and the articles of association – have been lodged with the Registrar of Companies. For all companies, a *Certificate of Incorporation* is issued by the Registrar, but a public company requires, in addition, a *Certificate to Commence Business*.

17.3 The Memorandum of Association

This document contains six clauses:

(*a*) the name of the company, the last words usually being 'limited' or 'public limited company';
(*b*) the part of the United Kingdom where the company's registered office is situated (England, for instance, or Scotland);
(*c*) the objects of the company;
(*d*) a statement that the liability of the members is limited;
(*e*) the amount of nominal capital and how it is divided; and
(*f*) a statement signed by the subscribing members that they wish to form a company.

Of these clauses the most important is (*c*), the objects clause. This clause determines what the company can legally do, and is usually drawn extremely widely, so as to allow the company to undertake a range of different operations. Transactions outside the objects are said to be *ultra vires* but the European Communities Act 1972 provides that, for a person dealing with a company in good faith, the transaction shall be treated as being within the company's capacity even though the objects clause itself would not allow it.

17.4 The Articles of Association

The Articles of Association contain the *internal* regulations of the company. The Companies Act 1948 contains model articles known as *Table A* which many companies adopt unamended; these apply to any company that does not register its own articles.

The principal matters covered by the articles are as follows:

(*a*) the issue of shares and the rights and obligations of members;
(*b*) transfer of shares;
(*c*) alteration of capital;
(*d*) meetings;
(*e*) voting and proxies;
(*f*) directors: their qualifications, powers and duties;
(*g*) dividends, reserves and capitalization of profits;
(*h*) accounts and audit; and
(*i*) winding-up.

The articles are binding on both the company and its members but it is unlikely that many members will have any knowledge of a company's articles unless these are brought to their attention in a company announcement or in the press.

Some matters may be dealt with in both the memorandum and the articles. Where the two are in conflict it is the memorandum which prevails. Either document can be altered on the passing of a special resolution.

17.5 Directors

In theory the control of a company is exercised by the shareholders. They do in fact exercise ultimate control but Table A, the model set of articles, provides that the business of the company shall be managed by the directors.

Until the passing of the Companies Act 1980, statute law was not specific about the duties of directors, but the courts had recognized two duties: a *fiduciary duty* (a duty in relation to money and kindred matters) and a *duty of care*. When representing the company, the directors are said to be agents of the company. Their position in relation to the shareholders is not quite clear. In some circumstances they are agents, in others more akin to trustees. But it is certainly true that in relation to the shareholders the directors occupy a position of trust and so, for example, must inform the members of any contracts involving the company in which they have a personal interest. A company cannot, generally, lend money to its directors and it is well-established law that where the interests of the company and those of individual shareholders are in conflict the interests of the company shall prevail. The 1980 Act imposes a special duty on directors in requiring them to have regard to the interests of their employees as well as their shareholders.

Every public company must have at least two directors. Directors are elected each calendar year at the annual general meeting and normally retire by rotation every three years and on reaching the age of 70, but in both circumstances they can be re-elected.

17.6 The Quorum

There are different kinds of members' meetings and, before looking in turn at the business of each, we shall consider several matters some of which may be common to more than one class of meeting.

For any meeting there must be a *quorum*, that is a specified minimum number of shareholders that must be present before the meeting can be valid. For general meetings this number is usually set at three.

17.7 Resolutions

Matters at meetings are determined by *resolutions* which are voted upon. There are three kinds of resolution. An *ordinary* resolution, not defined by the Companies Act 1948, is sufficient for most purposes including all the routine matters dealt with at an annual general meeting. Ordinary resolutions are passed by a simple majority of those voting, and require at least fourteen days' notice.

Certain important matters, however, require the passing of a *special* or an *extraordinary* resolution, for both of which a 75 per cent majority of those voting is required. Such resolutions are decided at an extraordinary general meeting (see Unit 17.10). Special resolutions are required, for instance, for the following:

(*a*) to alter the objects clause in the memorandum or any of the articles;

(*b*) to change the name of the company;

(*c*) to reduce capital, under section 66 of the Companies Act 1948, with the consent of the court;

(*d*) to have the company wound up voluntarily;

(*e*) to sanction a winding-up, under section 287 of the Act, whereby the company's property is exchanged for shares in another company.

Twenty-one days' notice is required for a special resolution.

Among the most important matters requiring an extraordinary general resolution is the winding-up of a company on the grounds that, by reason of its liabilities, it cannot continue business. The period of notice required is not specified but must be at least fourteen days, which is the period of notice required for an extraordinary general meeting.

17.8 Voting and Proxies

In order that a member may vote at a meeting at which he cannot be present, the Companies Act provides for the appointment of proxies. A *proxy* need not be a member of the company. A proxy cannot vote except on a *poll* and he can only speak to demand a poll. Corporate bodies can appoint a proxy or,

alternatively, a *representative* who has for the duration of the meeting all the rights of a member.

Normally voting is by a show of hands. A poll can, however, be demanded either by five or more members, or by members representing one-tenth of the voting capital. On a poll the usual procedure is to allow one vote for each share held. Companies, when sending out proxy forms, usually suggest the names of directors of the company who will then act as proxies, voting as they see fit unless otherwise instructed.

17.9 The Annual General Meeting

The principal meeting of the shareholders is called the *annual general meeting*. It is laid down that one must be held in every calendar year, and that the interval between meetings should not exceed fifteen months. At least twenty-one days' notice must be given.

The usual business transacted at an annual general meeting consists of the following routine matters:

(*a*) the consideration of the audited accounts;
(*b*) the declaration of a dividend;
(*c*) the election of the directors;
(*d*) the appointment and remuneration of the auditors.

All such matters are designated *ordinary business*. Any other matters are deemed *special business*.

17.10 Extraordinary General Meetings

All general meetings of shareholders other than the annual meeting are referred to as *extraordinary general meetings*. These can be called by the directors at any time, and shareholders representing one-tenth of the voting capital can require them to convene one. If the directors do not comply with the request, the shareholders themselves can call a meeting and charge the company with the expenses incurred. The period of notice required is not less than fourteen days, unless a special resolution is to be passed, in which case the period is twenty-one days.

17.11 Class Meetings

These are meetings held to consider matters which are of special concern to persons other than the ordinary shareholders. Such matters might include a proposal to reduce the level of the preference dividend, or to vary in some way the rights of debenture-holders. At such meetings the parties concerned would be those entitled to vote.

17.12 Special Business and Special Notice

All items of business at an annual general meeting, other than the routine matters (see Unit 17.9), and all matters laid before the members at an extraordinary general meeting are termed *special business*. Certain business requires *special notice* of twenty-eight days. Some such business may be particularly appropriate as items of special business, at an annual general meeting – for instance, a resolution to appoint as auditor a person other than the retiring auditor. Other matters requiring special notice would be more appropriate at an extraordinary general meeting, such as resolutions to remove directors or auditors before the expiration of their terms of office. (The terms 'special resolution', 'special business' and 'special notice' have no necessary connection with each other.)

17.13 Auditors

The role of the auditor has become increasingly important since audit was first made compulsory under the Companies Act 1948. An audit must be carried out by accountants belonging to a body recognized by the Department of Trade. Auditors are guided in the presentation of accounts not only by the legal requirements but also by (*a*) the Recommendations on Accounting Principles and (*b*) the Statements of Standard Accounting Practice.

The *Recommendations on Accounting Principles* were first published in the 1940s and are of persuasive authority only, allowing in many cases considerable flexibility. Many accountants believed that greater uniformity was necessary and in 1969 an Accounting Standards Committee was set up to attempt to standardize many areas of accounting.

Some seventeen standards have now been issued, of which two have subsequently been withdrawn or superseded. Auditors must comply with them, or qualify the accounts. If, therefore, the directors of a company decide to depart from a particular standard, the auditors cannot give the usual satisfactory report stating that the accounts have been examined and that they give a 'true and fair' view of the company's position. Qualification used to be tantamount to a statement that all was not well with the company, but in recent years many leading companies have had their accounts qualified because of non-compliance with a particular standard.

The Companies Act 1976 requires that auditors must be re-appointed by ordinary resolution at the Annual General Meeting. If they are to be replaced, twenty-eight days' special notice is required. If the auditors resign, they must state whether or not there are circumstances that should be reported to the shareholders and, if so, what these are. The auditors can demand that an extraordinary general meeting be held at which they can state the circumstances surrounding their resignation. This legislation strengthens the position and independence of the auditor.

17.14 The Audited Accounts

Before the Companies Act 1948, disclosure requirements were not onerous and, while many companies had for several years complied with enlightened accounting practices – for example, in producing consolidated accounts – many others sought merely to comply with the law. Today not only has the law been greatly strengthened but the widespread, if not wholehearted, compliance with standard accounting practice means that accounts now provide much more information than formerly, which certainly makes the professional investor's task easier. But smaller investors often feel oppressed by the sheer quantity of information, so that many companies are now endeavouring to present it in ways that are more easily assimilated, and some also prepare a separate report for their staff. Sometimes these take the form of a simplified set of accounts, perhaps illustrated by pie diagrams, charts and so forth.

The report and accounts must be sent to all shareholders and holders of debenture and loan stocks not less than twenty-one days before the annual general meeting. A copy must be lodged with the Registrar of Companies not more than seven months after the company's financial year ends. The content of the published accounts is discussed in Unit 15.

17.15 Stock Exchange Requirements

The Stock Exchange requires listed companies to provide shareholders, through the audited accounts, with more information than the minimum required by law. The directors are also required to state the reasons for any significant departures from standard accounting practice and to explain any material failure to meet a published forecast. This last requirement is intended to discourage company chairmen from making rash prophecies.

In addition to the audited accounts, listed companies are required by the Stock Exchange to publish an interim report covering the activities of the company for the first six months of each financial year. The information required is not extensive, the main items being turnover, profit after tax and dividends paid and proposed. Comparative figures are, of course, also required but the interim report is not subject to audit.

17.16 The Rights of Shareholders

The rights of the ordinary members are necessarily limited by the considerable powers which the directors exercise on their behalf and on behalf of the company itself. Since, in law, a company is a person with its own rights, the directors are bound to regard the company's interests as paramount. Thus, for example, while the shareholders can reduce a proposed dividend they cannot increase it, for this might create insurmountable liquidity problems for the company. The principal rights of ordinary shareholders are:

(*a*) to receive the annual report and accounts;
(*b*) to attend, vote and speak at meetings;
(*c*) to appoint a proxy to attend meetings, to request a poll and to vote on a poll;
(*d*) to share in the profits of the company either in the form of dividends or by an increase in the reserves;
(*e*) to subscribe for any new share capital or convertible loan stock in proportion to their existing holdings;
(*f*) to transfer their shares freely (except in the case of private companies).

17.17 Disclosure of Shareholders' Interests

Recent legislation has imposed an obligation on voting shareholders to notify the company whenever a purchase or sale of their shares affects in any way a substantial interest in that company. Section 33 of the Companies Act 1967 as amended by the Companies Act 1976 (section 26) requires any person acquiring a 5 per cent interest in the voting capital, or reducing or increasing such an interest, to notify the company within five days of the details of such transactions. Section 27 of the Companies Act 1976 enables companies to require shareholders to reveal the beneficial interest in holdings. Prior to the Act, where shares were registered in the name of a nominee, the company had no means of knowing where the real ownership lay. This meant that a company could be facing a gradual take-over by another company without being aware of it, particularly if the use of several different nominee names masked the same beneficial ownership.

17.18 Attendance at Meetings

The annual general meeting is the only regular opportunity for directors and shareholders to meet each other. The power of the individual shareholder is generally very limited, although he may be in a position to exercise significant influence, as illustrated by the activities of anti-apartheid shareholders at meetings of companies with South African interests. In many companies, interests are widely spread so that even a 2 or 3 per cent holding can be influential at a meeting where less than 10 per cent of the shares, and a far smaller proportion of members, are represented. Some substantial public companies, however, are still controlled by the family that formed the business.

In many companies little effective control is exercised over the directors and there is substantial support for the view that, as in some other countries, every board should include some non-executive directors, part of whose responsibility would be to look after the interest of the shareholders.

A number of companies have, in recent years, attempted to encourage shareholders to attend the annual general meeting by offering inducements such as a buffet lunch, product samples or vouchers for use in their retail outlets. Other companies simply provide the shareholders with benefits whether or not they attend meetings. One, for example, offers half-price dry-cleaning in its retail shops; another, a funeral company, provides a free burial or cremation for deceased shareholders.

Today, with the growth of institutional shareholding, there have been several notable instances of the institutions having been able to effect changes in company policy. The members of a company do not determine company policy directly but they can effectively do so by getting their own nominees on to the board of directors. The institutional shareholders now find themselves in something of a cleft stick. On the one hand some critics see their increased power as a threat to market forces and the independence of the directors, while on the other they may find themselves criticized for being supine.

17.19 Capital Reconstruction

In previous Units we examined those internal changes in capital structure that arise from an expansion of the undertaking, such as the issue of loan capital increasing the gearing of the company and the rights issue which has the opposite effect. Both of these have the important effect of increasing the financial resources of the company. A bonus issue, on the other hand, has no effect on total capitalization, gearing or financial resources. The structure of the equity capital is, however, affected when it is the revenue reserves (those available for distribution) that are capitalized.

In the remainder of this Unit we turn to those developments which usually arise following a period of adverse trading. These may have a profound effect on both the creditors and shareholders, and collectively are sometimes referred to as *reconstructions*, a vague term with no precise legal meaning.

17.20 Reduction of Capital

The capital of a limited company can be reduced on various grounds. The company may, for example, have paid-up capital in excess of its requirements and it may wish to return a portion to the shareholders, or it may extinguish or reduce the liability of any of its shares in respect of capital not paid. The usual cause, however, is that the company has made substantial losses.

A capital reduction is often the course chosen by a company when it has returned to profitability and wishes to be able to pay dividends, for it cannot do so until any adverse balance on profit and loss account has been cleared. The Companies Act 1980 has clarified the nature of distributable profits by defining them as the aggregate of undistributed realized profits less accumulated realized losses.

The Act also requires the directors of any public company to convene an extraordinary general meeting if they become aware that the company's net assets have fallen in value to less than half of the company's capital.

17.21 Sale of the Company under Section 287 of the Companies Act 1948

This remedy is often used when a company requires more capital which cannot be raised in the normal way. A new company is registered, to which the old company, through its liquidator, sells the assets in return for shares in the new one. These are issued as partly paid shares so that the shareholders must be prepared to pay the balance of the nominal value of the shares if so required, or relinquish them. This provision of the Companies Act 1948 applies also where the sale of the company is for fully paid shares where it is essential that the old company be wound up.

If any member who has not voted to wind up the old company expresses his dissent in writing to the liquidator at the company's registered office within seven days after passing the special resolution, he may require the liquidator either (*a*) to abstain from carrying the resolution into effect or (*b*) to purchase his interest at a fair price. The price for the shares must be paid before the company is dissolved. If a shareholder (or his executors) does not dissent in the manner provided in the Companies Act 1948, he loses his rights in the old company.

17.22 Scheme of Arrangement under Section 206 of the Companies Act 1948

This section of the Act enables a company to remain in existence and make compromises or arrangements with certain of its creditors and its members. In each case the compromise involves giving up some immediate right in the hope that the fortunes of the company will improve and that something will in due course be salvaged from the arrangement. Generally speaking, the creditors give up least, the preference shareholders rather more, but the principal sacrifice, as always, has to be made by the equity shareholders.

If the proposals are approved by a majority representing three-quarters of the value of the class of creditors or members concerned, they will, when sanctioned by the court, be binding on the various classes of creditors or members.

17.23 Questions

1. Summarize briefly the provisions of the Companies Acts in relation to:

   (*a*) the requirements for the passing of a resolution at an extraordinary general meeting;

   (*b*) the disclosure of ownership under section 33 of the 1967 Act and sections 26 and 27 of the 1976 Act.

2. (*a*) What is the nature of the business dealt with at the annual general meeting?

(*b*) What information and documents can the shareholder expect to receive before the AGM? What action (if any) is he required to take?

3. (*a*) What are the rights of the ordinary shareholders? How are these protected (i) by law, and (ii) by the Stock Exchange?
   (*b*) What rights do preference shareholders have? Can they vote at company meetings?

Unit Eighteen

Investor Protection

18.1 Introduction

L.C.B. Gower, in *The Principles of Modern Company Law*, comes to four main conclusions on the subject of investor protection:

(*a*) that English law is based on a philosophy of disclosure rather than supervision;
(*b*) that the existing system is inadequate in that it is difficult for investors and others to check the truth of the information disclosed;
(*c*) that the efficiency of company law depends to a large extent on private enterprise and extra-legal techniques;
(*d*) that the rules are remarkably irrational and confusing, there being several different statutes and innumerable institutions dealing with the single problem of protecting the investor.

There is indeed strong resistance to bureaucratic involvement in the securities industry. The huge Securities and Exchange Commission in the United States is often cited as an example of this, and the Take-over Panel and the Council for the Securities Industry (see Units 18.6 and 18.7) are both examples of low-profile regulatory bodies which are perhaps more typical of the British way of doing things! It is assumed that if the investor is given the fullest possible information he will be able to make up his own mind – 'a large assumption', says Gower.

Disclosure is all very well if the information disclosed is true. Companies' accounts are subject to audit, which affords the investor a large measure of protection, but the overburdened Registrar of Companies does not check the accuracy of prospectuses, merely that they comply with the statutory regulations. Many of the scandals affecting companies and their shareholders are revealed, not by the Department of Trade, but by the investigations of publications as diverse as the *Sunday Times* and *Private Eye*.

Finally, what Gower had in mind is the mish-mash of existing law. There has been no major Companies Act since 1948, but there have been the Companies Acts of 1967, 1976 and 1980, the Prevention of Fraud (Investments) Act 1958, the Protection of Depositors Act 1963 (now replaced by the Banking Act 1979), several statutes dealing with the rights of policyholders, and a host of statutory regulations and rules. We shall examine some of the more important statutory and voluntary protections of the investor.

18.2 Take-overs and Mergers

The shareholder may at any time encounter a take-over bid, either for a company whose shares he owns or by his company for the shares of another. The small shareholder is unlikely to be able to exercise very much influence in the latter case, but where an offer is made for the shares which he owns, he and his fellow shareholders will have a significant influence on the result of the bid.

Take-overs came in for heavy criticism during the 1950s and 1960s, not only for the methods used to attain them but also of the take-over as a means of business expansion.

Many of today's great companies have been built up by means of take-over, however, and governments of both political complexions have encouraged them. The motives for this type of expansion are many and various, the more important of them being:

(i) to enable the company to diversify its interests;

(ii) to obtain an increase in the share of a particular market (that is, a degree of monopoly power);

(iii) to ensure supplies by the acquisition of a company involved in providing essential materials, components or services;

(iv) to facilitate the distribution of a company's products by acquiring retail outlets.

These activities are illustrated in Fig. 18.1.

All these activities make economic sense, even though the social consequences in terms of redundancies may be serious. Take-overs are not always motivated by the desire for expansion, however. Frequently they arise from pressures on profit margins, and may then be considered defensive rather than aggressive.

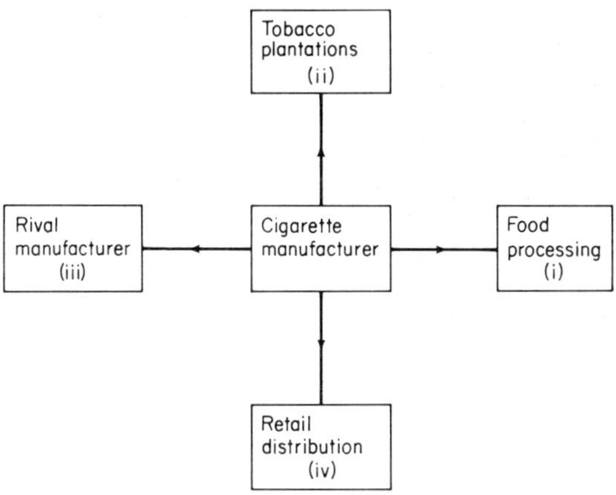

Fig. 18.1 The chief motives for take-over, illustrated in the case of a cigarette manufacturer

Often take-over bids arise when a company's earnings are too low to maintain a market price at or near the asset value. This situation prompts a second company to bid for the first company's voting capital at a price more in line with asset value, in order that it may use the assets to expand its own business. This is often a far cheaper and quicker way of expanding than issuing new capital for cash and then setting up new factories to extend operations. When it takes over another company, a bidding company acquires not only assets but an existing market and an experienced work force. By merging the interests and operations of the two companies it should be possible to effect economies and to produce greater efficiency than could be achieved by the two companies operating separately.

Take-overs and mergers are usually considered together. While most people know what is meant by the former, the latter are more difficult to define. In this book we treat the *merger* as the creation of a new company to acquire the assets of two or more existing companies. Frequently, but not always, the two companies being merged are of approximately the same size. Mergers are usually agreed at the outset but this is by no means always the case with the take-over.

18.3 Take-overs: Strategy and Information

The classic defence of a company that is the subject of a take-over bid is to announce profit forecasts for current and future years, in an attempt to prove that the depressed market price is based on a mistaken view of its prospects. Usually increased dividends are forecast, often a bonus issue is announced, and the company sets out to re-establish a higher market rating in order to persuade its shareholders not to accept the bid. Not all bids are defended in this way and many take-overs go through quietly, but a sufficient number become take-over 'battles' to feed the headlines of the popular press. Often more than one company is bidding at the same time for the shares of the same company.

Uneasiness has been expressed about the amount of information available to directors which is not passed on to shareholders, because a considerable number of take-overs either fail, or the bids have to be raised before they are successful. If a company can defeat a bid by announcing profit forecasts that raise the share price substantially, it is reasonable to ask why these forecasts were not given to shareholders before the bid was made. It may be argued that it is not in the interests of shareholders to disclose detailed forecasts and information except when they are being asked to accept a bid which is too low. But the ordinary shareholders of a company are its proprietors and have a right to be informed of a company's situation, especially if ignorance might cause them to sell their shares on the market too cheaply. Directors have as much duty to shareholders who wish to sell their shares as to those people who are buying and may be acquiring shares at a price that would be too low if all information were available. Sometimes a take-over defence reflects more the directors' fear for their jobs than the interests of the shareholders who might benefit from exchanging their shares for those of a more dynamic company.

18.4 Take-overs: the Shareholders' Response

Take-over bids are certainly of short-term benefit to the shareholders of the company bid for. Whether the bid succeeds or not, the price of their shares will rise and, if they do not wish to accept the bid, they have the opportunity to dispose of their holdings on the market at an enhanced price. In any event, the affairs of the company bid for are ventilated and this can rarely do harm to the shareholders.

If the proposal is for a merger, it is likely to be beneficial to the former shareholders of both companies, in the long run. In the short run, one company's shareholders may gain at the expense of the other's as market prices reflect the merger terms. If the merger really seems to make economic sense, however, the merger will be a 'bull point' and the shares of both companies could rise reflecting the market's view of improved business and profits prospects. A merger will result in an exchange of shares in the old company for shares in the new one, and there are no capital gains tax considerations.

With a take-over bid the position is rather different. Because the bidding company is offering more than the current market price for the shares of the other company, its shares usually fall in price in the short run. If the directors have got their sums right, however, this should not depress the bidding company's shares unduly, since in due course an expansion of profits should justify the bid. In many contested bids, however, the price ultimately paid is determined more by corporate rivalry than by economic logic.

The main difference between the two offers is in the terms. In a merger only shares are offered in exchange for shares. In a take-over the bid may be entirely for cash, or for cash and shares, or it may include a fixed-interest element, perhaps a convertible loan stock.

If the offer is for cash, the shareholder can easily calculate the immediate profit in prospect, taking into account the fact that a cash sale represents a disposal for capital gains tax purposes. Of course the offer, while being immediately attractive, may still fall below the price originally paid.

If the offer is in shares only, the calculations are fairly straightforward. Suppose, for example, that Company A, whose shares stand at 200p offers one of its shares for every two of Company B, whose shares are quoted at 80p; the bid is worth 100p a share and there are no capital gains tax considerations. The shares of Company A will not remain at 200p, however, nor will Company B's automatically rise to 100p. There are two main possibilities. If the bid seems likely to fail, the market may not mark up the shares much beyond the initial 80p. On the other hand, the shares could rise well beyond 100p in the belief that either an increased offer or other bidders will appear on the scene, and at this point the shareholders must decide whether to sell in the market or wait in the hope that a better offer will materialize.

If the bid is accepted the shareholder must make another important decision, namely whether to keep the new holding or sell in the market. This decision will depend very much on his view about the bidding company.

Where the offer is in cash and shares, the cash element is subject to capital gains tax. Suppose that Company A's terms were two shares and £1 cash for every five shares of Company B – the same offer based on the 200p valuation of Company A's shares – and consider the holder of 2 000 Company B shares purchased at 60p:

Original cost:		*Acquisition value of Company A shares*	*Capital gain*
2 000 shares of Company B at 60p	£1 200		
Acceptance of offer:			
800 shares of Company A at £2	£1 600	£ 960 (£1 200 × $\frac{1\,600}{2\,000}$)	Deferred until sale of Company A shares
Cash	£ 400	£ 240 (£1 200 × $\frac{400}{2\,000}$)	£160
	£2 000	£1 200	

Where the offer also concerns, say, a fixed-interest stock the position is still more complicated. A new loan stock is something of an unknown quantity and valuing it is not always easy, especially if conversion rights are attached. Many shareholders will not want it, anyway.

18.5 Obtaining Control

Legally a company has control of another when it has an absolute majority of the voting shares. We saw in Unit 17.7, however, that a company needs 75 per cent of the votes to pass special and extraordinary resolutions. In practice, however, it does not need anything like such a large proportion of the shares to obtain effective control. The Take-over Code, discussed in Unit 18.6, suggests 30 per cent is sufficient. Nonetheless many companies, for various reasons, like to obtain total ownership and there are provisions in the Companies Act (section 209) which prevent a small minority of shareholders from defeating this aim.

For the bidding company to obtain absolute ownership it must have received acceptances of 90 per cent of the shares other than any that it holds at the date of the bid. If, for example, it already holds 5 per cent of the shares it must receive further acceptances of at least 85.5 per cent of shares (90 per cent of 95 per cent) to invoke section 209. If it already holds 10 per cent or more of the shares the Act is still more stringent, and the bidder must also obtain the assent of 75 per cent of the remaining shareholders. Consider, for example, the following situation relating to the ordinary shares of a target company:

	Number of shares held
Bidding company	120 000
8 shareholders each holding 100 000 shares	800 000
8 shareholders each holding 10 000 shares	80 000
	1 000 000

The bidding company could achieve the 90 per cent requirement by acquiring only the eight larger holdings, but to satisfy the 75 per cent rule it must also obtain acceptances from four of the smaller holders.

Whatever the situation, the bidding company must receive the required acceptances within four months of the bid. It must then give two months' notice to the remaining shareholders to acquire their shares, any dissenting shareholders having one month to apply to the court to retain their holdings.

18.6 The City Code on Take-overs and Mergers

Take-over activity is both necessary and healthy in an advanced economy. Sometimes a proposed take-over may seem sensible when viewed from the economic aspects of efficiency and resource allocation, but may be questioned because of its adverse effect on jobs. The activities of the 'asset-strippers', who obtain control of companies only to wind them up and make quick profits for themselves, come into this category.

Because the take-over, by its very nature, involves the making of an offer above the current market price for the shares, it is clearly a prime area for activities and manipulations by the unscrupulous. Adverse publicity resulting from this kind of activity does the Stock Exchange and City institutions no good whatsoever, and in the late 1960s the larger institutions, encouraged by the Bank of England, formed the *Panel on Take-overs and Mergers* to regulate take-over activity. In March 1968 the first City Code was published by the Panel. This has now been revised and strengthened several times, most recently in 1981.

The Code does not prescribe the manner in which take-over bids should be made. Instead it states certain general principles and elaborates these in some specific rules. Its four main principles are:

(*a*) that all shareholders of the same class should be treated equally;

(*b*) that shareholders should be given adequate information to form a proper judgement;

(*c*) that directors of the offeree company (the company whose shares are being bid for) should act in the best interests of their shareholders and obtain independent advice;

(*d*) that creation of false markets in the shares should be avoided.

It is a cardinal rule that the spirit of the Code, and not merely its letter, be observed. The underlying principle is that there should be equal treatment of all shareholders. For instance, before the Code was introduced a company might make a generous offer for the directors' and their families' shares, thus acquiring control, and then at a later date make a lower offer to the other shareholders; such practices are not permitted by the Code.

If any company (including its associates and other parties 'acting in concert') acquires more than 15 per cent of any class of shares in the twelve months before it makes a take-over bid, then it must offer a cash alternative to all shareholders of that class at the highest price paid during that period. Moreover, if any company acquires more than 30 per cent of the shares in another company (this proportion being regarded as sufficient to give it effective control), then it is required to make a general offer to all shareholders at the highest price paid for these shares in the past twelve months.

The behaviour of directors is one of the main concerns of the Code, since it is essential that, as they are in a position of trust, they should always put the interest of shareholders before those of themselves and their associates. The dangers of the unscrupulous use of price-sensitive information (what is widely known as *insider dealing*) were brought out clearly in the Panel's Annual Report covering the year ended 31 March 1977:

> Lack of care about security, loose talk, the observation from outside of unusual activity at a company's offices, speculative hunches and dealings by insiders are just a few of the causes of sharp rises in the market price of securities before the announcement of price-sensitive matters. . . . The major objectives are to prevent small shareholders from parting with their shares just before the shares become especially valuable and to stop unethical practices.
>
> That there are great difficulties is indisputable and these have been experienced in all countries where sophisticated stock market systems exist. The view of the Stock Exchange and the Panel that true insider trading should be the subject of legislation is well known and the Government's recent confirmation that insider dealing legislation will be introduced as soon as opportunity permits, is warmly welcomed.

Insider dealing is now a criminal offence under the Companies Act 1980.

In October 1977 the Stock Exchange drafted a *Model Code for Securities Transactions by Directors of Listed Companies*. The report went on to mention an important result of one of several joint initiatives taken with the Stock Exchange:

> The Stock Exchange and the Panel now encourage companies to apply to the Stock Exchange for a temporary trading halt. This is a particularly appropriate step when an announcement of importance is imminent but full details are not available perhaps because certain formalities remain to be

settled. In the five months since the joint announcement was issued thirty companies have applied for a trading halt in the context of a merger or take-over proposal. This is an encouraging development and it has generally been noticeable that there have been fewer cases of speculative activity in the shares of companies which subsequently announced merger or take-over plans.

Since the authority of the Panel is not statutory its powers are strictly limited. It can, however, (*a*) admonish the offender in private, (*b*) reprimand the offender publicly and (*c*) refer the matter to the offender's own professional body for disciplinary action. The public reprimand or the professional body's disciplinary action can both have a severe effect and could result in depriving the offender of his usual means of earning a living. Appeals against disciplinary rulings can be made to an Appeals Committee. Critics of the Panel argue that its sanctions are not effective enough and that in any case certain other practices, not just insider dealing, ought to be made criminal offences.

18.7 The Council for the Securities Industry

In the past, the main task of non-statutory regulation has rested with the Stock Exchange. In recent years the Panel on Take-overs and Mergers has become an important second force, but its brief is clearly limited. Other developments in the securities industry, such as ARIEL (see Unit 9.7) and the over-the-counter market (see Unit 9.8(*c*)), involve activities that may be outside the scope of the Stock Exchange or the Panel. There has also been an increasing internationalization of the securities industry since the foundation of the Eurobond market in the mid-1960s.

All these developments, and others, prompted the formation in 1978 of the *Council for the Securities Industry*, with the full backing of the Bank of England and in consultation with all representative City institutions. Some idea of the new body's scope is given in Fig. 18.2 (page 303).

Of considerable concern in 1980 were the so-called 'dawn raids' whereby one company, through its stockbrokers, acquired just under 30 per cent of the shares of another, and were thus not obliged to bid for the remainder of the shares. This practice was taken up by the Council for the Securities Industry, which ruled that in future a bidder aiming to buy 5 per cent or more of a company so as to take his holding over 15 per cent but under 30 per cent must give notice of his intentions and make a general tender offer to the shareholders.

18.8 Other Voluntary Bodies

A number of other voluntary bodies also act as protectors of the investor in different ways and to different extents. They include the Building Societies

Association, the Unit Trust Association, the British Insurance Association, the Association of Investment Trust Companies, the Issuing Houses Association, the recently formed Association of Licensed Dealers in Securities and many others; a detailed study of each is beyond the scope of this book, however.

18.9 The Prevention of Fraud (Investments) Act 1958

To trade in shares an individual or firm must be licensed by the Department of Trade under the Prevention of Fraud (Investments) Act 1958 or be exempt from licensing.

This Act developed out of a 1939 law designed to protect the investor from share-pushing and fraudulent prospectuses but its scope is wider than the prevention of fraud and it is possibly not very aptly named. The Act, which is administered by the Department of Trade, requires intending licensees to provide copious personal details, references and a £500 deposit in exchange for a licence. Section 13 of the Act prescribes a penalty of up to seven years' imprisonment for any person who induces another person to invest money by means of statements, promises or forecasts which he knows to be misleading, false or deceptive. The same penalty applies to anyone attempting such inducement or conspiring to do so, and to the concealment of facts and reckless statements. The section covers not only securities, but also agreements that purport to secure a profit from the fluctuations in the value of any other property.

The Act also places restrictions on the distribution of circulars inviting investment and prescribes a penalty of up to two years' imprisonment or a fine of up to £500, or both, for a breach of those restrictions (section 14). There are exceptions to this provision, including prospectuses issued under the Companies Acts and documents issued by the managers of authorized unit trusts, members of the Stock Exchange, building societies and exempted and licensed dealers in securities as defined in the Act.

The Act lays down provisions for the compulsory licensing of all dealers in securities. Any person who is neither licensed nor specially exempted from licensing but who nonetheless deals in securities with the general public is liable to imprisonment for up to two years or a fine of up to £500, or both. Exempted dealers include joint stock banks, merchant banks, insurance companies and trustee savings banks. Also exempted from licensing are members of recognized stock exchanges and the trustees and managers of authorized unit trusts. Under a power given to the Department of Trade under the Act, the Department issued the Licensed Dealers (Conduct of Business) Rules 1960 to which licensed dealers must conform. These however have been greatly strengthened by the requirements of the Take-over Code. The Act also includes provisions for the registration of industrial and provident societies, and for the control and investigation of building societies and unit trusts.

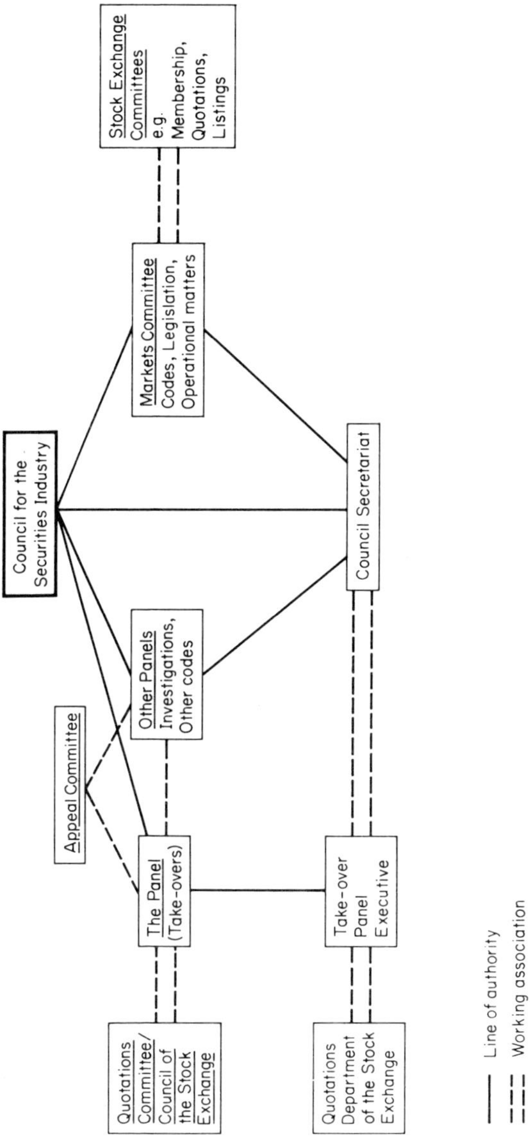

Fig. 18.2 The scope of the Council for the Securities Industry

18.10 The Banking Act 1979

This Act not only repealed the Protection of Depositors Act 1963, but considerably extended control over banks and other financial institutions receiving deposits. It arose from a number of developments in the previous two decades, in particular the fringe banking crisis of the mid-1970s and the need for EEC harmonization of banking law. For centuries the major financial institutions of the United Kingdom operated within a framework of voluntary and informal controls set by the Treasury and the Bank of England. Under the Community banking directive, however, all banks and other deposit-taking institutions must be licensed. The directive leaves the enforcement to the national legislative body. Under the Banking Act, deposit-taking institutions are divided into two kinds: *recognized banks* and *licensed deposit-taking institutions*.

The chief purposes of the Act are:

(*a*) to control the use of banking names and descriptions;

(*b*) to distinguish banks proper from other deposit-takers and to provide for their supervision and licensing by the Bank of England;

(*c*) to lay down criteria which must be satisfied before an institution is licensed;

(*d*) to make it a criminal offence for any unlicensed institution to advertise or accept deposits;

(*e*) to provide some protection for depositors by means of a Deposit Protection Scheme.

Every applicant for recognition must satisfy the Bank of England as to its solvency and the competence of its management. New deposit-takers require a capital base of £5 million for recognition, but only £250 000 for a licence. Although the Act is much more comprehensive than previous legislation, there are still important exemptions from its requirements. Apart from the Bank of England these include National Girobank, the National Savings Bank, the trustee savings banks (for the time being) and the local authorities. The insurance companies and the building societies are covered by other legislation.

Much of the debate about the new legislation turned on the two-tier licensing system. Some banks, including many of the smaller foreign banks, while permitted to use the word 'bank' in their title, have had to add the words 'licensed deposit-taking institution'. Many other institutions settled for the secondary designation alone: the Act, however, makes provision for promotion to the first rank.

Most important for depositors is the *Deposit Protection Scheme*. A fund is to be set up, financed by cash subscriptions from all recognized banks and deposit-takers. The fund is only intended to protect depositors of sums up to £10 000 and then only to the extent of 75 per cent of their deposits. But this goes well beyond the scope of the Protection of Depositors Act which, by means of regulation, sought only to prevent losses to depositors.

18.11 Insurance Policyholders and the Law

By the early 1970s insurance law was in an untidy state. The failure of some small life assurance companies, together with concern over the widespread practice of door-to-door selling of life assurance, resulted in a comprehensive review of unit-linked insurance by a committee chaired by Sir Hilary Scott.

The Insurance Companies Act 1974 consolidated nearly all the legislation contained in the acts of 1958 and 1973 but most of its real powers involve delegated legislation through the Department of Trade. The chief provisions of interest to investors are:

(*a*) the Department can regulate the content of advertisements (although no such action has been taken at the time of writing);

(*b*) issuing misleading, false or deceptive statements or sales material is made a criminal offence subject to two years' imprisonment or a fine, or both;

(*c*) the insurer must issue a statutory notice setting out the terms and benefits of the contract, and the notice must have annexed to it a form enabling the proposer to cancel the contract;

(*d*) cancellation must be within a period of ten days – the 'cooling-off' period – or on the earliest day the proposer knows the contract has been entered into or the first or only premium paid;

(*e*) any person selling a policy must reveal his connection with the company.

Shortly afterwards another act, the Policyholders Protection Act 1975, came into force. This Act is concerned not with the writing of the contract but with the possible aftermath, and established a Policyholders' Protection Board which can impose a levy on insurance companies and accountable intermediaries. The Board can thus ensure that in the event of the collapse of a company registered under the Act, policyholders will in general receive 90 per cent of the value of their policies; alternatively, it can arrange to have the business transferred to another company.

Finally, the Insurance Brokers' (Registration) Act 1977 established the Insurance Brokers' Registration Council which, among other things, deals with the registration, training, qualification and professional standards of brokers. As a result, it is now a criminal offence for a person to describe himself as an insurance broker unless he is registered with the Council. The Council has since drawn up a code of conduct and the disciplinary procedures also required under the Act.

18.12 Questions

1. What are the main objects of the City Code on Take-overs and Mergers? How effective is it?
2. In what circumstances can an offering company legally enforce the purchase of shares in a company for which it has made a take-over bid?
3. Discuss briefly the protection given to investors by legislation and otherwise in each of the following cases: (i) deposits, (ii) unit trusts, (iii) life assurance.

Unit Nineteen

Investment Advice and Professional Management

Many investors may consider that they do not have the time or inclination to manage their own investment portfolios, and will employ professional investment managers to do this for them. Every investor needs advice in one way or another. There are various places from which an investor can get advice; some are free, some are not, and there are a few types of organization which offer specialized investment management.

19.1 Advice

The investor cannot be protected from advice that proves to be bad, or from his own ignorance or stupidity. Every financial adviser has met someone who has put his life savings into the ordinary shares of a third-rate company and has lost most of them as a result. Other people, having purchased units in a unit trust investing exclusively in fixed-income stocks, have become very upset because its capital value did not improve in a bull market in line with other trusts run by the same group. Still others apply for units in a unit trust by cutting a coupon out of a newspaper, in the mistaken belief that it refers to a new issue of shares which would be substantially oversubscribed, and are dismayed to receive a full 'allotment'.

There is no remedy for losses incurred from following bad advice, if that advice is given in good faith. If your financial adviser tells you that an allotment letter is a circular only and can be destroyed, a claim against him for negligence may possibly be upheld. On the other hand, if he advises you that the allotment should be sold as the share price is too high, and the share price promptly doubles overnight, no claim for negligence will succeed. Anyone can be wrong, and there is no comeback as long as the opinion expressed is honestly and genuinely held, and the person giving advice is not exceeding the scope of his professional expertise. This is why an investor should familiarize himself with the range and use of the various types of investment, and be aware of the current investment climate, so that he can evaluate and assess the advice he receives.

Advice on investment matters is plentiful. There are as many people prepared to advise on investment as there are people prepared to advise the Government on its policies. Investment is a popular hobby, and where hobbies are concerned expense is rarely a major factor. So many people, having a few shares, and having had one success, come to believe that they have a flair for investment that can be developed to make fortunes for themselves and for all their friends and acquaintances. When questioned about their less-successful purchases, they maintain a discreet silence.

The investor should beware of such amateurs. However convincing the take-over story based on 'inside' knowledge seems, however much the friend employed by a large company claims to know about its current progress and however much the man on the train has made out of a particular share, he should either ignore what they say, or at least evaluate it carefully. The tale about the take-over may be true; it may merely be a rumour. Few people in large companies can see the whole picture of their company's activities. And a large profit on a purchase may only mean that the top price has been reached rather than that further appreciation is indicated.

(*a*) The Bank Manager

Many investors look to their bank manager for their general financial and investment advice. Usually this is as good a source as any, since bank managers see a good deal of the financial world in their day-to-day dealings with a wide range of customers and business associates. They are not, however, specially trained in investment matters. Bank managers vary considerably in their knowledge of investments but many of them have investment portfolios of their own which compel them to keep abreast of market trends and thinking. Many others, however, do not have the 'feel' of investments and are not able to give advice other than of a very general kind.

The well-known case of Woods *v.* Martins Bank Ltd and Another 1958 hangs over them like the sword of Damocles, although that case, which resulted in judgment against the bank concerned for loss resulting from a customer following his bank manager's advice, was decided on very special circumstances. The customer invested in preference shares in a private company which banked at the same branch and which was in financial difficulty. In his judgment, the judge said that in giving investment advice, the only obligation on the bank manager was 'to advise with the ordinary care and skill which the ordinary bank manager in his position might reasonably be expected to possess.' Here there was clearly a gross dereliction of that obligation.

It is desirable that the average bank manager should become more investment-orientated. Certainly he must know what rival organizations such as the National Savings Bank and the building societies are currently offering depositors. He should be familiar with the returns available on the National Savings investments and their suitability for customers in different tax situations. He will be mindful of his customers' needs for life assurance, and in particular the many advantages of unit trusts and insurance bonds. The investor himself should be aware that the manager's advice is unlikely ever to be wholly disinterested. Bankers like having deposit accounts; and it is only natural for them to prefer their own bank's unit trust and insurance subsidiaries to those of their rivals, even if the track record does not always justify that preference!

By training the bank manager is not an expert in investment and while he may be able to give excellent general advice he generally steers clear of giving specific advice on marketable securities. Banks will ask their brokers for advice on portfolio construction and individual investments if their customers wish. Today, however, they are much more likely to recommend the investment portfolio management services of their own banks (see Unit 19.2(*c*)).

(*b*) Stockbrokers

The best available advice on the purchase of equities probably comes from stockbrokers with experienced and able teams of analysts at their disposal. Only the largest firms can afford large research departments and generally these are the firms least willing to take on the small client. They do most of their business with the large institutions such as the insurance companies, merchant banks and pension funds, where the size of the individual orders produces commission for the brokers large enough to justify intensive research on a limited number of companies.

The same applies to fixed-interest investment. A number of brokers have specialized fixed-interest departments working on yield curves, anomaly positions and the like, and provide a service to institutions in return for the very large bargains which this section of the market produces.

Nevertheless, the smaller investor should have no difficulty in finding a broker. The Secretary of the Stock Exchange will provide the names of several firms, if he does not already have an introduction (see Unit 9.3). The amount of research and analysis done by these smaller firms will be less than that done by the big firms because of the nature of their business. But firms willing to accept the smaller investor can offer a personal service to their clients which many big firms, with their demanding institutional clients, cannot. And the advice that many of them give is excellent. As with all professions, the quality of the service one obtains depends on the ability of the particular person with whom one deals. Investment advice can only be evaluated in the medium term, and when dealing with a new broker it is necessary to take certain things on trust until sufficient time has gone by to be able to assess the advice given.

(*c*) Other Informed Sources

Many investors rely on their solicitors, accountants and insurance brokers for investment advice. The reservations made as to advice given by bank managers apply broadly here also. People whose principal activity is not directly related to investment can hardly be expected to be aware of all the latest developments in that area and to be fully in touch with market trends and opinion.

Unfortunately, the number of professional investment advisers whose services are available to the small investor is shrinking. The cost of all services is continually rising and the small investor cannot pay for expensive advice. What he needs is a good supply of general information that he can apply to his own circumstances. The number of newspapers and journals recognizing this need is increasing; some are listed in 'Further Reading' at the end of this book.

All-round financial services, including tax planning and insurance of all kinds, are frequently required as well as investment advice. The number of companies setting out to supply this need is rising, although they still include only a few recognized institutions. There is a need not only for more advisers, but for a greater awareness among the public of how much they need these services.

19.2 Professional Management

There is probably no other activity where the expert is so often wrong as in the field of investment. If the investment is absolutely straightforward – putting funds on deposit or into some form of life assurance, for instance – the matter is relatively simple, but there are no foolproof ways of making money out of risk investments like ordinary shares. The individual investor will therefore be wise to consider appointing professional managers to look after his investments, possibly even a full discretionary management service. Any recommendations will only be given by the competent manager in the context of an investor's overall strategy, and that always means considerable attention being paid to the need to diversify his interests.

We shall consider the services given by stockbrokers, merchant banks, clearing banks and others.

(*a*) Stockbrokers

Some stockbrokers offer a service to clients which goes beyond the mere giving of advice. They are prepared to take over the management of portfolios, dealing with them at their discretion. The size of portfolio which will be taken on varies with the firm, and so also does the amount of commission required from the portfolio. Some brokers make a charge for this service and others make no charge over and above their commissions. As the standard of advice varies throughout the range of firms offering this service, it is impossible to generalize on the quality of this type of investment management.

(*b*) Merchant Banks

Merchant banks offer investment management services to private clients and institutions. They all have a minimum size of portfolio which they will take on. Most merchant banks are not interested in portfolios of less than £100 000. Charges vary considerably, from 50p to £1.25 per annum per £100 managed. There are usually reduced rates for the largest portfolios. All merchant banks require full discretionary powers in their portfolio management and obviously the funds are largely, if not exclusively, invested in equities. Where pension funds have a fixed-interest section this is usually managed separately, with decisions taken periodically as to the proportion of the fund to be invested in this sector.

Merchant banks manage very substantial sums and they all have their own analytical departments. In addition, by using many firms of brokers for their business, they receive the output of most of the research departments of the large stockbroking firms. Their management services should therefore produce better results than those of other institutions with smaller business and consequently less resources. The only way in which it is possible to judge performance overall is to compare the records of unit trusts managed by merchant banks against those managed by other institutions. In fact, such a comparison does not show that the investment management of merchant banks is much better than any other. The ownership of the unit trusts concerned, and therefore the institutions responsible for investment, changes from time to time and strict comparison is difficult. However, the performance records for unit trusts over the seven years to the end of 1979 show only three trusts out of the top ten that had the investment management of merchant banks for most of the period. Similar results are obtained from a comparison over three years and five years, also to the end of 1979. Not all unit trusts managed by merchant banks concentrate on capital growth any more than those managed by other institutions, but there are enough of them for the above comparison to be useful.

(*c*) Clearing Banks

The investment portfolio management services offered by the clearing banks are generally in a lower key than those offered by merchant banks. Their analytical departments are smaller than those of the merchant banks and their expertise depends largely on their assessment and modification of the advice and recommendations received from the stockbrokers allocated to each client's portfolio. Usually the investment management service is operated by the executor and trustee departments of the banks concerned. It forms part of a financial service offered by those departments principally to the bank's general customers and which covers estate planning, personal tax advice, executorship and family trust administration as well as private portfolio management. The banks also have a measure of institutional business such as pension fund trusteeship and custodian services.

The minimum portfolio requirements for the investment management services of clearing banks range from £20 000 to £50 000. Charges are around the 50p to 75p per £100 level with minimum fees at about £100 per annum. Generally speaking, the service is geared more to the individual circumstances of the customer than those of the other institutions. The banks will recommend investments other than stock exchange securities if they feel that these are best suited to the customer's requirements, whereas the services offered by other institutions are primarily for the management of stock exchange portfolios. For this type of service knowledge of the whole of the customer's circumstances is necessary. The investment policy pursued by the banks is less active than many of the other portfolio management institutions, with the emphasis on the purchase and regular review of holdings suitable for the investor's requirements in the medium to long term. Maximizing of capital growth and comparison of performance against recognized indices take a secondary place to portfolio planning and maintenance. The service offered, therefore, is similar to the portfolio management which a private investor might do himself. For this reason the banks tend to attract those people who do not have the time or inclination to look after their own portfolios, rather than those knowledgeable investors who are looking to an institution for superior investment expertise.

The unit trusts run by the clearing banks, with a few exceptions, show unspectacular performances with rare appearances in either the top or bottom of the performance tables. Given the attitude of the clearing banks to investment policy generally, this is hardly surprising. In fairness, however, it should be borne in mind that medium-term performance is not achieved by spectacular success in one short period followed by spectacular failure in another. Trusts with the best long-term performance are not always in the 'top twenty' over short periods.

(*d*) Other Management Services

Advice and management have been available for many years from investment counsellors in the United States and from independent investment managers in the United Kingdom. As a result of the sharp escalation in costs over the past few years the availability of professional management from banks for the smaller investor has been considerably reduced. This has led to an increase in the number of companies able to provide an individual and comprehensive service. These independent investment managers are usually small firms giving a highly personal service with continuity of management by a known individual – a service more personal than that of the clearing banks and not requiring the high minimum portfolio value required by a merchant bank.

The Association of Independent Investment Managers now exists to establish and enforce standards of professional conduct and for the protection of investors. Any investor seeking management advice outside the better known sources will be wise to ensure that the firm he deals with belongs to this Association.

19.3 Questions

1. A customer holds British Government stocks and United Kingdom equities valued at about £100 000, the majority of which he has recently inherited. His brokers inform him that the investments held represent a sound, well-balanced portfolio with good long-term prospects. He is in his forties with a well-paid executive position in a large company based in the United Kingdom, but has little time to give to his own affairs.

   He asks you whether a periodic review of his investments by his stockbroker would be adequate supervision or whether he should place them in the hands of an institution for discretionary management. What would be your reply and what reasons would you give in support of your view?

2. Assess the position of the bank manager as an investment adviser. How well do you think he fits this role?
3. Discuss the investment portfolio management services offered by the clearing banks and the merchant banks. Do they differ in any important respects?

Unit Twenty

Investment by Trustees

The approach of trustees in general to the problems of investment differs from that of the individual in two respects. First, the investment powers of trustees may be limited whereas an individual, or an investment manager acting on behalf of individuals, can usually choose investments unhampered by artificial restrictions. Secondly, the interests of the persons entitled to the trust property may conflict, and in his investment policy the trustee must give consideration to the interests of all the parties concerned. The choice of investments and the interests of the beneficiaries of the trust will vary considerably, depending on the nature of the trust and the persons entitled to benefit. The circumstances of a large pension fund or charitable trust are clearly different from those of a small family trust; the investment policies to be followed by each will also differ.

20.1 The Investment Powers of Trustees

Powers of investment are given to trustees in two ways: by the trust instrument, and by statute. The investment powers, if any, contained in the deed (or will) setting up the trust override the powers given to trustees by law. The statutory powers come into effect in cases where the trust instrument is silent or gives powers less wide than those contained in the relevant Act of Parliament, and in cases of intestacy.

In modern wills and settlements and in the trust deeds of charitable trusts and pension funds, a clause is customarily included giving the trustees the widest powers of investment. This does not necessarily mean that the trustees will use these powers but it increases their flexibility of investment. The wording of clauses varies but most often they include a power for the trustees to invest 'in all respects as though they were the beneficial owners . . .' of the trust property. Such clauses are therefore commonly known as *beneficial owner clauses*.

In older trust deeds, beneficial owner clauses are less usual. Some deeds contain lengthy clauses specifying the types of investment than can be purchased. Others include a power to retain the investments originally settled, but limit any reinvestment of the proceeds of their sale. Wills often direct that the property settled shall be sold, but give the trustees power to postpone that sale for as long as they think fit. Some deeds and wills have clauses authorizing the retention of, or the investment in, specific companies, often family companies. All these clauses are known as *special powers of investment*, and stand beside the statutory powers.

Some trust deeds or wills authorize investment according to the law for the time being in force, while others are completely silent on investment powers. Then there are cases of statutory trusts in favour of dependants which arise on an intestacy. In all these situations the statutory powers have full effect. It is possible, though rare, for the investment powers of trustees to be limited by clauses naming certain types of investment or certain companies which the trustees may not invest in, notwithstanding any statutory power to the contrary. It is also possible, though even rarer, for the powers of investment to be limited to a specific investment or type of investment, overriding the statutory powers in the opposite way to a beneficial owner clause. The statutory powers of investment are contained principally in the Trustee Investments Act 1961.

20.2 The Trustee Investments Act 1961

Prior to this Act, trustees restricted to statutory powers of investment could generally purchase only fixed-interest investments specified in the Trustee Act 1925 or the Trusts (Scotland) Act 1921, which were mostly gilt-edged stocks. The principal exception to this restriction was the Settled Land Act 1925, which gave additional powers to trustees of settled land to purchase land and buildings, and to invest capital moneys in carrying out certain alterations and improvements to land and buildings owned.

There was a prolonged period after the passing of the Trustee Act 1925 during which prices were falling, but inflation was substantial during the war and apparently endemic thereafter. There was thus an urgent need to give trustees powers to make realistic investments – particularly in equities – during periods of inflation. The Trustee Investments Act 1961 was passed to meet this requirement. It is significant that it was passed not long after the reverse yield gap (see Unit 6.11) appeared, but the Act itself is only one of several factors contributing to the extent of yield differentials today. The proportion of the fund permitted to be invested in equities is limited and the equities purchased must fulfil certain requirements. The Act also for the first time permitted investment in certain industrial debenture and unsecured loan stocks.

Trustees do not have to invoke the Act but unless they do so, their investment powers are limited in the same way that they were before the Act was passed. Use of the investment powers granted by the Act involves the division of the trust fund initially into two equal parts, namely *narrower-range* property and *wider-range* property. In certain circumstances a third category of property, *special range*, may also be held.

20.3 Investments Authorized by the 1961 Act

The First Schedule to the Trustee Investments Act 1961 authorizes the following investments in the narrower-range and wider-range parts of trust funds:

Narrower-range Investments

Without advice (defined in section 6(4) of the Act and discussed in Unit 20.7), a trustee may hold or invest in:

(*a*) National Savings Certificates and their Northern Ireland counterparts;
(*b*) deposits with the National Savings Bank, ordinary deposits with trustee savings banks and deposits with banks and bank departments.

With advice, a trustee may invest in:

(*a*) other fixed-interest securities issued by the Governments of the United Kingdom or the Isle of Man, and Treasury bills;
(*b*) securities, the interest on which is guaranteed by the Government of the United Kingdom;
(*c*) fixed-interest securities issued in the United Kingdom by public authorities or nationalized industries;
(*d*) fixed-interest securities, issued in the United Kingdom by the government of an overseas Commonwealth territory or by any public or local authority within such territory, and registered in the United Kingdom;
(*e*) fixed-interest securities issued in the United Kingdom by the International Bank for Reconstruction and Development and the Inter-American Development Bank and registered in the United Kingdom;
(*f*) debentures registered in the United Kingdom and issued in the United Kingdom by a company incorporated in the United Kingdom (debentures include, for this purpose, debenture stocks, whether charged on specific assets or not, and loan stocks);
(*g*) stock of the Bank of Ireland;
(*h*) debentures issued by the Agricultural Mortgage Corporation and its Scottish equivalent;
(*i*) loans to local authorities in the United Kingdom and certain other authorities;
(*j*) debentures, guaranteed and preference stocks of water boards which have paid a dividend on their ordinary shares of at least 5 per cent per annum in each of the ten years preceding the investment;
(*k*) investment accounts with a trustee savings bank;
(*l*) building society deposit accounts (the societies must be designated under section 1 of the House Purchase and Housing Act 1959, generally referred to as having *trustee status*);
(*m*) mortgages of property in England, Wales or Northern Ireland which is freehold or leasehold with sixty years or more unexpired, and loans on heritable security in Scotland;

(*n*) perpetual rent-charges on land in England, Wales or Northern Ireland, fee-farm rents issuing out of such land, and feu duties or ground annuals in Scotland.

Wider-range Investments
With advice a trustee may invest in:

(*a*) any securities issued in the United Kingdom not being narrower-range investments, by a company incorporated in the United Kingdom and which are registered in the United Kingdom;
(*b*) shares in building societies of which the deposits qualify as narrower-range investments;
(*c*) authorized unit trusts.

Securities of companies, both shares and debentures, must meet four criteria to qualify as investments under the Act:

(*a*) they must be quoted on the Stock Exchange;
(*b*) any shares must be fully paid, except for new issues to be paid up within nine months;
(*c*) the company must have a paid-up share capital of at least £1 million;
(*d*) the company must have paid a dividend on all classes of share capital in each of the five years preceding the investment.

Two criticisms may be levelled at these criteria. The capital requirement of £1 million, adequate in 1961, represents quite a small company today and trustees, especially professional trustees, may well set themselves a more stringent requirement. Secondly, the Act only requires that a dividend is paid in each of the last five years. Therefore a company does not lose its trustee status even if its dividend falls in five or more successive years.

While the securities must be registered in the United Kingdom, the Trustee Act 1925 authorizes the purchase and retention of bearer securities if the issuing body meets the requirements for authorized registered securities.

Although at first sight the list of investments may appear quite comprehensive, there are several important omissions. There is no mention of freehold or leasehold land and buildings – the most outstanding major investment by far since 1961 – nor are trustees permitted to invest without specific power in any of the many insurance-based investments.

20.4 Division of the Fund

(*a*) Narrower-range and Wider-range Property
The Trustee Investments Act 1961 requires trustees wishing to include equities or unit trusts in the portfolio to divide the fund into two or three parts, the narrower range, the wider range and if applicable, the special range. The narrower-range and wider-range parts of the fund must be equal in value at the

time when the division is made and the division, once made, is final. The original allocation of securities between the two ranges can be made in any way the trustees think fit as long as they are equal in value at that time. After the fund is divided, only investments authorized as narrower-range investments under the First Schedule to the Act may be held in the narrower-range part of the fund. Any other investments in that range must be disposed of for re-investment in authorized investments. Narrower-range investments may be held in the wider-range part of the fund in addition to authorized wider-range investments. Any investment in the wider range not authorized as either a narrower-range investment or a wider-range investment must be disposed of for reinvestment in authorized investments.

(*b*) **Special-range Property**

The trust instrument may give no general powers but it may give the trustees specific power to retain or acquire investments that would not be allowed under the Act, such as unquoted shares. Any such investments must be allocated to the special-range part of the fund. Sometimes the trust deed specifies certain property which does come within the Act. If it comes within the definition of narrower-range property, it can be included either in the narrower-range or the wider-range part of the fund; but any property coming within the definition of wider-range property must, notwithstanding, be placed in the special-range part of the fund.

If a special power to invest is contained in the trust instrument, the proceeds of either narrower-range or wider-range investments may be used to buy investments authorized by that special power, and the investments so purchased will be transferred to the special-range part of the fund. This would immediately make the narrower and wider range of the fund unequal but no compensating transfer is required. When special-range investments are sold the proceeds may be used to purchase other special-range investments if a power to do so exists in the trust instrument. Otherwise the proceeds must be divided equally between the narrower- and wider-range parts of the fund for investment accordingly.

Table 20.1 (page 318) shows how a trust fund with special power to retain 'any bank securities' might be divided under the Act.

20.5 Transfers, Additions and Withdrawals

Once a trust fund has been divided, transfers from the narrower range to the wider range can only be made by making compensating transfers of equal amounts from the wider range to the narrower range, and vice versa. Suppose, for example, that the three unauthorized investments in Table 20.1 have been sold, realizing £5 900 (rather less than their value at the date of division), and it is desired to invest a total of £8 500 in equities. This could be effected in at least two ways: (*a*) by drawing £2 600 from the building society share account, or (*b*)

Table 20.1 Division of a trust fund under the Trustee Investments Act 1961

Security	Price	Valuation	Narrower range	Wider range	Special range
		£	£	£	£
£5 000 Funding 5½% 1982–84	89	4 450	4 450		
£4 000 Treasury 14½% 1994	119½	4 780	4 780		
£10 000 3½% War Loan	35	3 500	2 399	1 101	
£5 500 New Zealand 7½% 1983–86	82⅝	4 544	4 544		
£7 000 Canadian Pacific 4% Debenture	33	2 310		2 310*	
1 000 Barclays Bank £1 Ord	465	4 650			4 650
£5 000 Midland Bank 10¾% Loan 1993–98	91¼	4 562	4 562		
100 Unilever NV Fl 12	£22	2 200		2 200*	
2 800 M & G Dividend Units	145	4 060		4 060	
200 British Petroleum £1 Ord	1 182xd	2 364		2 364	
500 Rio Tinto Zinc 25p Ord (bearer)	300	1 500		1 500	
2 000 J.W. Winter Ltd £1 Ord (75p paid)	80	1 600		1 600*	
£5 600 Halifax Building Society Share Account				5 600	
Total		£46 120	£20 735	£20 735	£4 650

Notes

1. The investments marked with an asterisk are all unauthorized – two are not United Kingdom securities and the third is partly paid and also unquoted. Since these must be sold, they would normally be allocated to the wider-range part of the fund.
2. Although the trust instrument gives a special power in respect of bank securities, the Midland Bank loan stock must be placed in either the narrower-range or the wider-range part of the fund.
3. Rio Tinto Zinc Ltd is a United Kingdom company which also issues registered shares.
4. The equal division of the fund is facilitated by allocating part of the War Loan to the wider-range part of the fund.

by selling sufficient War Loan to realize £2 600; assuming for the sake of simplicity that War Loan is unchanged in value this will involve realizing (i) £1 101 from War Loan in the wider-range part of the fund, and (ii) £1 499 from War Loan in the narrower-range part of the fund. It will then be necessary to transfer £1 499 from the Halifax Building Society Share Account to the narrower range, reinvesting it in an appropriate security.

If any investments are added to the fund they must be divided in the same way as if they comprised the fund at the date of the division. Thus if the settlor were to add equities to the value of £10 000 this would involve a compensating transfer of £5 000 from the wider-range to the narrower-range part of the fund. In our example this would mean that some of the equities would have to be sold. Any additions such as a bonus issue or a rights issue will accrue to that part of the fund that includes the underlying holding. Any capital moneys that need to be paid out of the fund may be taken from any part of it and no compensating transfer will be necessary.

During the passage of the Act through Parliament it was described as 'nearly as incomprehensible to a layman as an Act of Parliament can be'. The need to maintain the division of funds certainly makes the Trustee Investments Act complex to administer, and it is highly desirable that, where at all possible, trustees are given the widest possible powers.

Despite the insistence in the Act on maintaining the division of trust property, once the division has taken place the two funds invariably cease to have the same value because (among other reasons):

(*a*) market forces affect fixed-interest stocks and equities differently;

(*b*) if there are special powers to invest then either of the two statutory funds can be used;

(*c*) payments to beneficiaries can be made from any part of the fund without compensating transfers.

Additions to the statutory funds, however, whether of new property or resulting from the sale of special-range properties, are made equally.

20.6 Retention and Postponer

Some testators, while limiting the trusts set up under their wills to the statutory powers of investment, nonetheless give their trustees power to retain any investments held at the date of death and postpone the sale thereof; others direct that they shall be sold but give the trustees power to postpone their sale indefinitely. In cases like these all such investments (except any narrower-range ones) should be treated as special-range property and it only remains to divide the cash between the two other parts of the fund. On the sale of any of the special-range property, however, the proceeds must be allocated equally between the two statutory funds.

20.7 Expert Advice

Apart from the few narrower-range investments which can be purchased or retained without advice, all investments coming within the ambit of the Trustee Investments Act require the attention of an 'expert'. An investment expert is defined in the Act as one 'who is reasonably believed by the trustee to be qualified by his ability in and practical experience of financial matters'. This is almost unbelievably vague in a modern statute, and it has been said that the investment expert should be 'something of an actuary, an accountant, an economist, a stockbroker, a man of affairs. . . . Above all he must have the ability to make up his mind quickly on the merits and demerits of an investment, then to act quickly'. The requirement to obtain advice always applies. If the sole trustee is a stockbroker or a trust corporation the advice can be given by an employee of that person or corporation.

The expert must be made fully aware of the objects of the trust and must make or confirm his recommendations in writing. Specifically the trustee, insofar as he is not an expert, must seek advice:

(*a*) as to the suitability to the trust of the investments;
(*b*) as to the need for diversification;
(*c*) as to the continued retention of any investments.

If a trustee makes an investment without seeking appropriate advice he must make good any loss arising from it, even if he makes a profit on all the other investments. He will therefore ignore expert advice at his peril. A trustee in doubt as to his powers should consult the Act itself and take legal advice if necessary.

20.8 The Trustee Act 1925

The Trustee Investments Act 1961 repealed section 1 of the Trustee Act 1925 entirely, as well as portions of sections 2 and 5. Certain important statutory powers of investment given to trustees by the 1925 Act remain in force, however. Section 7 authorizes the purchase and retention of bearer securities, providing that they would also have been authorized if registered. Sections 8, 9 and 10 of the Trustee Act 1925 contain powers and duties of trustees in lending money on mortgages in exercise of the power contained in the Trustee Investments Act. They provide, among other things, that no more than two-thirds of the value placed on a property by an independent valuer ought to be advanced by a trustee, and that if a property owned by the trust is being sold, two-thirds of the proceeds may be left on a mortgage of the property without an independent valuation being made. Like the Trustee Investments Act, the 1925 Act is highly complex, and a trustee wishing to invest in a mortgage ought to be legally advised as to his powers.

Section 10 of the 1925 Act also concerns powers relating to stock and share investments. Section 10(3) authorizes trustees to concur in any scheme or arrangement for the reconstruction, amalgamation or take-over of a company in which the trust holds authorized investments and for the release or modification of any rights attaching to any authorized securities held. Section 10(4) authorizes trustees to exercise any conditional or preferential right to subscribe for any securities which may be offered to them by reason of the trust having any authorized holding. Any proceeds of sale of any such right accrue to the capital of the trust. Retention of securities received under this clause was specifically authorized by an amendment contained in the 1961 Act.

20.9 Questions

1. What do you understand by a special power of investment in relation to the investment powers of trustees? In what ways can a special power be created?

2. Arthur bequeathed his estate to pay the income to his wife for life with remainder to his children. No investment powers are contained in the will. You are not concerned with the investment merits of the particular holdings, which are as follows:

		Price	*Value (approx.)* £
£5 000	Treasury 'A' 12½% 1993	94	4 700
£2 000	North of Scotland Hydro Electric 4% 1983–88	91	1 820
£2 000	Australia 5½% 1981–82	82	1 640
£2 000	Agricultural Mortgage Corpn 5% 1959–89	47	940
£2 000	Midland Bank 7½% Convertible Subordinated Loan 1983–93	80	1 600
200	Royal Dutch Petroleum Fl 20 shares	£34¾	6 950
100	Hudsons Bay n.p.v. shares	£14¼	1 425
400	Consolidated Gold Fields Ord 25p	180	720
200	British Petroleum Ord	590	1 180
500	ICI Ord	380	1 900
200	Hambros Ltd Shares of £10, £2½ paid	£18	3 600
200	British American Tobacco Deferred Ord 25p	350	700
100	XYZ Co Ltd (unquoted)	100	100
1 000	Guardian Royal Exchange Assurance Co 25p	205	2 050
			£29 325

(*a*) Having completed the administration of the estate you are required to divide the investments in accordance with the Trustee Investments Act 1961.

(*b*) State what further action (if any) you would take. *Note. Values quoted may be assumed to be proceeds of sales if appropriate and expenses may be ignored for the purposes of the question.*

3. (*a*) What are the requirements of the Trustee Investments Act 1961 for shares in a company to qualify as an authorized investment under Part III of the First Schedule?

(*b*) A trust has a holding of ordinary shares in a particular company in both the wider-range and the special-range parts.

(i) If the company is the subject of a take-over bid on a share-for-share basis, what are the powers of the trustees if they wish to accept the bid in respect of all the shares held by the trust? Quote the authority for your answer.

(ii) What action does the Trustee Investments Act require the trustees to take before accepting such an offer?

(iii) If the trustees do not accept the offer what are the powers of the bidding company in connection with the trust holding if the offer is accepted by holders of 90 per cent of the shares in issue?

Unit Twenty-One

Investment Portfolios for Trustees

As we said in the previous Unit, the choice of trust investments varies with the nature of the trust and the persons entitled to benefit. This Unit will be concerned with three specific kinds of trust: the family trust, charitable trusts and pension funds. (Unit trusts are dealt with in Unit 11.) We shall also consider the valuation of investments for taxation purposes.

21.1 Family Trusts

There are several different types of family trust. The most numerous are those created by will, where the testator has given a life interest to a surviving widow or widower, with the capital passing on the later death to children or other relatives. This was frequently done to reduce estate duty liabilities on the death of husband or wife for the benefit of the children of the marriage. Since the introduction of capital transfer tax, however, that part of an estate that passes to a surviving spouse has been totally exempt from tax.

Another reason for creating a life interest is where the testator does not wish to envisage the estate squandered by the surviving spouse or other relative, so despite the changed tax position there are still some trusts of this kind, although the number is diminishing. There are, of course, the statutory trusts arising on intestacy. Sometimes, too, a life interest is given so as to preserve the capital of the trust for the testator's immediate family or remoter issue, while in the meantime benefiting persons to whom the testator feels an obligation. Trusts creating life interests can also be created by deed.

In these cases the trustee has a duty to balance the interest of the *life-tenant*, who is entitled to the income of the trust for life, against those of the *remaindermen*, who become entitled to the capital of the trust on the death of the life-tenant. Clearly the remaindermen wish to see the capital of the trust grow as much as possible, which might require a total commitment to equities. Conversely, the life-tenant wishes to see the maximum income return from the trust's investments. Although equities should show a growing income over the medium term. it is often difficult to persuade a life-tenant to accept willingly a medium-term policy, especially where he needs a reasonably high income to maintain his standard of living. The life-tenant may not live to enjoy a reasonable return from the fund if a policy devoted to growth is vigorously pursued.

(*a*) Compromise

The policy to follow in these cases is a compromise. The funds available should be invested in such a way as to produce a moderate income coupled with prospects of maintaining the value of the fund over the medium to long term. This requires part of the fund to be invested in fixed-interest stocks giving a fair market return, and the balance in growth equities or, in the case of smaller estates, unit trusts. While the life-tenant has a reasonable expectation of life, the fixed-interest section can be managed on a basis of policy switching. When interest rates are considered to be low, the stocks held should be short- to medium-dated. On the other hand, when interest rates are high, the stocks should be dated to mature at intervals around the end of the normal life expectancy of the life-tenant, and bought to show profits to redemption. This policy should show growth in the fixed-interest section over the medium to long term. As the life-tenant gets older it is desirable to take profits on the equity section of the portfolio when markets are relatively high, for reinvestment in fixed-interest securities dated at around his life expectancy, until a fixed-interest fund large enough to meet the expected capital transfer tax liability is established.

Where the fund holds assets other than Stock Exchange investments, such as property, mortgages and private company holdings, generalizations on investment policy are impossible to make, and the trustees must judge the relative interests of the life-tenant, remaindermen and the Inland Revenue according to the circumstances of the fund.

(*b*) Trusts for Minors

Many family trust funds represent moneys held for minors and young adults until they reach a specified age. In these cases, unless the funds are small, a proportion of the trust fund should be invested in fixed-interest stock maturing at about, or within two or three years of, the date on which the capital becomes payable to the beneficiary. This is so that some spendable income is available to the beneficiary and also, where applicable, funds are available to meet any capital gains tax liability on the trust at that time. The choice of a fixed-interest stock should take account of any capital gains tax liability on maturity as this affects net redemption yield. The balance of the fund should be in equities. Where the trust funds are small, however, or where the beneficiary takes the funds within two or three years from the fund being set up, equity investment is often not desirable. It may be better to leave the beneficiary in a position to make his own decisions on investment or spending when he is able to do so.

(*c*) Indirect Investment

In all funds where equity investment is considered desirable, the trustees should decide, by the same criteria as individual investors, whether to choose direct or indirect investment.

In the absence of specific authority in the trust deed or will, none of the insurance investments is available to a trustee. This arises primarily from the difficulty of treating both classes of beneficiary – those entitled to the income and those entitled to the capital – in an equitable manner. There is no way of ensuring that the life-tenant does not receive part of the capital, or that the remainderman does not receive part of the income. (Withdrawal schemes do not provide an income, only regular distributions of capital.)

The capital shares of split-level trusts are also an unsuitable investment as they favour the capital of the trust at the expense of the income. Some 'beneficial owner' clauses include a power to invest in securities that do not produce income, but even then such an investment should not be made without the agreement of those entitled to the trust income.

One overriding factor relates to the investment powers of trustees of family trusts. Often all the beneficiaries who could be entitled to any part of the trust funds are identifiable and of full legal capacity. In these circumstances they may request the trustee to pursue a particular investment policy, even though this may involve breaches of trust. The trustee cannot be compelled to accede to their request, but he may agree against a suitable indemnity from the beneficiaries.

Trustees concerned with their powers and duties of investment should refer to the standard textbooks on trusts and take legal advice where necessary.

21.2 Valuation of Securities for Tax Purposes

Securities must be valued from time to time for tax purposes. The chief occasions are to determine the imposition of stamp duty, and to assess capital gains tax and capital transfer tax. Where full consideration is involved there is no problem, but where the ownership of securities changes because of a gift or on death, valuation is not so straightforward. The fundamental principle is that securities must be valued on an 'open market' valuation.

(*a*) Quoted Securities

Securities are valued on the basis of *the lower of*:

(i) the lower of the two prices quoted in the *Stock Exchange Daily Official List*, plus one-quarter of the difference between them – the so-called 'quarter-up' method. So if the prices listed were '99–101', the valuation would be $99\frac{1}{2}$ $(99 + \frac{1}{4}(101 - 99))$.

(ii) the middle-market price of ordinary bargains recorded. Thus if the prices of bargains were listed '98, 100, 101, 102', the valuation would be 100($(98 + 102) \div 2$).

Thus the shares would be valued at $99\frac{1}{2}$, the lower of the two valuations.

Where the Stock Exchange is closed on the date in question, the *Official List* for either the preceding or the subsequent business day can be used to determine the price – whichever gives the lower value.

(*b*) **Unquoted Securities**
Such securities must also be valued on an 'open market' basis, but this is much more difficult where there is no formal market. In making the valuation it is assumed that the notional purchaser has all the information available to make a prudent purchase from a willing vendor in an arm's length transaction. In many cases the transfer of unquoted shares is restricted, and this factor must be taken into account when trying to assess the open market value; so too must be the interests of any 'special purchaser' in acquiring the shares (for example, to give him a controlling interest). The valuation must have regard to the company's earnings and dividend record. The net asset value of the share is normally important only if liquidation is imminent, where a special purchaser is interested or in the case of any existing majority interest.

(*c*) **Unit Trusts**
The bid price (the lower of the two published prices) is taken.

(*d*) **Ex Dividend Valuations**
In the case of probate valuations for capital transfer tax, any dividend declared prior to the date of death, but not so paid, must be added to the value of the securities in question. It is the *net* dividend (that is, without tax credit) that must be added.

21.3 Charitable Trusts

The powers of investment of trustees of charitable funds are derived in the same way as for all other trusts, by the trust deed setting them up or by statute. The differences arise in three ways. First, the beneficial interests in capital and income are all charitable; second, the trust is free of all United Kingdom income and capital taxes; and third, the trusts often continue in perpetuity.

There is in fact no statutory definition of a charity but the rules determining charitable status were laid down by Lord Macnaughten in 1891. Charities are of four types:

(*a*) for the relief of poverty;
(*b*) for the advancement of education;
(*c*) for the advancement of religion;
(*d*) for any other purpose beneficial to the community.

The last section has been construed quite narrowly, and any body having any kind of political flavour will be refused charitable status. Charitable gifts must be made for the benefit of the public at large or a sufficiently important section of the community, and all of the income therefrom must be applied exclusively to the charitable object. Table 21.1 shows the relative frequency of trusts devoted to particular objects and the income generated in each group.

Table 21.1 The distribution of charities by objects and the income therefrom (1975)

Objects	Distribution	Income
	%	%
General and overseas	5.7	10.3
Relief of poverty	32.8	4.3
Children and youth	9.1	9.3
Old age	4.1	0.13
Health and sickness	9.3	23.5
Social welfare and culture	11.5	9.4
Moral welfare and reform	1.4	0.05
Advancement of religion	8.9	0.63
Advancement of education	13.4	42.1
Miscellaneous	3.8	0.2
	100.00	100.00

Source: *National Westminster Bank Review*

It is difficult to generalize about the different types of charitable trust. Some expend only the income, and the investment policy then often needs to be directed towards maximum immediate return. The desirability of pursuing a growth policy will be overridden by the immediate needs of the objects of the charity. Some have different objects as beneficiaries of the income from those which benefit from the capital, and the interests of both have to be balanced.

The Charities Act 1960 empowers the Charity Commissioners to set up *Common Investment Schemes* in which a number of charities can pool their property for investment and management by trustees appointed for the purpose. These schemes, such as the Charities Official Investment Fund and M & G's Charibond, are run rather like unit trusts except that the fund is divided into shares rather than units. Dividends are paid gross. The schemes rank as special-range investments, and a charity may transfer all its capital into such schemes without having to divide the fund under the Trustee Investments Act 1961. The schemes have unusually wide investment powers, being permitted to invest in securities or property of any kind, including real property.

In addition there is the authorized 'exempt' unit trust 'Charifund' (The Equities Investment Fund for Charities – M & G Group), restricted to charities, which pays dividends gross, and other exempt unit trusts restricted to pension funds and charities where dividends are paid net but tax can be reclaimed. These unit trusts rank as wide-range investments.

21.4 Pension Funds

Pension funds may be approved by the Inland Revenue as exempt or partially exempt funds. The benefits which members of a pension fund may enjoy with full tax reliefs are limited. Contributions to pension funds are allowable for tax relief and the Revenue permits funds to be free of all United Kingdom taxes only so far as the benefits obtained from contributions do not exceed certain limits. Where they exceed these limits, a tax liability remains on the fund to the extent by which benefits are deemed to be excessive and the fund will be only partially exempt from taxes. If a fund is described as 90 per cent exempt, 10 per cent of all income and capital gains is taxable.

The beneficiaries, that is the members, of pension funds are interested in both capital and income and there is therefore little need to distinguish between income and capital growth. A desired annual return is usually laid down by the actuary to a fund, however, and this is often interpreted by the committee of the fund as a required income yield, thus placing an artificial restraint on the trustees of the fund or on the investment managers. The income yield on pension funds therefore often tends to be somewhat higher than on other funds of similar sizes. To maintain yields, around 25 per cent of pension funds are invested in gilt-edged and other fixed-interest investments. It is now unusual for the investment powers to be less than those of a beneficial owner, as they can easily be widened. (The investment policies of pension funds and other institutional investors were discussed in Unit 14.16.)

'This land has been owned by generations of pension fund managers.'

21.5 Questions

1. As manager of a growing pensions fund which has unrestricted investment powers, you are asked to report to the trustees on the possibility of investing in property: (*a*) by way of shares in property companies, (*b*) by way of units in a tax-free property unit trust, (*c*) directly.

2. You are the manager of a pension fund with a value of about £20 million. The fund has wide powers of investment, and is growing at the rate of about £1 million per annum. It is currently fully invested in stocks and shares in roughly the following proportions: 35 per cent in gilt-edged stocks, 5 per cent in debentures and other fixed-interest stocks, and 60 per cent in UK equities. The trustees have raised the question of whether the fund should invest overseas – its liabilities are confined to the United Kingdom.

   Prepare a report for the trustees on the attractions and disadvantages of direct investment in overseas companies.

3. You are asked to review the portfolio of a charitable trust. You are informed that the capital of the trust is unlikely to be required for many years but that a high and growing income is desirable. The portfolio structure is as follows:

   20 holdings of British Government, local authority and water board stocks, well spread with redemptions from 1982 to 2015. Total value £2 000 000;

   120 holdings of UK equities, well spread across sectors. Total value £900 000;

   2 holdings of property unit trusts valued at £20 000 each;

   1 holding in an authorized unit trust, M & G Dividend Fund, valued at £60 000.

   (*a*) What advice would you give to the trustees on the structure of the portfolio, and in respect of each of the four areas of investment represented?

   (*b*) Are there any other types of investment which you consider ought to be included in the portfolio? Give details and your reasons for their inclusion.

   (*c*) How would you consider the portfolio should be managed, having regard to the nature of the trust?

   (*d*) What methods can the trustees adopt in order to assess the relative capital performance of the fund?

Unit Twenty-Two

The Successful Investor

22.1 A Sensible Approach

Success in investment can never be guaranteed. Too many factors lying outside the investor's control can influence the value of his investment. Inflation is one of these: yet it is essential that every investor has part of his capital in a cash investment which, by its definition, is not inflation-proof. Because market forces can bring down the price of ordinary shares in the short term, even while inflation is rampant, to depend on ordinary shares for additional cash in emergencies is foolhardy.

But the investor can be relatively successful if he sets out with a sensible approach, and if he is prepared to spend some time and trouble on the selection of investments and the taking of decisions concerning existing holdings. A summary of the requirements for a successful investment policy might be as follows:

(*a*) Suitability

Every investment, of whatever type, must be *suitable* for the investor and for inclusion in the investment portfolio. This presupposes that each investor is aware of the nature of a proposed investment, as only then can suitability be judged. Strangely enough, whereas hardly anyone buys an overcoat to protect him against the weather without trying it on to see if it fits, many people buy an investment to protect them against inflation without the slightest idea whether it fits their requirements or not.

(*b*) Crisis-proof

An investment portfolio should be free from the effects of *personal crises*. No foreseeable situation should ever cause the sale of an investment at a loss. Before setting out on a policy of investment in risk situations (and every ordinary share involves a risk) there should be enough provision for unforeseen circumstances. Thus the investor should have guarantees against loss of income through sickness or accident, life assurance cover to protect his dependants and to meet capital transfer tax liabilities. And he needs cash investments so that the need for a new car or household appliance, redundancy or unemployment do not cause financial embarrassment.

(*c*) Diversification

An investment portfolio needs to be *diversified* in two ways: in types of investment (to suit the needs of the investor), and across industries and areas. Concentration of interest can, of course, produce greater profits. Obviously having all one's capital in the company which is going to be the best market performer over the coming year will yield maximum profits. So will putting all one's possessions at long odds on the horse that is going to win the next race. Diversification will never make millionaires out of most people, but it does help them to sleep at night.

(*d*) Flexibility

The investment portfolio must be *flexible*. This means that holdings must generally be readily realizable, and the investor must be prepared to dispose of any holding if necessary. He should avoid holdings where he is 'locked-in' for any reason. Examples of unrealizable holdings are (i) a Finance For Industry term deposit (except on death), (ii) some offshore unit trusts which cannot be disposed of for a minimum period, and (iii) loans to, and interests in, private companies.

(*e*) Timing

The greatest art in investment is probably *timing*. Few investors know, except on rare occasions, just when to buy and when to sell individual equities, let alone when to back the market as a whole. The stockbrokers De Zoete and Bevan have shown that between 1946 and 1981 £1 000 invested in a building society would have grown steadily with net income reinvested to £4 677 and the same sum in equities would have amassed £16 480, but that a theoretical 'best performance' fund, in which every sale and every purchase was perfectly timed, would have grown to nearly £218 000!

(*f*) A Balanced View

The most inhibiting factor in the making of investment decisions is taxation. A successful investor will try to take a balanced view of the taxation and investment merits of a decision. Generally speaking, investment merit should override tax factors. If it is right to sell a share because it is overpriced, then the fact that capital gains tax is payable on a profit should not prevent the sale. A profit after tax is still a profit.

A balanced view should also be taken generally. The successful investor sees fashion trends for what they are and refuses to be swept along with the herd, willy-nilly, or to let the enthusiasm of others outweigh his own judgement. He is not to be persuaded by salesmen or advertisements to enter into a scheme which is not exactly what he requires. He realizes that no one is *always* right. And above all he knows that there is no guaranteed road to a fortune.

22.2 Conclusion

To end this book on a reflective note, there are three facts which you, as an investor, should never forget.

(*a*) A free market requires a balance of buyers and sellers. Therefore every time someone sells a holding of ordinary shares because he thinks the price is too high, someone else is buying those same shares, believing them to be cheap.

(*b*) The vast majority of investment decisions which result in purchases or sales on the market are made by professional investment managers and advisers. Therefore every time a professional investment manager sells a holding, the chances are that another professional is buying those same shares.

(*c*) Anyone who had the key to a fortune would not be advising others for a living. And that applies not only to investment managers and advisers, but also to authors of books on investment.

'He's an economic forecaster and I don't like the way he's eating, drinking, and being merry.'

Glossary

Note. Some of the terms that follow cannot be defined briefly. The reader is advised to refer to the text for fuller definitions and discussions.

Acceptance The paying of the first call on a rights issue, thereby accepting the allotment. See also **Letter of acceptance**.

Account A Stock Exchange dealing period, usually two weeks. All deals done for the account during the period are due for settlement on the settlement day relating to that account.

Accrued income The amount of dividend or interest deemed to have accrued during the period since the last distribution of income.

Ad valorem Means 'according to the value'. Used to describe the rate of transfer stamp duty payable on a transaction when stamp duty is payable on the value transferred.

Advance corporation tax Sum paid by a company to the Inland Revenue, equivalent to the tax credits issued to shareholders with their dividends, as an advance payment of corporation tax for the relative trading period.

Agent Any person performing an act on behalf of another person and in that other person's name.

Allotment The number of shares or amount of stock forming part of a new issue and due to an applicant or existing holder.

Allotment letter The document evidencing an allotment. It is a provisional letter in the case of a rights issue.

Amortization The provision for the replacement of a wasting asset out of the income or profits from that asset.

Annuity A guaranteed annual payment other than an interest payment, continuing for life unless otherwise restricted.

Anomaly The situation where the price of a stock or share is out of line with other similar stocks or shares, indicating an opportunity for a purchase or sale.

Arbitrage To switch between similar financial assets to take advantage of a price anomaly.

ARIEL (Automated Real-Time Investments Exchange) Computerized dealing system for large-scale investors, bypassing the Stock Exchange.

Assented Description of stocks or shares where an offer to acquire them or to modify their rights has been accepted.

Assets All items of value owned by a company or individual. See also **Current assets; Fixed assets**.

Asset value per share The value of the assets of a company on balance sheet figures after allowing for the repayment of prior charges and creditors, divided by the number of equity shares in issue.

Asset value The value of the assets of a company on balance sheet figures after allowing for the repayment of prior charges and creditors, divided by the number of equity shares in issue.

Associated company A company 20 to 50 per cent of whose shares are owned by another company.

Auditors' report Report attached to company accounts and required by the Companies Act, reporting on the accounts on behalf of the owners of the capital of that company, by auditors acting independently of the company.

Authorized capital The maximum amount of capital of a company which can be issued without the prior approval of shareholders.

Authorized unit trust A unit trust authorized by the Department of Trade under the provisions of the Prevention of Fraud (Investments) Act 1958.

Averaging The purchase of a further holding of shares at a lower price ('averaging down') or at a higher price ('averaging up').

Back-to-back loan One method of borrowing foreign currency. A deposit in one country is used to obtain a loan in another financed by a reciprocal transaction.

Backwardation The charge to a 'bear' (*q.v.*) for carrying over a transaction from one Stock Exchange account to the next.

Balance certificate Certificate representing balance of stock or shares due back to vendor after sale of part only of holding.

Balance sheet That part of the published accounts of a company showing the financial position on the last day of the accounting period.

Bar chart A method of displaying the price movements of a share, including highest and lowest prices reached in each period shown.

Bare trustee One who holds an asset to the order of the owner. Usually used where a trust has ended permitting a new owner to take control of the asset. See also **Nominee**.

Bargain Any transaction carried out by a stockbroker with a jobber.

Base portfolio Specimen portfolio against which the performance of a managed fund can be compared.

Bear One who takes the view that the price of a particular share will fall and sells a number of those shares, even though he may not own them when contracting to sell. See also **Covered bear**. Hence used to describe anyone who takes the view that stock market prices generally will fall.

Bearer Used to describe a stock or share which passes to a new owner without transfer formality, i.e. which belongs to the bearer thereof.

Bear market A period of falling prices on the Stock Exchange.

Bed and breakfast The selling of a security one day and buying it back on the following day, in order to establish a capital gain or loss for tax purposes

Best An instruction to a broker to deal 'at best' means to deal at the best price obtainable, that is, without imposition of a limit.

Best terms Broker's commission at rates which do not include sharing with an agent.

Beta coefficient The riskiness of a share relative to the stock market as a whole. A value of 1 implies the share is as risky as the market generally, provided it is held as part of a wider portfolio.

Bid The offer by a jobber to buy a stock or share. Hence 'bid price', the price at which stocks, shares or units in a unit trust can be sold by a holder. See also **Offer**.

Blue chips The ordinary shares of leading companies.

Bond A type of security. Also used to describe single-premium life assurance contracts issued for investment purposes.

Bonus issue An issue of shares fully paid to existing holders and with no payment to be made, representing an increase in issued capital by converting reserves into shares and thus only arising from an accounting change. Also called *capitalization issue* or *scrip issue*.

Book The day-to-day records of a jobber of shares bought and sold.

Book loss, book profit A loss or profit on paper, not realized.

Book value The value of an asset as shown in accounts, generally representing cost price plus additions, net of depreciation.

Bull One who takes the view that the price of a particular share will rise, and buys a number of those shares, even though he may not have the money to pay for them. Hence used to describe anyone who takes the view that stock market prices generally will rise.

Bull market A period of rising prices on the Stock Exchange.

Busted bonds Certificates of securities issued by famous companies which have gone into liquidation or countries which have repudiated their debts (e.g. Russian or Chinese bonds). Bought in hope of eventual repayment, or more commonly, as collectors' items.

Buying-in The action which can be taken by a purchaser who does not obtain delivery, namely repurchase at the expense of the first vendor.

Call The payment of part or all of the issue price of stock or shares, which were originally issued nil paid or partly paid. Also the right to buy under an option. See also **Put**.

Capital The total nominal value of all stocks and shares issued by a company. See also **Authorized capital; Issued capital; Loan capital; Share capital**. Also invested moneys as distinct from 'income', the return on investments. See also **Total return**.

Capital distribution A distribution by a company out of capital profits, or by way of reduction in the nominal value of the capital.

Capital gains tax A tax on certain realized capital profits.

Capital transfer tax A cumulative tax applied to gifts made during a lifetime and assets left at death.

Capitalization issue See **Bonus issue**.

Cash flow Usually equivalent to retained profits plus depreciation.

Cash investment An investment which can be converted back into the money originally invested on demand or after a short period of notice.

Cash-and-new When shares bought during the account are sold free of commission at the end of the account and are immediately repurchased for the new account.

Cash settlement Settlement for the purchase or sale of an investment which is due the day after the transaction.

Certificate The document of title to registered stock or shares.

Certificate of deposit Negotiable fixed-interest securities issued by banks in sterling or in some foreign currency.

Certified transfer A transfer form or deed certified to the effect that the certificate in respect of the stock or shares transferred is held at the offices of the registrar for the company awaiting the completed document.

Chart Visual display of the movement of prices or indices. See also **Bar chart; Line chart; Point-and-figure chart**.

Clawback The statutory reduction in life assurance tax relief when a qualifying policy is surrendered within four years.

Clean Describes the price of a stock after allowing for any accrued interest reflected in the market price.

Close company A company under the control of not more than five persons, or its directors.

Closing A bargain which reverses another carried out earlier, usually within the same Stock Exchange account.

Closing prices The prices ruling at the official close of the Stock Exchange at 3.30 p.m.

Conglomerate A company with subsidiaries operating in a variety of different industries.

Consideration The cost of purchase or the proceeds of sale before taking commission, stamp duty or other charges into account.

Consols Abbreviation for both 2½ per cent and 4 per cent Consolidated Stock.

Contango The charge to a bull for carrying over a transaction from one account to another; also used as a generic term to describe a *backwardation* (*q.v.*).

Contract An enforceable agreement to transact. Used loosely to describe a *contract note*, the evidence that a contract has been carried out.

Convertible A stock or share with rights to convert into another class of stock or shares.

Corporation tax The tax chargeable on all profits of a company.

Correlation coefficient A measure of the degree to which two variables (e.g. two security prices) move together. It is a measure of the degree to which knowing the value of one variable helps to predict the value of the other.

Cost-push inflation Inflation caused by increased costs (wages, imports, etc.) without excessive demand on a nation's resources.

Coupon Voucher attached to a bearer security entitling the holder to collect a dividend or interest payment. By derivation, the rate of interest payable on a fixed-interest investment.

Covenant A legally binding agreement under which one person agrees to make a series of payments to another.

Cover The amount of assets or earnings available to support the value of, or the dividend or interest payable on, a stock or share. See also **Asset cover; Dividend cover; Interest cover.**

Covered bear A bear who owns the shares sold in a bear transaction, and is therefore not at risk if the expected fall does not materialize.

Cum 'With'. Used to describe a bargain which entitles the purchaser to a forthcoming dividend or issue (see **Ex**). Used with 'div' for dividend, and with 'rts' for rights issue, etc.

Current assets Assets of a company expected to be utilized in the day-to-day operations of the company. See also **Fixed assets**.

Current cost accounting A system of inflation accounting based largely on the use of replacement rather than historic costs.

Current liabilities Debts of a company expected to be discharged in the day-to-day operations of the company. See also **Deferred liability**.

Dated Used to describe a fixed-interest stock or preference share with a final redemption date.

Debenture A charge on assets of a company. A mortgage.

Debenture stock A debenture issued as a fixed-interest stock.

Deferred liability A debt of a company not immediately payable.

Deferred stock A class of capital ranking after ordinary capital usually with restricted equity rights.

Delivery The passing of stock or shares from the vendor to the ultimate purchaser or through various intermediaries.

Demand-pull inflation Inflation caused by excessive demand on a nation's resources.

Depreciation The provision by a company for the replacement of fixed assets out of profits.

Distribution Any dividend payment or other payment of income. See also **Capital distribution**.

Dividend The income declared payable on share capital.

Dividend cover The number of times the declared annual dividend on share capital is covered by available earnings.

Dividend voucher Form accompanying dividend payment acceptable to the Inland Revenue as evidence of tax suffered.

Dividend warrant Form of cheque used for payment of dividends.

Dividend yield Annual grossed-up dividend per share as percentage of share price.

Double taxation relief Relief against the same income being taxed at the full rate in two countries.

Drawings Method by which some fixed-interest issues are redeemed (i.e. by ballot).

Drawn bond A bond for which notice has been given that it has been drawn for redemption.

Earnings Net profits of a company available for the ordinary shareholders and either declared as dividend or retained within the company.

Earnings yield Annual (full) earnings per share as a percentage of share price.

Easier Term used to describe a slight fall in market prices.

Endowment Type of life assurance policy giving a minimum payment at death or at a known date, with or without profits.

Enfaced Assented (*q.v.*). Implies the revised terms are indicated on the face of the bond.

Equalization Part of the first distribution received from a purchase of units in a unit trust, and representing a return of the purchase price. It is equivalent to income accrued to the date of purchase, and is therefore treated as a return of capital.

Equity The value of an asset or the assets of a company after all debts, mortgages and other charges attaching to the asset or assets have been discharged. Hence *equities*, the ordinary shares of companies. Also known as *net worth*.

Equity-linked Term used to describe an insurance policy, the final value of which is linked to the performance of a fund or ordinary shares.

Eurobond Interest-bearing stocks, not necessarily European, sold outside the country in the currency of which they are denominated.

Ex 'Without'. Used to describe a bargain which entitles the vendor to retain a forthcoming dividend or issue (see **Cum**). Used with 'div' for dividend, 'rts' for rights issue, 'all' for more than one item, etc. Also further abbreviated to 'x' as in 'xd', 'xr', 'xa', etc. Also 'xc' for 'without capitalization issue'.

Exempt Exempt from tax, either income, capital gains or both.

Exempt dealer Dealer in securities exempt from certain provisions of the Prevention of Fraud (Investments) Act.

Exempt fund A fund which is exempt from all taxes, e.g. a pension fund or charitable trust.

Final dividend The final dividend payment declared in respect of a trading period. Requires sanction of the annual general meeting of the company before payment can be made.

Finance house An institution engaged in lending money for hire purchase and similar transactions.

Firm Stock Exchange term used to describe the state of the market where prices are generally higher when changed, but an overall rise is not seen.

Fixed assets Those assets of a company not absorbed in the day-to-day operations of the company's business, e.g. plant, machinery and buildings. See also **Current assets**.

Flat yield Yield on a stock ignoring any profit or loss to redemption.

Floating charge A debenture, mortgage or other charge secured not on specific assets of a company, but on all its assets for the time being.

Flotation The bringing of an unquoted company to a stock market and the obtaining of a quotation.

Franked income Income which has suffered corporation tax before receipt and is therefore exempt from a charge to the same tax in the hands of a company or other institution.

Freehold The ownership of land nearest to absolute ownership.

Free market Term used to describe the ability to deal easily in large numbers or amounts of a particular share or stock.

Front-end loading The burden of charges or repayments at the outset.

Fundamental analysis The study of a company to determine the correct value of its ordinary shares in current market conditions and thus to arrive at an investment decision concerning those shares. See **Technical analysis**.

The Funds A collective term sometimes used for stock issued by the United Kingdom Government.

Gearing The relationship of loan capital and preference capital to the ordinary or total capital of a company.

Gilt-edged The stock of British and Commonwealth Governments, local authorities and public boards.

Go short Sell something one does not own in order to buy it back at a lower price before one needs to deliver.

Good names Recognized names in which American and Canadian shares can be registered for delivery without transfer formalities.

Gross Before deduction of tax.

Grossed-up net redemption yield Net redemption yield (*q.v.*) on a gross equivalent basis: a method for comparing returns on securities which are subject to differential tax treatment.

Gross fund A fund not liable to tax, such as a pension fund or charitable trust.

Ground rent Rent paid by the owner of leasehold property to the owner of the freehold.

Growth stock The ordinary share capital of a company able to increase its earnings per share at a much faster rate than the stock market as a whole.

Harder Term used to describe a slight rise in market prices.

Head and shoulders Term used to describe a chart pattern roughly equivalent to a drawing of a person's head and shoulders, indicating a fall in share price.

Heavy Term used to describe a highly priced share.

Holding company A company which does not necessarily engage in any trade or industry and which has a controlling interest in one or more subsidiary companies.

The House Colloquial expression for the Stock Exchange.

House fund A managed fund other than an authorized unit trust, used for the funds of small clients of the institution concerned.

Impact day The first day on which any publicity may be given to a new issue.

Index A measure of the movement of market prices produced by calculation of the movement of a sample of prices. 'The Index' generally refers to the *Financial Times* Industrial Ordinary (30 Share) Index.

Index fund A fund designed to replicate a stock market index in terms of constituents and performance.

Indicated dividend, indicated yield Shows that figures quoted are not historic, but are based on statements made by the company as to a dividend yet to be declared.

Indirect investment Investment through a managed fund.

Insider dealing The buying or selling of any security or option on the basis of privileged price-sensitive information, now a criminal offence under the Companies Act 1980.

Institutional investors Large-scale investors, such as insurance companies, pension funds, unit and investment trusts.

Insurance-linked Describes a managed fund linked to an insurance scheme.

Interest The income paid on a loan or loan capital.

Interest cover The earnings available to pay interest compared with the interest payable.

Interest warrant Form of cheque used for the payment of interest.

Interim report A statement of company profits, etc., for a period less than a trading period.

Introduction Method for obtaining a quotation of a new issue: no formal sale of shares is involved.

Investment trust A company investing in other companies as its principal business.

Irredeemable A stock which, by its terms of issue, cannot be repaid. Used loosely to describe a stock with no final redemption date.

Issued capital The amount of the authorized capital of a company which has been issued.

Jobber A member of the Stock Exchange who deals in stocks and shares exclusively on his own account, and only with brokers or other jobbers.

Leasehold Land or buildings held on lease from the freeholder.

Liability A debt. See also **Current liabilities** and **Deferred liabilities**.

Licensed dealer A dealer in securities licensed under the provisions of the Prevention of Fraud (Investments) Act.

Life-tenant Beneficiary of a trust fund entitled to the whole or part of the income received during his lifetime.

Limit A price specified when giving an order to a broker, above which he is not to execute a purchase order or below which he is not to execute a sale order.

Limited liability Liability of shareholders for the debts of a company is limited to the nominal value of their shares. A company described as 'Limited' or 'Ltd' or 'p.l.c.' is incorporated with limited liability.

Line Any number of shares or amount of stock of one issue.

Line chart A method of displaying the price movements of a share, an index, or relative movements, by means of a simple line joining points on a graph.

Liquidation The winding-up of a company whereby its assets are realized and creditors and holders of capital paid out according to their priority. Also the reduction of the number of units in issue in an authorized unit trust.

Liquidity A measure of the ease and certainty of switching an asset into cash.

Liquidity ratio Ratio of liquid assets to current liabilities.

Loan capital That part of the capital of a company representing debentures, debenture stock or loan stock.

Long-dated Describes a stock with, generally, more than fifteen years to redemption.

Managed bonds (or **Flexible** or **Three-way bonds**) Single-premium life assurance policies linked to a fund comprising equity, property and fixed-interest elements.

Managed fund Term used to describe a fund under active investment management where the owners of the moneys making up the fund have no control over the investment policy. Includes investment trusts, unit trusts, pension funds, insurance funds, house funds, etc.

Margin trading The purchase of securities with largely borrowed funds, usually with the intention of holding for a short period. More frequent in the USA than in the United Kingdom.

Market A market is said to exist in a stock or share when there are regularly enough buyers and sellers to enable a price to be arrived at on the basis of supply and demand. In the absence of a 'market' deals may have to be negotiated with jobbers.

Market capitalization The equity market capitalization is the value at current market prices of all of a company's ordinary shares. Sometimes the expression 'market capitalization' includes the market value of borrowed funds as well.

Marking (or **Mark**) The recording of a price at which a bargain is struck in the Stock Exchange for publication in the *Daily List* (this is only applicable to non-Talisman securities). Also, indication on an American or Canadian share certificate that a dividend has been claimed from the 'marking name' in which the shares are registered.

Marking name An institution recognized by the Stock Exchange as suitable for the registration of American and Canadian shares in its name, and for the subsequent collection and distribution of dividends.

Maturity The final redemption date of a stock.

Medium-dated Describes a stock with, generally, between five and fifteen years to redemption.

Middle price Price midway between bid price and offered price.

Mortgage A loan secured on land or buildings.

Narrower range That part of a trust fund subject to the provisions of the Trustee Investments Act 1961 which may be invested only in investments authorized as narrower-range investments by the First Schedule to the Act, principally fixed-interest securities.

Net asset value Total assets (excluding goodwill) less either total liabilities or simply current liabilities.

Net redemption yield Yield to redemption after deducting income tax and capital gains tax (if any) at appropriate rates.

Net worth The ordinary share capital of a company (i.e. issued capital plus reserves).

New time Dealings at the end of a Stock Exchange account for settlement at the same time as any dealings in the following account.

Nil paid A new issue, usually a rights issue, on which no payment has yet been made.

Nominal value The denomination in which stocks or shares are issued.

Nominee One who holds in his name an asset belonging to another.

No par value Often shown as 'n.p.v.'. A share which does not have a nominal or par value but which represents one part of the equity of a company out of as many parts as there are shares in issue. Not permissible in the United Kingdom.

NTP 'Not to press'. Delivery of certificate will be delayed.

Offer The offer by a jobber to sell a stock or share. Hence *offer price*, the price at which stocks, shares or units in a unit trust can be bought. See also **Bid**.

Offer for sale Principal method whereby new issues of equities are marketed.

Offshore fund Generally used to refer to a fund in the Channel Islands or the Isle of Man.

One-way option stock Stock with no firm date for redemption; redeemable at the option of the borrower only.

Opening prices Prices ruling at the official opening of the Stock Exchange each day – 9.30 a.m. for the market generally, 10 a.m. for gilts.

Option The right to buy or sell at a stated price within a stated period.

Ordinary share The type of share which gives the holder the residual ownership of the assets and earnings of a company.

OTC markets The buying and selling of securities 'over the counter'. The expression originates from the USA. In the United Kingdom it means markets for securities without a formal Stock Exchange listing.

Paid up The amount of calls paid on partly paid shares.

Par The nominal value of stock or shares.

Pari passu Ranking in all respects, equal to.

Partly paid Shares or stock on which the full issue price has not yet been paid.

Payout ratio The proportion of a company's earnings paid out as dividends. It is the reciprocal of the **Dividend cover**.

Personal representative The executor or administrator of the estate of a deceased person.

Placing The sale of a line of stock or shares, by arrangement, direct to institutions and others by the selling brokers, without going through the market.

Point and figure chart A method of displaying price movements of a share or index without a time axis.

Portfolio The total investments of an individual or fund.

Position The state of the book of a dealer in a particular share or other investment.

Pound cost averaging The investment of a fixed sum at regular intervals thus levelling out fluctuations in price.

Preference share Type of share carrying a fixed-income return ranking in priority to ordinary shares for both earnings and assets.

Preferential form Special application forms usually given to existing shareholders and employees when companies offer shares for public subscription. They are easily identifiable by their pink colour, hence they are also known as 'pink forms'.

Preferred share Type of share equivalent to a preference share, or otherwise having some priority over ordinary shares.

Premium The amount by which the quotation of a new issue exceeds the amount paid up. Also the sum paid to an insurance company to maintain an insurance policy in force.

Price–earnings ratio The ratio of a price of a share to the last published(net) earnings per share for a trading period.

Prior charge Stock ranking in priority to another. Used generally to describe the loan capital of a company.

Priority percentage The proportion of profits or assets needed to satisfy the income requirement or capital repayment of a stock or share.

Profit and loss account That part of the published accounts of a company showing income and expenditure over a trading period.

Property Generally any asset of whatever nature. Restriction of use to freehold and leasehold land and buildings is common but not correct.

Property bond An insurance scheme where the sum payable is linked to the performance of a fund invested principally in freehold and leasehold property.

Prospective Used in relation to earnings, dividends, etc.; means that they are based on projections of future results and declarations.

Prospectus Document giving details of company required to support a new issue or quotation.

Public limited company A company meeting the requirements of the Companies Act 1980.

Put The right to sell under an option. See also **Call**.

Put through When a broker can directly match a buy and sell order for the same security he nonetheless puts the shares through a jobber, i.e. sells them to the jobber and buys them back at a marginally higher price.

Qualifying policy Life assurance policy that qualifies for tax relief.

Quarter-up One-quarter of the difference between bid and offer price added to the bid price. Basis of valuation of shares and stock for capital transfer tax and capital gains tax purposes.

Quotation The acceptance of a stock or share by the Stock Exchange permitting dealings to be carried out in the Exchange in that stock or share. Hence the price quoted in the Exchange for that stock or share.

Rack rent The full rental value of land and buildings.

Random walk hypothesis The belief that changes in share prices are completely unsystematic in the short to medium term.

Redeemable Describes a stock with a redemption date.

Redemption Repayment of a stock on maturity.

Redemption yield Income return and annual profit or loss to redemption as a percentage of the cost of a dated stock.

Register The record of holders of registered stock or shares.

Registered stock Stock which passes by transfer as opposed to bearer stock which passes by delivery.

Registrar The keeper of a register.

Remainderman Beneficiary of a trust fund entitled to a whole or part of the capital of the fund on the death of a life-tenant.

Renunciation The giving up of the right to be registered as the holder of a new issue, enabling the issue to be transferred to another.

Reserves That part of the equity of a company in excess of the nominal value of the issued equity capital.

Retained profits That part of the profits of a company belonging to the holders of the equity and not distributed by way of dividend.

Revaluation surpluses Increases in the replacement costs of fixed assets and stock held since the last valuation. These are credited to shareholders' funds under current cost accounting.

Reverse yield gap The excess of the interest yield of $2\frac{1}{2}$ per cent Consols over the dividend yield of the *Financial Times*– Actuaries All Share Index.

Rights Preferential rights to take up a new issue offered to existing holders.

Risk capital Equity capital.

Running yield See **Flat yield**.

Savings bank A bank not offering a full range of services but designed particularly for the collection of small savings and the payment of interest thereon.

Scrip issue See **Bonus issue.**

Sector The shares of an industry or group of industries.

Security Strictly a secured stock, that is, a gilt-edged stock or debenture. Used generally to describe any stock or share. Also the assets charged to secure a loan.

SEDOL Abbreviation of *Stock Exchange Daily Official List* (*q.v.*).

Selling out The action which may be taken by a seller of a stock or share on a stock exchange if he does not get delivery instructions to enable him to complete. The holding is sold again and the original purchaser is liable for any difference in proceeds.

Settlement The completion of a stock exchange transaction.

Settlement/account day The day appointed for the settlement of transactions carried out in an account. This is the Monday ten days after the end of each account.

Share capital Those types of capital of a company ranking after loan capital.

Shorts Term used for Government stocks redeemable within five years.

Short-dated Describes a stock that is redeemable within five years.

Short-term When used to describe prospects or capital appreciation, it generally means a period of up to about one year.

Sinking fund A fund provided for the early redemption of a dated stock.

Special ex dividend Certain gilts may be so purchased or sold twenty-one days before normal ex dividend date.

Special range That part of a trust fund subject to the provisions of the Trustee Investments Act 1961 which may be invested in investments authorized by the trust instrument.

Speculation The dealing in assets with the sole object of short-term capital gains.

Split An allotment letter issued with others in exchange for a renounced allotment letter for a larger amount.

Split-level An investment trust with more than one type of share capital, each entitled to a different part of the profits of the trust.

Spot price The current price of a commodity or rate of exchange of a currency for immediate settlement.

Spread The obtaining of diversity of interest in investments.

Stag One who applies for more shares in a new issue than he can afford to retain, in the hope of receiving an allotment which can be sold at a profit soon after dealings begin.

Stale bull One who has bought shares in anticipation of a short-term rise which has not materialized.

Stamp duty A tax payable on certain transactions.

Standard deviation A measure of the dispersion of values around the mean, or expected, value.

Stock Part of the capital of a company. May be loan capital or share capital depending on the company's capital structure.

Stockbroker A member of the Stock Exchange dealing with jobbers on behalf of clients.

Stock exchange A recognized market in stocks and shares. 'The Stock Exchange' refers to the single stock exchange of Great Britain and Ireland.

Stock Exchange Daily Official List A daily publication of the prices of the majority of the stocks and shares quoted on the Stock Exchange.

Stock transfer form Form used to effect change of ownership of registered stock or shares (except those covered by Talisman).

Stock unit The unit of quotation of a stock not quoted as a percentage.

Stop-loss order An order to a broker to sell a security immediately should the price drop to a specified level.

Striking price The price at which an option is granted.

Subordinated loan stock A loan stock repayable only after all other creditors.

Subscription list The list of applicants for a new issue.

Subscription right The right to subscribe for a stock or share at a certain price at some time in the future.

Subscription share A type of building society investment designed for small savers who wish to save on a regular basis.

Subsidiary company A company the majority of whose ordinary shares are owned by another company, the **Holding company** (*q.v.*).

Sweetener A high-yielding security included in a portfolio to raise the average yield overall.

Switch A purchase and sale of investments carried out at the same time to change the composition of a portfolio.

Systematic risk The volatility of a share's price with respect to changes in the *Financial Times*–Actuaries All Share Index.

Take-over One company acquiring control of another by obtaining a majority of the voting capital, either by cash purchase or share exchange.

Talisman (Transfer Accounting Lodgement for Investors, Stock Management for Jobbers) The Stock Exchange computerized settlement procedure.

Talon Voucher detachable from bearer security used to claim new sheet of coupons.

Tap Stock of which there is more available than the demand but supply is controlled to match demand or to influence price.

Technical analysis The study of price movements and the forecasting of future movements from past prices. See **Fundamental analysis**.

Tender Issues offered which are allotted to the highest bidders. Also, to bid for stock from the cheapest sellers.

Term assurance Life assurance contract whereby premiums are payable for a limited period only and the sum assured is payable only on death before expiry of the term.

Top half The counterfoil attached to a dividend or interest warrant. See also **Dividend voucher**.

Total return The return from an investment or portfolio. Equivalent to dividends or interest received plus capital gain or loss.

Trade investment Investment made by an industrial or commercial company in its suppliers, customers or competitors.

Trading period Period for which accounts of a company are usually made up. Mostly it is a period of one year.

Trend line Movement of prices shown by a chart indicating a definite trend either upwards or downwards.

True Actual as opposed to 'indicated' or 'prospective'.

Trust Obligation binding a person to deal with property of which he has control for the benefit of others.

Trust deed; trust instrument Document defining powers of trustee and objects of a trust. May be a will or deed.

Trustee Person with control of the subject matter of a trust.

Trustee status Term applied both to (i) investments authorized for the investment of trust funds under the Trustee Investments Act 1961, and (ii) building societies meeting the minimum liquidity ratio (7½%) laid down by the Chief Registrar of Friendly Societies.

Turn The difference between bid price and offer price, especially as in 'jobber's turn'.

Undated No fixed date for redemption.

Underlease A lease granted by a leaseholder to another party.

Underwriting Agreement to take up part of new issue not applied for in consideration of a commission on the total possible liability.

Unfranked income Interest paid out of moneys which have not borne corporation tax.

Unit-linked An insurance scheme where the sum payable is linked to the performance of an underlying fund.

Unit trust An indirect investment in the form of a trust with the investors as beneficiaries.

Voting capital That part of the capital of a company which has control of it through the right of holders to vote at general meetings.

Warrant A negotiable right to subscribe for stock or shares at some time in the future. See also **Dividend warrant**.

Whole life Life assurance contract under which premiums are payable throughout life and sum assured is payable only on death.

Wider range That part of a trust fund subject to the provisions of the Trustee Investments Act 1961 which may be invested only in investments authorized by the first schedule to the Act as narrower-range or wider-range investments.

Winding-up Liquidation of a company.

Working capital Generally used to refer to 'net' working capital – current assets minus current liabilities.

X See **Ex**.

Yearling bonds Local authority quoted investments redeemable one year after issue.

Yield curve Curve produced by plotting on a graph the yields of stocks with different redemption dates.

Further Reading

General

Day, J. G. and Jamieson, A. T.: *Institutional Investment* (6 volumes). Institute of Actuaries (London, 1975).

Report of the [Wilson] Committee to Review the Functioning of Financial Institutions. Cmnd 7937. HMSO (London, 1980).

Rowlatt, J.: *Guide to Savings and Investment*. Pan (London, 1979).

Stock Exchange Investment

Firth, M: *Investment Analysis – Techniques of Appraising the British Stock Market*. Harper and Row (London, 1975).

The following are written from a more academic viewpoint:

Lorie, J. H. and Hamilton, M. T.: *The Stock Market: Theories and Evidence*. Irwin (New Chicago, 1973).

Sharpe, W. F.: *Investments*. Prentice-Hall (New Jersey, 1978).

Smith, A.: *The Money Game*. Pan (London, 1970).

Property Investment

Curzon, L. B.: *Land Law*. Macdonald and Evans (Plymouth, 1979).

Alternative Investment

Duthy, R.: *Alternative Investment*. Michael Joseph (London, 1978).

Indirect Investment

Gilchrist, C.: *How to Plan Your Life Insurance*. Martin Books (Cambridge, 1979).

The Investment Trust Yearbook. Financial Times Business Publishing (London, annually).

The Unit Trust Yearbook. Financial Times Business Publishing (London, annually).

Company Law

Arden, M. and Eccles, G.: *Tolley's Companies Act, 1980*. Tolley Publishing Company (Croydon, 1980).

Pennington, R.R.: *Pennington's Company Law*. Butterworths (4th edn., London, 1979).

Magazines, Journals and Newspapers

The *Financial Times* and the business pages of *The Times*, the *Daily Telegraph* and the *Guardian* contain much that is of interest to the student of investment. Articles concerning the personal investor generally appear on a Saturday. The business sections of the *Sunday Times*, the *Sunday Telegraph* and the *Observer* include similar material. More specialized publications include the weekly journals the *Economist*, the *Investors' Chronicle* and the *Financial Weekly*, the monthly *Money Management* and *Planned Savings*, and the quarterly *Money Which?*

There are also regular investment articles in the *Journals of the Institute of Bankers*, the *Bankers' Magazine*, and in the accountancy journals, particularly *Accountancy*. Television and radio programmes concerned with money matters are broadcast regularly.

Index

Italicized page numbers refer to definitions of terms in the Glossary.

Absolute ownership, 298–9
Acceptance, *332*
Accepting Houses Committee, 118
Account, 122–3, *332*
Accountants, 308
Account Day, 122–4, 136
Accrued interest, 40, 49, 54, 266, *332*
Accumulation units, 160, 161
'Acid test' ratio, *see* Quick assets ratio
Activity ratio, 250, 255–6
Advance corporation tax (ACT), 75, 241–4, *332*
Advertising of unit trusts, 153–4, 157
Advice
  for investors, 166, 184, 219–21, 306–9
  for trustees, 319–20
  on capital transfer tax, 210
Age
  of insured person, 173, 175, 176, 177, 178
  of investors, 213
Agents, 41, 134, *332*
  commission paid to, 41, 125, 128, 129
  directors as, 285
  overseas, 139–40
Aggressive shares, 76
Allotment letters, 106–7, 122, *332*
  provisional, 102, 104–5
Alternative investments, *see* Chattels
American securities, 74, 122, 127, 139
Annual general meeting, 75, 285, 286, 287, 288, 290
Annual report and accounts, 94, 238–58
Annuities, 177–9, 182, 218, 221, *332*
Anomalies, 269–71, *332*
'A' ordinary shares, 75, 107
Apportionment
  for capital gains tax, 206
  of jobbers' stock, 136
Arbitrage, *332*
ARIEL, 118–19, 301, *332*
Arithmetic scale, 234
Articles of association, 63, 84, 284–5
  of investment trusts, 166, 167
Assented bonds, 61, 62, *333*
Asset cover, *333*
  see also Capital cover
Asset turnover, 257
Asset values, 73–4, *333*
Associated companies, 240, 256, *333*
Association of Independent Investment Managers, 311
Association of Investment Trust Companies, 302
Association of Licensed Dealers in Securities, 302
'At best', 115, *334*
Attendance at meetings, 290–91
Auditors' report, 97, 238, 249, 288, *333*
Authorized investments, 315–16
Authorized unit trusts, 152, 153, 302, *333*
Average collection period, 256
Averaging, *333*
  see also Pound cost averaging

Back, 141
Back-to-back loan, *333*
Backwardation, 141, *333*
Balance certificate, 137, *333*
Balanced funds, 160
Balance sheet, 73, 87, 238, 244–7, 248–9, *333*
Ballot
  for shares, 95, 96
  repayment by, *see* Drawings
Bank borrowings, 10, 230, 247, 250, 251–2, 256
Banking Act 1979, 29, 294, 304
Banking names, 304
Bank of England, 15
  control of banking system, 304
  control of new issues, 7, 97
  role in stock transfer, 137
Banks, 13, 29, 39, 63, 101, 138, 139, 147, 153, 302
  advice and information from, 258, 307–8, 310–11
  and Treasury bills, 33

depository, 140
deposits with, 27–8, 163, 216
foreign currency accounts, 89
funds, 156, 311
investment through, 115, 148; *see also* Agents, commission paid to
see also Merchant banks; Trustee savings banks
Bar chart, 234, 235, *333*
Base (model, notional) portfolios, 265, 279–81, *334*
Base rate, 27
Bearer deposit receipts, 140
Bearer securities, 43, 122, 126, 131, 138–9, 320, *334*
Bears, 80–87, 140, 141, 158, 159, 164, 231, *334*
Bed and breakfast transactions, 208, *334*
Beneficial interest, 290
Beneficial owner clauses, 313, 324,
'Best terms', 129, *334*
Beta coefficients, 76–9, 231, *334*
Bid price, 112–13, *334*
Blue-chip companies, *334*
Board dealer, 144
Bond switching, 183
Bonus issues, *334*
see also Capitalization issues
'Book', jobbers', 113, *334*
Book value, 251, *334*
Break-out, 235, 237
British Insurance Association, 15, 302
British Rail pension fund, 198–9
Brokers' transfer forms, 137
'B' shares, 167
Building lease, 187, 191
Building societies, 29–30, 31, 39, 201, 216, 302
deposit accounts, 29
mortgages, 192
share accounts, 25, 29
subscription shares, 30, *347*
term shares, 30
trustee status, 30, 315, *349*
Building Societies Assocation, 301–2
Building-society-linked life assurance, 173, 183–4, 211
Bulls, 80–81, 140, 141, 158, 159, 231, *334*
Business risk, 75–6
'Busted' bonds, 198, *335*
'Buy-and-hold' policy, 267, 269
Buying-in, 145, *335*

Call options, 142, 143, 144–5, *335*
Calls, 101, 106, *335*
Canadian securities, 74, 122, 127, 139
Capital accumulation sterling deposit funds, 196–7
Capital cover, 252
Capital employed, 245, 256, *335*
Capital gains and losses, 72, 208–9, 269
options, 143
warrants, 88
Capital gains tax, 124, 205–9, 278–9, 297, *335*
and mergers, 297, 298
and share exchanges, 159
exemptions, 47, 162, 167, 173, 174, 192, 199, 202, 203, 205–6, 207
on British Government stocks, 47
on capital accumulation sterling deposit funds, 197
on fixed-interest stocks, 65
on local authority stocks, 59
on options, 143
on preference shares, 83
valuation for, 116, 324–5
Capital gearing, 251–3
Capital gearing ratio, 251–2
Capital growth, 166, 196, 198, 212
Capitalization issues (bonus issues, scrip issues), 87, 93, 99–100, 291, *334*
and capital gains tax, 207
'B' shares, 167
fractional allotments, 107
on 'A' share enfranchisement, 75
Capital priority percentages, 252–3
Capital reduction, 291
Capital risk, 271
Capital shares of split-level trust, 166–7, *324*
Capital structures, 69–70, 251
Capital transfer tax, 13, 93, 208, 209–11, 213, *335*
family trusts, 322, 323
valuation for, 116, 324
Capital World Index, 267
Cash-and-new, 142, *335*
Cash flow, 86, 247, *335*
Cash investments, 20, 24–5, 30–31, 214, 215, 329, *335*
Cash offers, 297, 298
Cash settlement, 122, 127, *335*
Central Government Borrowing Requirement (CGBR), 33
Certificate of Incorporation, 284
Certificate of tax deducted, 55
Certificates, *335*
shares, 133, 136, 137–8, 283

units, 149–50, 153
Certificates of deposit, 27, 138, *335*
Certificate to commence business, 284
Certification Office of the Stock Exchange, 137
Chain index, 265, 281
Chairman's letter, 97
Chairman's statement, 238–9
Channel, 235, 237
Charges
clearing banks, 310
investment bonds, 180
investment trusts, 165
merchant banks, 309
offshore funds, 196
unit trusts, 150–51, 156
see also Commission
Charibond, 326
Charitable trusts, 11, 67, 130, 195, 205, 313, 325–6
Charities Official Investment Fund, 326
Chartism, 232–8, 267
Chattels, 16, 19, 20, 198–202
Children, 210–11, 213
investment income, 203–4
trusts for, 323
City Code on Take-overs and Mergers, *see* Take-over Code
Class meetings, 287
Class of option, 144
Clawback, 174, 182, 183, *336*
'Clean' balance sheet, 76
'Clean' quotation, 40, 49, 54, *336*
Closed funds, 164
'Close' index, 163
Closing bargain, 127, 271, *336*
Coins, investment in, 201
Commission
ARIEL, 119
insurance policies, 184
National Savings Stock Register, 42
offshore funds, 196
see also Stockbrokers' commission
Commodities, 197–8
Commonwealth stocks, 38, 58, 61, 122, 126, 130
Companies Acts, 97, 240, 244
1948, 7, 63, 97, 239, 284, 286, 289, 292, 298–9
1967, 239, 290
1976, 288, 290
1980, 164, 284, 285, 300
Companies House, 259
Company flotation, 92–3, *339*
cost of, 98
see also New issues
Company formation, 284
Company funds, 4, 5, 6, 9, 11
Company management, 14–15, 74, 291
Company's registered office, 259
Composite 500 Stock Index, 267
Compulsory savings, 5
Consideration, *336*
Consolidated balance sheet, 246
Consolidated profit and loss account, 239, 240, 244
Consols, 78, 80, 223, 271, 273, *336*
Consols Index, 79
Contango, 141–2, *336*
Contango Day, 123
Continuation, 127
Contract note, 115, 123–4, 130, 148, *336*
Contract Stamp Duty, 131
Contractual savings, 5
Conversion premium, 84–5, 86, 87
Conversion price, 84, 86
Conversion ratio, 84
Convertible securities, 63, 65, 84–6, 165
see also Warrants
'Cooling-off' period, 305
Corporation and county stocks, 38, 58–9, 122, 125
Corporation tax, 82, 240–44, *336*
offshore funds exempt from, 196
on insurance company profits, 174
on unit trust profits, 162
see also Advance corporation tax
Correlation of returns, 215, *336*
Cost of share adjustment (COSA), 248–9
'Cost-push' inflation, 224, *336*
Council for the Securities Industry, 294, 301, 303
Coupons, 39, 46, 48, 82, 273, *336*
bearer securities, 138–9
Covenant, 210–11, *336*
of tenants, 190
Cover, 241, *336*
Covered bear, 140, *336*
Creditors, 251, 291, 292
'Cult of the equity', 168, 223
Cum, 114, *337*
Cum dividend (cd), 40, 114, 269
Cumulative preference shares, 83
Current assets, 245, 247, *337*
Current cost accounting, 248–9, *337*
Current cost operating profit, 248–9
Current liabilities, 247, 250–51, *337*
Current ratios, 76, 250, 251

Dated securities, 24, 39–40, 45, 48, *337*

'Dawn raids', 301
Dealers in securities, 129–30, 269, 302
Death, capital gains tax at, 205, 209, 324
Debenture stocks, 63–4, 126, 314, *337*
  rights of holders, 287, 289
Debtor turnover, 256
Declaration Days, 142
Deed of covenant, 210–11, *336*
Defensive shares, 76
Deferred equity, 86, 88
Deferred ordinary shares, 69, *337*
Delivery, 138, *337*
'Demand-pull' inflation, 223, *337*
Denomination of shares, 74
Department of Trade
  control of insurance companies, 305
  control of property bonds, 194
  control of unit trusts, 148, 150, 152–3, 155, 157
  licensing of dealers, 302
  recognition of auditors, 305
Deposit accounts
  bank, 27
  building society, 29
  foreign currency, 89
Depositories, 138, 140
Deposit Protection Scheme, 304
Deposit rate, 27
Depreciation, 247, 248, *337*
Direct investments, 21
Directors, 258, 285, 289, 290, 296–7, 299–300
Directors' report, 249
Disclosure
  of information, 294
  of shareholders' interests, 290
Discounted future dividends, 227–9
Discretionary savings, 5
Disposal of assets (for capital gains tax purposes), 205, 207, 208–9, 297
Diversification (spread) of interests, 12, 21, 76, 77, 89, 155–6, 164, 214, 215–16, 276, 330, *347*
Dividend cover, 242, 244, 249, 254–5, *337*
Dividend rate, 100
Dividends, 102, 154, 224, *337*
  effect of SSAP 16 on, 248–9
  ex and cum, 144
  on bearer securities, 138
  on preference shares, 82, 83
  paid in dollars, 139
  payment of, 75
  per share (DPS), 70, 242
  SEDOL record, 116
  shareholders' control of, 289
Dividend yield, 70, 72, 218, 223, 229, *337*
Division of trust fund, 316–21
Document that has value, 107–8
Double bottom, 233, 236
Double options, 142
Double taxation relief, 90, 242, *337*
Double top, 236
Dow-Jones Index, 91, 263, 267
Downside protection, 86
Drawings, 40, 41, 66, *337*
Dual-capacity firms, 118
Dual trust, *see* Split-level trust
Duration of stock, 273

Earnings, 71, 72–3, 74, 229, *338*
  nil, net and full, 241–2
  per share (EPS), 71, 73, 242
Earnings yield, 71, 73, 223, *338*
Efficient Market Hypothesis (EMH), 259, 274–7
Elderly people, 177, 178–9
Endowment element of bank funds, 268
Endowment insurance policies, 21, 171–3, 174, *338*
  tax-exempt, 183
Enfaced (assented) bonds, 62, *338*
Equalization, 161, *338*
Equities, 69–70, 214, 223, *338*
  capital growth, 212, 215, 219
  compared with other investments, 25, 78–80
  cost of issue, 98
  deferred, 86, 88
  overseas, 89–91
Equity Income Index, 79
Equity-linked insurance, 172, 180, *338*
Equity Price Index, 79
Equity switching, 267–9
Equity valuation ratio, 257–8
Equivalent warrant, 88
Escalating annuity, 177
Escalator-style building society bonds, 221
Estate duty, 209
Eurobonds, 62, 126, 301, *338*
European Communities Act 1972, 284
Evens, 141
Ex, 114, *338*
Ex all (xa), 114
Ex capitalization issue (xc), 114
Excess ACT, 242, 243, 244
Exchange controls, removal of, 89, 201, 266
Exchange Telegraph Company, 258

Ex distribution, 161
Ex dividend (ex div, xd), 40, 43, 114, 269
Ex dividend valuations, 325
Exempt dealers, 129–30, 302, *338*
Exempt funds, *338*
Exercise price, 87, 142, *338*
Expectations theory, 271
Expert advice, 319–20
Ex rights issue (xr), 114
Extel cards, 258
Extraordinary general meeting, 286, 287, 288
Extraordinary resolution, 286

Family trusts, 322–4
Fashion in investment, 199–200
Federation of Stock Exchanges, 110
Filter rules, 231–2
Final dividend, 75, 338
Finance for Industry (FFI), 62, 92
Finance houses, 28, 30, *338*
Financial gearing, 77, 239
Financial intermediary, 2
Financial risk, 75, 76
Financial structures, 251
Financial Times, 54, 121, 143, 144, 258, 264, 266
'Firm', 103, 106, *339*
Fixed assets, 245, *339*
Fixed-income investments, 19, 70, 82
Fixed-interest securities, 2, 7, 78, 148, 215, 218, 323
  issue of, 96, 98
  non-Government, 58–68
  taxation of interest from, 162, 167
  yield on, 48–56
  see also Gilt-edged securities
Flat yield, 49, *339*
Flexibility of investment, 330
Flexible (three-way) fund, 181
Floating charge, 64, 339
Floating-interest loan, 44
Foreign currency bank accounts, 89
Foreign governments' bonds, 61–2
Form of renunciation, 105, 106
Fractional allotments, 107
Fractions (in quotations), 114
Franked income, 67, 82, *339*
Freehold property, 186–7, 188–91, *339*
Friendly societies, 45, 183, 205
FT-Actuaries Indices, 264–6
  All Share, 78, 264, 265–6, 276, 279
  Investment Trust, 168
FT Industrial Ordinary (30 Share) Index, 81, 224, 262–3, 264

'Full' distribution earnings, 71, 242
Full repairing lease, 190
Fully paid shares, 102, 283
Fundamental analysis, 227–9, 239, 268, 275, *339*
Fund for the Banks for Savings, 26
Futures, 197–8

Gambling, 4
Gearing, 102, 192, *339*
  commodity dealing, 197, 198
  gold futures and options, 202
  investment trusts, 164–5
  options, 143
  property shares, 193
  split-level trusts, 168
  unit trusts, 148
  warrants, 87
Gearing adjustment, 248, 249
Gearing ratios, 76, 248, 251–5
General meetings, 84, 88
  see also Annual general meeting; Extraordinary general meeting
General undertaking, 119
Gifts, 208, 209–10
  of shares, 131, 134, 324
  to shareholders, 214
Gilt-edged securities, 38–47, 58–61, 62, 79, 118, 208–9, 223, 225, *339*
  commission, 126, 129
  quotation, 113–14
  recording bargains in, 116, 137
  risk, 22, 24
  switching, 269–74
Giver, 141
  see also Bulls
'Go-go' funds, 267
'Going concern', 73, 245, 258
Gold, 201–2
Good delivery, 136
Good for the day (GD), 144
Good marking names, 139, *339*
Good till cancelled (GTC), 144
Goodwill, 246, 257
'Go short', 198, *339*
Government borrowing, 133–47
  see also Gilt-edged securities
Government Broker, 43, 97
Government policy, 6, 8, 10, 223
Grandparents, 210
'Granny bonds', 36
'Greenhouse' schemes, 220
Grossed-up net redemption yield, 53–4, 55, *339*
Gross funds, 55, *339*

Gross redemption yield, 50, 53, 55, 270, 272–3
Ground rents, 187, *340*
Growth funds, 159–60
Growth rates, 72
Growth stocks, 72, *340*
Guaranteed growth bonds, 182–3
Guaranteed income bonds, 36, 182, 218

Hard commodities, 197
Head and shoulders chart, 234–6, *340*
Heavy shares, 100, *340*
Higgledy-piggledy growth, 229
High-rate taxpayers, investments for, 212, 216, 217
  building-society-linked insurance, 184
  low-coupon short-dated gilts, 203, 217
  National Savings, 25
  single-premium investment bonds, 179–80, 218
  split-level trusts, 167
  warrants, 88
High-yielding sterling funds, 197
Hire-purchase companies, 28
  see also Finance houses
Historic cost, 252
Holding gains, 248
Home-income plans, 178–9, 193, 218
'Home-made' dividends, 217
House funds, 195, *340*
Housing Act 1980, 192

Immunization, 271, 273
Impact Day, 97, *340*
Imputation system of corporation tax, 82, 240–44
Imputed rent, 192–3
Income, investing for, 217–18
Income and Corporation Taxes Act 1970, 167, 197
Income bonds, *see* Guaranteed income bonds
Income cover, 254
Income gearing ratios, 251, 253–5
Income position of investor, 211–13
Income priority percentages, 254–5
Income risk, 271
Income shares of split-level trust, 166–7, 218
Income statement, 239–44
Income tax, 37, 46, 92, 174, 202, 203–5
Income unit trusts, 159, 163
Income yield, 49
Indemnity, 138
Independent (unsystematic) risk, 77, 215, 216
Index funds, 276–7, 281, *340*
Index-linked gilt-edged stock, 45
Index-linked National Savings Certificates, 36, 217, 218–19, 221
Index-linked Save as You Earn, 34–5, 218
Indicator rate, 44
Indifference level, 76–7
Indirect investments, 21–2, 323–4, *340*
Industrial property, 188, 189, 191
Inflation, 10, 24, 36, 177–8, 188, 192, 218–19, 223, 224 230, 314
Inflation accounting, 248–9
Information sources, 160–61, 258–9
'Inside' knowledge, 14, 276
Insider dealing, 300, *340*
Inspector of Foreign Dividends, 46, 271
Instalments, payment by, 45
Institutional investors, 11–16, 113, 136, 211, 215, 222–5, 279, 291, *340*
  dealings through ARIEL, 118–19
  in chattels, 198–9
  in fixed-interest stocks, 67, 98
  in gilts, 38–9
  in investment trusts, 164, 166
  in National Savings, 34
  in property, 188, 189–90, 193–4
Institutional Shareholders Committee, 15
Insurance Brokers (Registration) Act 1977, 305
Insurance Brokers' Registration Council, 305
Insurance companies, 10–12, 80, 101, 103, 138, 153, 211, 222–5, 268, 272, 279, 281, 302
  investment in property, 189–90, 194
  unit trusts managed by, 186
Insurance Companies Act 1974, 305
Insurance-linked investments, 157, 171–84, 276, 323, *340*
  see also Life assurance
Intangible assets, 246
Inter-American Development Bank, 62, 126
Interest, 82, *340*
Interest payments, 55, 138
Interest rates, 10, 223, 268, 271, 273–4
Interest times covered, 253–4, *340*
Interest yield, 49–50, 86, 218
Interim dividends, 75, 258
Interim report, 289, *341*
Intermediate Days, 123
International Bank for Reconstruction and Development, 62, 126

Intestacy, 205, 313, 314, 322
'In the money', 144
Intrinsic (true) value of shares, 227–8, 229, 275
Introductions, 96–7, 98, *341*
Investment (defined), 1
 types of, 2–4
Investment analysis techniques, 227
 see also Fundamental analysis; Technical analysis
Investment bonds, 179
 see also Single-premium insurance policies
Investment companies, 164
Investment expert (defined), 319–20
Investment income surcharge, 205
Investment-linked assurance policies, 175–6
 see also Managed bonds; Property bonds
Investment management, 12–13, 156, 164, 309–11
Investment policies, 267–74, 276–7
Investment powers, 313–21
 charities, 325–6
 family trusts, 322–4
 house funds, 195
 investment trusts, 166
 pension funds, 327–8
 unit trusts, 152
Investment trusts, 21, 94, 164–9, 196, 222, 224, 232, 279, 281, *341*
Investor protection, 294–305
Irish securities, 125, 126, 127
Irredeemable stocks, 48, 58, 82, *341*
Issued share capital, 99, *341*
Issuing house, 7, 94, 95, 98, 103
Issuing Houses Association, 95, 302

Jobbers, 96, 110, 111, 112–13, 115, 116, 117–18 134–6, 145, *341*
Jobbers' book, 113, *334*
Jobbers' quote, 112, 113
Jobbers' turn, 113, 116, 117, 118, 208, *349*
Joint and survivor annuities, 177, 218
Joint brokers' and jobbers' books, 117

Land and buildings, 186, 314, 316
Landlord and Tenant Act 1954, 187
Leading indicators, 230
Leasehold ground rent, 187
Leasehold property, 186, 187, 190, 191, *341*
Leasehold Reform Act 1967, 187
Leasing, 29, 252,
Legal personality of company, 283
Letter of acceptance, 106
Leverage, 251
 see also Gearing
Licensed dealers in securities, 129–30, 302, *341*
Licensed deposit-takers, 304
Life assurance, 2, 12, 21, 157, 163, 168, 171–84, 205, 210, 213
Life-tenant, 322–4, *341*
Limited liability, 283, *341*
Limit order, 115, *341*
Line (chart), 235, 237
Line chart, 232, 233, *341*
Lines of shares, 111, *341*
Liquid assets (defined), 2
Liquidation, 83, 251, 258, 283, 292, *341*
Liquidity, 215, *341*
 of property funds, 180–81
Liquidity ratios, 250–51, *341*
Liquid ratio, *see* Quick assets ratio
Listed securities, 7, 116, 120, 134
Listing Agreement, 94
Loan capital, 62–3, 83, 84–7, 114, 122, *341*
Local authorities, 304
Local authority securities, 24, 30, 38, 58–61, 218
 see also Corporation and county stocks
Logarithmic scale, 234
Long-dated stocks, 39, 273–4, *341*
Long-term debt, 247, 251
Long-term investment, 217, 222, 229, 274

Mainstream corporation tax, 241
 see also Corporation tax
'Make a market', 111
Making-up Day, 123
Making-up price, 141
Managed bonds, 175, 176, 181, 193, *342*
Managers of unit trusts, 147, 148–53, 154, 155
Margin trading, *342*
Market, *342*
Market capitalization, 9, 94, *342*
Marketability of securities, 65, 66, 99, 166
Market yield, 229–30
Marking name, 139, *342*
Markings, 116, *342*
Married couple
 division of assets, 211
 gifts between, 209
 responsibilities, 213

taxation of, 203, 204
Matching bargains, 207
Matching maturity structures, 222
Maturity period, 266, 270, *342*
McCarthy Information Services, 258
Mean
arithmetic, 263
geometric, 263
harmonic, 277
weighted arithmetic, 265
Medium-dated stocks, 39, *342*
Medium-term investments, 217
Memorandum of association, 167, 284, 285
Merchant banks, 92–3, 95, 156, 195, 302, 309–10
Mergers, 296, 297
'Middle-of-the-road' funds, 160
Minimum lending rate, 27
Minors, *see* Children
Model Code for Securities Transactions by Directors of Listed Companies, 300
Monetary Working Capital Adjustment (MWCA), 248–9
Money, distinct from wealth, 3
Money supply, 230
Money-weighted rate of return, 278–9, 280
Mortgage debenture stocks, 63
Mortgages, 342
local authority loans, 60
on house property, 16, 178, 192
private, 187–8, 320

Name Day, 123, 134
Name ticket, 148
Narrower-range investments, 86, 315–19, *342*
National Debt, 33–4
National Girobank, 26, 33, 304
National Savings, 33–4, 37, 163
National Savings Bank, 25–6, 30–31, 33, 304
investment accounts, 26, 216
ordinary accounts, 25
National Savings Certificates, 24, 34, 35–6
Retirement Issue, 36
Second Index-linked Issue, 36, 218–19, 221
National Savings Stock Register, 42, 43, 46, 55
Neckline, 235, 236
Negotiable warrant, 55
Net acquisition of financial assets, 3, 4
Net asset format of balance sheet, 245
Net assets, 247, *342*
Net asset value per share, 247–8
discount on, 165
Net current assets, 247
Net dividends, 240
'Net' earnings basis, 241, 242, 243, 244
Net funds, 55
Net-of-tax returns, 203, 208, 216
Net present value, 51
Net redemption yield, 53, 59, *342*
Net worth, 76, *343*
Neutral zone, 207
New-issue market, 7, 8, 9, 10
New issues, 7, 92–108, 122, 127
New time, 123, 142, *343*
M.J.H. Nightingale and Co Ltd, 121, 277
'Nil' earnings basis, 241, 243, 244
Nil-paid shares, 102, *343*
Nil-taxpayers, 197, 216
Nominal values of shares, 74–5, *343*
Nominees, 290, *343*
Non-cumulative preference shares, 83
Non-discretionary savings, 5
Non-executive directors, 290
Non-residents of United Kingdom, 43, 46, 55, 61, 62, 67, 130, 205, 271
Non-voting shares, 75
No-par-value shares, 74–5, *343*
Not to press (NTP), 145, *343*

Objects clause, 284, 286
Offer price, 112, 113, *343*
Offers for sale, 95, 97, 98, 103, 106, *343*
Office property, 188, 189, 190–91
Offshore funds, 195–6, 202, *343*
One-way option stocks, 39, 45, *343*
'On tap', 43
Open-ended fund, 148
Operating gains (profits), 248
Option cost, 85
Option money, 142
Options, 1, 4, 127, 142–5, *343*
see also Convertible stocks; Warrants
Ordinary resolutions, 286, 288
Ordinary shares, 7, 9, 69, 74, 92, 96, 100, 114, 115, 329, *343*
'Other names', securities in, 139
'Out of the money', 144
Overriding commission, 103
Overseas corporation taxes, 242
Overseas profits, 242
Overseas securities, 89–91, 96
Oversubscription, 95, 96, 98
'Over-the-counter' (town hall) bonds, 61

Over-the-counter market, 121, 301, *343*
Over-the-counter securities, 116
Owner-occupied house property, 2, 16, 20, 191–3, 205–6, 219

Page Committee on National Savings, 26
Paid-up shares, *343*
Panel on Take-overs and Mergers, 294, 299, 300–301
'Paper' investment, 1
Participating preference shares, 83–4, 196
Partly paid shares, 283, 291, 292, *343*
Par value, *343*
Pass by delivery, 106
Payout policy, 70, 71
Payout ratio, 229, 249, *343*
Pension funds, 22, 45, 67, 163, 168, 189, 195, 198–9, 205, 211, 222–5, 268, 279, 281, 308, 326–7
Performance of investments, 80
measurement of, 168–9, 264, 277–82
Personal feelings of investors, 214
Personal possessions, *see* Chattels
Personal sector savings, 4, 5, 10, 11, 12, 80–81
Personal tax allowances, 203, 204–5
Placing an order, 115
Placings, 96, 97, 98, *344*
Point-and-figure chart, 235, 236, *344*
Policyholders Protection Act 1975, 305
Policyholders' Protection Board, 305
Policy switching, 271–4, 323
Poll of shareholders, 286, 287
Portfolio planning, 329–30
Post Office, 30, 42
Post Office Savings Bank, *see* National Savings Bank
Pound cost averaging, 157–8, 277, *344*
Powers of investment, *see* Investment powers
Powers of retention and postponer, 319
Preference shares, 19, 69, 70, 82–4, 100, 114, 160, *344*
Preferred ordinary shares, 84, *344*
Preliminary Day, 123
Premiums, 101, 171, 172, 173, *344*
Premium Savings Bonds, 19–20, 34, 36–7, 206
Present value of annuity, 52
Press comment, 54, 97, 113, 258
Press cuttings service, 258
Prevention Fraud (Investments) Act 1958, 152, 175, 195, 294, 302
Price–earnings ratios, 71–3, 229–30, 242, *344*
Price-relative, 263, 265
Prices
of gilts, 43
of investment bonds, 180
of investment trust shares, 165
of shares, 15, 73, 88–9
of units, 148, 150–51, 154
Primary market, 7
Prime property, 190–91
Principal (defined), 12
Prior charge, 83, 108, 252, *344*
rent as, 188–9
Private companies, 284
Probate, delayed, 143
Probate valuations, 127, 325
Profitability ratios, 250, 256–8
Profit and loss account, 248, *344*
see also Consolidated profit and loss account
Profit forecasts, 230–31, 296
Profit margin, 256–7
Property, 16, 186–94, 219, 223, 224, *344*
not permitted to unit trusts, 152
Property bonds, 21, 175, 176, 180–81, 194, *344*
Property company shares, 193–4
Property-linked annuities, 221
Property unit trusts, 195, 326
Proprietary ratio, 253
Prospectus, 106, 294, 302, *345*
Prospectus issues, 43, 94, 95, 96, 97, 98, 106
Protected shorthold tenancy, 192
Protection of Depositors Act 1963, 304
Provisional letter of allotment, 102, 104–5
Proxies, 286–7
Public board stocks, 38, 58, 61, 114, 116, 126
Public limit book, 144
Public limited companies, 92–3, 283–4, *345*
Public sector, 4, 5, 6, 8
Public Sector Borrowing Requirement, 6, 10, 274
Pull to maturity, 40
Put options, 142, 143, 144, *345*
'Put-through', 118, 125, *345*

Qualifying life assurance policies, 173–4, 178, 182, *345*
Quality of earnings, 229
Quartering-up, 324 *345*
Quick assets ratio, 250, 251

Quorum, 286
Quotation, 93–4, 96, 113–14, 116, *345*
Quoted investments, 20, 31–2
  valuation of, 324

Rack rents, 186, 188–91, *345*
Random Walk Hypothesis, 274, *345*
Rates of return, 76, 77, 279, 280–81
Ratio analysis, 250–58, 259
Real assets, 1, 2, 186–202
Real investment, 1, 3, 4, 10, 21
Receiver, 64
Recognized banks, 304
Recognized (good marking) names, 139
Recommendations on Accounting Principles, 288
Reconstructions, 291
Recovery stocks, 277
Redemption date, 218, 273
Redemptions, 65, 66, 67, 84, *345*
Redemption yield, 51–2, 85, 270, *345*
  see also Grossed-up net redemption yield; Gross redemption yield; Net redemption yield
Registered securities, 42–3, 131, 137, 139, 316, *345*
Register of shareholders, 114, 134, 137, 259, *345*
Register of unit-holders, 147, 155
Registrar of Companies, 284, 289, 291, 294
Registrar of shareholders, 133, 134, 136, 137, 138, 139, *345*
Registration of application form, 105, 106, 107
Regular savings plans, 175, 176
Relative strength, 231, 268
Reinvestment scheme, 160
Remainderman, 322–4, *345*
Renounceable share certificate, 100, 122
Rental yields, 188, 189
Renunciation, 106, *345*
Reports
  annual, 94, 238–58
  auditors', 97, 238, 249, 288, *333*
  directors', 249
  unit trusts', 161
Representative at shareholders' meetings, 286
Reserves, *345*
Residential property, 186, 189–90
  see also Owner-occupied house property
Residual securities, 116, 145
Resistance level, 235, 237
Resolutions, 286, 288
  see also Extraordinary resolutions; Ordinary resolutions; Special resolutions
Retained earning, 4, 6, 73, 99, 247, *345*
Return on capital employed, 256, 257
Returns to shareholders, 77, 78, 257
Revaluations, 99, *346*
Reverse yield gap, 78, 218, 223, *346*
Reversionary bonuses, 172, 216
Rights issues, 101–3, 106, 107, 108, 164, 207, 320, *346*
Rights of shareholders, 244, 289–90
Rights premium, 85
Risk, 1, 2, 3, 4, 13, 22, 24, 45–6, 65, 66, 69, 75–8, 79, 83, 214, 215–17, 222, 281–2, 283
Roll-over relief, 205, 208
Rules of the Stock Exchange, 125 (163), 90, 121
Running yield, 49, *346*

Save As You Earn (SAYE), 34–5, 218
Savings, 1, 4
Savings schemes, 157, 175, 176
Schemes of arrangement, 292, 320
School fees, 213
Scrip issues, *see* Capitalization issues
Secondary market, 7, 8
Sectors, 267–9, *346*
Secured loan, 63
Securities, 7, *346*
Securities and Exchange Commission, 294
Security of stocks, 65
Self-employed people' pensions, 22
Selling-out, 145, *346*
Separate entity of companies, 283
SEPON Ltd (Stock Exchange Pool Nominees), 134–5, 136
Series of options, 144
Settled Land Act 1925, 314
Settlement Day, *346*
  see also Account Day
Settlement period, 123
Settlements, 122–3, *346*
Share capital, 62, 99
Share certificates, 136, 137–8, 283
Share exchange schemes, 159
Share-for-share exchange, 297, 298
Shareholder democracy, 14
Shareholders, 70, 88, 244, 283, 285, 289–90
Shareholders' benefits, 214, 290
Shareholders' meetings, 94, 283–92

Share premium account, 247
Share price, 15, 73, 88–9
Shares, 7, 114, 201, *346*
see also different types of share
Share split, 100
Sharpe, W.F., 281–2
Shops, 188, 189, 192
Short-dated securities, 39, 43, 45, 54, 116, 127, 273, *346*
Short-term investments, 217
Single-capacity system, 117
Single-premium insurance policies, 179–80, 182, 183, 218
Sinking funds, 41, 65–6, 270, *346*
Sixteen-day options, 143
Small bargains, 127
Small companies, 277
Small investors, 12, 13, 14, 59, 125, 155
Small unit trusts, 80
Soft commodities, 197
Solicitors, 308
Sources and application of funds statement, 247
Special business, 288
Specialized funds, 160, 194, 216
Specially ex dividend, 42, 43, 269, *346*
Special notice, 288
Special powers of investment, 314, 317, 318
Special-range property, 314, 316–19, *346*
Special resolutions, 285, 286, 287, 288, 292, 298
Speculation, 3–4, 98, 143, *347*
Split-capital company, 166
Split-level trusts, 166–7, 221, *347*
Split tickets, 134
Splitting, 106, *347*
Spot prices, 197, *347*
Spread of interest, *347*
see also Diversification of interest
Stags, 98–9, *347*
Stale bull, 140, *347*
Stamp duty, 347
see also Contract stamp duty; Transfer stamp duty
Standard and Poors Indices, 267
State benefits, 216
Statements of Standard Accounting Practice (SSAP), 239, 248, 288
Statutory trusts, 314, 322
Sterling certificates of deposit, 27, 138
Sterling commodity funds, 197–8
Stock, 250
Stock and Bonds Office, 42
Stockbrokers, 31, 41, 96, 107, 110–12, 115–18, 134, 137, *347*
and small investors, 13
house funds, 195
information and advice from, 166, 258, 308–9
Stockbrokers' commission, 41–2, 65, 90, 98, 120, 122, 125–31, 143, 157
concessions, 125, 208, 271
Stock Exchange, 7–10, 14, 31–2, 110–21, 136, 302, *347*
Buying-in and Selling-out Department, 145
control of new issues, 75, 94, 96
control of take-overs, 300, 301; *see also* Take-over Code
options trading on, 144
recognition of 'names', 139
requirements for companies, 88, 239, 289
see also Rules of the Stock Exchange
Stock Exchange building, 110
Stock Exchange (Completion of Bargains) Act 1976, 136
Stock Exchange Daily Official List (SEDOL), 7, 59, 116, 119–20, 324, *347*
Stock Exchange Fact Book, 259
Stock Exchange Official Year Book, 40, 259
Stock Exchange Weekly Official Intelligence, 59
Stockjobbers, *see* Jobbers
Stock Market Indices, 76, 78, 230, 262–7, *340*
Capital World, 267
Dow-Jones, 91, 263, 267
FT-Actuaries, 168, 264–6, 267; All Share, 78, 264, 265–6, 276, 279
other FT, 266
Standard and Poors, 267
Times, 266–7
Stock markets, choice of, 90–91
Stocks, 7, 113–14, *347*
see also different types of stock
Stock Transfer Act 1963, 43, 134
Stock Transfer form, 132–3, 134, 137, *347*
Stock turnover, 255
'Stop-loss' order, 86, *347*
Straight loan stock (defined), 85
Striking price, 96, 142, 144, *347*
Subordinated loan stocks, 63, *347*
Subscription rights, 87, *347*
Subsidiary companies, 239, 244, 249, *348*
Subunderwriters, 103

Sum assured, 171
Support level, 235, 237
Surrender of policies, 173–4, 183
Survey of published accounts, 249
Switching, 278–9, *348*
  equities, 267–9
  gilt-edged, 269–74
    anomaly, 269–71
    policy, 271–4, 323
    tax, 269
  investment bonds, 183
Systematic risk, 77, 78, *348*

Table A, 284, 285
Take-over Code, 14, 298, 299–301, 302
Take-overs and mergers, 14, 15, 74, 86, 94, 207, 257, 290, 295–301, *348*
Taker, 141
  see also Bears
Talisman, 116, 132, 134–7, *348*
Talon, 139, *348*
Tap stocks, 43–4, 270 *348*
Taxable income, 203
Tax credits, 161, 241
Taxes, *see* Capital gains tax; Capital transfer tax; Corporation tax; Income tax
Tax-exempt investments, 35, 183
Tax-exempt investors, *see* Charities; Pension funds
Tax position of investors, 203, 212–13, 330
Tax relief, 12, 22, 173, 175–6, 183, 192, 193, 205, 210, 326–7
Tax switching, 269
Technical analysis, 231–8, 268, 274–6, *348*
Tender issues, 45, 95–6, *348*
Term assurance, 21, 171, 173, *348*
Terminal bonuses, 172
Three-way fund, 181
Ticket Day, 123, 134
Tickets, 134
Time element in investment, 1, 2, 3, 24
Times stock market indices, 266–7
Time-weighted rate of return, 279, 280–81
Timing, 4, 80–81, 156–7, 330
  of new issues, 108
  of unit trust purchases, 156–7
Top-slicing, 179, 183, 194
Total return on share, 72, 78, 79, *348*
'Town hall' bonds, 61
Trade cycle, 81
Trade debtor turnover, 255–6
Traded options, 142, 144–5
Trade investments, 73, 246–7, *348*
Trade unions, 205
Trading profit, 256
Transfer deed, 134
Transfer of securities, 131–7
Transfer stamp duty, 65, 90, 130–131, 133, 134, 139, 150
  exemptions, 59, 61, 62, 102, 106, 122, 131, 139
Treasury bills, 33, 34, 80, 223
Trend line, 235, 237, *348*
Triple trust, 167
'True and fair view', 244–5, 288
Trust deed, 313, 314, 317, 325, *349*
  debentures, 64
  investment trusts, 222
  unit trusts, 147, 148, 150, 153, 154, 161, 166, 222
Trustee Act 1925, 314, 316, 320
Trustee Investments Act 1961, 86, 223, 314–20
Trustees, 67, 86, 131, 136, *349*
  directors as, 285
  for debentures, 64
  for house funds, 195
  for unit trusts, 147, 149–50, 152, 153–5
  investments for, 223, 313–27
Trustee Savings Bank Act 1976, 26
Trustee savings banks, 26, 30, 31, 302, 304
Trustee status, 30, 315, *349*
Trusts, 188, 210, 322–4, *348*
Trusts (Scotland) Act 1921, 314
Turn, *see* Jobbers' turn

Unallocated accounts, 202
Unassented bonds, 62
Unauthorized clerks, 110
Unauthorized investments, 317–18
Unauthorized unit trusts, 162, 194–8
Uncovered ('naked') bear, 142
Undated stocks, 7, 82, 83, 271, *349*
Underleasehold properties, 187, *349*
Undersubscription, 95
Underwriting, 94, 95, 103, 106, *349*
Underwriting commission, 98, 103
Unfranked income, 82, 196, *349*
United Kingdom Government securities, 34, 56, 58, 122, 125, 126 130, 138
Unitization, 168, 280
Unit-linked life assurance, 175–6, 216, 305, *349*
Unit-linked savings, 277

Unit Trust Association, 153, 302
Unit trusts, 21, 119, 127, 147–63, 164–6, 194–8, 216, 222, 224, 279–81, 282, 310, 311, 325, *349*
Unit trust settlement duty, 150
Unit Trust Year Book, 161
Unlisted Securities Market (USM), 116, 119, 120, 121, 277
Unquoted investments, 20, 325
Unrelieved advance corporation tax, 242, 244
Unrelieved foreign tax, 242–4
Unsecured loan stock, 63, 64, 65, 107, 314
Unsystematic risk, *see* Independent risk

Valuations
  for tax purposes, 324–5
  of chattels, 199–200
  of property investments, 180–81, 190, 195
  of unit trusts, 151, 325
Value-added tax on bullion, 202
Variable-income investments, 19
Variable-interest loan, 44
Vendor shares, 94
Volatile securities, 76–7, 167, 193, 214, 216
Volatility of securities, 45–6, 76–8, 273–4, 281
Voting, shareholders', 84, 286–7, *349*

Wall Street, 91, 234
Warehouses, 191
3½% War Loan, 22, 38, 39, 43, 46, 55, 223, 271
Warrants, 1, 87–9, *349*
Wasting assets, 143, 206
Water boards, 62
Wealth, distinct from money, 3
Whole life assurance policy, 171, 172, 173, *349*
Wider-range property, 86, 316–19, *349*
Wills, 205, 313, 314, 319, 322
Wilson Committee, 9
Winding-up, 286, 292, *349*
Wines, as investment, 198, 201
Withdrawal plans, 158–9, 194, 218
Withholding tax, 90
Without-profits policies, 171
With-profits policies, 171–2, 216
Woods *v.* Martins Bank Ltd and Another 1958, 307
Working capital ratio, *see* Current ratio
World Bank, *see* International Bank for Reconstruction and Development
Writer of option, 144

'Yearling' bonds, 59, *349*
Yield, 48–9, 65, 66–7, 78
Yield curves, 55–6, 215, 270, 271–4, *350*
Yield structure, 66